D0025143

Family Therapy Approaches with Adolescent Substance Abusers

CONTRIBUTORS

HARLENE ANDERSON, Ph.D.
THOMAS C. AYERS, M.Div.
INSOO KIM BERG, M.S.S.W.
GUILLERMO BERNAL, Ph.D.
DAVID R. CHABOT, Ph.D.
DON COLES
MICHAEL DURRANT
YVETTE FLORES-ORTIZ, Ph.D.
MICHAEL R. FOX, M.D.
DAN GALLAGHER, M.Div.
ANTHONY W. HEATH, Ph.D.
HARVEY P. JOANNING, Ph.D.
KATHRYN R. KAMINSKY, R.N., M.A.
BRUCE P. KUEHL, Ph.D.
ROBERT A. LEWIS, Ph.D.
DARIO J. LUSSARDI, M.A.
MARGHARITE C. MATTEIS, Ph.D., R.N.
DUSTY MILLER, Ed.D.
NEAL A. NEWFIELD, Ph.D.
FRED P. PIERCY, Ph.D.
WILLIAM H. QUINN, Ph.D.
LARRY L. RUHF, Ed.D.
DOUGLAS H. SPRENKLE, Ph.D.
TERRY S. TREPPER, Ph.D.
ELIZABETH HEMLEY VAN DER VELDEN, Drs.

Family Therapy Approaches with Adolescent Substance Abusers

THOMAS C. TODD, Ph.D.

Chief Psychologist, Forest Hospital, Des Plaines, IL
Training Faculty, Family Institute of Chicago, Chicago, IL

MATTHEW D. SELEKMAN, M.S.W.

Family Therapy Supervisor, Des Plaines Valley
Community Center, Summit, IL
Adjunct Faculty, Marriage and Family Therapy Program,
Northern Illinois University, Dekalb, IL

ALLYN AND BACON
Boston London Toronto Sydney Tokyo Singapore

Series Editor: Susan Badger
Editorial Assistant: Dana Lamothe
Manufacturing Buyer: Louise Richardson
Editorial Production Services: Louise A. Gelinas, Mac + Me Production Services, Inc.

A Division of Simon & Schuster, Inc.
160 Gould Street
Needham Heights, Massachusetts 02194

Library of Congress Cataloging-in-Publication Data

Family therapy approaches with adolescent substance abusers / [edited by]
Thomas C. Todd, Matthew D. Selekman.
p. cm.
Includes bibliographical references.
Includes indexes.
ISBN 0-205-12505-0
1. Teenagers—Substance use. 2. Family psychotherapy. 3. Substance abuse—Treatment. I. Todd, Thomas C. II. Selekman, Matthew D.
[DNLM: 1. Family Therapy—methods. 2. Substance Abuse—in adolescence. 3. Substance Abuse—therapy. WM 270 F1976]
RJ506.D78F35 1990
616.86—dc20
DNLM/DLC
for Library of Congress 90-842
CIP

Printed in the United States of America
10 9 8 7 6 5 4 3 2 1 95 94 93 92 91 90

CONTENTS

PREFACE

As the two of us have conducted training and consultation in a variety of mental health and chemical dependency programs across the country and abroad, we have been constantly impressed by the split between addiction therapists and mental health professionals. Family therapists are clearly not immune to this—indeed it often seems that the split is even more severe.

This book evolved as an effort to bridge this gap. It is aimed at clinicians practicing in the chemical dependency, family therapy, and psychotherapy fields who work with drug-involved adolescents. Since it offers state of the art practice in the family therapy of adolescent chemical dependency, we hope that even the most sophisticated practitioner will find much that is new and thought-provoking.

We also hope that this book will do more than have an impact on individual practitioners. We hope that it will help to generate a dialogue between those predominately in the chemical dependency field and those in family therapy and mental health disciplines. Beyond that, we hope to have an impact on the larger treatment delivery systems including employee assistance counselors, program administrators, funding agencies, and those who license substance abuse and alcoholism counselors.

Chapter authors have been asked to address controversial issues in order to encourage this dialogue. We hope that the material is not inflammatory or overly provocative; on the other hand, we do hope that any reader, regardless of experience or theoretical persuasion, will find their beliefs critically challenged by some of the viewpoints presented.

It may not surprise the reader to learn that we continue to find that our own work, based particularly on the structural-strategic model of Stanton and Todd, provides a solid framework for the treatment of adolescent substance abusers and their families. Our own evolving views are well represented in the book, as are the views of several authors who have both influenced our approach and been influenced by the Stanton and Todd model.

We hope, however, that the reader will agree that we have welcomed a diversity of approaches and have avoided the temptation to have one point of view dominate. We have sought prominent experts in the field of family therapy and chemical dependency to contribute to this book. Our criteria were simple—to represent a wide variety of viewpoints, to find those working on the "cutting edge" of this specialty area, and most of all to find authors whose work would be interesting for all of us to read.

T.C.T
M.D.S

ACKNOWLEDGMENTS

The authors would like to acknowledge the Herculean efforts of Mary Knauss and Brenda Shifrin in wrestling with this manuscript, various computer glitches, and all of our revisions. We would like to express our continued appreciation to our spouses and bosses for their patience and flexibility during this process. Finally, we would like to thank M. Duncan Stanton, Bill O'Hanlon, and Vince Foley for their helpful editorial comments.

FOREWORD

Drug abuse has become a central concern of modern-day society. Since the generational split that emerged in the 1960s, drugs have served as both a symptom of society's problems, and as a battleground for struggles between parents, youth, professionals, politicians, and others. Recent years have, however, seen the internecine battle subside. The various protagonists have backed away from the fray and, in unison, shifted their gaze to a single direction. They have begun to see drugs as a common enemy that must be eradicated from the society. The voices of young, old, and in-between have begun to rise in a chorus of protest: "Enough!," they cry; "No more drugs! No more alcohol!"

This book joins that chorus. Its authors are saying that something must be done. More important, they are saying that they have already begun to *do*. They are announcing that "we think we can help," and "here are some of the ways we have found."

The book is both thoughtful and generous. It accepts that families have their own competencies. It acknowledges the place of self-help groups. It invites the clients' friends into the therapy room. Many useful clinical techniques and guidelines are proffered for getting through therapeutic impasses. In short, the book tells us there is hope.

This book is also courageous. It faces up to the monsters and beasts that can emerge in the therapy experience. It questions the initiation rites that are sometimes required for clients to receive treatment, and points out the Catch-22 of providing treatment only to those who are drug-free. It challenges the notion of "once an addict, always an addict" as it pertains to adolescents.

As I finished reading this book, I was reminded of a conference I attended in 1973, on the family and schizophrenia. One of the plenary speakers was the noted, family psychiatrist, Ross Speck. At the conclusion of his talk, Speck observed that, "There are at least 53 major theories in psychiatry today. . . . And if we are doing our job, that number should increase." At the time, I was both amused and disturbed by Speck's proclamation. I was amused at his inconoclasm, and disturbed by its implication. I thought, "Shouldn't we be trying to pare down that number, and look for the one truth that is *true*r than the others?" Eventually, however, the wisdom of his thinking began to sink in: We are far from the point of having all the answers, and extensive and diverse exploration will be needed before the field can begin to coalesce toward an identifiable whole.

Likewise, this book. It presents a stimulating diversity of approaches to the family treatment of adolescent substance abuse. More than a book on substance abuse, however, it gives us a grand tour of the present-day thinking of various family therapy schools, accompanied by the background music of healthy empiricism. Through it all, though, one theme keeps returning: The tune of "No One Thing Works with Everybody." It is a tune that makes the tour through *Family Therapy Approaches with Adolescent Substance Abusers* all the more worth taking.

M. Duncan Stanton, Ph.D.
Professor and Director
Division of Family Programs
University of Rochester Medical Center

PART 1

Perspectives in Family Therapy with Adolescent Substance Abusers

This section of the book introduces the reader to the current treatment delivery system for adolescent substance abusers and exposes readers to a variety of family therapy approaches that can be utilized with this treatment population. Each of the family treatment chapters provide comprehensive theoretical overviews of the various family therapy approaches being presented, as well as useful case examples to help illustrate major therapeutic techniques and strategies.

In Chapter One, Selekman and Todd present some of the critical and controversial issues in the treatment of adolescent substance abusers and their families and offer several useful recommendations to help remedy some of the major gaps in the present treatment delivery system. The chapter is filled with important empirically-based research findings and innovative therapeutic ideas.

Chapter Two, "The Purdue Brief Family Therapy Model for Adolescent Substance Abusers," presents a brief integrative family therapy approach that was recently utilized in a major multi-year National Institute On Drug Abuse study with adolescent substance abusers. The Purdue model is unique in that it offers clinicians an effective, empirically-based, family treatment approach that logically integrates several different family therapy models.

The Mental Research Institute's Brief Problem-Focused model is applied to adolescent substance abuse problems in Chapter Three. The chapter authors present a challenging case in which there were multiple chemical abusers in the family.

In Chapter Four, Guillermo Bernal and Yvette Flores-Ortiz present their Contextual Family Therapy model and apply it to adolescent substance abuse presenting problems. The authors provide two excellent case examples to help illustrate major therapeutic techniques in clinical practice.

Chapter Five, "Solution-Focused Brief Therapy with Adolescent Substance Abusers," provides the reader with a highly pragmatic and strength-oriented brief therapy model for adolescent substance abusers. This family wellness approach capitalizes on the strengths and resources of family members to co-construct solutions.

In Chapter Six, Chabot and Matteis present their Systemic Intergenerational family therapy approach to adolescent substance abuse problems. Following a thorough overview of their treatment approach, the authors provide a case illustration of their therapeutic methods.

1

Crucial Issues in the Treatment of Adolescent Substance Abusers and Their Families

MATTHEW D. SELEKMAN, M.S.W.
Family Therapy Supervisor
Des Plaines Valley Community Center
Summit, Illinois

THOMAS C. TODD, Ph.D.
Chief Psychologist, Forest Hospital, Des Plaines, Illinois
and
Training Faculty, Family Institute of Chicago, Chicago
Illinois

Over the past two decades adolescent drug use in the United States has grown considerably. Alcohol is the most commonly abused chemical substance, with approximately 90 percent of adolescents drinking before they finish high school (Harrison & Hoffman, 1987). According to national statistics, approximately one in seven high school seniors report drinking to the point of inebriation on, at least, a weekly basis. Nationally, 40 percent of high school seniors report using drugs other than marijuana, with cocaine, amphetamines, and look-alike substances being the other major drugs of abuse. Several large surveys conducted with adolescents have found that youngsters using drugs perceive their chemical use as primarily a social activity—influenced mainly by peer and parental use (Blum, 1987; Glassner, Carpenter, & Berg, 1986; Glassner & Loughlin, 1987).

Across the country, adolescent drug prevention and inpatient chemical dependency programs have been created to help combat this growing epidemic. The majority of these programs are based heavily on the traditional disease model of chemical dependency, that is frequently utilized with adult alcoholics and drug addicts. Despite the popularity of the disease model of addiction, there is presently little outcome data to support its effectiveness with adolescent substance abusers. In this chapter, the authors will critically examine the current treatment delivery system for adolescent substance abusers and their families.

RELAPSES: DO THEY REALLY HAVE TO BE A PROBLEM?

We believe it is crucial to educate adolescent substance abusers and their families early in treatment about the fact that relapses are practically inevitable, but that their occurrence can be an "opportunity for comeback practice" (Tomm & White, 1987). The normalization and reframing of relapses can instill client hope, disrupt ineffectual patterns of interaction, and challenge family members' beliefs that a relapse means the family has returned back to square one. We have found that in addition to normalizing and reframing relapses, the use of relapse prediction and restraint from immediate change are effective interventive tools for mobilizing and strengthening family problem-solving capacities.

It is our contention that relapse prevention should be a family affair. When working with adolescent substance abusers and their families, we stress team work and group responsibility for the prevention and management of relapses. Many hospital-based and residential treatment programs for adolescent substance abusers fail to actively involve the families of these clients in relapse prevention, which in turn, sets the stage for disaster on therapeutic passes and following discharge. Through the use of family relapse prevention strategies, families can learn more productive ways of interacting and problem-solving. Similar to fire drill training, we have families practice both in sessions and at home how they would either diffuse a near relapse situation or prevent a brief relapse from escalating into a crisis situation.

Several empirically-based studies have clearly demonstrated a strong association between family support and the prevention of relapses, either following treatment or once the substance abuser achieved abstinence without treatment (Billings & Moos, 1983; Daley, 1987; Harrison & Hoffman, 1987; Levy, 1972; Marlatt & Gordon, 1980; Tuchfeld,

1976; Wermuth & Scheidt, 1986; Wille, 1980). Harrison and Hoffman (1987) found in their treatment outcome study with 493 male and female adolescent substance abusers that active parental involvement in Al-Anon or a similar group was strongly associated with the adolescent's abstinence. For example, those adolescents whose fathers attended Al-Anon or similar group meetings for one year after the adolescents were discharged from residential treatment achieved a remarkable abstinence rate of 63 percent.

A truly systemic approach to relapse prevention would take into consideration the circular interplay between the cognitive, familial, peer group, and the larger systems' impact on the adolescent's use of alcohol and street drugs. Social-learning theorists and researchers have identified the role of environmental cues and thought processes in precipitating relapses (Donovan & Chaney, 1985; Ludwig, 1988; Marlatt & Gordon, 1980, 1985; Wesson et al., 1986; Wikler, 1973). Adolescent clients can be taught to identify high risk situations and self-defeating thoughts that get them into trouble with chemical use. Ludwig (1988) found, in his research with over 1000 alcoholics in varying stages of recovery, nine common thoughts and attitudes (scripts) that seem to predispose toward drinking including the:

- Escape script
- Relaxation script
- Socialization script
- Improved self-image script
- Romance script
- Sensual pleasure script
- To-hell-with-it script
- Self-control script
- No-control script

Cognitive-restructuring and coping skills training can be utilized with adolescent clients to help them manage these high-risk situations and erase self-defeating scripts. Some of our adolescent clients have found it quite useful to carry cards in their wallets that list positive behaviors and past solutions that can be utilized when high-risk situations occur.

Selekman (1989) has developed a systemically-oriented relapse prevention group model for adolescent substance abusers participating in day treatment and residential settings. The group relapse prevention model is based on the cybernetic-systemic approach of Michael White (Durrant, 1985; Durrant & Coles, this volume; Menses & Durrant, 1987;

Tomm & White, 1987). Relapses are normalized and externalized into either *Just Keeping You Honest Friends* or *Relapse Beasts and Monsters*. On a daily basis, adolescents record which type of relapse they interact with, and the various things they do to avoid being pushed around by the Relapse Monster. Systemic roleplays are utilized to assist clients in gaining access to newsworthy information regarding the different ways they, themselves, their families, the peer group, and larger systems (e.g., the probation department), all mutually interact in such a way as to invite the Relapse Monster to reign over them. The treatment team employs circular and cybernetic questioning in their daily interactions with the adolescent client to help highlight differences in thinking and behavior. The team is also responsible for recording the clients' and the Relapse Monsters' victories over one another. At the end of each school semester, clients receive medals, plaques, trophies, and a special party to celebrate their victories over the Relapse Monster. This relapse prevention approach can be used in a multiple family therapy group context as well.

At this point, we would like to focus more specifically on how the traditional chemical dependency treatment delivery system contributes to the high rates of relapse during and following substance abusers' inpatient treatments. In reviewing the current alcoholism and drug addiction research literature, it may come as a surprise to our readers to discover that only 10 percent of the inpatient treatment population manage to maintain chemical abstinence for six months beyond treatment (Gorski, 1982; Gottheil et al., 1982; Maddux & Desmond, 1986; Miller & Hester, 1980; Valliant, 1983). Daley (1987), in a thought-provoking paper, identified three major variables that contribute to the problem of relapse, namely, client-related variables, common erroneous beliefs and myths held by professionals regarding relapse, and treatment system problems. Daley argues for a comprehensive approach to relapse prevention that would consist of a careful assessment of client variables (such as, cognitive factors), active family involvement, a cooperative treatment team/client relationship, and the modification of agency policies to accommodate relapsing clients.

In many hospital-based chemical dependency treatment programs, clients are immediately discharged for getting intoxicated on the unit or while on a therapeutic pass. If the client is not discharged, the treatment team will most likely discipline the client by taking away privileges for a designated period of time. Clients who relapse chronically tend to be viewed by the treatment team as being "unmotivated," "uncooperative," "resistant," or failing to "hit bottom" yet. In other words, these clients are not regarded as being suitable for treatment if they show evidence of their diagnosis, namely, loss of control. The Catch-22 is that these clients must remain abstinent in order to receive treatment. Once abstinent, clients are never expected to use chemicals again, despite the fact that an inability to refrain from using alcohol or street drugs is a major symptom of the diagnosis they received (Ludwig, 1988).

THE MYTH OF NEGATIVE PEER PRESSURE

Historically, social scientists have argued that peer pressure plays a major role in the initiation and reinforcement of adolescent drug use (Glynn, 1981; Kandel, 1978, 1981). The nationwide "Say No! To Drugs" campaign has served to perpetuate this traditional view. Recently, several important research studies have produced substantial findings that challenge this traditional peer pressure view (Glassner & Loughlin, 1987; Meier et al., 1984; Tec, 1974; Weinstein, 1978). All of these studies have demonstrated that adolescents typically are active participants, rather than passive respondents to social influences. Tec (1974) reports that adolescent drug users tend to be less dependent on their friends' expectations than are non-users. Peers are often positive influences who aid in the control and abandoning of drug use. Weinstein (1978) and Meier and his colleagues (1984) found that pressure from peers is provided as a reason for never using drugs and for discontinuing use. These researchers also report that adolescent drug users select friends based on their usage preferences, rather than changing their drug-taking patterns to respond to friends' pressure. Glassner and Loughlin (1987) found in their indepth interviews with adolescent drug users that to reinforce or model use of chemicals for non-users or experimenters was viewed as damaging to the important role-reciprocity that these youth see as essential to friendship and dating.

In some cases, adolescent substance abusers' peers can serve as a valuable resource for therapists to utilize in the context of family therapy. Haber (1987) has identified several creative ways to employ clients' friends in family therapy. We have found it useful to enlist the services of our adolescent clients' friends in helping to provide added support while the former are struggling to remain drug-free and leave the drug scene. In some instances, the presence of members of adolescent clients' peer group in family sessions can help put parents at ease regarding their misconceptions and fears surrounding their adolescent's involvement with these young people. The use of the peer group can greatly assist adolescent clients and their parents in rebuilding trust in their relationships. The peer group can also be utilized as a helpful consultation team to the adolescent client and parents in sharing how they resolved similar difficulties and conflict issues with their own parents (Selekman, 1989b).

It would be naive to assume that all peer groups are of the positive variety. We would not deny the fact that many of our adolescent clients were first introduced to street drugs by their close friends. However, like most family therapists, we are not interested in the history or underlying motivations behind drug-abusing behavior. Instead, we focus most of our attention on accessing and utilizing family strengths and resources to co-create a context for change. When peers are negative influences, therapy can include returning to non-using friendships or developing strategies for making new ones.

TREATMENT SYSTEM DILEMMAS

Earlier in this chapter, we discussed how the traditional chemical dependency treatment delivery system often fails to prepare substance abusers to deal with relapses during treatment and following discharge. In this section, we will examine four additional treatment system problem areas of inpatient and residential treatment programs for adolescent substance abusers. They include failure to engage and actively involve the adolescent clients' family in the treatment program; exclusion of the adolescent client and parents from the treatment planning process; treatment team replication of the adolescent clients' family dynamics in the milieu; and the failure of the treatment team to include extra-familial significant others and larger systems as part of the treatment system. In discussing each problem area, we will present suggestions on how these treatment system dilemmas can be remedied.

Failure to Involve the Family

Although many traditional drug abuse programs for adolescent substance abusers stress the importance of family therapy as a major component of treatment, it is questionable how important this modality is in actual practice. Coleman and Davis (1978) found in their national survey of drug abuse programs that not only was family therapy a peripheral component of substance abuse treatment, but when it was used, the therapists providing this modality were often inexperienced. Thus, the brand of family therapy provided in many of these programs tends to be traditional family drug education combined with communications skills training. Family members, if invited in for family therapy at all, will learn a great deal about their survival role behaviors (Black, 1981; Wegscheider, 1981), signs and symptoms of adolescent chemical dependency, enabling behaviors, and the importance of each family member getting actively involved in their own individual recovery program—

such as Al-Anon. Family sculpture techniques may be employed by therapists to help facilitate family communications, particularly the expression of "frozen feelings" (Wegscheider, 1981). For some highly motivated and higher functioning families, this educationally-oriented family therapy may produce important changes in their family relationships. It has been our experience, however, that the majority of posthospitalized adolescent substance abusers and their families that we have been involved with felt that much of their inpatient treatment experience failed to produce differences that made a difference (Bateson, 1980). Changes were of the first-order variety (Watzlawick et al., 1974). Outmoded belief systems and problem-maintaining patterns of interaction were left untouched while the adolescent substance abuser was in the hospital or residential treatment program. Considering the lack of impact on the families to which adolescents return, it is no surprise to us that close to 56 percent of the adolescent substance abusers who receive inpatient treatment resume chemical use following discharge (Harrison & Hoffman, 1987).

We believe that if inpatient treatment teams spend more time and energy engaging families at intake, premature drop-out rates and family resistance would decrease. Several clinicians and researchers have identified the importance of engaging the substance abuser's family at intake (Kaufman & Kaufmann, 1979; Sorensen et al., 1985; Sorensen & Bernal, 1987; Stanton & Todd, 1981; Van Deusen et al., 1980; Wermuth & Scheidt, 1986). Harbin (1985) routinely conducts family admission interviews as a means of engaging families and capitalizing on their readiness for change while in a state of disequilibrium. The therapist's active use of relationship skills can greatly reduce family resistance (Barton & Alexander, 1977, 1981; Piercy & Frankel, 1985). The use of client language, normalizing, reframing, and complimenting can further enhance cooperation between treatment team and family (de Shazer, 1985). Menses and Durrant (1987) include the entire treatment team in admission interviews and family therapy sessions as a powerful and respectful way to foster a cooperative relationship with families.

Once families are engaged in individual family therapy, multiple family group therapy and Strategic Parenting (Efron & Rowe, 1987) groups can serve as valuable adjunctive treatment modalities. Kaufman and Kaufmann (1979) have found mutliple family therapy groups to be the treatment of choice for substance abusers and their families. Wellisch, DeAngelis, and Bond (1979) argue that family change occurs more rapidly in the multiple family group context because of the weight of the group, which therapists can use for leverage. The authors have had a great deal of success utilizing Strategic Parenting groups in both inpatient and outpatient treatment settings. This innovative parenting group model provides parents with creative, hands-on techniques for intervening with difficult and challenging behaviors of their children and adolescents.

Many of the intervention strategies mentioned previously are primarily used in outpatient and inpatient treatment settings that have a strong family systems orientation. Unfortunately, the majority of drug abuse programs in this country continue to utilize the traditional disease model exclusively and lack the funding to expose clinical staff to techniques of family therapy which could enhance program effectiveness. According to O'Connell (1986), 75 percent of the psychiatry departments of hospitals in this country regularly use outside consultants for clinical training, while less than 8 percent of the chemical dependency programs can afford this service. These statistics help explain why the majority of family counselors in Twelve Step programs lack the knowledge and skills to provide effective family therapy. Since staff training budgets are often quite low in these programs, family counselors may be limited to attending one or two workshops per year. In many ways, family counselors and other clinical staff who work in these programs are set up to fail with their clients due to the lack of emphasis on staff development.

We believe that one major way inpatient clinical teams can keep adolescent clients and their parents invested in their treatment programs is to actively involve them all in the treatment planning process. Research on motivation indicates that clients are most likely to persist in an action when they perceive that they have personally chosen to do so. In order to perceive that one has a choice, there must be alternatives among which the client/family can choose (Miller, 1986). One research study suggests that any particular alcoholism treatment approach is more effective when clients choose that approach from among alternatives than when that approach is imposed on clients as the only option (Kissin, Platz, & Su, 1971). Along these same lines, when clients perceive freedom of choice in their treatment, there appears to be a decrease in resistance and a reduction in drop-out rates (Costello, 1975; Parker, Winstead, & Willi, 1979).

At times, Twelve Step residential and hospital-based programs seem too quick to diagnose adolescents as addicted and too ready to use exactly the same treatment package with all their adolescent clients. Gawlinski and Otto (1985) have found that programs serving alcohol abusers tend to lack clear goals and simply respond to whatever comes in the door. Similarly, Emrick and Hansen (1983) found that clients who reported to alcoholism clinics with any type of concern about their drinking were invariably welcomed for treatment. This is particularly obvious in many Twelve Step programs for adolescents. Once adolescent substance abusers receive their diagnoses, they will be confronted by peers and staff to admit that they are addicts or alcoholics. If adolescent clients refuse to acknowledge they have a disease and are addicted to chemicals, most likely they will be viewed as being in a state of denial.

The standard treatment regime for adolescent clients consists of attending daily Alcoholics Anonymous (AA) or Narcotics Anonymous (NA) meetings and educational groups. Physicians and clinical staff rarely consider adolescents' and parents' views of the problem, or what they would like treatment to achieve. Shapiro (1980) has identified how hospital treatment teams are more invested in treating the patient's illness, rather than his or her social context. As a result, the clinical staff often assume adversarial relationships with families. Polak and Jones (1973) argue that inpatient hospital programs function on the basis of staff values and social needs, while ignoring those of the patients. Often families refuse to accept the treatment team's authority and seek allies on the staff, which creates confused hierarchies in the treatment system (Schwartzman, (1985).

As we reported earlier, Harbin (1985) and Menses and Durrant (1987) have abandoned the traditional expert/patient hierarchical approach to inpatient care of adolescents and replaced it with a family-treatment team collaborative approach. Fox (Chapter 9 this volume) has developed an innovative inpatient treatment model for adolescent substance abusers which consists of empowering parents by placing them in charge of their adolescents' treatment. With the Fox System, the psychiatrist and treatment team serve only as consultants to the parents, while the latter are in charge of all treatment decisions. These previously mentioned clinicians recognize that families do have the resources and strengths to greatly assist the treatment team in resolving presenting problems. A collaborative, rather than hierarchical relationship is established with families (Hoffman, 1985). We believe that if programs can adopt this kind of treatment philosophy, there will be a considerable decrease in premature drop-out rates, less family resistance, and more effective treatment provided to adolescent substance abusers and their families.

In order for treatment teams to be effective helpers, there needs to be quality supervision and regular weekly clinical staff meetings to discuss cases. By clinical staff meetings, we mean having the treatment team carefully examine the interactions between themselves, the families they service, and the larger systems that impact the treatment process. If possible, the inpatient treatment program should contract with a reflecting consultation team (Andersen, 1987; Lussardi & Miller, this volume; Roberts, et al., 1989) to be present in clinicial staff meetings and for live family therapy case consultations. Reflecting consultation teams can be useful in providing treatment program staffs and other members of the family-multiple helper system (Coppersmith, 1985) with new and alternative ideas about presenting problem situations. As Anderson and Goolishian (1988) have pointed out, once members of the family-multiple helper system or problem organizing system begin to entertain new ideas about the identified problem, or communicate about it differently, the problem will rapidly dissolve.

Inpatient and residential treatment teams need to recognize that they are part of the same problem systems of their client families. Keeney and Ross (1983) refer to this view as "cybernetics of cybernetics" or "second-order cybernetics." Unfortunately, most drug abuse program personnel have not been exposed to this kind of systemically-oriented technology, and thus, are blind to the various ways other helpers and themselves contribute to the maintenance of family problems. Treatment teams may end up replicating the same ineffectual family patterns in the milieu that occur in the adolescents' families.

Staff Replication of Family Patterns

Schwartzman and Kniefel (1985) have identified three types of staff-replicated family patterns that occur in state mental health treatment centers for children: too richly joined, too poorly joined, and normal systems. The first two family patterns serve to maintain the problems they are trying to change by creating family structures in the milieu that are analogous to the children's present family systems. A similar staff replication dynamic frequently occurs in methadone maintenance clinics. Bokos and Schwartzman (1985) have identified family patterns that are not only replicated between the staff and clients, but are also the same family dynamics that occur between paraprofessionals, clinicians, and administrative staff. In the methadone clinic, problems begin with a lack of agreement between clients, families, paraprofessionals, and clinical staff regarding definitions of addiction. Conflict develops among staff, clients, and families. As a result of this conflict, there is a lack of consistent limits and rules, and no clear expectations for clients (Schwartzman, 1986). All of these treatment system problems lead to staff apathy, high staff turnover rates, paraprofessionals relapsing, and clients graduating to chronic patient status. Similar processes occur in alcoholism treatment facilities as well (Davis, 1980; Miller, 1983; O'Connell, 1986; Schwartzman, 1985, 1987).

Failure to Include Other Helping Systems

Although many programs for adolescent substance abusers often involve outside school personnel and probation officers in the treatment planning aspect of their programs, the treatment team is oblivious to the fact that these key members of the problem system need to be actively included in the treatment process as well. By conducting a macrosystemic assessment at intake with families, treatment teams can determine with their client families who should be included as part of the family-multiple helper problem system. This complex problem system can include the following individuals: extended family members, close family friends, the adolescent's peers, school personnel, probation officers, and past and present helping professionals. According to Goolishian and Anderson (1981), therapeutic planning should include all of those individuals who have participated significantly in defining the family's problems and their attempted solutions. This is most apparent in the context of adolescent substance abuse problems. Many of these adolescent clients who are referred to inpatient programs have had a long history of outpatient and residential treatment experiences. While on the treatment circuit, these adolescents may have accumulated a long list of diagnoses from several different therapists with varying treatment orientations. In some case situations, past therapists may remain actively involved with adolescents' families long after the conclusion or failure of therapy.

After securing families' written consents, it can be most advantageous for inpatient treatment teams to include past and presently involved therapists and other helpers in the adolescents' milieu activities and family therapy sessions. Not only can these key members of the problem systems provide treatment teams with invaluable information regarding their attempted solutions with the identified clients, but their active participation in the treatment process will serve to maximize opportunities for these other helpers to notice differences and changes in the adolescent's behavior and in each family. Thus, when these other helpers become less concerned about the adolescent's behaviors and family, they will no longer feel compelled to organize themselves around the previously perceived substance abuse problem.

CONTROLLED USE VERSUS TOTAL ABSTINENCE AS A GOAL FOR TREATMENT

Since the majority of inpatient and outpatient chemical dependency programs in this country are based heavily on Jellinek's disease model (Jellinek, 1960) and the principles of Alcoholics Anonymous, adolescent clients are often left with no choices of treatment goal other than total abstinence. Clinicians who operate from this traditional treatment perspective often seem to believe that once their clients stop using chemicals, their individual problems will stop as well. One major difficulty with this line of thinking is that it implies a response to the clients' problems which separates the substance abuse behavior from the wider social context in which it occurs (Thorley, 1985). We believe that the disease approach can focus too much on the client's chemical abuse and need for immediate abstinence. Surprisingly, chemical dependency programs continue to employ complete abstinence as the major goal of treatment despite the fact that long-term follow-up studies indicate that 90 percent of those individuals who received services in these programs resume chemical use in the future (Emrick & Hansen, 1983; Helzer et al., 1985; Miller, 1986; Polich et al., 1981).

Now, we would like to discuss the strengths and limitations of pursuing controlled use goals with adolescent substance abusers. Depending on parental goals for adolescents, cutting back appears to be more palatable to most youths as an initial treatment goal, particularly in outpatient treatment. In some cases, therapists will serve as arbitrators in negotiating an initial goal of controlled use with parents and adolescents. This should include agreement on criteria for whether adolescents have been successful in moderating use.

Cutting back as a treatment goal fits more closely with the developmental norms and values of the adolescent culture. Several studies with regular and heavy substance abusers support this view (Brook & Whitehead, 1983; Glassner & Loughlin, 1987; Jessor & Jessor, 1977; Kandel, 1981; Miller et al., 1981; van Dijk, 1980; Winick, 1961). Jessor and Jessor (1977) argue that most drug use by adolescents can best be understood as transitional behavior that occurs within normal development from adolescence into adulthood. Glassner and Loughlin (1987) found that heavy adolescent drug users plan to give up most or all drug use in adulthood specifically because they imagine the social worlds they join in the future as having no place for drugs. Kandel (1981) and Miller, et al. (1981) found in their longitudinal research that most adolescent drug users greatly reduce or fully abandon drug-taking when they became young adults. Two studies have suggested that adolescents use drugs as displays of independence (Jessor & Jessor, 1977; van Dijk, 1980). Brook and Whitehead (1983) found that heavy drug users were able to envision their lives ten years down the road as being drug-free.

There are a number of societal obstacles preventing total abstinence goals from being useful with adolescent substance abusers. Our society permits and encourages chemical use of legal psychoactive drugs for adults through media advertisements which glamorize the use of alcohol as making one more seductive, macho, or sociable. Taking pills for quick relief is another popular message provided by the media. These advertisements not only stimulate adolescent curiosity, but convey a strong message that chemical use is good for you (Carroll, 1986). Contradictory findings concerning some of the immediate and long-term physical, mental, and social effects of chemical substances may contribute to some adolescents generalizing these research findings to all drugs including alcohol (Gordon & McAllister, 1982).

Politicians at all levels of government often contribute to the maintenance of ineffectual treatment strategies for adolescent substance abusers. These important officials are not familiar with the research literature and effective intervention strategies with this population. It appears that government officials are satisfied with the traditional drug education approach with adolescents because it is easy to deliver and fairly inexpensive to provide (Rhodes & Jason, 1988).

Little has been written in addiction literature on controlled chemical use as a treatment goal for adolescent substance abusers. Carpenter, Lyons, and Miller (1985) found that behavioral self-control training can be a useful primary and secondary prevention approach for adolescents at high risk for developing alcoholism problems. Adolescents are taught specific guidelines and goal-setting procedures for achieving responsible drinking behavior. The major focus of this approach is on self-control, an internal-attribution framework that has been found to be associated with better maintenance and generalization of gains in a wide range of problem areas (Kopel & Arkowitz, 1975).

Smith (1983) has found the goal of moderate use to be most useful with adolescent substance abusers who refuse to discontinue marijuana use. He offers the following five guidelines to such adolescent marijuana abusers.

1. Moderate use is 4–5 marijuana joints per week.
2. Use would be limited to after school and weekends.
3. Marijuana would not be used before driving a motor vehicle.
4. Use should be inconspicuous, since unusual or disturbing behavior can lead to legal involvement.
5. Multiple drug use is hazardous.

Although Smith's treatment approach would be considered by most therapists as being quite radical, he speaks a language that more closely fits with the values and norms of the social world in which regular and heavy substance abusers are very much a part of. Several studies have clearly demonstrated that a proscriptive approach—total and permanent abstinence from all chemicals—is not effective with adolescents who use drugs on a regular basis (Blizzard & Teague, 1981; Dembo et al., 1978; Nathan, 1983; Swisher & Hoffman, 1985).

While controlled use is also controversial with adult problem drinkers, a number of studies support controlled drinking as a legitimate goal. Sobell and Sobell (1973) found, in their major outcome study comparing behavioral treatment approaches with hospital treatment in groups having either an abstinence or a moderation goal, that the latter group of subjects showed superior improvement up to three years following treatment. Caddy, Addington, and Perkins (1978) in replicating the Sobells' research, found that harm-free drinking goals, when negotiated with physically dependent clients after an initial period of abstinence, actually resulted in more client compliance and, ultimately, more abstinence. Miller and his colleagues have repeatedly demonstrated that both therapist-directed and self-directed behavioral control training can produce successful outcome rates with problem drinkers (Buck & Miller, 1981; Carpenter et al., 1985; Miller & Hester, 1988; Miller & Munoz, 1982).

At this point in our discussion we would like to examine some specific case situations where controlled use treatment goals would be contraindicated. It has been our clinical experience that in family therapy cases where one or both parents are either adult children of alcoholics, or are recovering from addiction problems themselves, total abstinence may be the only treatment goal these parents would accept for their adolescents. These very same parents may be actively involved in self-help groups such as Alcoholics Anonymous which preach total and permanent abstention from all chemicals for life. In case situations where one or more family members besides the adolescent client are heavily abusing chemicals, it is not likely that controlled use will be achieved. We would not pursue controlled chemical use treatment goals with adolescent substance abusers who display signs of severe physical withdrawal or who fail to comply with contracts for moderate use. Finally, adolescent substance abusers who are on probation are court-ordered to abstain from using alcohol and other drugs while in the legal system, which makes therapeutic goals less flexible.

If controlled chemical use is ever to become a respected and useful treatment goal for adolescent substance abusers, further research will be needed to empirically legitimize the effectiveness of such a treatment goal with this population. Through rigorous research efforts, we may be able to determine which type of adolescent substance abusers would best benefit from moderation of use as a treatment goal.

CONTROVERSIES REGARDING THE DISEASE MODEL OF ADDICTION

The popular disease model of addiction has its roots in the pioneering work of E.M. Jellinek (1952, 1960). Jellinek devised a rather elaborate classification system for diagnosing alcoholics. For Jellinek (1960), alcoholism is a progressive disease characterized by biochemical alterations, loss of control, intense craving, and traumatic withdrawal. Once considered physically dependent on alcohol or other drugs, individuals' original reasons for using chemicals do not matter because the psychobiological factors have taken over (Shaw, 1985).

Numerous research studies have attempted to find empirical evidence for Jellinek's diagnostic classification system of alcoholism (Miller, 1983; Pattison et al., 1977; Room, 1983). Some authors believe that these studies have failed to demonstrate that alcoholism follows any identifiable path in its development or that it is a unitary entity (Peele, 1985). These authors also point to the lack of an empirically demonstrated internal mechanisms that would account for an alcoholic's loss of control (Peele, 1985; Robinson, 1972). Instead, laboratory studies in which alcoholics were observed while consuming alcohol have found that these individuals do regulate their drinking (Heather & Robertson, 1981; Marlatt, 1978; Mello & Mendelson, 1971; Nathan & O'Brien, 1971). Finally, contrary to the longstanding traditional view of the progressive nature of alcoholism, alcoholics with varying degrees of drinking problems have been found to recover without treatment and to return to nonproblematic use (Heather & Robertson, 1981; Knupfer, 1972; Peele, 1985; Polich et al., 1981; Shaw, 1985; Vaillant, 1983). Vaillant (1983), in his important longitudinal study with over 1000 alcoholics, found the following: Alcoholism occurs along a continuum, which includes a variety of drinking disorders; alcohol problems frequently reverse themselves without medical treatment or the support of Alcoholics Anonymous; a genetic basis for alcoholism is questionable; alcoholics generally engage in harm-free drinking in the future (Peele, 1985).

The widely held belief that addiction is the result of a particular "biological mechanism that locks the body into an invariant pattern of behavior—one marked by intense craving and traumatic withdrawal when the drug of choice is not available—is disputed by considerable research evidence" (Peele, 1985, p. 6). Several studies with regular and heavy opiate users have challenged a purely biological view of addiction. This is most evident with the large number of Vietnam veterans who heavily abused heroin while overseas, but who were able to give up their drug habits completely upon returning to the states (Jaffe & Harris, 1973;

Peele, 1978). The high recovery rates of many of these veterans helps to demonstrate that any harm that heroin may have engendered is not necessarily permanent or irreversible (Robins, 1980). Winick (1961) has observed a "maturing out" of opiate use phenomena that occurs with many young addicts as they get older. Finally, another study found that occasional use of narcotics without becoming addicted appears possible even for individuals who would have previously been considered dependent on narcotics (Robins et al., 1974).

Advocates of the disease model of addiction point to the genetic research findings of Goodwin et al. (1973) as providing support for a genetic and biological explanation for alcoholism. Goodwin (1985) found that children of alcoholic parents are four times as likely to become alcoholic as children who were reared in nonalcoholic family environments. However, two other genetic research groups that attempted to replicate Goodwin's study failed to produce similar findings or any further evidence for the existence of a genetic predisposition for alcoholism (Knop et al., 1984; Partanen et al., 1966). These contradictory findings have led genetic theorists and researchers to propose that the inherited genetic predisposition factor for alcoholism takes the form of some "probabilistically greater risk of developing drinking problems" (Peele, 1985, p. 49). We tend to adopt this probabilistic assumption in our work with adolescents who have a strong family history of chemical dependency. It seems justified to warn adolescents that they are likely to be at greater risk for developing an addiction than their peers who lack such a history. This does not seem terribly different from our practice of warning adolescents from such families that they are at risk for choosing chemically dependent partners.

Implications for Adolescent Substance Abuse

Despite all of the contradictory research findings to support the use of a disease-oriented treatment approach for adolescent substance abusers, the majority of adolescent chemical dependency treatment programs are strongly committed to this treatment philosophy. This situation is perpetuated, at least in part, by the fact that many of these programs were founded or are run by recovering alcoholics or drug addicts. The clinical staffs in these programs often may consist primarily of adult children of alcoholics and recovering counselors. Since many of these treatment programs are heavily based on the principles of Alcoholics Anonymous, the major thrust of treatment is lifelong abstinence and active confrontation of clients regarding their denial. The physicians and the clinical staffs in these programs teach their clients what to say, and chemical dependence is no exception to this. Clients who regularly attend AA or NA meetings will strongly express widely held beliefs about loss of control and will value abstinence more than those clients who do not. Thus, it may be that clients trained in AA or NA thinking will find a chemical dependence diagnostic label more useful than others (Thorley, 1985). Many substance abusing clients attending social service agencies and mental health clinics are not particularly inconvenienced by or aware of their substance dependence. More significantly, clients do not express their difficulties or problems in terms of dependence or complain of physical dependence (Freed, 1976). Thorley (1985) has observed that "the assumptions of the therapist rating his patient's dependence and proceeding with the appropriate treatment regimen do seem to overlook the most powerful and significant factor in the system—the patient or *client himself*" (p. 83). Thorley and other leading anti-disease model theorists vehemently oppose the kind of standardized treatment that occurs in many traditional Twelve Step programs.

Often adolescent substance abusers are misdiagnosed as being chemically dependent or as displaying the symptomatic profile of some popular *DSM III* diagnosis, such as Conduct Disorder (*Diagnostic and Statistical Manual: Revised Edition,* 1987). Often the context in which adolescent clients receive treatment dictates the diagnostic label and treatment regimens received. If adolescent clients are admitted into Twelve Step programs, they will have to acknowledge that they are either an alcoholic or an addict, with little choice in the matter. At the other extreme, adolescent substance abusers may be misdiagnosed and placed on inpatient psychiatric units. Psychiatrists, psychologists, and other clinical staff members will endlessly search for characterlogical explanations of why adolescent clients abuse chemicals. For example, substance-abusing behavior may be viewed as a symptom of an underlying depression by psychiatrists and clinical staff.

The theory that substance abuse is symptomatic of some underlying psychopathology is largely unproven. Despite numerous studies, no specific psychological predisposition factors for substance abuse have been identified. As Glassner and Loughlin (1987) have pointed out, "drug-taking is simply too widespread among adolescents today for it to be reasonable to expect that this behavior grows out of individual psychopathology" (p. 239).

Few studies have focused on the positive traits of adolescent substance abusers. Glassner and Loughlin (1986, 1987) have found that heavy adolescent drug users place a strong emphasis on being independent, value self-control when using chemicals, and have the capacity to feel competent and master their environment. Adolescent marijuana users have self-imposed rules about drug usage versus addiction. Even frequent drug users do not accept the labels of addiction or addicts; instead they value self-control (Glassner & Loughlin, 1987). We believe strongly that an optimal treatment program should capitalize on these positive qualities, rather than assuming that adolescent substance abusers are deficient.

REFERENCES

Andersen, T. (1987). The reflecting team: Dialogue and metadialogue in clinical work. *Family Process, 26*(4), 415–429.

Anderson, H. & Goolishian, H. A. (1988). Human systems as linguistic systems: Preliminary and evolving ideas about the implications for clinical theory. *Family Process, 27*(4), 371–395.

Barton, C. & Alexander, J. (1977). Therapist skills as determinants of effective systems—behavioral family therapy. *International Journal of Family Counseling, 5,* 11–20.

Barton, C. & Alexander, J. (1981). Functional family therapy. In A. S. Gurman & D. P. Kniskern (eds.), *Handbook of family therapy.* New York: Brunner/Mazel, 403–443.

Bateson, S. (1980). *Mind and nature: A necessary unity.* New York: Bantam Books.

Billings, A. & Moos, R. (1983). Psychosocial processes of recovery among alcoholics and their families: Implications for clinicians and program evaluators. *Addictive Behaviors, 8,* 205–218.

Black, C. (1981). *It will never happen to me.* Denver: M.A.C. Printing & Publications.

Blizzard, R. A. & Teague, R. W. (1981). Alternatives to drug use: An alternative approach to drug education. *International Journal of the Addictions, 2,* 371–375.

Blum, R. W. (1987). *School survey results: The Minnesota adolescent health survey database project 1986-1987.* Minneapolis, MN: University of Minnesota.

Bokos, P. J. & Schwartzman, J. (1985). Family therapy and methadone treatment of opiate addiction. In J. Schwartzman (ed.), *Families and other systems.* New York: Guilford Press.

Brook, R. C. & Whitehead, P. C. (1983). Values of adolescent drug users. *International Journal of the Addictions, 18,* 1–8.

Buck, K. & Miller, W. R. (1981). Why does biblio-therapy work? A Controlled study. Paper presented at the annual meeting of the Association of Advancement of Behavior Therapy, Toronto, Ontario.

Caddy, G. R., Addington, H. J., & Perkins, D. (1978). Individualized behavior therapy for alcoholics: A third year independent double-blind follow-up. *Behavior Research & Therapy, 16,* 345–362.

Calahan, D. (1970). *Problem drinkers.* San Francisco: Jossey-Bass.

Calahan, D. & Room, R. (1974). *Problem drinking among American men.* Monograph 7. New Brunswick, NJ: Rutgers Center of Alcohol Studies.

Carpenter, R. A., Lyons, C. A., & Miller, W. R. (1985). Peer-managed self-control program for prevention of alcohol abuse in American Indian high school students: A pilot evaluation study. *International Journal of the Addictions, 20*(2), 299–310.

Carrol, J. F. (1986). Secondary prevention: A programmatic approach to the problem of substance abuse among adolescents. In I. Beschner & A. I. Friedman (eds.) *Teen drug use,* Lexington, MA: Lexington Books.

Clark, W. B. (1982). Public drinking contexts: Bars and taverns. In T. C. Harford & L. L. Gains (eds.). *Social drinking contexts.* Research Monograph 7. Rockville, MD: National Institute on Alcohol Abuse & Alcoholism.

Coleman, S. b. & Davis, D. (1978). Family therapy and drug abuse: A national survey. *Family Process, 17*(1), 21–31.

Coppersmith, E. I. (1985). Families and multiple helpers: A systemic perspective. In D. Campbell & R. Draper (eds.), *Applications of systemic family therapy: A Milan approach.* London: Grune & Stratton.

Costello, R. M. (1975). Alcoholism treatment and evaluation: In search of methods. *International Journal of the Addictions, 10,* 251–275.

Daley, D. C. (1986). *Relapse prevention workbook for recovering alcoholics and drug dependent persons.* Holmes Beach, FL: Learning Publications.

Daley, D. C. (1987). Relapse prevention with substances abusers: Clinical issues and myths. *Social Work,* 138–142.

Davis, D. I. (1980). Alcoholics anonymous and family therapy. *Journal of Marital and Family Therapy. 6*(1), 65–74.

de Shazer, S. (1985). *Keys to solution in brief therapy.* New York: W. W. Norton.

Dembo, R., Burgos, W., Babst, D. V., Schneidler, I., & La Grand, L. E. (1978). Neighborhood relationships and drug involvement among inner city junior high school youths: Implications for drug education and prevention programming. *Journal of Drug Education. 8*(3), 231–252.

Diagnostic statistical manual of mental disorders. 1987. Spitzer, R. L. & Williams, J. B. (eds.). Washington, DC: American Psychiatric Association.

van Dijk, W. K. (1980). Biological, psychogenic, and sociogenic factors in drug dependence. In D. Lettieri (ed.), *Theories of drug abuse.* Washington, DC: National Institute on Drug Abuse.

Donovan, D. M. & Chavey, E. F. (1985). Alcoholic relapse prevention and intervention: Models and methods. In S. A. Marlatt & J. R. Gordon (eds.), *Relapse prevention.* New York: Guilford Press.

Durrant, M. (1985). Temper taming. Unpublished manuscript.

Efron, D. & Rowe, B. (1987). *The strategic parenting manual.* London, Ontario: Journal of Strategic & Systemic Therapies.

Emrick, C. D. & Hansen, J. (1983). Assertions regarding effectiveness of treatment for alcoholism: Fact or fantasy? *American Psychologist, 38,* 1078–1088.

Falk, J. L., Dews, P. B., & Schuster, C. R. (1983). Commonalities in the environmental control of behavior. In P. K. Levinson, D. R. Gerstein, & D. R. Maloff (eds.) *Commonalities in substance abuse and habitual behavior.* Lexington, MA: Lexington.

Fillmore, K. M. (1975). Relationships between specific drinking problems in early adulthood and middle age: An exploratory 20 year follow-up study. *Journal of Studies on Alcohol, 38,* 882–907.

Freed, A. (1976). Alcoholism: The interaction of alcoholics in a therapeutic community. Unpublished manuscript.

Gawlinski, G. & Otto, S. (1985). The anatomy of organizational melancholia, or treatment works on some occasions and not on others. In N. Heather, I. Robertson, & P. Davies (eds.). *The misuse of alcohol: Crucial issues in dependence treatment and prevention.* New York: New York University Press.

Glassner, B., Carpenter, C., & Berg, B. (1986). Marijuana in the lives of adolescents. In G. Beschner & A. S. Friedman (eds.), *Teen drug use.* Lexington, MA: Lexington Books.

Glassner, B. & Loughlin, J. (1987). *Drugs in adolescent worlds: Burnouts to straights.* New York: St. Martin's Press.

Glynn, T. J. (1981). From family to peers: A review of transitions of influence among drug using youth. *Journal of Youth & Adolescence, 10,* 363–378.

Glynn, T. J (1984). Adolescent drug use and the family environment: A review. *Journal of Drug Issues, 4,* 271–295.

Goodwin, D. W., Schulsinger, F., Hermansen, L., Guze, S. B., & Winokur, G. (1973). Alcohol problems in adoptees raised apart from biological parents. *Archives of General Psychiatry, 28,* 238–243.

Goodwin, D. W. (1985). Alcoholism and genetics. *Archives of General Psychiatry, 42,* 171–174.

Goolishian, H. & Anderson, H. (1981). Including non-blood-related persons in family therapy. In A. S. Gurman (ed.), *Questions & answers in the practice of family therapy.* New York: Brunner/Mazel, 75–80.

Gordis, E., Dorph, D., Sepe, V. & Smith, H. (1981). Outcome of alcoholism treatment among 5578 patients in an urban comprehensive hospital-based program: Application of a computerized data system. *Alcoholism: Clinical & Experimental Research, 5,* 509–522.

Gordon, N. F. & McAllister, A. L. (1982). Adolescent drinking: Issues and research. In F. J. Coates, A. C. Petersen, & C. Perry (eds.), *Promoting adolescent health: A dialogue on research and practice.* New York: Academic Press.

Gorski, T. T. (1982). *Gaining a perspective on relapse in alcoholism.* Hazel Crest & Alcoholism Systems Associates.

Gorski, T. T. & Miller, M. (1986). *Staying sober: A guide for relapse prevention.* Independence, MO: Independence Press.

Gottheil, E., Thorton, C. C., Skoloda, T. E. & Alterman, A. I. (1982). Follow-up abstinent and nonabstinent alcoholics. *American Journal of Psychiatry,* 139, 560–565.

Haber, R. (1987). Friends in family therapy: Use of a neglected resource. *Family Process, 26*(2), 269–283.

Harbin, H. T. (1985). The family and the psychiatric hospital. In J. Schwartzman (ed.), *Families and other systems.* New York: Guilford Press, 108–131.

Harbin, H. T. (1978). Families and hospital: Collision or cooperation. *American Journal of Psychiatry, 135,* 1496–1499.

Harrison, P. A. & Hoffman, N. G. (1987). *CATOR 1987 report: Adolescent residental treatment intake and follow-up findings.* St. Paul, MN: Chemical Abuse/ Addiction Treatment Outcome Registry.

Heather, N. & Robertson, I. (1981). *Controlled drinking.* London: Methmen.

Heather, N., Winton, M., & Rollnick, S. (1982). "An empirical test of a cultural delusion of alcoholics." *Psychological Reports, 50,* 379–382.

Heather, N., Rollnick, S., & Winton, M. (1983). A comparison of objective and subjective measures of alcohol dependence as predictors of relapse following treatment. *British Journal of Clinical Psychology, 22,* 11–17.

Helzer, J. E., Robins, L. N., Taylor, J. R, Carey, K., Miller, R. H., Combs-Orme, T. & Farmer, A. (1985). The extent of long-term moderate drinking among alcoholics discharged from medical and psychiatric treatment facilities. *New England Journal of Medicine, 312,* 1678–1682.

Hoffman, L. (1985). Beyond power and control: Toward a second order family systems therapy. *Family Systems Medicine, 3*(4), 381–395.

Hoffman, L. (1988). A constructivist position for family therapy. *Irish Journal of Psychology, 9(1),* 110–129.

Jaffe, J. H. & Harris, T. G. (1973, August). As far as heroin is concerned, the worst is over. *Psychology Today,* 68–79, 85.

Jellinek, E. M. (1946). Phases in the drinking history of alcoholics: Analysis of a survey conducted by the official organ of Alcoholics Anonymous. *Quarterly Journal of Studies on Alcohol, 7,* 1–88.

Jellinek, E. M. (1952). Phases of alcohol addiction. *Quarterly Journal of Studies on Alcohol, 13,* 637–684.

Jellinek, E. M. (1960). *The disease concept of alcoholism.* New Haven: Hillhouse Press.

Jessor, R. & Jessor, S. L. (1977). *Problem behavior and psychosocial development: A longitudinal study of youth.* New York: Academic Press.

Kaufman, E. & Kaufmann, P. N. (1979). *The family therapy of drug and alcohol abusers.* New York: Gardner Press.

Kandel, D. B., Kessler, R. C. & Margulies, R. Z. (1978). Antecedents of adolescent initiation into stages of drug use: A developmental analysis. In D. B. Kandel (ed.), *Longitudinal research on drug use.* Washington, DC: Hemisphere.

Kissin, B., Platz, A., & Su, W. H. (1971). Selective factors in treatment choice and outcome in alcoholics. In N. K. Mello & J. H. Mendelson (eds.). *Recent advances in studies of alcoholism.* Washington, DC: U.I. Government Printing Office.

Kandel, D. B. (1981). Drug use by youth: An overview. In D. J. Lettieri & J. P. Ludford (eds.), *Drug abuse and the American adolescent.* Washington, DC: National Institute on Drug Abuse.

Keeney, B. P. & Ross, J. M. (1983). Cybernetics of brief family therapy. *Journal of Marital and Family Therapy, 9*(4), 375–382.

Knop, J., Goodwin, D. W., Teasdale, T. W., Mikkelsen, N., & Schulsinger, F.

(1984). A Danish prospective study of young males at high risk for alcoholism. In D. W. Goodwin, K. T. va Drusen, & S. A. Mednick (eds.). *Longitudinal research in alcoholism.* Boston: Kluwer-Nijhoff.

Knupfer, G. (1972). Ex-problem drinkers. In M. A. Roff, L. N. Robins, & M. Pollack (eds.), *Life history research in psychopathology.* Minneapolis, MN: University of Minnesota Press.

Kopel, S. & Arkowitz, H. (1975). The role of attribution and self-perception in behavior change: Implications for behavior therapy. *Genetic Psychologist Monograph, 92,* 175–212.

Lennard, H. L., Epstein, L. J., Ransom, D. (1971). *Mystification and drug misuse.* San Francisco: Jossey-Bass.

Levine, E. M. & Kozak, C. (1979). Drug and alcohol use, delinquency among upper middle class pre- and post-adolescents. *Journal of Youth and Adolescence, 8,* 397–413.

Levy, B. (1972). Five years after: A follow-up of 50 narcotic addicts. *American Journal of Psychiatry, 7,* 102–106.

Ludwig, A. M. (1988). *Understanding the alcoholic's mind: The nature of craving and how to control it.* New York: Oxford University Press.

Lukoff, I. F. & Brook, J. S. (1974). A socio-cultural exploration of reported heroin use. In C. Winick (ed.), *Sociological aspect of drug dependence.* Cleveland, OH: CRC Press.

Maddux, J. F. & Desmond, D. P. (1986). Relapse and recovery in substance abuse careers. In F. M. Tims & C. S. Leukefeld (eds.), *Relapse and recovery in drug abuse.* Rockville, MD: DOHHS, NIDA Research Monograph 72.

Marlatt, G. A. (1978). Craving for alcohol, loss of control & relapse: A cognitive-behavoral analysis: In P. Nathan, G. A. Marlatt, T. Loberg (eds.). *Alcoholism: New directions in behavioral research and treatment.* New York: Plenum.

Marlatt, G. A. (1982). Relapse prevention: A self-control program for the treatment of addictive behaviors. In R. B. Stuart (ed). *Adherence, compliance and generalization in behavioral medicine.* New York: Brunner/Mazel.

Marlatt, G. A & Gordon, J. R. (1980). Determinants of relapse: Implications for the maintenance of behavior change. In P. O. Davidson & S. M. Davidson (eds.). *Behavioral medicine: Changing health lifestyles.* New York: Brunner/Mazel.

Marlatt, G. A. & Gordan, J. R. (1985). *Relapse prevention.* New York: Guildford Press.

Meier, R. F., Burkett, S. R., & Hickman, C. A. (1984). Sanctions, peers, and deviance. *The Sociological Quarterly, 25,* 67–82.

Mello, N. K. & Mendelson, J. H. (1971). A quantitative analysis of drinking patterns in alcoholics. *Archives of General Psychiatry, 25,* 527–539.

Menses, G. & Durrant, M. (1987). Contextual residential care: The applications of the principles of cybernetic therapy to the residential treatment of irresponsible adolescents and their families. *Journal of Strategic and Systemic Therapies, 6(2),* 3–16.

Miller, D. (1983). Outlaws and invaders: The adaptive function of alcohol abuse in the helper-supra system. *Journal of Strategic and Systemic Therapist,* 2(3), 15–27.

Miller, W. R. (1983, May). Haunted by the Zeitgeist: Reflections on contrasting treatment goals and concepts of alcoholism in Europe and America. Paper presented at the Conference on Alcohol and Culture, Farmington, CT.

Miller, W. R. & Hester, R. K. (1980). Treating the problem drinker: Modern approaches. In W. R. Miller (ed). *The addictive behaviors: Treatment of alcoholism, drug abuse, smoking, and obesity.* New York: Pergamon press.

Miller, W. R. & Hester, R. K. (1988). The effectiveness of alcoholism treatment: What research reveals. In W. R. Miller & N. Heather (eds.), *Treating addictive behaviors: Processes of change.* New York: Plenum Press.

Miller, W R. (1986). Increasing motivation for change. In R. K. Hester & W. R. Miller (eds.), *Handbook of alcoholism treatment approaches: Effective alternatives.* New York: Pergamon Press.

Miller, W. R. (1983). Controlled drinking: A history and critical review. *Journal on the Study of Alcohol, 44,* 68–83.

Miller, W. R. & Munoz, R. F. (1982). How to control your drinking. Albuquerque, NM: University of New Mexico Press.

Miller, W. R., Gribskov, C. J. & Nortell, R. L. (1981). Effectiveness of a self-control manual for problem drinkers with and without therapist contact. *International Journal of the Addictions, 16,* 1247–1254.

Nathan, P. & O'Brien, J. S. (1971). An experimental analysis of the behavior of alcoholics and nonalcoholics during prolonged experimental drinking: A necessary precursor of behavior therapy? *Behavior Therapy, 2,* 455–476.

Nathan, P. (1983). Failures in prevention: Why we can't prevent the devastating effect of alcoholism and drug abuse. *American Psychologist, 38*(4), 459–467.

O'Connell, K. R. (1986). Counseling the counseling family. *Alcoholism & Addiction,* 21–22.

Parker, M. W., Winstead, D. K., & Willi, F. T. (1979). Patient autonomy in alcohol rehabilitation: I. Literature review. *International Journal of the Addictions, 14,* 1015–1022.

Partanen, J., Brunn, K., & Markkaners, T. (1966). *Inheritance of drinking behavior.* New Brunswick, NJ: Rutgers University Center on Alcohol Studies.

Pattison, E. M., Sobell, M. B., & Sobell, L. C. (1977). *Emerging concepts of alcohol dependence.* New York: Springer.

Peele, S. (1978, September). Addiction: The analgesic experience. *Human nature,* 61–67.

Peele, S (1985). *The meaning of addiction: Compulsive experience and its interpretation.* Lexington, MA: Lexington Books.

Piercy, F. P. & Frankel, B. R. (1985). *Training Manual: Purdue Brief Family Therapy.* W. Lafayette, IN: Purdue University.

Polak, P. & Jones, M. (1973). The psychiatric nonhospital: A model for change. *Community Mental Health Journal, 9*(2), 123–131.

Polich, J. M., Armor, D., & Braiker, H. B. (1981). *The course of alcoholism: Four years after treatment.* New York: Wiley & Sons.

Rhodes, J. E. & Jason, L. A. (1988). *Preventing substance abuse among children and adolescents.* New York: Pergamon Press.

Roberts, M., Caesar, L., Perryclear, B. & Phillips, D. (1989). Reflecting team consultations. *Journal of Strategic and Systemic Therapies, 8*(3), 38–47.

Robins, L. N. (1980). The natural history of drug abuse. In D. J. Lettieri, M. Sayers, & H. W. Pearson (eds.), *Theories of drug abuse: Selected contemporary perspective.* NIDA Research Marograph 30. Washington, DC: National Institute on Drug Abuse.

Robins, L. N., Davis, D. H., & Goodwin, D. W. (1974). Drug use by U. S. Army enlisted men in Vietnam: A follow-up on their return home. *American Journal of Epidemiology, 99,* 235–249.

Robinson, D. (1972). The alcohologist's addiction—some implications of having lost control over the disease concept of alcoholism. *Quarterly Journal of Studies on Alcohol, 33,* 1028–1042.

Room, R. (1983). Sociological aspects of the disease concept of alcoholism. In R. G. Smart, F. B. Glaser, H. Kalant, R. E. Popham, & W. Schmidt (eds.), *Research advances in alcohol and drug problems,* Vol. 7. New York: Plenum Press.

Schaps, B., Bartolo, R. D., Moskowitz, J., Palley, C. S., & Churgin S. 1981). A review of 127 drug abuse prevention program evaluations. *Journal of Drug Issues,* Winter, *17*(48), 17–43.

Schwartzman, J. (1985). Alcoholics anonymous and the family: A systemic perspective. *American Journal of Drug and Alcohol Abuse, 11(1&2),* 68–89.

Schwartzman, J. (ed.) (1983). *Families and other systems,* New York: Guilford Press.

Schwartzman, J. (1987). Continuities and discontinuities in the family treatment of substance abuse. *Journal of Psychotherapy & the Family, 3*(3), 105–127.

Schwartzman, J. & Kneifel, A. W. (1985). Familiar institutions: How the child care system replicates family pattern. In J. Schwartzman (ed.), *Families and other systems.* New York: Guilford Press.

Schwartzman, J. (1986). Ritual as staff intervention. *Journal of Strategic and Systemic Therapies, 5*(3), 60–71.

Selekman, M. (1989a). Taming chemical monsters: Cybernetic-systemic therapy with adolescent substance abusers. *Journal of Strategic & Systemic Therapies, 8*(3), 5–10.

Selekman, M. (1989b). Engaging Adolescent Substance Abusers in family therapy. *Family Therapy Case Studies Journal,* in press.

Shapiro, J. (1980). Changing dysfunctional relationships between family and therapist. *Journal of Operational Psychiatry, 11*(1), 18–26.

Shaw, S. (1985). The disease concept of dependence. In Heather, N., Robertson, I., & Davies, P. (eds.), *The misuse of alcohol: Crucial issues in dependence treatment and prevention.* New York: New York University Press.

Smith, T. E. (1983). Reducing adolescents' marijuana abuse. *Social Work in Health Care, 9*(1), 33–44.

Sobell, M. B. & Sobell, L. C. (1973). Individualized behavior therapy for alcoholic. *Behavior Therapy, 4,* 49–72.

Sorensen, J. L. & Bernal, G. (1987). *A family like yours: Breaking the patterns of drug abuse.* San Francisco: Harper & Row.

Sorensen, J. L., Gibson, D., Deitch, D. A., & Bernal, G. (1985). Methodone application dropouts: Impact of requiring involvement of friends or family in treatment. *International Journal of the Addictions, 20,* 1273–1280.

Stanton, M. D., & Todd, T. C. (1981). Engaging "resistant" families in treatment: II. Principles and techniques in recruitment. *Family Process, 20,* 261–280.

Stanton, M. D., Todd, T. C. & Associates (1982). *The family therapy of drug abuse and addictions.* New York: Guilford Press.

Swisher, J. D. & Hoffman, A. (1985). Information: The irrelevant variable in drug education. In Corder, B. W., Smith, R. A., & Swisher, J. D. (eds.), *Drug Abuse prevention: Perspectives and approaches for educators.* Dubuque, LA: William C. Brown.

Tec, N. (1974). *Grass is green in suburbia: A sociological study of adolescent usage of illicit drugs.* Roslyn Hts., NY: Libra.

Thorley, A. (1985). The limitations of the alcohol dependence syndrome in multidisciplinary service development. In N. Heather, I. Robertson, & P. Davies (eds.). *The misuse of alcohol: Crucial issues in dependence treatment and prevention.* New York: New York University Press.

Tomm, K. & White, M. (1987, October). Externalizing problems and internalizing directional choices. Training Institute presented at the Annual Conference of the American Association for Marriage and Family Therapy, Chicago, IL.

Tuchfeld, B. (1976). Spontaneous remission in alcoholics: Empirical observations and theoretical implications. *Journal of Studies on Alcohol, 42,* 626–641.

Vaillant, G. E. (1983). The natural history of alcoholism. Cambridge, MA: Harvard University Press.

Van Deusen, J. M., Stanton, M. D., Scott, S. M., & Todd, T. C. (1980). Engaging "resistant" families in treatment: I. Getting the drug addict to recruit his family members. *International Journal of the Addictions, 15,* 1069–1089.

Watzlawick, P., Weakland, J., & Fisch, R. (1974). *Change: Principles of problem formation and problem resolution.* New York: W. W. Norton.

Wegscheider, S. (1981). *Another chance: Hope and health for the alcoholic family.* Palo Alto: Science & Behavior Books.

Weinstein, R. M. (1978). The avowal of motives for marijuana behavior. *International Journal of the Addictions, 13,* 887–910.

Wellisch, D., DeAngelis, G. G., & Bond, D. (1979). Family treatment of the homosexual adolescent drug abuser: On being gay in a sad family. In E. Kaufman & P. N. Kaufmann (eds.), *Family therapy of drug and alcohol abuse.* New York: Gardner Press.

Wermuth, L. & Scheidt, S. (1986). Enlisting family support in drug treatment. *Family Process, 25,* 25–33.

Wesson, D. R., Havassy, B. E., & Smith, D. E. (1986). Theories of relapse and recovery and their implications for drug abuse treatment. In F. M. Tims & C. G. Leukefeld (eds.), *Relapse and recovery in drug abuse.* Rockville, MD: National Institute on Drug Abuse, NIDA Research Monograph 72.

White, M. (1985). Fear busting and monster taming: An approach to the fears of young children. *Dulwich Centre Review,* 29–34.

Wikler, A. (1973). Dynamics of drug dependence: Implications of a conditioning theory for research and treatment. *Archives of General Psychiatry, 28,* 611–616.

Wille, R. (1980) Process of recovery among heroin users. In G. Edwards & A. Arif (eds.), *Drug problems in the sociocultural perspective.* Geneva: World Health Organization Public Health Paper No. 73.

Winick, C. (1961). Maturing out of narcotic addiction. *Bulletin of Narcotics, 14,* 1.

Zinberg, N. (1984). *Drugs, set and setting: The basis for controlled intoxicant use.* New Haven, CT: Yale University Press.

2
The Purdue Brief Family Therapy Model for Adolescent Substance Abusers

ROBERT A. LEWIS, Ph.D.
Professor, Department of Child Development and Family Research Institute

FRED P. PIERCY, Ph.D.
Associate Professor, Department of Child Development and Family Studies

DOUGLAS H. SPRENKLE, Ph.D.
Professor, Department of Child Development and Family Studies

TERRY S. TREPPER, Ph.D.
Professor, Behaviorial Sciences Department
Purdue University, West Lafayette, Indiana

THE GROWING EFFECTIVENESS OF FAMILY-BASED DRUG INTERVENTIONS

Until ten years ago very few drug treatment programs involved spouses or other family members directly in the treatment of the identified patient (Stanton, 1979a; 1979b). According to Stanton, although 93 percent of drug treatment programs acknowledged some interest in the clients' families, very few directly included any family members in their

*Authors have been listed alphabetically. All are core staff researchers on the project, **FAMILY THERAPY FOR DRUG ABUSING ADOLESCENTS,** funded by the National Institute for Drug Abuse, Grant DA/MH 03703-03.

treatment. For example, Farkas (1976) found that, even though 25 percent of his adult addicts were living in a marriage or common law relationship, their spouses were never included in the treatment.

Since then more recent research (including Stanton & Todd, 1979; 1982) has revealed that systemic (family-systems centered) drug interventions and treatments are effective in getting family members off drugs and keeping them off (Lewis et al., 1981; 1983). In contrast, if adolescents are treated individually and their family systems are not changed, adolescents may return to their homes and resume the same roles which earlier fostered their addictive behaviors. As some researchers have suggested, drug abuse, however costly or painful, may be subtly serving a function or role in the family such as keeping the parents together (Stanton & Todd, 1982) or serving as an attention getting device to get parents to stop fighting (Haley, 1980).

Although the inclusion of other family members may add greatly to the complexity of interventions, their involvement often provides greater leverage for sustained and successful drug treatment (Lewis & McAvoy, 1983). For example, in a study by McAuliffe (1975) one-third of a group of addicted heroin users in Baltimore, Maryland, were involved in stable marriages or common-law relationships. These respondents noted that their primary motivation for eliminating their drug use was to maintain their love relationship.

In other words, family love bonds can be utilized to work *for* successful drug treatment. To be sure, there are those cases where the addiction of a spouse or family member may contribute to the contagion/addiction of another. However, *effective* family relationships may be used to fight a family member's drug abuse. It is only when drug treatment professionals view the interplay between relationships and drug abuse that the professionals make full use of the motivations inherent in good relationships which may aid abusers in overcoming their reliance on drugs (Lewis & McAvoy, 1983).

HISTORICAL ROOTS OF FAMILY-BASED DRUG INTERVENTIONS

Systemic family therapy appears to be a viable prevention and treatment alternative for several reasons. For one, Tramontana's (1980) review of individual psychotherapy with adolescents suggested that adolescence may be a critical prevention and treatment period. Also, a variety of family relationship characteristics have been found to correlate strongly with adolescent drug abuse (e.g., Kovach & Glickman, 1986; Simcha-Fagan et al., 1986). In addition, Gurman and Kniskern (1981) have suggested that family therapy is at least as effective as individual therapy with children and may be even more effective when the identified patients are children.

But what types of family-based interventions might be most effective? At this stage in our knowledge, the most promising family interventions appear to be those that integrate theoretically compatible procedures from family therapies that have previously demonstrated their effectiveness. Four potential, well-defined family therapies with impressive empirical foundations are the structural, strategic, functional and behavioral family therapies.

Stanton and Todd's research (1979; 1982) with adult heroin addicts has been identified as one of the best controlled studies in family therapy (Gurman & Kniskern, 1981). To summarize, Stanton and Todd (1982) demonstrated structural-strategic family therapy to be an effective treatment modality for adult heroin addicts. Specifically, they found a significant decrease in adult heroin usage when structural-strategic family therapy was employed. Similarly, Szapocznik and his colleagues at the University of Miami School of Medicine found strategic therapy effective in decreasing adolescent drug abuse (Szapocznik et al. 1983, 1986).

Likewise, Minuchin and his colleagues (1978) found that structural family therapy significantly decreased symptoms of psychosomatic illnesses such as asthma and anorexia nervosa. The emphasis on a strong parental hierarchy in both structural and strategic family therapy appears particularly useful in the prevention and treatment of adolescent drug abuse, since many of the studies examining the families of adolescent drug abusers report ineffective parental authority and control.

Secondly, Alexander (1974) and his colleagues have repeatedly found functional family therapy, which incorporates aspects of behavioral and strategic family therapies, to be effective in the treatment of juvenile delinquents. Specifically, functional family therapy has been shown to positively affect outcome measures such as recidivism rates, family communication patterns, and premature termination from therapy.

Thirdly, behavioral family therapy often includes empirically validated procedures that are theoretically compatible with those of structural, strategic, and functional family therapies. For example, Patterson (1982) and his colleagues have repeatedly demonstrated the effectiveness of behavioral contracting with delinquent adolescents. Similarly, assertion training has been shown to positively affect interpersonal relationships in a variety of contexts. Assertion training would seem to be a particularly useful procedure in family therapy, to help drug abusing adolescents and their siblings learn skills to resist peer pressures related to drug use, as well as to learn to communicate with family members in appropriate, nonaggressive ways.

While the above family therapies appear promising for the prevention and treatment of adolescent drug abuse, prior to our Purdue Brief Therapy Model, they had not been integrated into one operational, replicable, and teachable family therapy treatment program. We developed in 1982-83 such an integrated family-based therapy. We are currently testing the effectiveness of the PBFT Model on one-third of approximately 150 families within a newly developed system of community networks in Indiana and Illinois.

The Purdue Brief Family Therapy Model

In brief, the Purdue Brief Family Therapy Model (PBFT) is a twelve-week program that integrates some of the most effective elements of structural, strategic, functional, and behavioral family therapies to change family systems into healthier environments, to stem the current drug abuse by adolescents and to prevent the development of drug abuse by younger siblings. Our integrative treatment model is intended to decrease familial resistance to drug treatment, redefine drug use as a family problem; establish appropriate parental influence; interrupt dysfunctional sequences of behavior; assess the interpersonal function of drug abuse; implement change strategies consistent with the family's interpersonal functioning; and provide assertion training skills for both adolescents and siblings to resist peer pressures leading to chemical abuse.

BASIC ASSUMPTIONS

The remainder of this chapter describes more fully the PBFT model. As described earlier, the PBFT model employs selected, theoretically compatible, and teachable skills from the structural, strategic, functional, and behavioral family therapies. These family therapies are suitable for integration because of their pragmatic and theoretical similarities. Specifically, we assume that the structural, strategic, functional, and behavioral family therapies all:

1. Monitor behavior and interpersonal interactions,
2. Conceptualize problems interactionally rather than in terms of individual pathology,
3. Note the function of problem behaviors,
4. Conceptualize the family process as maintaining problems,
5. Emphasize the present over the past,
6. Attempt to change behaviors and/or behavioral sequences,

7. Employ instruction and coaching in therapy,
8. Assign homework to generalize change, and
9. See their goal as restructuring interactions by way of behavioral or cognitive change, in order to change the presenting problem.

Finally, these family therapies were chosen for integration also because of their applicability to issues related to adolescent substance abuse (e.g., hierarchical confusion, poor communication), because of the impressive empirical data associated with each therapy (e.g. Arnold et al. 1975; Barton & Alexander, 1981; Minuchin et al., 1978; Stanton, 1981a, 1981b, 1978; Stanton & Todd, 1982) and because of other successful attempts at integrating these therapies with other models (e.g., Birchler & Spinks, 1980; Foster & Hoier, 1982; Liebman et al., 1974; Stanton, 1981a).

PHILOSOPHICAL STANCE

Although the disease concept of chemical dependency is not explicitly stated in the PBFT Model, it is one of the implicit philosophical assumptions of most of its authors. Our position coincides with the statement of the National Council on Alcoholism that alcoholism (and other forms of chemical dependency) is a chronic, progressive and potentially fatal disease. It is characterized by tolerance and physical dependency, pathologic organ changes, or both, all of which are the direct or indirect consequence of the alcohol (or other chemicals) ingested. In other words, even though most adolescent abusers of alcohol and other chemical substances do not die from the abuse during the relatively short period of adolescence, we believe that substance abuse is a potentially fatal disease, which is chronic, progressive, and morbid. Chemical addiction will eventually lead to death, unless checked. However, as we will discuss more fully in the final section of this chapter, we believe that the dichotomy some professionals hold between a *disease model* and a *systems model* is misleading and not useful.

In summary, most of our own and our therapists' philosophical approaches to drug abuse assume abstinence to be the goal. In actuality, however, our family therapists effectively pursue abstinence as the ultimate therapeutic goal only when it becomes one of the family's goals.

ASSESSMENT CONSIDERATIONS

In our drug program, therapists use an assessment model that provides a framework for understanding the complexities of adolescent drug use and its relationship to the family (Piercy & Nelson, in press). Therapists use both formal test data and on-going, in-session assessment to evaluate the nature and extent of the teenager's drug use, family functioning, and social-environmental contributors.

Nature and Extent of Drug Use

Since the presenting problem is adolescent drug use, it is important to accurately assess the types of drugs being used, how often they are used, and to what extent they are used. It is also essential that drug use be reliably evaluated during the course of treatment to ensure both adequacy of the treatment and the ultimate safety of the adolescents.

We use full spectrum urinalysis of adolescent abusers and their siblings before beginning the program and at its conclusion along with random urine testing during therapy. This provides us with accurate and objective measures of drug use. We also give each family member the Polydrug Use History Questionnaire (Lewis, 1979), which measures self reports of the extent to which a person has taken any of 15 classes of drugs during the previous month. Preliminary data from our study show an unexpectedly high correlation between the self-report data from adolescents and the more objective, biochemical data from the urinalysis. Finally, we ask family members throughout therapy about the types and amounts of drugs used by the adolescents to more fully assess their drug use and to provide important information about the family's willingness and motivation to cooperate in therapy.

Family Functioning

We assess various components of family functioning in our program. A number of formal tests help provide objective information about family structure, interaction, and communication. Besides these, therapists informally gather information on the hierarchies within the family, the appropriateness and flexibility of boundaries among subsystems, and the effectiveness of parental discipline. Therapists are also constantly alert to the sequencing of behaviors, particularly around the drug use. Finally, therapists assess the functions of the drug abuse: Is it serving a closeness function or a distancing function? (See treatment goal number four under the Major Treatment Goals section.)

Family Structure.

FACES III, based on Olson's Circumplex Model (Olson et al., 1979), provides information on family cohesion (the amount of emotional bonding among family members) and family adaptability (the degree of flexibility to change present within a family). This paper and pencil test also provides an inferential estimate of family satisfaction felt by individuals within the family. The *Kvebaek Family Sculpture Test* (Cromwell et al., 1980) is also used to measure family structure. Individuals in a family place small, wooden blocks, each symbolizing a different family member on a large checkerboard to spacially represent the relative position of each family member to the other. This test then can be objectively scored. This and other tasks performed by all family members are routinely videotaped for additional, behavioral assessment of family structure.

Family Interactions.

An inventory that assesses various dimensions of the marital relationship, the *Dyadic Formation Inventory* (Lewis, 1973; Lewis et al., 1981), provides important information on the couple's dyadic interaction, commitment to the relationship, and identity as a couple. We also review videotapes of family interactions and objectively score them using the *Social Interaction Scoring System* (Conger & McLeod, 1977). This allows us to code categories of verbal and physical responses, affects, commands, and compliant behaviors. Finally, we use the *Family Problem Assessment Scale,* adopted from Feldman (1982) as a goal attainment method that allows families to consensually identify and describe the severity of problems within their family.

Family Communications.

As a self-report measure of family communications, we use the *Parent-Adolescent Communication Inventory* (Barnes & Olson, 1982). This paper and pencil test evaluates how the adolescents and parents view each other with regard to their communication.

Social Environmental Contributors

Although no formal tests are used, therapists assess social-environmental contributors and/or buffers to drug abuse by specifically asking about friends, school and work conditions, and the extended family. Also, we assess the types and extents of involvement with outside agencies, such as the police and protective services, primarily to evaluate the possible resistances these agencies might have about our treatment program, which may send confusing messages to our clients.

PHASES OF TREATMENT AND KEY TECHNIQUES

This twelve-session PBFT treatment program is composed of four general phases. Although the phases are presented as discrete for the purpose of training, in actuality, there is considerable overlap and the phases vary from family to family.

Phase One (Joining) During this phase, the therapist decreases a family's initial resistance by promoting rapport, demonstrating relationship skills, and positively connoting certain problematic behaviors or relationship patterns. The therapist also attempts to restrain the family from immediate change, begins to establish greater parental influence, and starts to gather systemic information about the presenting problem. The therapist will begin to track behavioral sequences and will make an initial assessment of the function (interpersonal payoff) of drug use in the family.

Phase Two (Implementation) In Phase Two, the therapist first gives directives designed to interrupt dysfunctional sequences of behavior, then, offers change strategies consistent with interpersonal functions (such as distance or intimacy), and finally, initiates assertion skill training.

Phase Three (Facilitating/Monitoring) This phase entails the therapist's monitoring, revising, and facilitating progress on the aforementioned strategies.

Phase Four (Termination) In the last session, the therapist evaluates a family's progress and highlights positive changes. The therapist also works with the family to develop a plan to both preserve their gains and to generalize those gains to other areas of their lives (Piercy & Frankel, 1987).

As previously mentioned, components of the therapy model are not new, but have been borrowed from existing models proven effective with juvenile delinquents (Barton and Alexander, 1981; Patterson, 1982) and adult heroin addicts (Stanton et al., 1982). In the following material, the six major goals of the model are identified and described along with the specific skills associated with each goal. For a more detailed discussion of these points, see Piercy & Frankel (1987; 1988).

MAJOR TREATMENT GOALS

1. Decrease a family's resistance to treatment. By reducing family defensiveness, therapists increase their potential influence. Especially since many clients are court-referred, their families are often less than enthusiastic about being in therapy.

Previous research has shown that therapists' *relationships skills* are not only important to the process and outcome of family therapy (Gurman and Kniskern, 1981), but also are related to low drop out rates (Alexander et al., 1976). PBFT emphasizes those ten skills (such as empathy, warmth, self-disclosure, and humor) described in the Family Therapist Rating Scale (Piercy et al., 1983). Although these joining skills may seem obvious to most therapists, their importance cannot be overstated.

Positive connotation (Selvin et al., 1978) is the positive relabeling of behaviors that were previously considered negative. Even self-destructive behaviors, such as drug abuse, or obnoxious behaviors can have a positive *intent* that can be understood and appreciated, even if not condoned. For example, the therapist can relabel a parent's hostility as "concerned interest" or can describe a teenager's drug abuse as "a way of sacrificing yourself to pull the family together."

2. Restrain Immediate Change. One "no lose" strategy emphasized by PBFT is asking family members to discuss possible negative *consequences of change.* Either families find a "silver lining" when the lack of change is discussed (e.g., "It's true. When Johnny goes out and gets high it's peaceful around here. If we put our foot down, all hell would break loose.") or families will disagree and mobilize to prove to therapists that they do indeed want change. Some possible disadvantages of solving drug problems might include a renewed focus on other painful family problems or parents' decreased involvement with their children (Piercy and Frankel, 1987). Such possibilities are not forced on families, but are discussed tentatively, as possible concerns that might come with change. If families reject such possibilities, this may be "filed away" by therapists and brought up again later in therapy if families neglect to proceed with assignments, progress slowly, or otherwise get stuck.

Go slow (Fisch et al., 1983) messages are typically coupled with "consequences of change" messages in order to deal respectfully with the natural ambivalence that these families (like most families) have about change. These "go slow" messages also prevent therapists from working harder than the families.

3. Establish Appropriate Parental Influence. Families with drug abusing adolescents typically have a hierarchical structure that is reversed or confused. Adolescents' motivations and abilities to abuse drugs are often stronger than the parents' capacity to stop these behaviors. Establishing parental influences, then, are tantamount to making parents more effective "executives."

Making parents better managers can be accomplished directly or indirectly. Piercy and Frankel (1986) have offered guidelines concerning decisions to intervene directly or indirectly. They also provide clear illustrations of the classes of interventions. For example, direct interventions include a) encouraging and supporting the power of parental subsystems, b) marking boundaries, c) seeing parents without the children for portions of some sessions, d) providing parents opportunities to practice more effective executive skills, and e) developing change strategies that put parents in cooperative, executive roles.

Indirect strategies are more paradoxical in nature. They might include pattern prescriptions where parents are encouraged to continue their interactional discipline patterns with their children so that therapists can gain more information about how this works within their families. Or, therapists may employ positioning, paradoxical procedures in which therapists take even more extreme positions than those of their families and encourage the families to take complementary, less extreme positions (Weeks & L'Abate, 1979). For example, if parents refuse to take charge of their acting out children, therapists may adopt the extreme positions that the police, probation officer, or training school should take charge. Hopefully, parents will decide to establish the limits themselves (Piercy & Frankel, 1986).

4. **Systemic Assessment of the Presenting Problem.** Therapists ask questions about what happens before, during, and after drug abusing incidents in order to identify predictable cycles of family interactions (Piercy & Frankel, 1988). The ways in which families organize around drug abuses provide important information for therapists as they devise plans to disrupt dysfunctional sequences.

Therapists also try to identify interpersonal *functions* (Alexander, 1974) of drug abusing behaviors in families. The abuse (and the behaviors surrounding it) may serve either distancing or intimacy functions for families depending on whether behavioral payoffs result more in closeness or distance. As Piercy and Frankel (1987) note:

> Therefore, if familiar interaction surrounding the adolescent's drug abuse continually result in sustained involvement with one or more parents (e.g., long lectures, groundings, trips to therapists with family), an intimacy function would be hypothesized. If, on the other hand, drug abuse results in the disengagement of the adolescent from his/her parent(s) (e.g., leaving the house for long periods of time), then a distancing function would be surmised (p. 15).

5. **Interrupting Dysfunctional Sequences of Behavior.** Perhaps the greatest skill required of therapists is to interrupt previously identified dysfunctional sequences in ways that are also consistent with families' previously identified interpersonal functions. For example, if drug abuse serves to engender intimacy (i.e., sustained contact) in families, therapists must substitute adaptive behaviors that will produce the same

interpersonal payoff (namely, more closeness in the family). There are no set interventions and PBFT therapists frequently draw upon strategies typical of structural, strategic, and behavioral therapies.

The matching of interventions to family functions are described by Piercy and Frankel (1988).

> For example, if a family generally draws together in response to a drug abuse incident (e.g., through long lectures) the therapist would design a strategy to alter the behavioral cycle in a way that allows the family to maintain closeness but without drugs (e.g., home token economy or contingency management). If, on the other hand, *less* involvement among family members occurs after a drug abuse incident (e.g., the adolescent spends a week at a friend's house) then the therapist would try to devise an intervention that respects the adolescent's need for separation from his/her parents (e.g., a contract that raises the youth's curfew as he/she becomes more responsible) (p. 10).

One major choice therapists must make is whether to intervene directly or indirectly. Two factors typically influence the decision about which of these two strategies should be employed (Madanes, 1984). First, therapists determine if families are strongly committed to change. Direct strategies are typically used when there is clear motivation. If families are unsure or are resistant to therapy, indirect methods are employed. Second, therapists should determine if they are in positions of strength relative to their client family and hence have leverage for direct interventions. This is determined by such factors as age, gender, professional degrees and personal characteristics of therapists. If families have little leverage, indirect strategies may be more useful (Madanes, 1984).

To summarize, therapists must learn to develop strategies that a) families will buy, b) that are consistent with the family functions, and c) are potent enough to disrupt the dysfunctional sequences of behavior and substitute reasonably attractive functional alternatives.

6. Provide Assertion Skill Training. In PBFT, assertion training techniques are used with drug abusing adolescents and their siblings in order to help them to say "No" to peer pressures concerning drug use and other negative behaviors. Assertion practice is also seen as a form of communication training in that teenagers and families need alternatives to either aggressive or passive communication patterns that have proven unproductive.

The heart of the approach is to model for adolescents more appropriate responses and, after feedback and discussion, to encourage the adolescents themselves to practice the new behaviors within their sessions. Then, following feedback from the therapist and additional discussion, there is more *in vivo* practice both in new situations within the sessions and through structured homework assignments. In situations where drug abusing adolescents have gained control over the drug abuse, they may be asked to roleplay effective ways of saying "No" for younger siblings.

CHANGE

Our theory cannot be understood apart from the crucial importance given to the presenting problem in our model. We agree with Todd and Stanton (1983) that change in the presenting problem is the *sine qua non* of successful therapy. While changes in cognitions, affective expression or interaction patterns may be interesting and useful, our goal clearly is to eradicate, or at least significantly diminish, adolescent substance abuse. We emphasize change in the presenting problem because

1. This respects the family and the reason they came to therapy,
2. The presenting problem gives the therapist the most leverage because it is the issue about which the family is usually most willing to work, and
3. It offers the most concrete and specific index of change.

Although there are several subfactors noted below, the major curative factor in the PBFT model is *the specific action of the therapist to engender change* in the presenting problem. The authors agree with Haley (1976) that therapeutic changes come about ". . . through interactional processes set off when a therapist intervenes actively and directly in particular ways in the family system" (p. 7). While we do not argue that clients are active partners in the change process and indeed must do the work that counts, therapists have the primary responsibility for creating the context in which that work is done.

In theory, the process of change is a simple one: Since presenting problems are embedded in dysfunctional sequences of behaviors and in dysfunctional family structures, therapists must gain enough leverage to help families substitute functional behaviors and structures for the dysfunctional ones. The following are the curative factors which therapists keep in mind as they proceed with these tasks.

Curative Factors

It is curative when:

1. The family feels the therapist is "with them" or "on their side." It is important to note that many of our families had attended a variety of unsuccessful drug programs before PBFT. As previously noted, many were court mandated and quite skeptical. A few were simply exhausted and demoralized. Beyond technical abilities related to joining, we have come to believe that certain intangibles, such as commitment and being there for our families may be highly significant. One therapist, for example, noted that visiting a client in jail made a real difference in therapy. Several therapists, who were former substance abusers themselves, used limited self-disclosure to demonstrate their understanding of the issues involved. Others made special visits to clients' homes.

2. The therapist engenders hope. This is crucial since most families are demoralized or at least stuck. Hope is engendered in the model through positive connotation and the relabeling of behaviors that had led to demoralization. Family members' discoveries of positive intent can make decisive differences. Also, the re-establishing of parental influence or other interventions that make a difference add credence to the adage that "Nothing succeeds like success." When vicious cycles are replaced by virtuous cycles, the resulting hope helps to foster progress.

3. The therapist diminishes the family's fear of change. Although most families that come to therapy sincerely want change, there are parts of them that do not. Not only are changes often painful and difficult, but there are typically silver linings associated with things remaining the same. PBFT's emphasis on consequences and "go slow" messages are ways of addressing the natural ambivalence that most families have about change. Paradoxical directives often provide a respectful way of attending to these fears.

4. The therapist avoids resistance. We believe it is disrespectful, as well as unproductive, to spend time arguing with clients or pushing ideas to the point where we are engendering resistance. Therapy is one of those areas in life where therapists can be right yet wrong. Our therapeutic interventions are no better than the willingness of our clients to buy into them and utilize them. If our ideas are not accepted, this means that either a) we have not joined effectively with particular clients, or b) we need to make changes in our own direction.

5. The therapist respects the family's uniqueness. The model demonstrates this focus by ascertaining the families' functions or interpersonal styles and tailoring interventions accordingly. Decisions regarding the appropriateness of direct versus indirect interventions also attend to uniqueness.

6. The therapist mobilizes the family's resources. The PBFT Model assumes families have the abilities and resources to solve their problems but not know how to mobilize them. In establishing appropriate parental influence, for example, single parents were specifically helped to negotiate alliances with other family members, friends, neighborhood adults, probation workers, and other professional helpers to strengthen the single parents' influence with their drug abusing teenagers. In many cases where the parents' own substance abuse problems got in the way of treatment, therapists mobilized their own concern for their children to get them to act more responsibly themselves. In short, PBFT therapists look for resources wherever they can find them. They may be particular family strengths, hidden positive intentions, or other resources within church, community, school, and so on.

Indicators of Family Change

Although changes in presenting problems are our bottom line criteria, we view the following indicators (linked to the goals of the model described above) as positive indicators that presenting problems will abate.

1. Families demonstrate that therapists have joined with them. Behavioral indicators include laughter, verbal and nonverbal displays of affection toward therapists, head nods, etc. Families also indicate an acceptance and appreciation of the positive intent behind their negative and/or destructive interactions.

2. Families either accept that there are some silver linings to maintaining problems and seriously discuss their ambivalence about changes or they actively rebel against ideas that there are negative consequences of change or that they should go slow. That is, they take *active* steps to show that they are indeed motivated to bring about changes.

3. Parents demonstrate greater competence and confidence in adolescent behavioral management and discipline.

4. Closely related are changes in the family hierarchies which put parents in positions to influence teenagers and children and work cooperatively with one another. There are no cross-generational coalitions.

5. Needs for intimacy and distance in families are met in functional ways as dysfunctional behavioral sequences are disrupted.

6. Family members, especially teenagers, learn to communicate assertively as opposed to aggressively or passively. There is clear communication of sufficient duration and intensity to keep family members informed. Teenagers say "No" to negative peer pressure and restructure friendships around straight peers.

CASE EXAMPLE

Therapists working with families of drug abusing adolescents invariably face a variety of challenges. Here we will highlight a few of these challenges by presenting a slice of therapy with one family, we will call the Nelsons. We will also discuss how interventions from our present-centered, problem-focused model were used to address these challenges.

Seventeen-year-old Jimmy Nelson and his ten-year-old brother, Bob, are the sons of Judy and Ralph Nelson. Jimmy was recently found driving drunk and was consequently court ordered to attend family therapy in lieu of a jail sentence. (He had had other alcohol-related incidents at high school.) The two boys and their mother attended the first session (their father had refused to come). The therapist, Matt Eastwood, attempted to join with each, and complimented Mrs. Nelson on her concern for her children. He also attempted to determine the extent of the presenting problem and determine how it was embedded in the fabric of the family's interactions. This was difficult since Jimmy denied any problem, and stonewalled any questions about his alcohol use.

The therapist discovered from Mrs. Nelson, however, that the family did indeed have a history of alcohol abuse. Mr. Nelson had been an active alcoholic until ten years ago when he "decided to quit and did." (Alcoholics Anonymous would call him a white knuckle alcoholic.) Mrs. Nelson reported that her husband contends that "If Jimmy wants to quit drinking, he should just do it. Neither therapy, nor anything else can help him do what he has to do on his own." The therapist also found that Mrs. Nelson had five brothers, four of whom were recovering alcoholics.

The therapist ended the first session with a message to go slow in attempting any changes until Mr. Nelson could be consulted and until possible consequences of change could be examined more closely.

During the next few sessions, the therapist encouraged Mrs. Nelson, without success, to have her husband come to therapy. The therapist finally called Mr. Nelson, who reiterated that "when Jimmy's ready to clean up his act, he will." Again, Mr. Nelson refused to come in.

Also in the initial sessions, the therapist attempted to track sequences of behavior around Jimmy's drinking. Jimmy was less than forthcoming, and his mother was unable to be specific. The therapist did try to make use of Jimmy's insistence that he could be trusted and did not have an alcohol problem. The therapist asked Jimmy to "convince his mother" that he was responsible and how he would prevent future drinking problems.

The negative consequences of change that were discussed with Jimmy and his mother related to the tradition of alcoholism that seemed to exist in this family. Could Jimmy be a man and be loyal to the family without going through this rite of passage? Would he be disowned if he decided *not* to become an alcoholic? Would his brother Bob also have to follow suit? The family denied such thinking, but not too much.

Generally, Mrs. Nelson was worried and overinvolved with Jimmy and his father who still refused to attend therapy and was distant and sardonic. The major task the therapist faced was to marshal greater parental/extended family influence. To this end, the therapist devised an elaborate homework assignment. Jimmy was asked to interview all the recovered alcoholics in the family, starting with his uncles, and to take detailed notes on what they might tell him. He was to ask each of them the following questions.

- How they got involved in heavy drinking?
- How their alcoholism had affected their own family life?
- How and why they stopped drinking?
- What their lives have been like since they stopped drinking?
- Whether they had any suggestions for Jimmy?

This task was intended to productively involve Mr. Nelson and the extended family with Jimmy. Jimmy was instructed *not* to schedule the next therapy session until all interviews were completed. (The therapist had leverage in assigning this task since the court required a statement of client compliance when therapy was completed and the family knew it.) Jimmy also roleplayed (assertion training) with the therapist how he could approach each of these family members so they would cooperate. Mother and Bob looked on quietly but intently.

Jimmy left the session intrigued with the task, and eventually followed through on it. The court is still out (literally and figuratively) on whether Jimmy's case can be considered a success. We are not sure either. Cases such as his are not always tied up in neat bows and stamped cured. Still, we believe that Jimmy's case illustrates the flexibility of our model. Most of the components of the model were eventually employed with Jimmy's family. His therapist mobilized both the influence of his extended family system and the leverage of the courts to help Jimmy sidestep his family tradition. Only time will tell.

LIMITATIONS AND EFFECTIVENESS

We are presently analyzing data on over 150 families to determine the differential effectiveness of our PBFT model as compared to other treatments. We are particularly interested in determining for which families and adolescents our model is most effective. As illustrated above, the model appears to be flexible enough to be employed with a wide range of challenging clients. Among our biggest challenges are families with multiple chemical abusers, families with single parents, and families where we have minimal external leverage such as court or school. However, our colleagues across the country report that such cases generally seem to be their biggest challenges as well.

ROLE OF ADJUNCTIVE THERAPIES AND/OR SELF-HELP GROUPS

Self-help groups such as Alcoholics Anonymous and Narcotics Anonymous can provide wonderful complements to family therapy, provided that adolescents or family members are sufficiently committed to make use of them. Our families are routinely informed of the existence and function of these programs at the beginning and end of therapy. Self-help groups can be a useful supplement during therapy and/or excellent after-care programs.

Over the last several years, however, we have noticed the development of certain stereotypes in the addictions field for both systems therapists and addictions counselors. Systems therapists are popularly stereotyped as disavowing a disease model and ignoring vital information on the use and abuse of drugs and alcohol. Addictions counselors, on the other hand, are stereotyped as recovering alcoholics or addicts wedded to an AA tradition that some believe ignores vital interactional dynamics of the family. Both stereotypes are unfair and tend to blind therapists to the values in both traditions.

As we stated earlier, we believe that any dichotomy between a disease model and a systems model is misleading. We have no trouble accepting that a person may have a genetic predisposition toward an addiction (i.e., a disease), and that a disease concept makes sense on many levels. (See previous section entitled Philosophical Stance.) The more important issue, as we see it, involves what to do *now.* For us, the family is a useful entry point in bringing about change for many individuals. This is not to say that other entry points (e.g., courts, schools) or other interventions (e.g., AA, individual education, or hospitalization) might not also be effective. As professionals, we need to complement each other and learn from each other, and to minimize misleading and destructive stereotypes that may prevent finding the best interventions for particular persons.

REFERENCES

Alexander, J. F. (1974). Behavior modification and delinquent youth. In J. C. Cull & R. E. Hardy (eds.), *Behavior modification in rehabilitation settings.* Springfield, IL: Charles Thomas.

Alexander, J. F., Barton, C., Schiavo, R. S., & Parsons, B. V. (1976). Systems-behavioral intervention with families of delinquents: Therapist characteristics, family behavior, and outcome. *Journal of Consulting and Clinical Psychology, 44,* 656–664.

Alexander, J. F. & Parsons, B. V (1982). Functional family therapy. Monterey, CA: Brooks Cole.

Arnold, J. E., Levine, A. G., & Patterson, G. R. (1975). Changes in sibling behavior following family intervention. *Journal of Consulting and Clinical Psychology, 43,* 683–688.

Barnes, H. & Olson, R. H. (1982). Parent-adolescent communication. In D. H. Olson, H. I. McCubbin, H. Barnes, A. Larsen, M. Muxen, & M. Wilson, (eds.), *Family inventories.* St. Paul, MN: University of Minnesota.

Barton, C. & Alexander, J. F. (1981). Functional family therapy. In A. S. Gurman & D. Kniskern (eds.), *Handbook of family therapy.* New York: Brunner/Mazel.

Birchler, G. R. & Spinks, S. H. (1980). Behavioral-systems marital and family therapy—Integration and clinical application. *American Journal of Family Therapy, 8,* (6).

Conger, R. D. & McLeod, D. (1977). Describing behavior in small groups with the datamyte recorder. *Behavior Research Methods and Instrumentation, 9,* 418–424.

Cromwell, R., Kvebaek, D., & Fournier, D. (1980). *The Kvebaek family technique: A diagnostic and research tool in family therapy.* Jonesboro, TN: Pilgramage.

Farkas, M. I. (1976). The addicted couple. *Drug Forum, 5,* 81–87.

Feldman, L. (1982). Mimeographed paper. Chicago Family Institute. *Family Problems Assessment/Family Strengths Assessment.*

Fisch, R., Weakland, J. H., & Segal, L. (1983). *The tactics of change.* San Francisco: Jossey-Bass.

Foster, S. L. & Hoier, T. S. (1982). Behavioral and systems family therapies: A comparison of theoretical assumptions. *American Journal of Family Therapy, 10*(3), 13–23.

Gurman, A. S. & Kniskern, D. P. (1981). Family therapy outcome research: Knowns and unknowns. In A. Gurman & D. Kniskern (eds.), *Handbook of family therapy.* New York: Brunner/Mazel.

Haley, J. (1976). *Problem-solving therapy.* San Francisco: Jossey-Bass.

Haley, J. (1980). *Leaving home: The therapy of disturbed young people.* New York: McGraw-Hill.

Kovach, J. A. & Glickman, N. W. (1986). Levels of psychosocial correlates of adolescent drug use. *Journal of Youth and Adolescents, 15*(1), 61–77.

Lewis, R. A. & McAvoy, P. (1983). Improving the quality of relationships: Therapeutic intervention with opiate abusing couples. In S. Duck (ed.), *Personal relationships: Repairing personal relationships. Vol. 5.* Academic Press.

Lewis, R. A. (1973). The Dyadic Formation Inventory: An instrument for measuring heterosexual couple development. *The International Journal of Sociology of the Family, 3,* 207–216.

Lewis, R. A. (1979). A mimeographed paper. *The polydrug use history questionnaire.*

Lewis, R. A., Filsinger, E. E., Conger, R. D., & McAvoy, P. (1981). Love relationships among heroin-involved couples: Traditional self-report and behavioral assessment. In E. E. Filsinger & R. A. Lewis (eds.), *Assessing marriage: New behavioral approaches.* Beverly Hills, CA: Sage Publishing.

Liebman, R., Minuchin, S., & Baker, L. (1974). An integrated treatment program for Anorexia Nervosa. *American Journal of Psychiatry, 131,* 432–436.

Madanes, C. (1984). *Behind the one-way mirror.* San Francisco: Jossey-Bass.

McAuliffe, W. E. (1975). Beyond secondary deviance: Negative labeling and its effects on the heroin addict. In W. R. Gove (ed.), *The labeling of deviance: Evaluating a perspective.* New York: Halsted Press, pp. 205–242.

Minuchin, S., Rosman, B., & Baker, L. (1978). *Psychosomatic families: Anorexia nervosa in context.* Cambridge, MA: Harvard University Press.

Olson, D. H., Russell, C. S., & Sprenkle, D. H. (1979). Circumplex model of marital and family systems II: Empirical studies and clinical intervention. In J. Vincent (ed.), *Advances in family intervention, assessment and theory,* Greenwich, CT: JAI Press.

Patterson, G. R. (1982). *A social learning approach to family intervention: Coercive family process. 3* Eugene, OR: Castalia.

Piercy, F. P. & Nelson, T. S. (in press). Adolescent substance abuse and the family. In C. R. Figley & H. I. McCubbin (eds.), *Stress and the family, Volume III.* New York: Brunner/ Mazel.

Piercy, F., & Frankel, B. (1988). The evolution of an integrative family therapy for substance abusing adolescents. *Journal of Family Psychology, 3*(1), 5–6.

Piercy, F. & Frankel, B. (1986). Establishing appropriate parental influence in families with a drug-abusing adolescent: Direct and indirect methods. *Journal of Strategic and Systemic Therapies, 5*(3), 30–39.

Piercy, F., & Frankel, B. (1985). *Training manual: Purdue brief family therapy.* West Lafayette, IN: Center for Instructional Services, Purdue University.

Piercy, F., & Nelson, T. (In press). Adolescent substance abuse. In C. Figley (ed.), *Treating stress in families.* New York: Brunner/Mazel.

Piercy, F., Laird, R., & Mohammed, Z. (1983). A family therapist rating scale. *Journal of Marital and Family Therapy, 9,* (1), 49–59.

Selvini-Palazzoli, M., Boscolo, L., Cecchin, G. F. & Prata, G. (1978). *Paradox and counterparadox.* New York: Aronson.

Simcha-Fagan, O., Gersten, J. C., & Langner, T. S. (1986). Early precursors and concurrent correlates of patterns of illicit drug use in adolescents. *The Journal of Drug Issues, 16.* (1), 7–28.

Stanton, M. D. & Todd, T. C. (1979). Structural family therapy with drug addicts. In E. Kaufman & P. Kaufmann (eds.). *The family therapy of drug and alcohol abuse.* New York: Gardner.

Stanton, M. D. & Todd, T. C. & Associates (1982). *The family therapy of drug abuse and addiction.* New York: Guilford Press.

Stanton, M. D. (1978). Some outcome results and aspects of structural family therapy with drug addicts. In D. Smith, S. Anderson, M. Buxton, T. Chung, N. Gottlieb, & W. Harvey (eds.), *A multicultural view of drug abuse: Selected proceedings of the national drug abuse conference, 1977.* Cambridge, MA: Schenkman Publishing.

Stanton, M. D. (1979a). Family treatment approaches to drug abuse problems: A review. *Family Process, 18,* 251–281.

Stanton, M. D. (1979b). Drugs and the family. *Marriage and Family Review, 2,* 1–8.

Stanton, M. D. (1981a). An integrated structural/strategic approach to family therapy. *Journal of Marital and Family Therapy, 7,* 427–439.

Stanton, M. D. (1981b). Strategic approaches to family therapy. In A. S. Gurman & D. P. Kniskern (eds.), *Handbook of Family Therapy.* New York: Brunner/Mazel.

Szapocznik, J., Kurtines, W. M., Foote F. H., Perez-Vidal, A., & Hervis, O. (1983). Conjoint versus one-person family therapy: Some evidence for the effectiveness of conducting family therapy through one person with drug-abusing adolescents. *Journal of Consulting and Clinical Psychology, 51,* (6), 889–899.

Szapocznik, J., Kurtines, W. M., Foote, F. H., Perez-Vidal, A., & Hervis, O. (1986). Conjoint versus one-person family therapy: Further evidence for the effectiveness of conducting family therapy through one person with drug-abusing adolescents. *Journal of Consulting and Clinical Psychology, 54,* (3), 395–397.

Todd, T. & Stanton, M. D. (1983). Research on marital and family therapy: Answers, issues, and recommendations for the future. In B. Wolman & G. Striker (eds.), *Handbook of family and marital therapy.*

Tramontana, M. C. (1980). Critical review of research on psychotherapy: Outcome with adolescents, 1967–1977 *Psychological Bulletin. 88.* 429–450.

Weeks, G. R., & L'Abate, L. (1979). A compilation of paradoxical methods. *American Journal of Family Therapy, 7,* 61–76.

3

MRI Brief Therapy with Adolescent Substance Abusers

ANTHONY W. HEATH, Ph.D.
Coordinator, Marriage and Family Therapy Program, Department of Human and Family Resources, Northern Illinois University, DeKalb, Illinois

THOMAS C. AYERS, M.Div.
Private Practice and Consultation Services, Elgin, Illinois

This chapter is about the theory, approach, and techniques developed and practiced in the Brief Therapy Center of the Mental Research Institute (MRI) of Palo Alto, California, as applied to the treatment of substance abusing adolescents and their families. Certain aspects of MRI methods may, to some, seem radical. The MRI brief therapy approach is based upon presuppositions and premises that are not consistent with traditional psychotherapy, or what has become (or is becoming) conventional family therapy. Yet, as system purists, MRI theorists still see interactions as the basis of those concerns for which people seek professional assistance. They do not attach importance to intrapsychic or linear causal formulations of clients' problems.

For substance abuse treatment specialists who come upon this therapy for the first time, the MRI brief therapy model described in this chapter may seem unusual. Its conceptualization of therapy and substance abuse and its intervention strategies with substance abusers and their families are different from mainstream substance abuse treatment models. For example, practitioners of the MRI brief therapy model assume that the substance abuse behaviors of adolescents must be maintained by current patterns of interaction in order to persist. However, the model rejects the thesis that substance abuse behavior serves a specific function for the family. In terms of the practice of MRI brief therapy, therapists avoid abstractions—including the term *substance abuse*—and deal with problematic and observable behaviors. Observing that adolescents rarely ask for help with substance abuse, MRI therapists (as therapists who practice MRI-oriented therapy are known) work with anyone with complaints about substance abusers, intending to influence the troubling behaviors through those most concerned.

It is the authors' intention to use this chapter to introduce the reader to the MRI model of brief therapy as it is used in treating adolescent substance abuse. Toward this objective the historical roots of the model, its assumptions, its practice, and a case study are discussed. Additional opportunities to understand the model are offered by the books and articles cited herein.

HISTORICAL ROOTS OF APPROACH

By all accounts, the MRI approach has its approach in the pioneering work of Gregory Bateson, Milton H. Erickson, and Don Jackson, the founder of MRI. Bateson, a naturalist and anthropologist, had been interested in communication—how messages qualify one another, and more significantly, how mammals communicate that certain messages are to be interpreted one way and not another. In late 1952, Bateson received a grant to study paradoxes in communication from the Rockefeller Foundation (Bateson, 1972; Lipset, 1980). The research was primarily interested in paradoxical forms of communication. Early investigations focused upon river otters' play, guide dogs for the blind, humor, ventriloquism, and hypnosis. Bateson invited John Weakland to join the project, and hired Jay Haley and William Fry as well. At the time this project began, Bateson had been involved for some time in the Macy Conferences on cybernetics (Lipset, 1980). He brought concepts, such as feedback, from those conferences into the study of the social sciences.

Initially, Bateson's project investigated paradox in communication (in a broad sense), and had nothing to do with mental illness. The connection with mental illness came about in part by accident—the project was housed in a V. A. hospital. As a result the researchers were exposed to schizophrenic patients and their communications, which soon began to appear paradoxical in their nature.

Early 1954, Bateson attended a lecture on homeostasis given by Don Jackson, a psychiatrist who had been influenced by Harry Stack Sullivan while at Chestnut Lodge in the late 40s. Later in 1954, Jackson joined Bateson's communication project as a consultant (Jackson, 1968; Lipset, 1980). Jackson brought to the Bateson project his growing belief that interactional processes in social groups, especially families, were significant in the treatment process. Jackson had become involved in the treatment of schizophrenia and was developing his concept of family homeostasis.

In 1953, Haley learned that Milton H. Erickson was to be in the San Francisco area conducting a seminar on hypnosis. Bateson, who had previously consulted with Erickson on some fieldwork film of trances in Bali, arranged for Haley to attend the seminar. This contact began an interaction between project members and Erickson which would span several years. Members of the project (namely, Haley & Weakland), made week-long trips to Erickson's office in Phoenix once or twice a year to discuss a variety of topics with Erickson. The topics covered the nature of hypnosis and trance induction, (including the communicational dimension of trance—a dimension long overlooked); the "similarity between the behavior of schizophrenics and hypnotized subjects; the similarity between the ways a hypnotist induces trance . . . and the ways a mother induces schizophrenia in a child" (Haley, 1976, p. 79); and the nature of therapy. All of this involved paradoxical aspects of communication.

It was in this context of investigation that the Brief Therapy Project at the MRI began. Started in 1967 as a research endeavor, it arose because

> like other therapists with orthodox training and many years of practical experience we found ourselves increasingly frustrated by the uncertainty of our methods, the length of treatments, and the paucity of their results. At the same time we were intrigued by the unexpected and unexplainable success of occasional "gimmicky" interventions—probably more than anything else by the fact that they were not supposed to have any beneficial effect (Watzlawick, Weakland, & Fisch, 1974, p. xiv).

Since its inception 20 years ago, the Brief Therapy Project has had a number of members, most consistently, Richard Fisch, John Weakland, and Paul Watzlawick. The major goal of the project was to do therapy as efficiently and as effectively as possible (Weakland, 1981). The MRI staff set out to investigate what worked and what did not work in therapy. Particularly wary of traditional procedures, they felt that traditional approaches were not as effective and as efficient as they could be. They wanted to try something different. They were not certain where it would lead, but they were convinced, at the very least from Erickson's clinical work, that therapy could be more efficient and effective.

BASIC ASSUMPTIONS

Three basic assumptions guided the work of the original MRI Brief Therapy Project team and continue to guide MRI therapists today. These assumptions reflect the beliefs of the founders of this approach.

First, MRI therapists are guided by a concern for what works. MRI therapy is a lot like scientific experimentation at least in this one way: Every attempt to solve a problem, every therapeutic directive, every idea is judged on its ability to lead to a solution to the problem at hand. Thus ideas and methods are continually tested for their effectiveness in context and are not compared to any standard of what is orthodox—what should be done.

This view is carried all the way to the MRI model itself. No claims are made that the model is true; its value is dependent on its usefulness and practicality (Fisch, Weakland & Segal, 1982). Similarly, no claims are made that truth is knowable in any form; this constructivist view has been advanced by MRI originators for over a decade (Watzlawick, 1976, 1984; Segal, 1986).

Naturally, then, MRI therapists rarely pursue the truth in or out of therapy. Rather, they seek the observable (behavioral) aspects of interpersonal communications and avoid inferential, linear causal explanations including historical and illness formulations.

Second, MRI therapists are wary of traditional theories and practices. Thus, assumptions made by most therapists are not accepted without careful examination. One of the factors that led to the development of family therapy approaches was a dissatisfaction with the results and methods of traditional therapy methods. There was some concern that this new *family therapy* was different in its basis and assumptions from the tradition of psychotherapy. The founders of family therapy, then, were naturally wary and skeptical of bringing traditional concepts and techniques into this new field without careful examination. More particularly, Bateson's anthropological orientation and emphasis upon context added to the break with traditional practices and techniques.

Third, MRI therapists value efficiency in resolving client problems. MRI therapy is brief—often limited to ten sessions—and is strictly focused on resolutions of the problem presented by clients. To be efficient, problems must be clearly defined in behavioral terms. Problems are not abstractions or states of being in the clients' minds or the therapists', but each is something that someone is doing. Once problems have been resolved, therapy is considered complete.

It is worth noting here that MRI therapy is both non-normative and non-pathological. It is non-normative in the sense that MRI therapists do not attempt to impose any standards upon clients. There is no ideal standard of family structures or communications, for example. Problems are considered to exist only when (and as) clients perceive them. This is not to say that MRI therapists will not make every effort to engage clients and families in therapy. Engagement is always focused around concerns or complaints of clients, not on the concerns of therapists or others. Thus, therapists work to identify clients' existing concerns as a means of engagement.

MRI therapy is non-pathological in that clients are seen as caught up in unhelpful or unsatisfactory (for the clients) interactional patterns. From this perspective, nothing is wrong with the clients, they are caught and unable—without outside help—to do anything but more-of-the-same. While family members or community members may believe that something is wrong, MRI therapists focus on interaction for both the problems and their solutions.

THE MRI VIEW OF ADOLESCENT SUBSTANCE ABUSE

MRI therapists view problems of adolescent substance abuse and dependency as they do other problems presented in therapy. Maintaining their value for ideas and methods that work, MRI therapists seek specific behavioral definitions of problems with adolescents, avoid causal (e.g., disease) explanations of problems, and work with those concerned to resolve problems attributed to substance abuse.

Since MRI therapy is non-normative and non-pathological, therapists seek to understand each case involving adolescent substance abuse from the perspective of those concerned and involved. MRI therapists respect other's constructions of the reasons for the problems seen as related to the substance abuse and consider arguments about *dependence, addiction, abuse, disease* and similar terms not useful within the MRI point of view. Further, they take positions that certain commonly held beliefs tend to cloud and confuse issues where adolescents and drugs/alcohol are concerned. According to Weakland (personal communication, September 3, 1987),

> We have seen a number of cases where, to our view, either actual or even presumed substance abuse was over-emphasized (mostly by parents, but it could be by teenagers themselves); that is, drugs or alcohol, made the reason and excuse for any and all undesired behavior, so that family members collude in avoiding matters of interpersonal influence and responsibility.

From the MRI perspective, then, it is considered inadequate to describe a problem as a substance abusing adolescent. Instead, a specific description of observable behavior would be a necessary first step toward defining the problem. In a sense, the term substance abuse (and all related terms) is an abstract explanation for the cause of troublesome events, actions, or behavior. Statements about causes of problems may be interesting or even true, but they rarely are useful in resolving the undesirable behaviors that bring people to therapy.

Finally, it should be emphasized that MRI therapists see all troubling behaviors of substance abusing adolescents in the context of interpersonal relationships. It has long been observed that substance abuse affects and is affected by family members and peers. This interpersonal conceptualization of substance abuse and dependence enables therapists to identify specific behavioral contributions to the perpetuation and solution of clinical problems.

THE BRIEF THERAPY MODEL

In this section we will describe the practice of MRI Brief Therapy, as it has been constructed on the assumptions described above. To present the model in traditional fashion, we have divided it into four phases: assessment, intervention, termination, and evaluation. What may be lost by this categorization is the recursive nature of the practice of Brief Therapy—the way the interventions test assessments leading to new assessments, new interventions and so on.

Assessment

A therapist's theory guides the process of data collection, assessment, and intervention. According to this approach, information must be collected concerning the problem, the handling of the problem, the goal, and the pertinent views, beliefs and values of those involved. As data are collected, the therapist must think about and organize the data in such a way as to make it useful for treatment planning and intervening.

The first three—problem definition, the handling of the problem, and goal setting—are inquired about directly. Data in the last category—pertinent views, beliefs and values—are gathered indirectly via observation and through what family members say in the course of providing other information.

In collecting data, MRI therapists are first concerned with an adequate description of the problems or complaints. For therapists, this means getting clear, concrete data on *how* the problems happen: Someone is doing something that someone else defines as undesirable, or, conversely, someone is not doing something that someone else defines as desirable. This concrete description of a problem involves the identified patient (IP), the action, and the complainant. Usually when adolescent substance abusers are considered, the IPs are the adolescents, the actions are some behaviors that concern parents (or significant others), and the complainants are parents, school officials, or law enforcement officials, who view problem behaviors as undesirable. Substance abusers rarely complain about their own behaviors.

To define problems, MRI therapists begin with questions like, "What is it that concerns you?", and work toward behavioral statements of the problems as seen by the complainants. Clients are asked to state specific *precipitating events* that brought them to therapy at this particular time and the effects that the problems have on the daily lives of those involved, to clarify the problems being presented. While it may be common to hear chemical dependence offered as the reason for therapy and aftercare requested, MRI therapists ask for more specific problem definitions.

Next, MRI therapists seek descriptive information regarding the way problems are handled. Again, they seek concrete data—descriptions of behaviors and interactions—rather than abstractions or generalities. Who is trying to solve the problems and what is being said and done? This is of particular importance since, in this view, it is the problem solving behaviors of those involved that perpetuate and maintain the problem behaviors. This information, therefore, provides the direction for planning and intervening.

In effect, descriptions of solution-oriented actions and events are sought which give MRI therapists clear pictures of what is being said and done by whom and in what situation. This often includes such details as which room of the house, what time of day, duration, who is present, and where they are. It is concrete descriptions of behavioral interactions that are sought; not general family interactions, but interactions focused around the problematic behavior and events.

MRI therapists attach particular importance to clients' views about or explanations of the causes of the problems. This information is placed into the category of client *position,* which includes the values and beliefs of the client. But, in this approach, it is understood that clients' views are just views, and it is seen as error to mistake those views for descriptions of problem situations. Interestingly, it seems that when clients are asked about problems, they often respond as if they had been asked for their views of the causes of the current troubles. Nevertheless, clients' positions about the causes of problems, when placed with their positions on the values, directions, and on how therapy should be conducted, the types of solutions that are needed, and other views, can be used to tailor interventions so that they can best be understood and accepted.

Position information is gathered over the course of therapy through listening to and observing families. Data on pertinent views, beliefs, and values are gathered indirectly via observations by listening to what family members say in the course of giving other information. For example, it is significant to know who is most worried and concerned about the problems. It is not uncommon for one parent to say that the IP is *just being a typical teenager,* while the other parent sees the problem as the *first step toward jail.* In this therapy, it is considered easier and more efficient to work with the parent that sees the problem as more serious—*first step toward jail*—rather than the parent that sees it as normal—*just being a teenager.* It is uncommon for substance abusing adolescents to be most concerned about the abuse behavior, although they may be concerned about how the problem is being handled. In any case, client positions are always considered legitimate and are never debated, challenged, or refuted by therapists. (Here and in the following material, the italicized phrases indicate position statements.)

An example may clarify the uses of client position information. A mother called for counseling because her son, Joe, age 16, had come home drunk twice within the preceding month. The most recent time was the day before she called. Mrs. J was concerned *that her son not be like his father* (her ex-husband). She said that *Joe thought she was making a big deal out of nothing.* Despite her concern with Joe's drinking, *Mrs. J described him as a good kid.* Although she was having no other problems with him—he was doing well in school and was otherwise a normal teenager around home—*she did not approve of his friends and said they were having a bad influence on Joe.* She wanted some help getting Joe back on the right track, but *wasn't sure what she could do.*

Mrs. J's views regarding her son are positive. He's not bad, but has come under the influence of some bad friends. She is hopeful that something can be done about the problem, is willing and able to help her son, but doesn't know what to do. This sort of information can be contrasted with the values and beliefs of another parent, Mrs. K.

Mrs. K, another mother, saw evidence that her son, too, had been drinking. Yet she thought that in this case, it was the *first sign of some medical problem. His condition,* she believed, *attracted him* to others who were *similarly ill* and related to *his denial* that there was *anything wrong with him.* Mrs. K believed her *son needed help,* but since he wouldn't accept it, *she felt helpless.*

The contrast here is significant, and while the problem behaviors may be identical, (a teenage son's drinking), therapists should not approach the mothers in the same way. The therapist should approach Mrs. J more positively, offering suggestions and directions. With Mrs. K, this approach would likely be less productive. An approach more in line with her views would be appropriate: A serious and pessimistic tone, a discussion of her son's symptomatology, a concern with his denial, a cautious exploration of any little things that mother could do to help prepare him for the real treatment.

Once therapists have working understandings of clients' positions, treatment goals can be set. MRI therapists handle goals in a unique manner; they set minimal goals. From this view, it is important to get clients doing something successfully. While many clients seem to want problems to go away overnight, they may also see problems as large and overwhelming, and thereby make their wishes impossible or unattainable. By setting minimal goals, MRI therapists reduce problems to manageable steps, thus, making the unattainable possible. Readers familiar with the AA approach to recovery, as captured in the "One day at a time" bumpersticker, will find a parallel in this step-wise conception of change.

In setting minimal treatment goals, MRI therapists raise questions such as: "What sort of small, but significant action or event would be a sign of progress or change?" All of the involved parties are asked questions of this nature, and while their responses are taken seriously, it is the ultimate responsibility of therapists to choose the goals of therapy. In a larger sense, goals are ways to interrupt the ineffective solutions that are being applied to the families' views of the manifestations of the adolescents' substance abuse problems.

Intervention

According to MRI therapists, problems take doing and the doing is part of social interactions. That is, problem behaviors are part of social interactions and further, problems are maintained by social interactions. Specifically, problems are maintained by clients' or others' attempts to solve them. So therapists believe that—for whatever reasons—clients are applying solutions to their problems that not only are *not* working, but are maintaining problems. The theory of change, therefore, is simple. Have those involved stop maintaining the problems. Get them to change behaviors that are, in fact, supporting the problems. If that can be done—and that is often a difficult task, and one central to the therapy—problems will be resolved.

Thus, MRI therapists work to interrupt the current, non-working attempts to solve problems. Rather than simply telling clients to stop what they are doing, which has been found inadequately convincing, therapists convince clients to do something different that, in so doing, will preclude what they had been doing. For example, if a parent explains and reasons with an adolescent about the evils of smoking and yet finds ashtrays full of cigarette butts, the therapist should urge the parent to cease the explanations and do something else.

When first exposed to the MRI model, many therapists make two mistakes. First they assume that logical arguments and explanations will help clients stop their attempted solutions. Second, they wonder how they will know what to suggest to replace the old attempted solutions With experience, these therapists come to realize that logic and explanations can motivate, but only when the therapist's argument is within clients' positions (or frameworks). In addition these therapists soon learn to explore alternatives that are 180 degrees from solutions already tried.

To create new, alternative solutions for clients, then, therapists must first learn the solutions that have been attempted or considered thus far. It is helpful to ask for attempted solutions that have worked, failed, those that have been advised (by others) but not tried, and those considered, but not tried. Occasionally clients have already discovered effective solutions, but somehow have forgotten to use them again. Generally these solutions should be given another chance. Similarly, clients who have been harboring a secret hunch about something that would work should be encouraged to try it, assuming it's different from the usual and ethically acceptable. Solutions advised, but not tried, provide information on client positions regarding what will not work and help therapists to know what to avoid.

While clients often say they have "tried everything," experienced therapists look for a theme among the various attempted solutions. It is the themes or main directions of previous attempts that provide the basis for interventions. Once the patterns or themes of ineffective attempted solutions are identified, therapists choose interventions and construct rationales that will convince clients to do something new. MRI therapists concentrate on constructing or framing rationales that are within clients' positions about problems and solutions. Thus, a mother who believes her son's refusal to clean his room and help with household chores is rebellious and defiant behavior—and finds herself arguing and becoming angry with him—might be directed toward solutions that are consequence-based, and away from angry arguments with him. Another mother who believes her son's apparent experimentation with drugs is because he is depressed—and finds herself trying to encourage him and cheer him up—might be urged to help him by telling him how bad his situation is. In both cases, new solutions should be chosen because they are 180 degrees from previous solutions, not because they are right and presented to clients in ways that they could be most easily accepted.

MRI therapists make their recommendations primarily to complainants in a well thought-out manner usually near the end of sessions. These suggestions or tasks are often given in detail. For example, when he says or does X, you do Y, then Z. Reports from clients during the next session about how they accomplished the tasks are essential since it is during the task reports that changes are revealed. Tasks are then modified or extended depending on performance by the clients. When clients report no change, the report is explored and evaluated, after which the task is modified, or at times abandoned for a new one. Once change has begun, the MRI agenda is to keep it going, and begin to terminate with the clients, often accomplished by spacing out appointments.

When substance abusing adolescents and their families are discussed, therapists often ask how AA, Al-Anon, Al-Ateen, and other self help groups, educational group, and residential treatment fit into MRI therapy. Such specialized treatment and support programs clearly have established their values in the eyes of many including many MRI therapists. Where clients are concerned, though, the relevant eyes are those of the clients, and many substance abusing families have opinions and experiences with such specialized programs. MRI therapists assess clients' use or potential use of adjunctive programs according to how the clients have used them before and to what extent they see these programs as potentially helpful.

Termination

Many psychotherapists unknowingly accept views of termination that were originally advanced by psychoanalysts. According to analytic thinking, therapy is appropriately ended when clients have worked through their disabling neuroses. Until this point of cure, any departure from therapy is viewed as premature and neurotic, and the therapy is considered incomplete. While many family therapists would avoid words like neurosis and even the assumption that clients are sick until therapy cures them, many seem to unexplainably allow therapy to go on and on and feel disappointed when clients leave without saying good-bye.

MRI therapists see therapy more like the practice of a general practitioner than the practice of a psychoanalyst (Heath, 1985). Clients are seen as entering and leaving therapy just as they would begin and end a series of consultations with their physicians. They go to the doctor when they hurt and stop going when they begin to feel better. Thus MRI therapists see clients over short intervals, consider cases open indefinitely, encourage people to stop therapy when specific problems end and return if other problems occur, interpret returns by clients as statements on their satisfaction, and expect that life goes on before, during, and after therapy.

The above beliefs and actions are clearly related to the MRI position that small changes made in therapy can be the beginning of beneficent cycles of interactional processes. Once systemic changes have begun, clients build on their successes as life becomes more satisfactory. Based on this view that change begets change, MRI therapists and their clients terminate therapy when change begins, not when it ends. Accordingly, adolescent substance abusers and their families are seen until change in their specific concerns have begun. Check-up visits are often scheduled four-to-six weeks hence to monitor the progress of the changes initiated during therapy.

CASE EXAMPLE

Rob Norton was in trouble with his school the spring he was referred to the local mental health center. Robert, age 13, had missed half of the days of school that year and no one knew what to make of it. He was bright, nicely dressed, and usually polite—even to the school authorities—as was his mother.

When the school truancy officer called to make the referral for six sessions of school district funded therapy, he had already become interested in the family.

> "There's an older sister who's in residential [drug] treatment, an alcoholic brother who's missing, and a drunk father who lives somewhere else. But the assistant principal says there's no evidence Rob is using drugs or alcohol. Oh, and I guess I should warn you, the mother says they've had all the family therapy she can take."

Mrs. Norton and Rob arrived for the first session 20 minutes late. The therapist greeted the Nortons and invited them into his office.

> "Those things happen to me too," he said to Mrs. Norton's apology for their late arrival. "We don't have much time left so why don't we just chat tonight and we'll really begin next week?"

The rest of the session was spent in casual conversation in order to initiate a collaborative, non-hierarchical relationship. The therapist's objective was to define himself as different from school authorities and the family's previous therapists.

In the second session, attended only by Becky—as the mother had asked to be called—the therapist began the process of defining the problem while assessing client position and her status as a complainant. Initial signs such as the mother's warning that she'd had enough therapy, and the type of the referral, suggested that Becky might not be the complainant. The therapist began by asking Becky, "What is it that concerns you?" She replied that she had divorced Rob's father three years previously. Her daughter, Rose (age 15), had gone to live with him at the time, but had been so spoiled (Becky's term) by her alcoholic father that she had ended up in a residential drug treatment program six months before Rob's problem at school surfaced. Becky's oldest son was also an alcoholic, she said, although she hadn't heard from him in several years.

The therapist redirected Becky by asking what she thought about Rob's truancy.

> "I just don't know what to make of it," she replied. "I've never seen any signs that he had any interest in drugs or alcohol. Rob's very intelligent. I think he's just bored."

Becky added that she didn't drink or take drugs but said that she considered herself addicted to her work.

Returning to the task of defining the problem, the therapist asked,

> "So what do you think has to change?" Becky replied, "He has to go to school."

Somewhat relieved to have a more specific problem statement, the therapist spent the remaining ten minutes of the session trying to determine whether Becky thought she had any influence over her son's school attendance and what she had tried to do to get him to school.

Several days later the therapist called Rob's school to make an appointment to talk with his teachers, counselor, and assistant principal.

> "You mean you haven't heard?", asked the counselor. "He's gone."

As it turned out, the assistant principal of Rob's school had made Rob an offer. Increasingly convinced that the inexplicable truancy of Rob was due to scrupulously concealed drug abuse, the administrator explained to Rob that only a voluntary admission to a hospital drug treatment program would save him from having to repeat seventh grade. Rob, who later told the therapist that he was bored in his classes and wanted to be an eighth grader, agreed to having a drug problem and was admitted to a hospital drug treatment program the next morning. According to the counselor, Rob's mother consented and was apparently pleased that Rob would be able to salvage his school year.

> "Did she seem to think he has a drug problem?" the therapist asked. "I don't know," the counselor replied.

Thinking about it later, it seemed to the therapist that he had missed an important point. While working to understand the family's definition of the problem, he had overlooked the assistant principal, who now seems to have been more devoted than the family to solving a problem of what to do with a truant student. With this lesson in mind and after talking with Rob's mother on the phone, the therapist administratively closed the case.

Five months later the therapist received a call from Becky Norton. Having begun work in a different agency, he was impressed that she had tracked him down. "I have a few things I need to talk about," she explained and an appointment was set.

The next morning, Becky updated the therapist on Rob's progress. Rob had been transferred twice before ending up in a nationally-known substance abuse treatment program in the Midwest.

> "I'm still not sure he ever really had a drug problem, but his father's insurance is good and Rob's enjoying it. And I'm enjoying the quiet at home alone, but that's about to end, and that's why I'm here." She paused. "Rose wants to come home."

Rose, now age 16, had been released from her substance abuse treatment program, dropped out of school, and had called her mother the night before to ask if she could come home. Living with a drinking father would be hard on her abstinence, she had explained to her mother. Becky knew how hard it could be to live with her ex-husband. Yet, somehow she worked up the nerve to tell her daughter that she would consider it and let her know in 48 hours.

> "It sounds like a tough decision," said the therapist. "How would you like me to help?"
>
> "I just don't want it to be like it was before," Becky replied. "I was always having to watch her. I couldn't trust her. I mean, what's she gonna do all day while I'm at work? All her old friends here are dopers, she'll get back on that stuff. I can't quit my job to watch her, I'm up for a promotion."

In the rest of the session with Becky, the therapist worked to define a clear, manageable problem. It seemed that Becky had already decided to allow her daughter to live with her. Becky wanted her daughter to stay off drugs, change her friends, get back into school, and begin therapy with a new therapist. While there were moments when the therapist thought that Becky really wanted the help of television's Equalizer, his gentle suggestions that her expectations were grandiose were immediately accepted. "But where should I start?" she asked.

Given this opening the therapist moved to define a small problem by suggesting that Becky probably would *not* be able to keep Rose from doing drugs while Rose was home alone. In addition, Becky probably could *not* make Rose go to school or therapy, and could *not* choose her friends for her. Becky accepted these parameters with some relief.

> "So what's left for you to do?" the therapist asked, beginning an inquiry to define possible, pragmatic actions by Becky and to determine what she has already tried.
>
> "I can set up some rules," she said tentatively.
>
> "I suppose so," he replied as cautiously. "Have you tried that before?"
>
> "Yes."
>
> "Have they worked?"
>
> "No."
>
> "Why not?"

"She hates authority and defies all rules."
"What have you done when she's defied rules?"
"Grounded her."
"Has that worked?"
"No."

Through such a process it was eventually agreed that Becky would focus her attention on changing her reaction when Rose broke a rule. Efforts to define the problem more specifically were hindered by the length of time since the two had lived together. Because there was little direct data on a pattern to intervene in, speculation was necessary. Becky was not so much interested in solving a specific problem as in preventing the old patterns from becoming reestablished. Becky's previous attempted solutions tended to be rational, carefully measured, and unenforceable. A workable solution would probably have to be radically different, perhaps even irrational and randomly scheduled, but certainly enforceable. The session ended with a suggestion:

> "Invite Rose to come live with you *for a while.* Tell her you are still thinking about the terms, and you'll let her know about them in a couple weeks. Then think about the consequences you really can impose for misbehavior."

The next three sessions were focused on helping Becky define new ways to deal with Rose when she misbehaved. Using between-session suggestions, which Becky was willing to carry out, she was encouraged to define house rules (get a job, pay a share of the car insurance, and get up for breakfast), to find an adolescent AA meeting for her daughter, and to adopt an I-don't-know-what-I'll-do-if-you-break-the-rules posture with Rose. When Rose broke a few rules, Becky was directed to respond irrationally. For example, when Rose took the car without asking, Becky lost the spare set of keys and forgot to leave her set with Rose; when Rose began sleeping past breakfast, Becky found reasons to call her as soon as she got to work with some sort of question or reminder. Rose, faced with such a strange and disorganized mother, began to act more responsibly. Becky reported that it was going as well as could be expected, and therapy was again concluded.

Seven months later, the therapist began preparing for a seminar he was going to conduct on substance abusing adolescents. In an effort to understand substance abuse from the perspective of an adolescent, he decided to find a known abuser who would talk candidly about his or her views on drugs, drug treatment, drug education, and recovery. Remembering Rose, Rob, and their mother, he knew he'd found a likely candidate.

First the therapist called Becky and asked her permission to contact Rose. Becky, who stated that things were still going fairly well, seemed to welcome the possibility.

> "I've been trying to get her to go talk to you or another therapist for a while. I think she could use someone to talk to. Maybe if she sees you're not like the others, she'll go back to see you after the interview."

The therapist called Rose, introduced himself, explained the purpose of the interview and its use, and asked for her help. Rose seemed interested in the opportunity to speak her mind and the meeting was set. "I'll be there," she stated in closing.

A week later Rose came into the office. Remarkably, she had walked the three miles from her house after a friend was unable to give her a ride. She arrived on time and was dressed neatly.

It would be impossible here to adequately represent the viewpoint that Rose expressed in the two hour interview which ensued. She described her reactions to the drug-related treatment she had received, her explanation of why adolescents take drugs, and her views of her family, friends, addiction, and the hazards of drug use. Rose was articulate and thoughtful; her opinions helped the interviewer/therapist and the audiences who have since heard the taped interview to understand substance abuse from at least one adolescent's perspective.

Six months later, the therapist received a call from Rose. This time she wanted to talk about a problem—what to do about her father who was drinking himself to death. The therapist again used the MRI approach, this time for three sessions, which Rose paid for herself. Similarly Rose's mother has returned for four hours of therapy concerning a relationship she was having with a man.

The therapist didn't hear from the family again—except for a Christmas card—for two years. At that time, he called Becky to follow-up on the status of Rob and Rose. After two years of residential treatment and private schooling, Rob had come home and was back in a public high school. Rose had left home the same spring she had returned to see the therapist and moved to the West Coast. Soon thereafter she began using hard drugs, nearly died of an overdose, and straightened out. At last report, Rose was working and happily engaged to a man her mother actually liked. Becky is remarried to her ex-boss, still climbing the corporate ladder, and more satisfied with her life than she's ever been.

The Norton family case may be considered characteristic of the MRI approach to cases with adolescent substance abusers, for the following seven reasons:

1. There were difficulties in reaching a workable problem definition.
2. There were difficulties in establishing who was the complainant and what the complainant was concerned about.
3. The problems presented were indirectly concerned with substance abuse.
4. The complainant and the substance abuser were not the same person.
5. There were no attempts to define the extent of the substance abuse in terms of its severity.
6. The therapy was focused on observable behavioral problems.
7. The clients entered and exited therapy according to *their* assessments of the situation.

EVALUATION

Critics of the MRI model of therapy have expressed their objections to the approach since its inception. Included in their criticism have been references to manipulation, the lack of emphasis on the therapeutic relationship, and superficiality, especially in regard to substance abuse—the model's apparent refusal to come to grips with the realities of substance abuse. Additionally, concern has been expressed that MRI therapists do not educate people about the disease of alcoholism or addiction, do not attempt to work through denial, do not perform standard assessments of substance abuse, and do not insist that clients use AA or related programs. While well-intended, these criticisms fail to take seriously the radical nature of the basis of MRI therapy. This model is radical and is so intentionally. It has been generated, at least in part, by a dissatisfaction with traditional conceptualizations of problems and therapy, and the resulting techniques and treatment. This model no doubt has shortcomings, certainly more can be done with vague clients, and clients who come to therapy under duress, and those whose positions seem to make therapy impossible. It is exactly these shortcomings as well as the development of means of applying the model to other problem areas that is the agenda for current and future MRI researchers and clinicians.

Other limitations seen as related to the model are more usefully seen as related to how the model is implemented. For example, some therapists have used the MRI model as an excuse to trick people into doing silly things, but well-informed MRI therapists rely on a respectful understanding of clients to develop creative suggestions that are different enough to make a difference. Other critics have said that the model turns away people who need help. Again, some therapists use MRI ideas less effectively than others, but skilled MRI therapists persist in determining what problem is of most concern to families which come for therapy.

To date there remains limited quantifiable information on the effectiveness of the MRI model. The first article on the Brief Therapy approach, (Weakland et al., 1974) published results of follow-up interviews with clients. The authors reported that of 97 cases on which follow ups were completed, 39 (40 percent) reported complete relief of the presenting problem, 31 (32 percent) reported clear and considerable improvement in the presenting problem, and 27 cases (28 percent) reported little or no change. In other words, 72 percent of the cases showed significant improvement at follow up. Additional research (de Shazer, et al., 1986) indicates similar results. However, in both cases the results were not specifically for a substance abusing population.

As this is being written, it seems likely that further research on the MRI model is underway. Since specific problem definitions—in the words of the clients—are always sought and recorded, therapy is usually brief, the model is widely accepted and practiced, and fairly well specified, follow-up research is both possible and practical. For example, a study on the effectiveness of this model is being conducted by researchers at Northern Illinois University. This study will result in a similar type of uncontrolled descriptive report, but the subjects are also being asked to respond to questions about their satisfaction with the therapy received. It has been observed by clinicians using this model that some clients seem satisfied with services when the presenting problem is resolved and some are satisfied even when the problem remains. In addition, some clients are not satisfied whether the problem is solved or continues. The relationship between these variables is being explored in order to further understand this apparent contradiction. Further research specifically concerned with assessing the value of this approach with a substance-abusing population is equally possible.

CONCLUSION

MRI therapy is problem focused. Problems are central to the therapy in that problems are what bring families in, problems are what families (or at least some of them) want changed, changes are what they will work toward (if anything), problems are the focus of data gathering—problems, attempted solutions, goals—an index of outcomes, criteria for determining the complainant, and central in position data. This approach to therapy is different in that therapists do not discover problems and then tell families what they are, instead families tell therapists what the problems are.

The approach seeks concrete interactional data: behavior, happenings, events, words, and actions. It stays away from causes, abstractions, and emotions. MRI therapists assume that for a problem to be a problem, someone must be doing something that another doesn't want him or her to do, or someone is not doing what another wants him or her to do. It assumes that problems have some components that are behavioral, interactional, and observable, and that when therapists focus upon these (behavioral) levels, therapy can become more efficient.

When the problem presented is one of substance abuse, MRI therapists want to know how the problem is manifested. They avoid the assumption that all of the IP's misbehavior is due to substance abuse. That is a causal formulation of the problem. MRI therapists want a behavioral/interactional formulation of the problem. They want to see the problem (behavior) in its family context. Further, MRI therapists assume there is a connection between the family context and the problem, and that the connection is the way the family is trying to solve the problem.

In many ways, MRI therapists are minimalists. First they collect data. The data include clear definitions of problems, straightforward lists of attempted solutions, and minimal goals. They also learn about the complainant status and positions of those involved. Then, after synthesizing the data collected, they plan interventions. The interventions are framed within pertinent positions and often include tasks which are 180 degrees from original solutions. Ensuing sessions check on task performances and alter further interventions in accordance with new data. MRI therapists begin to terminate therapy when significant change has begun.

The MRI approach does not claim to be a cure for substance abuse, but rather offers a different view of it and one that may be worth greater attention and research (Fisch, 1986).

REFERENCES

Bateson, G. (1972). *Steps to an ecology of mind.* New York: Ballantine Books.

de Shazer, S., Berg, I., Lipchik, E., Nunnally, E., Molner, A., Gingerich, W. & Weiner-Davis, M. (1986). Brief therapy: Focused solution development. *Family Process, 25*(2), 207–221.

Fisch, R. (1986). The brief treatment of alcoholism. *Journal of Strategic and Systemic Therapies, 5*(3), 40–49.

Fisch, R., Weakland, J., & Segal, L. (1982). *The tactics of change: Doing therapy briefly.* San Francisco: Jossey-Bass.

Haley, J. (1976). Development of a theory: A history of a research project. In C. Sluzki & D. Ransom (eds.), *DOUBLEBIND: The foundation of the communicational approach to the family.* New York: Grune & Stratton.

Heath, A. (1985). Some new direction in ending family therapy. In D. Breunlin (ed.), *Stages: Patterns of change over time.* Rockville: Aspen Systems.

Jackson, D. (ed.) (1968). *Communication, family, and marriage: Human communication volume 1.* Palo Alto, CA: Science and Behavior Books.

Lipset, D. (1980). *Gregory Bateson: The legacy of a scientist.* New Jersey: Prentice-Hall.

Segal, L. (1986). *The dream of reality.* New York: Norton.

Watzlawick, P. (1976). *How real is real?* New York: Random House.

Watzlawick, P. (ed.). (1984). *The invented reality.* New York: Norton.

Watzlawick, P., Weakland, J., & Fisch, R. (1974). *Change: Principles of problem formation and problem resolution.* New York: Norton.

Weakland, J. (1981). The focus of change in family therapy. Paper delivered at the symposium, Frontiers in family therapy. Los Angeles: American Psychological Association.

Weakland, J., Fisch, R., Watzlawick, P., & Bodin, A. (1974). Brief therapy: Focused problem resolution. *Family Process, 13*(2), 141–168.

4

Contextual Family Therapy with Adolescent Drug Abusers*

GUILLERMO BERNAL, Ph.D.
Associate Professor of Clinical Psychology
University of Puerto Rico, Rio Piedras

YVETTE FLORES-ORTIZ, Ph.D.
Clinical Core Faculty
California School of Professional Psychology
Berkeley, California

The theory and practice of Contextual therapy offers an alternative to behavioral, strategic, structural, communicational and other power-based models of family therapy. Contextual Family Therapy suggests a language for understanding and working with close relationships that transcends the ideology of power (Bernal & Ysern, 1986). A dialectical theory of relationships (Boszormenyi-Nagy, 1965) served as the base upon which a fairness model of therapy evolved.

In this chapter, we present part of our experience in applying Contextual Family Therapy (CFT) concepts, principles, and methods in the treatment of drug abuse. The context of most of our work was within the limits of a treatment outcome research project with late adolescents and adult heroin addicts. Cases from private practices, consultations, and

*Work on this chapter was supported, in part, by a grant from the National Institute of Drug Abuse (No. 5 RO1 DA03543) awarded to Guillermo Bernal, principal investigator and to James L. Sorensen and Yvette Flores-Ortiz, co-investigators, while the authors were at the University of California, San Francisco.

supervision on the treatment of adolescent drug abuse with other drug problems are also included as examples. The chapter aims to describe basic theoretical concepts, principles, and assumptions of the application of CFT to the problems of drug abuse.

HISTORICAL ROOTS OF THE CONTEXTUAL APPROACH

The theoretical principles and clinical foundations of Contextual therapy were developed by Ivan Boszormenyi-Nagy and collaborators (e.g., Boszormenyi-Nagy, 1987; Boszormenyi-Nagy & Framo, 1965; Boszormenyi-Nagy & Krasner, 1986; Boszormenyi-Nagy & Spark, 1973; and Boszormenyi-Nagy & Ulrich, 1981). The theoretical and philosophical roots of CFT may be found in three areas of development: Object-relations theory, existential psychology á la Buber (Buber, 1970), and dialectical thinking.

Recently, Boszormenyi-Nagy and Krasner (1986) have written about the historical development of CFT. They note that the Contextual Approach grew out of a quest of 25 years for answers to the question of clinical effectiveness. Indeed, the evolution of the conceptual scheme has undergone a number of transformations and it is beyond the scope of this chapter. Nevertheless, as early as 1962, Boszormenyi-Nagy wrote about the concepts of *need complementarity* and *counterautonomous superego* (Boszormenyi-Nagy & Krasner, 1986, pg. 34). These concepts served to link individuals to family systems. By 1965, a dialectical theory of relationships (Boszormenyi-Nagy, 1965) was presented expanding the understanding of relational dynamics. The concepts of the *unconscious contract, intersubjective fusion,* and *collusive postponement of mourning* were descriptive of relational dynamics of multiperson systems. With the publication of *Invisible Loyalties* in 1973 (with Geraldine Spark), a major step was taken toward the development of a model that integrated the psychology of the individual with levels of the relational system. The emphasis of the approach turned more toward loyalty and justice dynamics of human relationships. More recently with *Between Give and Take* (with Barbara Krasner) the model has undergone a significant recasting. A language for describing human relationships in social terms has been refined. The issue of *consequences* and the *ethics of due consideration* are concepts that help clarify contradictions of contemporary life. Examining consequences and considering the welfare interests of others goes against the values of family therapy and family psychology increasingly governed by concepts and values of the marketplace.

The terms referring to this modality of therapy have undergone several transformations. At one time the model was known as *dialogic*, emphasizing dialogues among family members. At another time, this modality was referred to as *dialectical* reflecting the notion that individuals could best be understood in relation to others. With the development of concepts such as loyalty and legacy, relational, dialogic, and dialectical aspects of the model became fused with what became known as an *intergenerational* approach to family therapy. However, during the last ten years, the term *contextual* has been settled upon.

Literally, the word contextual means with (con) or within the fabric (text) of relationships. Context is defined as part of a "written or spoken statement" which "leads up to and follows and often specifies the meaning of a particular expression" (Morris, 1970). Context is also the setting, situation, environment, or circumstance which gives meaning to an event. The roots of context come from the Latin *contextus* meaning coherence. The text, that is the spoken word, and that which gives meaning and coherence to the word (the fabric of family, social, and economic relations) is a central aspect of Contextual therapy. Thus, the term contextual is used to refer to the totality of human resources, as well as to the context of relational dimensions (factual, psychological, systemic, and ethical relational) available to individuals, couples, and families.

BASIC NOTIONS AND ASSUMPTIONS

One of the distinguishing features of CFT is that it addresses the equitable distribution of burdens and benefits in family relationships. *Justice* and *fairness* constitute a central dynamic. The goal of therapy is to examine and restore a balance of fairness. While not acting as judge, a goal for CFT therapists is to encourage family members to consider the fairness of each others' positions.

CFT is rooted in the notion that fairness is basic to all human systems. While fairness may be content-relative from system to system, it is considered a universal human process. The bedrock of human systems lies in the balance of human rights and obligations. When there are imbalances, symptomatology or dysfunction emerges as a means of restoring the balance of fairness.

Trust is a central notion of CFT. Trust is developed from the experience that life will be reasonably fair and that one's contributions will be acknowledged and reciprocated at some future time. CFT proposed an ethical criteria for close relationships, particularly intergenerational family relationships.

The prototypic relationship between a parent and a newborn illustrates that if the parent does not give, the child will not survive. If the child cannot receive the parent's care, the child will die. Herein lies a fundamental aspect of material reality, which is a matter of *consequences.* Caring about consequences in this prototypic human situation is basic to human existence. Thus, relational ethics and reality are inseparable. The existential context of the parent with a newborn determines that most of the giving is to come from parent to child (Grunebaum, 1983). When the child becomes an object for the gratification of parental needs, the ethical-relational asymmetry is disturbed. The child becomes parentified and exploitation develops.

The notion of *context* refers to the total realm of potential human resources for individuals, couples, and families including past, present, and prospective resources for the relating individuals. Context integrates both vertical (family of origin) and horizontal (family of procreation) resources, as well as individual and systemic perspectives on relationships. The systemic perspective includes communicational processes, interactions, and the dynamic of power in relationships. The multilateral perspective on the context recognizes the critical subjective universe of the individual, as well as, the importance of the individual's relationships. Context also refers to the social, economic, and political environment in which the family develops.

Entitlement is the accumulation of merits within a relationship in the form of credits that are a result of considering the welfare interests of the other. Entitlement is an important aspect of evaluating the fair distribution of burdens and benefits in close relationships; this is not the same as feeling entitled. Expressions of anger and hostility are often manifestations of entitlement issues in relationships.

Legacy are entitlements and obligations from prior generations that link the current generation to future ones. On the one hand, legacy is a transgenerational mandate, while on the other it is a generational dialectic. Considering welfare interests of past and present generations, as well as, the welfare interests of future generations are ways of contributing to the legacy. A central focus of contextual therapists is on helping individuals define and clarify the terms of contributing to the legacy.

Loyalty refers to the bonding in the relational context that develops either from fair consideration (earned merit) or by entitlement inherent in family of origin relationships. Loyalty is a triadic notion. Vertical (family of origin) loyalty commitments often clash with horizontal (family of procreation) ones, which are particularly critical at differing life cycle stages of the family. *Split loyalty* is a situation in which a child has to seemingly choose between one of his or her parents. Expressions of affection to one parent will offend the other and vice versa. *Invisible loyalty* is a related concept defining a pathological situation whereby the person is contributing to the legacy through destructive actions to oneself or others.

Multidirected partiality (MDP) is both a method and a goal of CFT. MDP is oriented toward eliciting dialogues among family members. As a process, MDP may be characterized as siding consecutively with one person after the other in order to help family members define their positions, tolerate opposing views, and acknowledge mutual efforts. Therapists are neither neutral nor unilaterally partial to any one family member. Rather, therapists' positions are directed to the multiple facets of relationships, that is, oriented to considering the fairness of each position based on concrete actions and the consequences of such actions for the family. MDP is also a treatment goal, since the long-term balance of fairness (burdens and benefits) for the family and across generations is basic in developing trust in relationships.

THEORY OF CHANGE

The CFT theory of change transcends individual psychology, systems, and cybernetic family psychology notions of change. Individual psychology whether behavioral or psychodynamic hinge on a need satisfaction (reinforcement or pleasure principle) principle as a goal for success in therapy (Boszormenyi-Nagy, 1987). The treatment contract is individual and success is defined in terms of the needs and satisfactions of the identified client. Change is viewed as either learning new patterns of behavior or as personality change. In both cases, the concept of change is a static one and centered on the person.

Systems theories expanded the notion of change to the family context (Burt, 1980; Glynn, 1981; Harbin & Mazier, 1975; and Kaufman & Kaufmann, 1979). Notions of structure, power, hierarchy, and communication entered into the language of change. Thus, we speak of a change in structure (Stanton and Todd, 1982); (Haley, 1980), patterns of communication (Watzlawick, Beavin & Jackson, 1967), and so on.

However, the implicit value in most family theories of change is an *interventionistic* one (Bernal, 1988). Therapists observe systems and tinker with them is one way. Another is to move a system along and "watch it jump" (Golann, 1988, p. 62). In CFT, the critical question of change is in whose interest is this change? Who benefits the most from a particular change? The implicit value of CFT is a participatory one, in which all family members are involved in contributing to a change that is desirable and beneficial to everyone. Indeed, rather than incorporating concepts of cures into the model with its emphasis on pathology, the preference is to consider the notion of freeing and liberation, a political (Bernal, 1988; Boszormenyi-Nagy & Spark, 1973) rather than a medical concept.

In CFT, change is considered an ongoing dynamic and multilateral process that is part of dialogue and relatedness. Change is viewed as a dialectical progression between conflicts of interest on the one hand and reflection linked to action on the other. Through the simultaneous consideration of "two antithetical sides of any relationship, the conflict between reciprocal need gratification efforts have to be transcended and resolved into an equilibrium of fairness, tolerance, concern, trust, and reliability—mutually needed for the survival of the relationship" (Boszormenyi-Nagy, 1987, p. 143). By directly addressing conflicts of interests and contradictions with the family, examining the burdens and merits of various family members and their limitations, a context for dialogue is woven. The greatest liberating possibility for posterity lies within dialogues of trust and mutual consideration.

The dialogue supported in contextual therapy has a dialectical structure of reflection in the service of action and action in the service of reflection. Action without a reflection of the social, family, political and economic context, hinges on activism. Similarly, reflection without a commitment to action and reciprocity is an empty sort of analysis. The dialectic between action and reflection is an essential element of intergenerational and relational change (Bernal, 1982).

MAJOR THERAPEUTIC TECHNIQUES AND STRATEGIES

In CFT, the therapeutic techniques and the goals of therapy are dialectically related and therefore inseparable. The goals are part of the methods and the methods are part of the goals. Nevertheless, a fundamental goal of CFT is to arrive at the most preventive design for the benefit of all the persons involved. As previously noted, context refers to the fabric of relationships giving emphasis to the balance of fairness in human relations. This context is characterized by the consideration of the welfare of all family members whom the therapy potentially affects in current, previous, and future generations. Therefore, consideration of the interests of the individuals involved is both a goal and a method of this approach.

The following principles of CFT are summarized from several sources (Bernal, 1982; Bernal et al., 1985; Boszormenyi-Nagy, 1987; Boszormenyi-Nagy & Krasner, 1986; Grunebaum, 1983; Stierlin et al.,

1980) and presented here to clarify some of the key therapeutic stances of the model.

1. The major methodological principle of CFT is multidirected partiality. The therapeutic aim is building trust.
2. CFT therapists foster a process of dialogue. Merited trust (or trustworthiness) is the key to healthy relationships.
3. The orientation is toward identifying resources rather than pathology. The whole context of a person's relationships is available for therapists and family members to examine for sources of trust. Often such an examination entails three generations.
4. Family relationships are ethically nonsubstitutable. Filial loyalty exists whether or not actual relationships have been severed.
5. CFT therapists are concerned with the validation and disconfirmation of individuals in relationships, particularly children who are most vulnerable.

Therapeutic strategies and interventions are based on challenging cut-offs (Bowen, 1978), supporting integrity in relationships, and encouraging the possibility of reconnections that build trust in family relationships. How such strategies evolve varies a great deal from family to family. The essence of CFT treatment strategies is to mobilize human resources to make them available to the family.

For example, we often make use of the genogram or family tree (Bowen, 1978). The genogram is given to the family as a task to complete for the next session. The use of the family tree is particularly helpful to introduce families to a reflection on their context. Similarly, tasks often emerge from the family, itself, of reconnecting with specific family members. A well-guided reconnection and dialogue with a significant family member can go a long way in establishing trust in close relationships. CFT strategies are based on building trust with a priority of positive outcomes for future generations. The therapist's challenge of cut-offs and support for rejunctive efforts are central aspects of these strategies.

ASSESSMENT CONSIDERATIONS

A comprehensive analysis of the relational determinants in family therapy must include four overlapping dimensions.

- Existential
- Individual

- Transactional
- Ethical-relational

These four dimensions were first proposed by Boszormenyi-Nagy and Ulrich (1981).

Factual or Existential Dimension

This dimension considers facts and events occurring in the physical, social and material environment of the family. These facts and events impose existential constraints or limiting conditions. They do not determine the future of the family. Such limiting conditions may be related to a variety of factors such as

1. One's origin (i.e. gender and nationality)
2. Societal or cultural determinants (i.e., ethnicity, race, religion, political, and economic context, etc.)
3. Individual conditions (i.e., biological determinants, stage of development, education, occupation, etc.)
4. Past events in the life of the family (i.e., immigration, loss of family members, physical illnesses, financial reverses, abandonment, etc.)
5. Family constellation (i.e., number of children and particular position in the order of birth) and
6. Stage in the family life cycle (i.e., marriage, childrearing, individuation of children, actual separation of children, aging)

Individual Dimension

This dimension refers to the psychological elements of individual family members. Clinicians may draw upon psychodynamic principles, personality theory, or any psychological framework useful in generating hypotheses about the functioning of individual family members. A person's contribution to the relational network of the family system can be highlighted by analyzing different aspects of the individual's dynamics such as

1. Feelings, which are inseparably connected to relational patterns
2. Needs, generated from biological, psychodynamic, social, political, spiritual frameworks
3. Identity and
4. Coping defenses significant for personal relationships

Transactional Dimension

This dimension examines family relations from a systemic orientation. Systems can be understood as wholes of mutually interdependent parts, characterized by an organization that

1. Responds to a specific set of rules which permits the system self-regulation; and
2. Is characterized by transformations that maintain a balance or equilibrium.

From the properties of wholeness, self-regulation, transformation, and equilibrium, it is not difficult to understand that anything affecting one part of the system, affects the system as a whole. If we consider the family as a system, all the properties of the system are applicable to the structure and functioning of the family as well. We will not elaborate further on this dimension since a number of chapters in this volume are entirely devoted to various systemic perspectives.

Ethical-Relational Dimension

The focus of this dimension is on examining the balance of equitable fairness in human relations. By *equitable* balance, it is understood that everyone is entitled to have his or her interests considered in a way that is fair. The ethical-relational dimension represents Boszormenyi-Nagy's unique contribution to the field of family therapy. In part, the approach is based on Buber's (1970) existentialism about "I-thou" relationships.

For Boszormenyi-Nagy (1976), human nature is a dialectical concept. A person cannot be understood in isolation, but only in relation to others. From this viewpoint, justice is an inherent quality of human relationships without which no long-term attachments would be possible.

Boszormenyi-Nagy and Spark (1973) translated this ethical-relational principle of justice into pragmatic thinking—there are obligations to fulfill in relationships. Recognition of such obligations are inherent as are efforts and willingness to fulfill indebtedness and maintaining satisfying relationships. The sources of these obligations vary a great deal. Debts may result from harmful acts of commission or of omission to another person. Merits represent credits earned by investing in a relationship on behalf of another person's welfare. The acknowledgment of a person's obligation to the other implies a recognition of the other's merit; this is a reciprocal process central to the CFT concept of change.

GOAL SETTING WITH THE CFT APPROACH

As previously mentioned, the aim of the CFT approach is to arrive at the most effective preventive design for benefit of all the persons involved. A treatment contract that follows from a position of multilateral partiality is necessarily multiperson-oriented. The contract between therapist and client includes the network of family relationships. Since the contract is multilateral or collective in nature, the goals of therapy are oriented toward maximizing the benefits for all family members.

At the outset of therapy, it is usually noted that other family members may be called upon as resources for therapists in trying to arrive at workable plans of action. The questions often asked to help in determining specific goals of treatment are:

- How have you tried to help the family?
- What kind of things have you tried to do to help?
- What goals do you have for yourself and your family in therapy?
- What family resources exist to help with these goals?
- Who in the family can be called upon as a resource to the parents and to the client?

In the context of our research, a brief 10-14 session model of CFT was developed. Usually, treatment consisted of ten sessions. Additional sessions (one to four) were offered when a crisis or special situation emerged and the family requested additional sessions. Specific procedures for each session are described in the treatment manual (Bernal et al., 1985). The protocol was designed to serve as a guide for therapists providing treatment. On the whole, three basic stages can be distinguished in the treatment process, namely, initial, middle, and final stages.

The specific goals of the initial stage are to engage the family in treatment, to establish a treatment contract which includes the identification of specific areas of conflict to work on during the therapy, and to define the problem.

The middle stage encompasses a large portion of the treatment. This stage focuses on helping the family to identify unhelpful patterns that maintain the problems (symptoms), and to examine the consequences of maintaining a status quo. The latter aspect is examined simultaneously as the elements that maintain the problems are identified. Identification of such factors is achieved by examining the family system from multiple perspectives:

1. Existential factors and events that affect the life of the family and impose limitations;
2. Individual psychological issues for different family members;
3. Structure and functioning of the system, such as composition of subsystems from the family system, losses in the family, and ways in which they have been handled;
4. Ethical-relational aspects of the relationship among family members including entitlements, obligations, merits, debts, and in general, the degree of fairness in the relationships among family members; and
5. Legacies, invisible loyalties, and destructive entitlements.

The final stage deals with two main issues.

1. Implementing a plan of action to make changes in conflictive areas; in this plan attention is focused on: finding ways in which fairness in the relationship could be rebalanced, building trust, and developing a support system for the family by helping the reconnection among members of the system.
2. Discussing issues concerning termination such as analysis of the process of therapy, evaluation of goals proposed in the treatment contract, and an examination of plans to work on the goals proposed during treatment, once the therapy terminates.

All sessions include an update of events. In most sessions, a task is assigned. This task deals with specific issues discussed during the session. As previously noted, one of the tasks given to all families in our research and most families in our practice is the construction of a family tree.

PHILOSOPHICAL POSITION ON ADOLESCENT CHEMICAL DEPENDENCE

The CFT approach views drug abuse as primarily rooted in social and community dynamics that impact upon the family and the person. Indeed, some social systems have completely eradicated drug abuse as it is known today in European and North American societies. Clearly, drug addiction is primarily a social and community problem requiring interventions at those levels.

Nevertheless, the CFT approach to addiction incorporates the contributions of other models or approaches; these are integrated as contextual dimensions. For example, the notion of biological predisposition to alcohol abuse and chemical dependency may be a factual reality for a person that the family and the therapist must face.

Additionally, contextual therapists are concerned with the possibility that addiction, itself, may be a way of showing concern and loyalty for the family. As Cotroneo and Krasner (1976) have asked, "What if a young person's addiction, however self-destructive, is an attempt to force parents to face the implications of an unsatisfactory marital relationship?" Sacrificial behavior like drug addiction can be a last-ditch attempt to make family members" (p. 518) accountable. Indeed, drug abuse can be an important resource when integrity and trustable parenting are either not available or have eroded.

ROLE OF ADJUNCTIVE THERAPIES AND SELF-HELP GROUPS

As a resource-oriented approach, CFT encourages participation in self-help groups and other modalities of treatment that have beneficial effects. For example, at a methadone maintenance clinic, a psychoeducational family modality was developed (Sorensen & Bernal, 1987); this program complemented the individual counseling and the methadone treatment. Community network groups were supported and a specific educational and training program was developed for clients and their families. We have found self-help groups to be extremely valuable in providing ongoing support to family members. This is particularly important once treatment ends.

Our experience with multifamily or substance abuse therapy groups working concurrently with family treatment is limited, particularly in the context of private practice. In hospital and public clinic settings, the use of psychoeducational multifamily groups generally occurred prior to family treatment. Indeed, it was often after participation in educational and informational programs about drug abuse that family members became interested in pursuing family therapy.

CASE EXAMPLE

The Jones Family

The Jones family consisted of four members: Mr. Jones, 38, a former professional football player who worked as a high school teacher and football coach; Mrs. Jones, 36, a writer, who worked as a substitute teacher at an elementary school and their two children. Eddie, the IP was 14 and his sister, Susan, was 7. The parents were both fifth generation British-Americans. The family was self referred with Eddie's experimentation with marijuana and barbiturates as the presenting problem.

Background Information

The couple met in college, lived together for several years, and married shortly before the birth of their son. They reported having an ideal marriage—they never argued, and always discussed their differences. They viewed each other as comrades in the struggles of life.

Mr. Jones was the youngest son of a working class family from the Midwest. His parents believed they were infertile, so they adopted two boys who were American Indians. Two years after the adoption, the couple became pregnant and Mr. Jones was born. He reported during therapy that he was always treated better than his brothers. In fact, the brothers were routinely beaten and slept on the floor when they misbehaved, while he was seldom if ever punished by his parents. His brothers, however, often retaliated by teasing Mr. Jones for his size (he was 6′5″ from the time he was twelve) and his skin color. When Mr. Jones was five, his mother was stricken with multiple sclerosis and spent the rest of her life in and out of hospitals. When he left for college at the age of 18, his mother committed suicide. Since that time, he maintained minimal contact with his father or siblings, both of whom are reported to be addicted to heroin.

Mrs. Jones is the youngest of two daughters. She described her father as the "typical bourgeois capitalist pig" and her mother as the prototypical "American housewife—bored, fat, and on valiums." Her sister was described as "Barbie" married to a "Ken doll" and living a capitalist life in Southern California. Mrs. Jones broke the family tradition of studying law, by leaving home at 17 and moving to San Francisco where she lived in a commune. She attended a regional college, mostly for the political activities, where she met Mr. Jones. Since she left home, Mrs. Jones has had a cordial but distant relationship with her parents; she reports rarely speaking to her sister who did not respect their political and cultural orientation.

For most of their marriage, the Jones have lived abroad where they taught English in the Peace Corps for several years. Six years ago, the couple was invited to work and live in Cuba. They returned to the United States one year ago. The decision to return was based on the parent's desires for their children to learn something about their native country. Eddie's problems began six months after the family returned.

Family Evaluation

The Jones were an attractive and easygoing family. All four were quite tall. The children, having been educated abroad, were fluent in three languages. Shortly after their arrival in this country, both were placed in classes for the gifted. However, the parents insisted they remain in regular classes so they would not adopt an elitist ideology. The daughter appeared to adjust to her new school fairly well. Eddie, however, began to experience difficulties soon after arrival. The children were in a racially mixed school. In Cuba, Eddie's friends were mostly black. In the States, however, he felt rejected by his black peers, alienated from his white classmates, and began having frequent fights at school. After one altercation, the teacher found marijuana in his possession. Eddie insisted that it did not belong to him. Initially, the parents believed Eddie and assumed the marijuana had been planted. However, Eddie eventually confessed to smoking regularly since their arrival.

During the course of a four session evaluation, the parents complained that Eddie had been a difficult child since birth. He was described as overly aggressive. Moreover, the examples given by the parents appeared quite normative (i.e., hair pulling and biting as a toddler). The parents also disliked what they viewed as overly-competitive behavior between siblings. The fact that the daughter was enurectic was not considered a problem by the parents. They both expected she would outgrow it.

Contextual Formulations and Treatment

Facts

There were a number of important facts to consider in the evaluation and treatment of this family. First, the family had recently returned to the United States after five years of living in Cuba. They reported to love Cuba, its people, and in particular its political system. They rejected the materialism of United States society and lived here in fairly austere conditions (no heat, television, washer, dryer, etc.). The only luxury they allowed themselves was a car. Thus, while rejecting United States culture and its way of life, they felt a need to reconnect and teach their children about their country. At best, their present feelings about the migration were ambivalent. Second, both adults were disconnected from their families of origin and the ways in which they were raised. Thus, the extent to which Eddie's symptoms were related to migratory stress, acculturative adjustment, or the parents' disconnection to their own families and culture merited evaluation.

Psychology

Both adults described their childhoods as troubled. Mr. Jones in particular felt he overly benefited by being "the real biological child." At the same time, he assumed responsibility and guilt for the unjust treatment of his brothers. Due to his height, color, and size, he always felt different and strange. Because of the physical abuse of his siblings, Mr. Jones was terrified of hitting his children, so he yelled a great deal. He described feeling impotent in the world except on the football field. Mrs. Jones' rejection of her socioeconomic privilege and adoption of proletarian values cost her the support and approval of her parents.

Systemic

A structural analysis of this family suggested a strong executive subsystem, a strong mother-daughter dyad, and an exclusion of Eddie, who from birth, was viewed as different and problematic. The couple married before Eddie's birth. The parents emphasized that they only married to legitimize his birth. Thus, implicitly, Eddie was blamed for the parent's adoption of a convention that neither valued. An analysis of the family's patterns of communication suggested that Eddie's behavior (perhaps even from birth) served to deflect marital conflict. Since the spouses strove to make their relationship an ideal of egalitarianism where there was minimal room for conflict.

Ethical Relational

From a contextual position, Eddie's symptom needed to be understood in terms of its intergenerational meaning. Specifically, an analysis of the genogram found that the first born male was always a problem in Mr. Jones' family. Furthermore, Mr. Jones' indebtedness to his brothers for their unjust treatment was being paid by not allowing Eddie to be OK. In this way, Mr. Jones revindicated and invisibly remained loyal to his father, who could not love, approve, or justly treat his sons. In addition, Eddie's symptom, epitomized for the Jones all that was wrong in the United States and thus allowed them to indirectly postpone the mourning for the losses associated with the migration, and perhaps the disconnection from their own families. In turn, Eddie's behavior could be seen as an act of rebellion, following in the tradition of his parents who also rebelled.

Treatment

The treatment of this family was brief (12 sessions) and focused on a rebalancing of obligations in the family (parental, spousal, ideological, political, and professional), a reconnection of each spouse with his and her family of origin, and an examination of values (Latin-American, British-American, socialist, and capitalist). The family's problems were acknowledged as normative for a progressive couple who was attempting to define and create a progressive family context with few models to emulate. Eddie's symptom was viewed as contributing to the family legacy of suffering, rebellion, and potential disconnection. Having examined their context, the couple began to actively make changes in order to contribute to their legacy.

The primary vehicle for examining this family's context was the genogram. Each spouse developed his or her own geneology focusing on a mutligenerational pattern of cut-offs, adolescent rebellion, and difficulties in parenting. Mr. Jones discovered that since his family's arrival (with the Mayflower), the eldest son had cut all ties with the family of origin; subsequent children had developed alcoholism and the youngest child was always the favorite. In addition, patterns of informal adoption and physical abuse of these children were common. Mrs. Jones' family similarly showed a tradition of cut-offs and political activism among the youngest daughters (suffragette, antislavery, and so on) with a pattern of political conservatism among the eldest daughters and the men.

By *contextualizing* their problem, the Jones began to contribute to their family legacy in a more constructive manner. Specifically, Mr. Jones re-established contact with his ailing father and his addicted brothers. He organized a reunion among the men which culminated with a visit to their mother's grave. Through this effort at reconnection, Mr. Jones was able to begin mourning his mother's death, the lack of parenting he received, and expiate his guilt over his brother's unfair treatment. As a consequence, Mr. Jones began to interact with his son in a loving and optimistic way, no longer believing his son was doomed to be a problem.

Mrs. Jones re-established a dialogue with her mother and sister, seeking commonalities that could transcend ideological differences. The women thus agreed to disagree while respecting each other's lifestyles. Having rebalanced relational difficulties with their families of origin, the Jones turned to their marital relationship and began to negotiate ways in which they could be separate yet a couple, disagree yet continue to love, and thus remain united without parentifying their children.

By the six month evaluation, both children were in gifted programs and Eddie was no longer smoking marijuana.

CASE EXAMPLE

The Soto Family

Background Information

The family consisted of Mrs. Soto, 35, a native of El Salvador, her common law husband, Raul, 30, and the couple's four children: Juan, 9, Paul and Mike, twins aged 5, and an infant daughter, six weeks. Mrs. Soto's two older children by a previous relationship, Tomas, 17, and Rita 14, were currently in foster homes. The maternal grandmother was currently visiting from El Salvador. She came to help her daughter with the new baby.

Referral Information

Rita was referred for an evaluation to this therapist by Child Protective Services. Rita was removed from the home and placed in a temporary foster home after a severe beating from her mother. The Soto family had been involved with the child welfare system for five years—since the arrival of the two older children from El Salvador. Both children have been in and out of home placements 12 times in the past four years. Tomas had been placed in a permanent foster home until age 18, at which time he will be expected to live independently of his parents and the court system. Rita on the other hand, because of her age, was evaluated to assess the suitability of permanent foster placement or another turn at home. Court records indicated that the last beating was prompted by the mother's discovery that Rita was sexually active with a 19-year-old friend of the family. Mrs. Soto broke a jar of peppers on Rita's head. A cousin who was visiting the family told a teacher at school and Rita was immediately removed from the home. In the hospital, a blood test uncovered high levels of methaamphetamine and cocaine. Rita then acknowledged daily use of cocaine and crack.

Family Evaluation

The therapist conducted a three-session family evaluation with the Sotos and a three-session evaluation of the Sotos and the foster parents. The following material was a result of the six family meetings.

Mrs. Soto left El Salvador 13 years ago for the United States shortly after Rita's birth. Her migration was prompted by economic need and a desire to escape a difficult family situation. Mrs. Soto had had two children out of wedlock with different men. Each time her own mother had beaten her severely throughout the pregnancies. Maria left her two children with her mother hoping to return for the children within a year. Mrs. Soto was unable to send for her children until eight years later. She never visited El Salvador, thus, Tomas and Rita did not remember their mother and considered their maternal grandmother their mother. When the children came to the United States, Mrs. Soto was living with Mr. Soto, had a two-year-old son, and was expecting twins. The family reunification was fraught with difficulties. Mrs. Soto complained that her children did not respect or love her. Both children had difficulties at school. A few months after the children's arrival, Rita was molested by a family friend. Mrs. Soto's reaction was to accuse Rita (then 9) of being a tramp and severely beat her. It was then that the family was initially referred to the protective agency. From then on, the children told a story of continual physical, verbal, and emotional abuse by their mother. The mother on the other hand, described her children as ungrateful, disrespectful, and denied any physical or emotional abuse.

Rita's current behavioral problems coincided with her mother's last pregnancy and the grandmother's arrival from El Salvador. Rita claimed that she began using drugs because all the kids at school were doing it and because it helps her cope with her mother's abuse. The mother viewed this behavior as further evidence of Rita's hypersexuality and prostitute-like conduct.

A contextual analysis of this family highlighted a number of multigenerational patterns: Daughters having children out of wedlock and leaving them with their own mothers as the young women leave to seek economic prosperity elsewhere, alcohol abuse, abandonment and illegitimacy among the men, parentification of children, extreme disciplinary practices. Furthermore, all the women (grandmother, mother, sisters, Rita) were molested by family friends at a young age and all have been accused of being tramps by family members.

While these were multigenerational patterns in the Soto family, the migration process, separation of family members, and involvement of social welfare systems all compounded the family dysfunction. Despite the fact that the Sotos were referred for child abuse countless times, they continuously refused to engage in therapy. The therapeutic strategy became not an offer for therapy, but an evaluation to facilitate the disposition of the case to which the family agreed.

The focus of the evaluation was then to:

1. Assess the safety of all the children as the family entered a crisis stage with the birth of the new child, the arrival of the grandmother, and the removal of two children into foster placement;
2. Identifying extrafamilial resources for Mrs. Soto to help prevent abuse of the infant and other children;
3. Contextualize the long history of abuse in terms of the family's own sociopolitical, cultural, and family history;
4. Determine the best possible outcome for Rita in the short- and long-term;
5. Understand Rita's drug use and other behavioral problems as embedded in a pattern of multigenerational legacies and migration-related difficulties; and
6. Evaluate the extent of Mr. Soto's contribution to the family dysfunction as a resource for change.

It was the therapist's position, that regardless of the eventual disposition of Rita's placement, family relationships needed to be rebalanced, specifically, mother and daughter needed to understand the historical basis of their conflicts and begin a reconstructive dialogue to foster trust, forgiveness of the abandonment, lack of protection, and difficulty expressing love. Furthermore, the children needed support in order to prevent future abuse and a continuation of these destructive multigenerational patterns of cut-offs, unplanned pregnancies, and drug abuse.

After the family evaluation meetings, the extended Soto family agreed to continue meeting for 10 additional sessions. The bulk of the treatment focused on trust-building, negotiation of cross-cultural and intergenerational conflicts between parents and children, and building resources for the family and Rita.

Having engaged the family in treatment and examined the multigenerational legacies of abandonment and neglect and abuse, the middle phase of treatment focused on the relationships of the three women. Grandmother, mother, and Rita began to engage in a reconstructive dialogue in which each woman's contributions (destructive and constructive) to the family legacy were examined. Rita was credited with bringing to the fore the suffering of all the women. In this way, Rita's addiction together with mother's and grandmother's physical and emotional abusiveness were acknowledged as contributions to the family legacy. Extrafamilial resources were identified, including the maternal aunt and uncle who were cut-off from their mother and sister, who would help the women generate fair and just ways to contribute to the legacy.

The theme of family suffering was used as a resource to shift the focus of attention away from abuse. Each woman's sacrifice (of motherhood, parenting, youth, etc.) was explored in detail eliciting validation, acknowledgement, and expressions of forgiveness from each other. Both grandmother and mother were encouraged to help find solutions for Rita and the infant daughter so that transgenerational suffering could be stopped.

In the final stage of treatment, the peripheral and often abusive role of men was examined with an aim to prevent such patterns from emerging within the Soto boys. The long history of sibling abuse, including incest and subsequent cutoffs, was rebalanced by the reconnection of Mrs. Soto and her siblings. Dialogues were focused on preventing patterns of abuse.

At the end of treatment, a ritual task was assigned to facilitate forgiveness, trust-building, and facilitate the search for a spiritual balance and integrity among family members. Consistent with the indigenous/Catholic background of this family, the task entailed building an altar and offering a symbol of each family member's sacrifice for the group. In this manner, each family member sought forgiveness for injustices and made resolutions to work toward establishing and maintaining fairer relationships. In this ritual, Mrs. Soto offered the belt she used to hit the children, the grandmother offered her long braids, and Rita surrendered her drugs.

At the end of treatment, Rita chose to continue living in foster placement for an additional six months and to continue working with her family on issues of reunification. Rita continued in individual therapy (mandated by the court) with monthly family meetings with the therapist. At the onset of treatment, Rita became drug-free, her school performance improved, and her depression decreased. She began to dress in a more age-appropriate manner and decided to stop being sexually active until the time she found someone who truly cared for her.

EFFECTIVENESS OF CFT

Clinical work with CFT has been well documented (Bernal 1982a; Bernal & Flores Ortiz, 1982; Boszormenyi-Nagy & Spark, 1973; Boszormenyi-Nagy & Krasner, 1986). To our knowledge, there has been only one treatment outcome study (Bernal et al., 1987) that has examined the question of effectiveness of CFT. While the final analyses of this study are not available, preliminary results will be summarized here.

Our research was a randomized clinical trial of brief CFT with methadone maintenance patients. The major purpose of the study was to evaluate a 10-session program of CFT in comparison to a 10-session psychoeducational program covering similar content but within a videotaped format of lectures and subsequent discussions.

Forty-one families were randomly chosen for each group and treated with a manual for each condition. Families were evaluated at multiple levels of outcome at pre, post, and six-month follow-up. The details of the methods and procedures are reported in Bernal et al. (1987).

The preliminary results demonstrated that addicts in both treatment programs showed significant beneficial improvements with the indices of drug abuse. However, families in the CFT condition showed greater improvement in the outcome measures of family and marital functioning than families receiving the psychoeducational control. In general, the findings were encouraging. CFT appears to be a treatment modality that has beneficial effects for a difficult population of adult and late adolescent drug abusers. These findings, while preliminary, may be generalizable to other populations with less severe drug problems.

LIMITATIONS OF THE CONTEXTUAL APPROACH

In considering the limitations of any approach, the model itself is questioned not only in terms of the available clinical and empirical evidence, but also in terms of its theoretical clarity. Perhaps, one of the limitations of CFT is its main contribution: a system of concepts about complex relational processes. The efforts of developing a language for therapy that are genuinely relational (such as beyond the psyche and the cybernetic system) that may appear to some as a jargon-riddled model of therapy.

A second limitation of the approach is the burden it places on therapists and families to consider the multiple sides of relationships. For example, it is certainly easier to side with and defend the interests of an abused and victimized child. Intrinsic to the CFT approach is a consideration of the interests of, at least, the abused and the abuser—the victim as well as the victimizer. Taking into account the interests of the victimizer may not only be unpopular but difficult to accomplish, particularly in cases of incest, child abuse, and so on. In other words, the CFT approach may tax the personal resources of many therapists with its basic rule of multidirected partiality.

A third limitation is often the inevitable consideration of how to impact on the social context itself (Bernal & Ysern, 1986; Bernal, 1988). For example, when the side of the victimizer is examined, the social roots of the victimization are often revealed. While an acknowledgement of the social, economic, and other contextual limitations are important, they are certainly not justification for the present abuse. Herein, the limits of CFT may be reached, particularly if the model presents no guidelines for social and community action beyond the family. Articulating such guidelines may be an important area of development in the CFT approach.

The other side of the issue of limitations within the CFT approach are the consequences of not considering the ethical, relational dimension of relationships. What are the consequences of assuming that a pattern of drug abuse is only a behavior or hierarchical family problem? What are the implications of a plan of therapy that assumes that the drug abuse has nothing to do with giving and receiving nurturance in a most fundamental way? What are the consequences of not acknowledging that adolescent drug abuse may be a way to express loyalty and or exonerate a particular family member? What of the *giving* of an adolescent, if his or her drug abuse is a way to help with a deep depression of a parent or a means through which the family avoids facing a catastrophic loss? The consequences of not acknowledging such efforts as legitimate ways to give, albeit destructive, may not only perpetuate the problem, but in the long run, may be as destructive as the drug abuse.

REFERENCES

Bernal, G. (1982). Parentification and deparentification in family therapy. In A. S. Gurman (ed.) *Questions and Answers in Family Therapy.* Vol. II. New York: Brunner/Mazel.

Bernal, G. (1982a). Cuban families. In M. McGoldrick, J. Giordano & J. Pierce (eds.) *Ethnicity and Family Therapy.* New York: Guilford Press.

Bernal, G. & Flores-Ortiz, Y. (1982). Latino families in therapy: Engagement and evaluation. *Journal of Marital and Family Therapy, 8*(3).

Bernal, G., Flores-Ortiz, Y., Sorensen, J. L., Miranda, J. M., Rodriguez, C., Diamond, G., & Alvarez, M. (1987). *Intergenerational family therapy with methadone maintenance patients and family members: Findings of a clinical outcome study.* Paper presented at the 18th annual meeting of the Society for Psychotherapy Research, Ulm, West Germany, June 1987.

Bernal, G., Rodriguez-Dragin, C., Flores-Ortiz, Y., & Diamond, G. (1985). *Intergenerational family therapy: A treatment manual.* Unpublished manuscript.

Bernal, G. & Ysern, E. (1986). Family therapy and ideology. *Journal of Marital and Family Therapy, 12*(2), 129–137.

Bernal, G. (1988). Latino families: Toward a progressive family therapy. *The Community Psychologist, 21,* 29–30.

Boszormenyi-Nagy, I., & Sparks, G. M. (1973). *Invisible loyalties.* New York: Harper & Row.

Boszormenyi-Nagy, I. & Framo, J. (1965). *Intensive family therapy: Theoretical and practical aspects.* New York: Harper & Row.

Boszormenyi-Nagy, I. (1976). Behavior change through family change. In A. Burton (ed.), *What makes behavior change possible?* New York: Brunner/Mazel.

Boszormenyi-Nagy, I. (1987). *Foundations of contextual therapy.* New York: Brunner/Mazel.

Boszormenyi-Nagy, I. & Krasner, B. R. (1986). *Between give and take: A clinical guide to contextual therapy.* New York: Brunner/Mazel.

Boszormenyi-Nagy, I. & Ulrich, D. N. (1981). Contextual family therapy. In A. S. Gurman & D. P. Kniskern (eds.), *Handbook of family therapy.* New York: Brunner/Mazel.

Bowen, M. (1978). *Family therapy in clinical practice.* New York: Aronson.

Buber, M. (1970). *I and thou.* Translated by W. Kaufman, New York: Charles Scribners' Sons.

Burt, M. R. (1980). *Family therapy: A summary of selected literature.* DHEW Publication No. (ADM) 80–944. Washington, DC: U.S. Government Printing Office.

Cotroneo, M., & Krasner, B. R. (1976). Addiction, alienation, & parenting. *Nursing Clinics of North America, 11*(3), 517–525.

Glynn, T. J. (ed.) (1981). *Drugs and the family.* DHHS Publication No. (ADM) 81–1151. Washington, DC: U.S. Government Printing Office.

Golann, S. (1988). On second order family therapy. *Family Process, 27,* 51–64.

Grunebaum, J. (1983). *Contextual Therapy: Trust-building through development of intergenerational resources.* Unpublished manuscript. Boston.

Haley, J. (1980). *Leaving home: Therapy with disturbed young people.* New York: McGraw-Hill.

Harbin, H. & Maziar, H. (1975). The families of drug abusers: A literature review. *Family Process, 14,* 411–431.

Kaufman, E. & Kaufmann, P. (1979). Multiple family therapy with drug abusers. In E. Kaufman & P. Kaufman (eds.), *Family therapy of alcohol and drug abuse.* New York: Gardner Press.

Morris, W. (ed.), (1970). *American heritage dictionary of the English language.* New York: American Heritage Company.

Sorensen, J. L. & Bernal, G. (1987). *A family like yours: Breaking the patterns of drug abuse.* San Francisco: Harper & Row.

Stanton, M. D., & Todd, T. C., and associates. (1982). *The family therapy of drug abuse and addiction.* New York: Guilford.

Stierlin, H., Rucker-Embden, I., Wetzel, N., & Wirschin, M. (1980). *The first interview with the family.* New York: Brunner/Mazel.

Watzlawick, P., Beavin, J. H., & Jackson, D. D. (1967). *Pragmatics of human communication.* New York: Norton.

5

Solution Focused Brief Treatment with Adolescent Substance Abusers

INSOO KIM BERG, M.S.S.W.
Co-Director, Brief Family Therapy Center
Milwaukee, Wisconsin

DAN GALLAGHER, M.Div.
Family Therapist, HealthShield HMO
Poughkeepsie, New York

INTRODUCTION

Adolescence is a period of great turmoil that can be a time of many positive changes. Since we believe change is inevitable and occurs constantly, the therapeutic task is to enhance and direct positive changes in the most useful and least intrusive way possible. Chemical abuse in adolescents comes in many different forms and, at times, it is only one of many issues—and not necessarily the primary one. At these times it can be more prudent to treat the other issues before addressing the chemical abuse, particularly when an adolescent is resistant to acknowledging the abuse as a problem.

It is useful to view the abuse as multi-causal and many-faceted. Rather than viewing the abuse as a manifestation of an individual personality defect or using the functional view that symptomatic behaviors serve a useful function for the family (usually the marital unit), we believe that it can be useful to view substance abuse as a continuum from serious addiction to just a tool to experiment with one's independence and autonomy.

Basic Assumptions

Solution Focused Brief Therapy (de Shazer, 1982, 1985, 1988) is constructed around the idea that *nothing always happens.* Substance abuse is no exception; there are times (sometimes few and far between) when the abuser chooses not to abuse (i.e., exceptions to the abuse rule). Viewed in this way, the therapeutic task becomes one of helping clients discover non-problematic patterns and helping clients to repeat those patterns, thus increasing the frequency of the patterns that include solutions. Substance abuse, like other behaviors, creates disturbances in adolescents and those around them lies within the person's control.

Milton Erickson's influence (Haley, 1967) is apparent in the model. Instead of dwelling on past problematic patterns, (which by and large tend to result in fault finding and blame placing), discovering the exceptions to the abuse and projecting clients into the future when the abuse is no longer a troublesome issue creates an expectation of change. Thus, paying attention to solution patterns, such as what instead of drug use happens on days when the youth decides not to use drugs, is sometimes more important than how often or how much he or she uses. When a solution pattern is found, the therapeutic task is to help the client find ways to repeat it even under adverse conditions in the coming days.

Of course, nothing always works, including those tasks built on exceptions. Whenever tasks do not lead toward the client's goal, the therapist must switch to tasks built around the idea that doing something different is required. Another way of viewing therapeutic tasks, then, is to avoid repeating tasks that are not working. In fact, the problems therapists are called upon to solve most often are the result of clients doing more of the same of what is not working.

When a therapist replicates the more of the same problem solving efforts that did not work, the therapist ends up frustrated and the client is called resistive. It appears that substance abuse problems more than most other problems tend to create more of the same ineffective attempted solutions that seem to go nowhere. Therefore, it is easy for clinicians to fall into patterns that others fall into, that is, trying to catch or prevent drug abusers' sneaking behaviors, repeatedly admonishing them, preaching to them, and checking up on their stories to verify their truthfulness—this not only increases frustration, but also increases the sneaking behaviors.

We believe that ensuring clients' cooperation for therapeutic endeavors are the therapists' responsibilities. This view, derived from the systemic, interactional view, gives therapists much latitude in initiating positive working relationships, even with clients who have a reputation of being resistive to treatment. Because we recognize the value of the positive feedback loop, we have come to appreciate the power of small changes and their potential ripple effects. It is always easier both for clients and therapists to aim for and accomplish small change; it is also easier to see the results. This is particularly so with adolescent clients who by nature tend to feel unsure about themselves.

Finding out what they are doing right, what they are good at, what they are interested in, and what they have been successful in, and so on, are not only good joining techniques, but also point out the strengths of adolescents and their parents.

When the cybernetic viewpoint is combined with a strong dose of pragmatic solution development, the therapeutic task becomes a process of constructing solutions rather than solving problems. This approach provides both clients and therapists with clues about how to invent and implement solutions. That is, building on exceptions helps clients find their unique way of developing solutions. In their stuck situation, clients often do not realize that they can and often have solved the problems on their own. Simply, therapists' roles become those of pointing clients in the right directions and then getting and staying out of their ways.

Assessment Consideration: Visitor or Customer?

More important than how much, when, and how long the abuse has been going on, the most important consideration in the assessment phase is the degree of client motivation. Substance abusers in general, and adolescents in particular, are often thought to be resistive to treatment and are viewed as more prone to denial (Miller, 1985).

More so than adults, adolescents are frequently forced to enter treatment by their parents, schools, or courts. Frequently, there are strong tendencies in treatment programs, or within therapists' definitions of their jobs leading therapists to become agents of social control; thus, therapists often become more their own customers than the abusers themselves (Berg, 1985).

When confusion arises between the therapeutic task and the role of social control, it is frequently the client who is blamed, for instance, the client is said to be unmotivated or not ready for therapy, or the therapist finds himself or herself doing the work for both of them.

Like any other interpersonal phenomenon, the client's motivation for change is the product of therapist and client interaction. Instead of viewing client motivation as an innate, characterological quality that the client brings to therapy, it is more useful to view motivation as a product of the therapist-client interaction (Lipchik, 1987). This is particularly true when an element of coercion is involved.

Since all substance abusing clients are familiar with repeated admonitions about the evils of substance abuse including how it is ruining their health, life, and so on, it is important to catch clients' attention by utilizing a different approach. In all likelihood, clients have become immune to repeated sermons. Until an individual client can clearly see the benefit of treatment, he or she is not likely to cooperate with it. That is, when he or she sees that therapy can help achieve what he or she wants the most, such as getting back into school, stopping parental nagging, having the desired girl or boyfriend, and so on, then the client is likely to cooperate. Even though the goal that the abusing adolescent sets may not represent the ideal or the real problem he should work on from the therapist's viewpoint, this is a pragmatic approach that emphasizes usefulness more than rightness.

We find the distinction between *visitor* and *customer* a useful clinical tool for describing the therapist-client relationship pattern in a quick, shorthand way. These are not static states the client is in, but rather, fluid states that change from session to session. Visitor or customer is the product of the therapist-client relationship thus, the therapist has a reasonable amount of influence on how the relationship develops.

Substance abusing clients who are forced to come to treatment against their wishes act like visitors. That is, they are unfamiliar with or uninterested in what therapy has to offer. Their sole interests appear to be fulfilling the obligations to come to sessions, but not to come for substance abuse treatment. Being sympathetic about the hassles of "being pushed around" and "being told what to do," while complimenting clients for caring enough to show up for an appointment, helps increase their cooperation and establish therapeutic relationships.

When an adolescent abuser refuses to participate in treatment, or the abuser is on the run and not available for treatment, or the parents are unable to get the abuser to come for treatment, we frequently work with the non-abusing members of the family, usually the parents. When parents are more customers than their child, that is, when parents are more upset or desperate for change—more willing and ready to take steps to bring about change—they can change their more of the same non-productive behaviors with their teenagers, thus producing different, more positive patterns of interaction.

Turning the visitor into a customer requires finding out what is important to the client whether it is to avoid going to jail or to improve grades by joining the client's world view and using the client's own language. Even though the parents or the referral source identified the drug use as the presenting problem, the adolescent client's main interest may be to use the car. Therefore, a client might be a customer to the goal of getting the car and a visitor to the issue of drug abuse. Accepting the goal of working toward using the car may lead the client to realize that his or her drug abuse interferes with that goal.

Treatment Goals

When a client's goal is accepted as legitimate and valid, even though it may seem unrelated to the substance abuse, frequently involuntary, and resistive clients become cooperative, hard-working customers of therapy. Treatment goals need to be specific and concrete. Therefore, "getting my parents off my back" must be developed through a description of what the client's life will be like when his parents stop bugging him. For example, after being kicked out of his parent's home (for abusing drugs), one young man's goal was to return home long enough to save money so that he could afford to get a place of his own. When this goal was accepted as valid, he became a willing customer of treatment. One of the many conditions for returning home was no more drugs. Thus, ending the drug abuse became only a step on the way toward his goal.

When goals between parents and adolescents are different (for example, the parents want the drug use to stop completely so that the teenager can do better in school while the abuser's goal is to cut down so that he or she can have more friends), it is frequently more productive to see the parents and adolescent separately. In fact, seeing them separately may allow the therapist more room to develop a solution that fits the family.

In situations where two or more members of the family are abusers, joint and separate assessment of each member's investment and goal for treatment is crucial. When both parties involved acknowledge the substance abuse behavior and are customers, they can be treated simultaneously since their goal is the same. However, when one member is a customer and the other is a visitor, it is more prudent to start working on the change process with the customer which in turn will ripple through the entire family.

Role of Therapist and the Team

The primary task of the therapist in the first phase of treatment is to join the client by learning the client's world view and language and to discover what matters to the client the most. Once the treatment goal is established, helping the client discover any exceptions to the problem becomes the second task. Even though the client tends to focus on the problem, perhaps out of the belief that the more they talk about the problem the sooner it will be solved, focusing on the future state *when* the problem is solved helps the client see that a solution can be achieved and that such a change is within his or her reach without having to turn his or her life around.

Once the change is initiated, the therapeutic task is to reinforce and monitor other changes that are taking place.

Even though the use of the team, the one-way mirror, and the telephone hookup are all essential tools for the training of clinicians and other creative processes, such equipment is not essential to treatment nor cost effective. Our guideline: When there is no movement in treatment by the third session, we suggest a consultation with the team. We have found that using the team as a consultant by an individual therapist is a pragmatic way to utilize our model.

From our experience using the team, we learned that the consultation break has a dramatic impact since client expectation about therapy rises and the client becomes more attentive to whatever the therapist has to say. When working alone we still take this break, informing the client that we need to take some time to think about things and that we will return with some feedback and maybe even with some suggestions. Our experience is that if a therapist's approach to the client is respectful and if the therapist takes the client's problems seriously enough, the client's refusal of the team approach is minimal.

Ultimately the most important product of the therapeutic endeavor is to empower clients, to enable them to see themselves as in control of their lives, and to see that they can run their lives effectively.

KEY INTERVENTION STRATEGIES

Since the focus of our treatment is future directed, we believe that the solution pattern is more important than the problem pattern. Asking questions to discover solutions that work and to construct the future state when the problem is solved becomes an important task.

1. Questions as Interventions

The following are some example questions that may serve as guides. Since most clients and therapists are not accustomed to such questions, effective use will take practice and persistence. The results are worth the effort.

A. Questions Designed to Find Exceptions.

"I have a good picture of what happens when there are problems. Now, in order to get a more complete picture of your situation, I need to know about when the problem does not happen.

When do you NOT have that problem?

How do you explain that the problem doesn't happen then?

What is different at those times when the problem doesn't happen?

What do you do that is different at those times? What else?

What has to happen for that to happen more often?

What will convince your parents (teacher, friend, etc.) that the problem is really solved?

How would your parent (teacher, friend, etc.) react as a result of the changes he or she notices in you?

How often does that happen now?

What will you have to do to make that happen?"

B. Scaling Questions. When the problem description and treatment goal are vague or too global, scaling questions helps focus the problem and the treatment goal. They also serve as useful tools for assessing change investment.

"On a scale of one to ten, with ten the highest and one the lowest, where would you put your desire to stop using drugs today?

On the same scale, where would your parents say you are today?

On the same scale, what would you say your chances of making it are? What would your parents say? Your teachers? Your friends?

What do you have to do to move from 5 to 6? What would your parents say you have to do?"

C. Miracle Questions. When a therapist is unable to identify exceptions and wants to obtain hypothetical solutions, or when exceptions have been identified and the task at hand is goal-setting, the miracle question can be useful. It is remarkable how clear, specific, and concrete most clients are as they give behavioral descriptions of their goals when these questions are asked.

"If a miracle happened overnight while you are sleeping and your problem is solved:

What would you notice tomorrow morning that tells you that there has been a miracle? What else?

Who else would notice that there's been a miracle? How?

What will your parents notice about you that is different?

How would your parents react as a result of the changes they notice in you?

What will you have to do to make that happen?

What would it take for you to start acting as if there has been a miracle?"

D. Coping Sequence Questions. When a client reports that nothing is going right, no matter how you search, and he or she persists in denying that anything positive happens about his or her parent or child, a good joining technique is to temporarily agree with his or her negative appraisal by asking the coping questions. The following examples are designed to point out to a client that he or she has the resources and strengths to manage and improve his or her life.

"It sounds like the problem is very serious. How come things are not worse?

What are you (or your family) doing to keep things from getting worse?

How has that been helpful? Would your parent (or adolescent) agree?

What are you doing to keep going when things are so bad?

What would tell you that things are getting a little better?

What would it take to make that happen?

What do you imagine yourself doing then?"

E. Questions for the Pessimistic Sequence. When the client insists that there is nothing good about his or her adolescent (or parent) and insist that only dire and disastrous consequences lie ahead, it is better to join him or her at this level by posing the following questions.

"The problem you describe is indeed serious and we need to think about how bad things can get.

What is the worst possible picture you can imagine if things don't get better?

What do you imagine your life would be like then?

What do you imagine yourself doing if it were to happen?

Who would be most upset if the worst things were to happen? Who next? Anybody else?"

If the client becomes a little more optimistic in response to this pessimistic picture, it can be used to construct a solution by asking these questions.

"So what would it take for you to make that happen just a little bit? What else?

Who will notice first when it is beginning to happen?

What will be a small sign that it is beginning to get a little bit better?

What would it take for you to make it happen?"

2. Past Successes

A client and/or therapist may often overlook a few days, a week or two, or a month of no drug use. Since even a journey of thousand miles begins one step at a time, even one or two days of control or abstinence before the start of treatment can be framed as an indication of the client's ability to solve the problem. The therapist's task then is to look at all the things the client did during that period that were part of his or her success. Since these are within the repertoire already, it is fairly easy for the client to initiate them again.

3. Current Successes

"Keep track of what you do instead, *when* you overcome the urge to use drugs."

The task here is to focus on control, not on the lack of control. This task implies that the client will overcome the urge by doing rather than passively waiting for things to happen. When he or she overcomes again implies that the client will overcome, and that it is only a matter of time. The question no longer is built around *if* he will overcome.

4. Compliments

A client may react with surprise and relief when the therapist points out the positive things he or she is doing, such as coming for therapy even though he was skeptical, wanting to get along with parents, wanting to avoid trouble with the law, and so on. It is often the first time any professional has ever said nice things to him or her and is probably the first time anyone really listened, especially if the client has been in a series of troublesome events in school, with the police, the courts, and/or parents. The content of the compliments may not be related to the presenting problem, but anything the client is doing that is good for him or her, that he or she is good at, and aspires for, should be pointed out.

5. Future Successes: Goal Setting

Clear, concrete, and measurable goals not only help the therapist know what needs to be done in order to solve problems, but also increase the chances of success for the client. At the point of entry into therapy most clients are so overwhelmed, confused, and frustrated by their problems that they may not be able to specify clear goals for therapy. Taking the time to establish specific goals and measures of success makes problems seem less overwhelming. Fifteen-year-old Jason, who is on probation for a weapons charge and disorderly conduct in school because of his drug use, spelled out his goals by answering the miracle questions: He will not have to go get medicine for his mother's nerves, will go to school, stay away from rowdy kids, and do his chores. At the end of the session, what he constructed as the result of the miracle questions can be suggested as tasks to get the solution pattern started.

6. Reframing

Since perceptions are negotiable, and since perceptions, in part, determine behavior, it is often helpful to offer a more positive viewpoint about an event rather than a negative one.

For example, one young man was angry at his parents for kicking him out of his family. After listening a while, I commented casually about how much his parents must love him. Startled to hear this, he was curious to hear more. I said that because they loved him so much they probably decided not to treat him like a little boy, nagging at him, telling him what to do, and giving him a little money which makes them entitled to demand that he follow their rules and so on. Perhaps they respected their son too much to treat him that way and maybe kicking him out was their ultimate way of showing love and respect for him as a growing young man with a mind of his own. He thought about this for a long time before agreeing that indeed his parents loved him very much.

LIMITATIONS AND EFFECTIVENESS

Since the model described here is not just a collection of techniques, but a way of looking at human problems in general and the therapeutic relationship in particular, it is difficult to describe the limitations of this model as a tool. Our followup indicates that we average about five sessions per case and that we are successful in meeting or exceeding clients' goals in approximately 80 percent of our cases regardless of the presenting complaint.

The following case illustrates a detailed description of the Solution Focused Brief Therapy model in practice.

CASE EXAMPLE

Alice called to make an appointment for her 15-year-old son, Joe, who was abusing drugs. The school and his probation officer wanted him in therapy because "he has a lot of anger inside him. If this [therapy] doesn't work, they will place him in a home."

Joe's father introduced Joe to the therapist and left. Joe seemed amused at the admission process. "If my dad knew all this was going to happen he would have stayed." The therapist responded jokingly, "And if your father had stayed, he would tell me what brings you here." Joe said that he was uncertain why he was here except that if he did not come, he would be sent away somewhere.

THERAPIST: What does your father think will happen here that will be helpful to you?

JOE: He just wants me to stay out of trouble.

THERAPIST: When you're not in trouble anymore, what will be different in your life?

Joe thought that people would leave him alone. He reported that he was being watched by everyone at school and his parents would probably be happier if he were somewhere else. The therapist continued to inquire about what will be happening when Joe is not in trouble. He wanted to graduate with his class and go on to college, but he did not think that likely anymore: there were the missed classes at school; the grades that seemed too low to bring up; the police record at 15 "for dealing drugs"; all of which led to his parents "fighting all the time about me."

As the therapist continued to ask Joe to describe how things will be without the problems, Joe provided information about his problems as well. Although the therapist and the team behind the mirror were mainly interested in solutions and potential solutions, Joe seemed to be more comfortable when he could give some other data about himself and the trouble he was in. This was accepted with interest. He had been experimenting with alcohol, marijuana, and cocaine since he was 13 years old. Just the previous year, Joe began smoking crack. Money for this came from selling drugs at school.

JOE: I loved it. It was my drug. I haven't wanted to use anything else since. But I was busted for dealing pot and they suspended me from school and gave me probation. My parents, the school, and probation officer made a deal that I can go back to school for the rest of the year if I don't step out of line. I can't even miss one class. I know I can handle that, but I haven't given up my crack. They'd die if they knew about this. They just think I'm some kind of delinquent dealing grass to kids.

THERAPIST: You gave up grass, booze, and coke! How did you do that?

JOE: I just stopped. All my friends are using crack, too. I use it once in a while but I haven't touched the booze and weed in over a year. I gave up cigarettes a week ago. That's the hardest. With all this going on, I want a smoke real bad.

THERAPIST: But you haven't smoked in a week. What have you been doing instead?

JOE: Whenever I get the urge, I do my homework.

Joe described listening to music, calling a friend (he smoked the most when he was avoiding giving in to urges to use crack in his home or other places where he might be caught), and going for a ride on his dirt bike as ways he successfully handled the temptations to smoke. He knew that sooner or later he had to give up the crack, too. The therapist agreed that it might be sooner rather than later, now that they are watching him more because of the probation.

At that point in the session, the team behind the mirror called to prompt the therapist to ask for more exceptions.

THERAPIST: When else do you not have all these problems Joe? When are things happening that you'd like to see happen more often?

Joe said that about the only time he was relaxed and happy these days was when he was listening to music, riding his bike, or talking to his girlfriend on the phone. The therapist asked how things are better at those times.

JOE: When I'm talking to her or listening to music, it's like a part of me wants to have a better life. I don't want to be fighting all the time like my parents do.

The therapist then asked Joe, "If a miracle happened tonight and your problems are solved, what will you notice tomorrow morning that tells you there has been a miracle?" Joe chuckled and said that everyone would back off and leave him alone. He would be doing well in school and not selling drugs. As they discussed what Joe will have to do to make that happen, the therapist asked, "Are they noticing anything even a little, now?" Joe said that he has only been back in school for two days, so he was uncertain, but agreed to try and find out.

THERAPIST: On a scale of zero to ten, with zero being pretty serious problems with crack and ten being no problems at all, where do you put yourself now?

JOE: About a six.

THERAPIST: And what will it be, say, six months from now?

JOE: A ten.

THERAPIST: What has to happen for you to get to, say, a seven or an eight?

JOE: I haven't used anything for two weeks. I was a little down at first and I had a short fuse. That's when they thought I needed to deal with my anger. I don't think I'm ready to stop smoking yet.

Consultation Break

The team members discussed whether Joe was a visitor or a customer. After deciding that he may be closer to being a customer (i.e., someone who is interested in doing something about the complaint), the team discussed what Joe needed to hear from them and how they could help him focus more on solutions. They agreed that Joe needed to know that they noticed how he had cooperated with his father by coming to therapy, had overcome serious drug use problems, and now was rising to the opportunity to solve serious problems despite the odds.

The following message was given following the consultation break.

> We are very impressed by how you came here and told us about your situation in a very open and honest way. That wasn't easy. And it looks like you have a lot more to do to convince people to back off and this is a good first step. We also noticed that you have solved difficult drug problems on your own and you are open to getting some help to solve this difficult problem now. In order to figure out how best to help you we need to know more about what happens when you aren't on the spot like this. Therefore, we would like you to keep track of everything you do when you overcome the urge to light up a cigarette. Keep track of what you do instead.

The following day, the therapist received two phone calls, one from Joe's mother, Alice, and the other from Joe's guidance counselor.

Alice impatiently informed the therapist that she had just received a call from the school telling her that Joe had skipped yet another class. "Where else can we send him? This is *not* working." The therapist agreed that "the problem is very serious and maybe our best hope is to try and get Joe into a more positive frame of mind." Alice said that she had tried just about everything and nothing had worked. The therapist commented that "two heads are better than one" and asked Alice to pay close attention to what is happening on days when Joe is "not a hassle." He asked her to come with Joe next time to discuss this "before we have our session with Joe."

The guidance counselor thought that Joe needed more help than "individual counselling." In our meeting here we decided to refer Joe and his whole family for therapy. Joe needs long-term treatment. There are no easy or short-term solutions to his problems. Are you going to see him and his family weekly? He also suggested a psychiatric consultation for Joe and that he be placed on medication.

The therapist asked him for a summary of the results of any testing the school had done. After some discussion, the therapist requested one more bit of information.

THERAPIST: We need to know what is happening on days when Joe is not in trouble. We are trying to get a more complete picture and need to know how he is on good days when the problem does not happen.

GUIDANCE COUNSELOR: He can do well when he wants to. His science teacher has no trouble with him.

THERAPIST: How does he do that? Do you have any clues?

GUIDANCE COUNSELOR: No. You'll have to ask the teacher.

The therapist thanked him and said that he would call from time to time for more information about how Joe is improving.

THERAPIST: We need to know when he is not conning us and our best measure is improvements.

GUIDANCE COUNSELOR: Then, you will put him on medication?

THERAPIST: If it's necessary, the doctor will. We'll be in touch.

Session 2: One Week Later

Joe and his mother came for the second session. They were seen together for the first part. Alice was asked what improvements she had noticed. She seemed confused. "Do you mean in Joe, or what?" The therapist asked, "Are things better . . . the same. . . ?" For her, things were better, but she was skeptical. She was reassured because she had not received any more calls from the school and Joe had been home more. Alice went on to list numerous things that happened at home and at school that she considered problematic.

After listening for a short time, the therapist took advantage of a pause in her account to say, "I think I have a good picture of what happens when there are problems. You have been very clear and specific. At this point, I need to know more about what's happening now that Joe is home more and you are not getting calls from school." Alice listed several areas of improvement, including Joe's taking out the garbage, treating his sister better, and talking with her more. The therapist asked Joe how they are talking more and how they can keep that going. He then said it was time to see Joe alone.

Joe reported that he was trying harder and things were better with his mother. But the people at school were even more vigilant now that he is attending classes regularly. After focusing on improvements, noticed and unnoticed by others, and ways to get parents and school authorities to notice more of the good things, the therapist asked about how Joe had overcome temptations.

JOE: I didn't stop.

THERAPIST: OK. When you overcame the urge, what did you do?

JOE: I did my homework. I killed two birds with one stone. Cut back on the smokes and did homework.

THERAPIST: What else did you do?

JOE: Nothing. I ate more. . . . Oh, I talked to my mother, too.

THERAPIST: What else?

JOE: That's it. I didn't do anything else. Have you talked to my probation officer?

When the therapist returned from the consultation with the team, he complimented Joe on getting his mother to notice some of his improvements. He told Joe that "of course, there will be good days and bad days. Two steps forward and one back. But, we want you to continue to pay attention to what you do when you overcome the urge to smoke."

The therapist then invited his mother in and, with Joe present, complimented her on "doing something right when you got Joe to talk to you more."

THERAPIST: It is a good idea to continue to be skeptical because when you raise your hopes too high, disappointment can be greater than before. Also, it's important to continue keeping track of what happens on good days—how Joe gets people to notice when he isn't in a scrape and how you get the good days to happen more often. And when you talk to Joe's teachers, guidance counselor, probation officer, and his father, get their opinions about what is happening when Joe is not in trouble.

Between sessions the therapist received a call from Joe's probation officer. She said she needed a full evaluation of Joe, including his progress (or lack of it) in therapy and had all the necessary signed release of information forms. The therapist told the probation officer, apologetically, that his evaluation would not be complete until he had more information about when Joe does not get into trouble. Further, progress in therapy was being monitored by the parents and it might be some time before the required information was processed and confirmed.

PROBATION OFFICER: How long do you think it will take?

THERAPIST: It depends on Joe and his parents. I'm not sure. You could help me move things along if, when you speak to the parents, you share your observations about how Joe is not getting into jams so they can report them in their sessions.

PROBATION OFFICER: Can't you just write when he began therapy and when the sessions were held?

THERAPIST: Sure. And I need some way in the therapy to know when he is not conning me. The best way I have found so far is to see a consistent pattern of improvements, taking into account, of course, any temporary setbacks.

Session 3: Two Weeks Later

Joe arrived alone for this session. The therapist asked him how things were improving.

JOE: The same, I guess.

THERAPIST: How come things aren't worse?

JOE: I'm not doing anything to make them worse.

THERAPIST: You mean they're backing off?

JOE: Some.

THERAPIST: How are you getting them to do that?

JOE: Not getting into trouble.
THERAPIST: Yeah, but how?
JOE: No drugs, mostly. Things are better when I don't do drugs.
THERAPIST: And how are you not doing drugs? It can't be easy.
JOE: I don't need any more trouble.

Joe went on to explain that his parents went away for the weekend without him and his sister, something they had not done previously. He said that his teachers were encouraging him, some giving him makeup work and extra help. The therapist wondered aloud what will convince Joe's parents, teachers, and probation officer he does not need to come here anymore. "What will be *enough* improvement? How are you *not* in a mess? What are you doing right? How can you do more of what's working?" Joe was complimented on his ability to convince the skeptics and was prompted to continue to do more of what is working.

Session 4: Three Weeks Later

The tone of this session was similar. Joe recounted improvements and the therapist complimented him on his continuing success in getting people to back off. Then he explored with Joe how he did that and what would have to happen for that to continue. Joe thought that time was a major factor. If he completed the term without further incident and was able to work over the summer, things should continue to improve. But, he said, he was far from certain whether he would be able to avoid getting himself into a corner that long. The therapist agreed that it may be very difficult to avoid further trouble, but it will be a more temporary setback when Joe keeps the focus on improvements.

A follow-up session was scheduled in a month. A week after the fourth session the therapist received a call from the guidance counselor who was alarmed to hear that Joe was not being seen weekly. "We think that the whole family should be in therapy. At our meeting, everyone present agreed that the family had serious problems that have to be brought under control before Joe will be out of the woods. The family agreed. Are you going to provide family therapy and see Joe weekly?" The therapist said that he is seeing improvements and family therapy has been utilized in the treatment, "but it is a slow, difficult, uphill battle. We need all the help we can get. We are still having difficulties telling if the progress we see from Joe here is realistic. We need to know more about how Joe is improving in school.

Could you let Joe's parents know how Joe is improving? That just might motivate them to come to our next family session." The guidance counselor said that there is "nothing I can put my finger on yet," but he would look into it.

Session 5:

The next day Joe called and asked if he could come in sooner. "I've been OK with the other drugs, but I got back into the crack this week. Things are beginning to fall apart."

In the session a day later, the therapist inquired about how this specific drug use was different. Joe said it felt like a setback rather than part of a habit. The therapist asked, "When you're back on track, how will things be different?" Joe said that he had only used once and felt like he was back on track already, but that he had found it hard to keep going. The therapist remarked that this just emphasizes Joe's need to develop even more alternatives—doing more things he is interested in instead of the drugs or the skirmish with the school. Joe mentioned playing baseball with a local team in past years and thought he would do so again.

The therapist also asked about when Joe overcame the urge to use. He said that it had been easier to overcome big urges than small ones. He could identify the temptation for what it was and distract himself by simply waiting five minutes, calling his girlfriend, going for a walk, watching TV, talking to his mother, and so on. He had also discovered that it was far easier when he was with friends who were not users.

The therapist took a consultation break even though the team was not available and returned with this message:

THERAPIST: I think we both know that this hasn't been easy. Yet, you have overcome a major hurdle and have taught me an important lesson. You have learned a lot about yourself from this temporary relapse which is a warning to you that you must be alert. The important thing is to go on and stay on the right track. I am glad that you had the courage to come in today and learn from this success. I want to hear more about how you are succeeding in about six weeks.

Joe did not come for his follow-up appointment. There were no more phone calls until six months later when the probation officer called and requested a report that Joe had been in therapy. She was updating her files. This was provided with no further comment. A call to Alice shortly after speaking with the probation officer revealed that the family was satisfied with Joe's behavior, he was doing well in school, and was doing more in sports. Alice said that things are generally going well for Joe and the whole family. We ended the conversation with the understanding that she could call back if the family needed further help.

CONCLUSION

The central task when working with adolescents who abuse drugs is to establish working goals with them that are salient to them. Once that is accomplished, cooperation in the therapeutic endeavor is possible. Of course, not abusing drugs may become only one step toward reaching their goals and thus the goals of larger, related systems can be met as well.

REFERENCES

Berg, I. K. (1985). "Helping referral sources help," *Family Therapy Networker,* 6.

de Shazer, S. (1982). *Patterns of brief family therapy.* New York: Guilford Press.

de Shazer, S. (1985). *Keys to solutions in brief therapy.* New York: W. W. Norton.

de Shazer, S. (1988). *Clues: Investigating solutions in brief therapy.* New York: W. W. Norton.

Haley, J. (1967). *Advanced techniques of hypnosis and therapy: Selected papers of Milton H. Erickson.* New York: Grune & Stratton.

Lipchik, E. (1987). "Purposeful sequence for beginning the solution focused interview," *Interviewing,* Eve Lipchik (ed.), *The Family Therapy Collections, 22,* Aspen Publications.

Miller, W. (1985). "Motivation for treatment: A review with special emphasis on alcoholism," *Psychological Bulletin,* 98(1), 84–107.

6

Adolescent Substance Abuse

A Systemic Intergenerational Approach

DAVID R. CHABOT, Ph.D.
Director of Clinical Services
Center for Family Learning
Rye Brook, New York
Director, Clinical Training
Psychology Department
Fordham University, New York, NY

MARGHARITE C. MATTEIS, Ph.D., R.N.
Training Faculty
Center for Family Learning
Rye Brook, New York
Assistant Professor
Nursing Department
Mercy College, Dobbs Ferry, NY

HISTORICAL ROOTS OF THE APPROACH

Historically, the transgenerational aspects of this approach are directly lodged in the work of Murray Bowen. Much has been written about the forces that have molded Bowen's theoretical ideas about family functioning and family therapy (Guerin, 1976; Kerr, 1981). Bowen's influence on us arises from his general contributions to the field of family therapy and his personal relationships with two of our colleagues, namely Philip Guerin and Thomas Fogarty. Guerin (1987) has focused on the extended family system and more recently, marital conflict and its treatment. Fogarty (1978) has made major theoretical contributions, particularly his focus on the individual within a systems context is just one.

In addition to being influenced by Bowen, Guerin, and Fogarty, we have education and clinical training in clinical-child psychology and psychiatric nursing, respectively. This has sensitized us to the individual and the developmental aspects of family functioning. Currently, we are members of the Child and Adolescent Project at the Center for Family Learning. The ideas from this interdisciplinary group have contributed significantly to the development of this approach for treating adolescent substance abusers from an intergenerational systems perspective.

BASIC ASSUMPTIONS OF THE MODEL

We strongly believe that multiple areas must be considered in understanding the dysfunction of the adolescent substance abuser. The following factors are important

- The transgenerational process from the husband's and wife's extended families;
- The level of anxiety in the family;
- The individual characteristics of family members (such as temperament, personality, and current emotional functioning);
- The peer relationships of family members; and
- The school and/or work systems of family members.

A transgenerational family systems perspective is used as the primary framework to understand and integrate information gathered on the aforementioned areas. The transgenerational family system has primary influence in the current and future experiences of all family members. While undertaking this perspective, we fully recognize the specific characteristics of individuals (their differences and uniqueness) who are members of the family system.

There is constant interaction between and among individuals in a family and this process extends across generations. The interchange of emotional energy extends at least three generations. These emotional forces at work in the transgenerational system are not only historical but current and ongoing, even though they may not be perceived as such.

A developmental perspective is also necessary for understanding the interaction of individuals and their transgenerational family system.

The individuals, the sub-parts of the system, and the entire transgenerational system are in constant developmental change. The progression through developmental change is stressful and often triggers vulnerability in the system and in its individuals. When working with a dysfunctional family, it is important to watch for the occurrence of difficulties in making developmental transitions. Often, stress and dysfunction occur when families move from one stage to another.

The process of conceptualization and analysis of the transgenerational system naturally leads one to place primary emphasis on the development of the individual in the system. Thus, the concept of differentiation is central to this theoretical orientation.

Similar to Bowen (1973) and Guerin (1978), we believe that there are two aspects to differentiation, that is, the differentiation of self from others (usually the family) and the differentiation of feeling from thinking processes. Lack of differentiation from others results in excessive conformity or pseudo-independence predicated on reactive behavior. On the other hand, a differentiated person is able to be more self-focused while remaining emotionally connected to others. Simultaneous with the need to become differentiated from others is the need to separate individual thinking and feeling systems. The differentiated person is able to strike a balance between thinking and feeling and to allow for appropriate expression of feelings without being governed by them.

Anxiety and stress are two other important concepts central to understanding individual and family functioning. The amount of anxiety an individual experiences is directly related to his or her level of differentiation. The lower the level of differentiation, the greater the amount of anxiety that an individual harbors or discharges through adaptive or maladaptive means.

The level of anxiety serves as an index of the level of functioning of the individual or family. Anxiety can also serve as an impetus for change. However, in attempting to produce constructive change, it is important that the level of anxiety not be too high. When situational or chronic anxiety is high and beyond the level of the dyadic relationship to contain, there is a tendency to reduce the anxiety by triangulation. Essentially, this involves moving away from the stress-producing source and involving an outside person, activity, or object to provide distance. The triangle is the basic building block to understanding how individuals are connected in a system (especially a family system) and how issues and themes are communicated transgenerationally.

In addition to considering multi-generational patterns and influences, it is important to gain knowledge about the characteristics of individuals within the system including such characteristics as operating styles in response to stress. When anxious, an emotional pursuer moves outside self and toward others to achieve relief; whereas, an emotional distancer moves inside self or toward objects to become calm. These individual aspects are important in terms of the emotional and behavioral processes surrounding them (Guerin & Gordon, 1984).

PHILOSOPHICAL VIEW ON ADOLESCENT CHEMICAL DEPENDENCY

Before a theoretical view of adolescent chemical dependency can be presented, it is important to conceptually outline the phenomenon of substance usage in this age group. Consumption of chemicals by teenagers can be depicted along a continuum starting with use and progressing to abuse, to problem usage, and ending with dependency.

Chemical dependence is often a result of intense substance abuse. The adolescent has compromised his or her ability to control the use of substances despite negative sequelae (American Psychiatric Association, 1987).

Symptoms of tolerance and/or withdrawal are associated with chemical dependency. Tolerance is characterized by the need for larger amounts of the substance to achieve the same effect or by a greatly decreased effect of the chemical with consumption of the same quantity (American Psychiatric Association, 1980). Withdrawal symptoms can occur when the addicted teenager stops consumption. However, one must remember that the exact point at which experimentation ends and dependence begins is unclear, even for mental health professionals to decide.

Various factors impact upon teenage chemical dependency. They include genetic, individual personality, and family systems.

Research (Collins, 1985) has shown that genetics may play a role in the development of chemical dependency. Efforts to uncover an inheritable base to this disorder have mainly focused on alcoholism. Studies (Cotton, 1979) have uncovered that offspring of an alcoholic mother or father have a much greater tendency to develop this problem than the non-alcoholic population.

There are many psychological reasons why teenagers use chemical substances. Adolescents under psychological distress have been found to abuse chemicals (Pandina & Schuele, 1983). Some teens use drugs as a temporary escape from depression (Niven, 1986). Teenagers with low self-esteem tend to abuse alcohol and/or drugs (Pandina et al., 1981).

Theoretically speaking, we take a systemic and multi-generational view of adolescent chemical dependency but keep in mind individual and genetic factors, as mentioned above. The development of adolescent substance abuse is indicative of failure of the multi-generational family system (Roberts, 1979). The chemically-dependent family has a low level of differentiation; thus, it is unable to adapt to the accumulation of past and present stressors throughout the generations. The system is not open to change and lacks nuclear and extended family and network support to deal with stress. Toxic issues and covert relationship conflicts have not been addressed. Unresolved temperamental conflicts between adolescent and parent or adolescent and sibling may be evident. Resultingly, the level of anxiety in the family is quite high, cannot be contained, and symptoms erupt. In adolescent chemically-dependent families, the system dysfunction is primarily focused on the adolescent.

Various stressors affect the level of anxiety and resultant functioning of the family. Transition times impose stress on the system. These include normative occurrences in the lifecycle of the family, such as births, marriages, and expected deaths (Guerin & Gordon, 1984).

Families with adolescents are often experiencing the stress of multiple life stage events. Teenagers are grappling with their own developmental issues; parents are confronting middle age; grandparents are beset with the difficulties of the latter stages of the aging process. The clustering of stress from these developmental changes and other life events can disturb the "emotional equilibrium of the family" (Guerin & Gordon, 1984, p. 161) leading to the formation of symptoms such as chemical abuse.

Thus, cluster stress, high anxiety, low level of differentiation, and compromised family functioning all impact upon the occurrence of chemical dependency in teenagers. If the adolescent experiences individual personality difficulties, he or she may not have the constitution or resilience to monitor self and change destructive patterns. Combined with a multi-generational pattern of substance abuse, the teenager would be targeted for chemical dependency.

ASSESSMENT CONSIDERATIONS

An integral part of the assessment of the adolescent chemically-dependent family is engagement. In addition to intense anxiety, the family presents with a myriad of other feelings, including "shame" (Leveton, 1984, p. 44), "guilt, ambivalence, confusion, and mistrust" (Finley, 1983, p. 125). Feelings of upset should be normalized.

Essential to engagement is keeping one's own anxiety level under control. The therapist also needs to listen to and to connect with each family member without aligning with anyone in particular. This can be especially difficult in a high stress family system.

In order to foster development of a relationship with the adolescent, a few individual evaluation sessions should be scheduled. The therapist needs to be able to knowledgeably discuss common areas of interest of teenagers such as sports, clothes, and music. It is important that a feeling of genuine interest be conveyed to the adolescent. An authoritarian stance should be avoided; however, appropriate therapeutic distance should be maintained (Chabot, 1984).

Once approaches have been made toward engagement, the therapist can focus on assessment of the presenting problem of the family. It is obviously important to obtain a careful picture of the adolescent's pattern of chemical usage; that is, type or types of chemicals, quantity, frequency, duration, and associated negative sequelae. The therapist should also obtain information as to the family's perception of the magnitude of this problem, including any steps taken (successful and unsuccessful) toward resolution. A family's reaction to teenage chemical usage can vary greatly. Parents and the adolescent may deny the seriousness of using alcohol and/or drugs. On the other hand, parents may have a disproportionate amount of emotional upset over their offspring's experimentation with substances.

It is important to gain an understanding of the family emotional process surrounding the chemical dependency. The configuration and flow of emotional energy in the primary parental triangle should be assessed. Usually, the mother has an over-close, ineffectual relationship with the adolescent, whereas, the father is in a more distant position. The father criticizes the mother's relationship with the adolescent, especially her meager attempts toward taking a firm stance. When the adolescent substance usage becomes intolerable for the system, the father angrily and critically moves toward the adolescent to eradicate the problem behavior. His stance is also unproductive because he does not have the groundwork of a personal relationship with the teenager to serve as leverage. The mother is critical of both the father's distant relationship with and the movement toward the adolescent (Sherman, 1982). Marital conflict often underlies and charges this intense emotional process.

After gaining information about the presenting problem, it is important to obtain a perspective as to its historical development in the family system. Mapping the family history in the form of a three-generational genogram is a useful way of accomplishing this.

Using this structure, the therapist obtains information about the formation and evolution of the nuclear family system and each spouse's extended family system. Alliances, boundaries, and degree of openness are outlined (Guerin & Pendagast, 1976). Temperamental synchrony of family members within and between the generations can be assessed.

The therapist evaluates how the multi-generational family system has dealt with toxic issues, relationship conflicts, transition times, and other stressors. Past and current functioning of the system as a whole and of individual family members is ascertained (Kerr, 1981). The level of chronic family anxiety is illuminated. Thus, dysfunctional familial patterns such as chemical dependency are often uncovered.

Special attention should be paid to the assessment of the individual functioning of the chemically-dependent teenager. In addition to the evaluation of substance usage and family relationships, the therapist needs to assess other major systems in the teen's life, such as peers and school. The teenager's social network can foster chemical usage. On the other hand, relationships with peers may become strained when the adolescent abuses chemicals. School performance often suffers. Lastly, the therapist should assess the degree of acute and chronic emotional upset of the adolescent, including the presence of low self-esteem, depression, and suicidality.

GOAL SETTING

After the preliminary evaluation has been completed, the therapeutic contract is developed. It provides a focus for treatment. Contracting is a mutual process between the therapist and the family.

The therapist presents his or her view of the presenting problem (the adolescent's chemical usage), of the related problems, and of the surrounding emotional family process. Goals, duration, session frequency, and membership are tentatively outlined.

Family members respond to the therapist's input by sharing their ideas and feelings about the nature of the problem and of its resolution. Then, terms and goals of treatment are developed by the therapist and the family. The therapeutic plan should be flexible enough to allow for revisions when changes occur within the family system.

Goal setting needs to take into account the family's view of the adolescent's chemical usage, especially its ability to systemically view the problem. The therapist inquires about the parents' degree of self-focus—their capacity to understand how they contribute to the emotional process surrounding their offspring's difficulties. Questions that attempt to uncover parental ability to take responsibility for self include the following.

- What do you think about your child's drinking and/or taking drugs?
- What needs to be changed? About your family? About your son/daughter? About yourself?
- How helpless do you feel about dealing with your child's drug and/or alcohol abuse?
- How do you show your helplessness?
- How does its expression help and hinder dealing with this problem?
- Are there other family problems that make dealing with your son/daughter's drug and/or alcohol use more difficult?

An assessment is made as to the degree to which the adolescent is willing to assume more control over his or her life, especially the pattern of chemical use. Questions focusing on this dimension include the following.

- "How do you see your life?; Who owns your life?" You? Your parents? (Sherman, 1984, p. 39)
- What goals do you have for yourself?
- How much is your drinking and/or taking drugs interfering with your accomplishing these goals?
- Do you want to stop taking drugs and/or drinking? If not, why not?
- If you do, do you have a *game plan* to accomplish this?, If you don't, how can you get one?

Assessing the family system's level of self-focus provides information about how to frame the problem and how to utilize motivated family members and work with resistant ones. Treatment strategies should be outlined in such a way that they are acceptable to the family. If parents do not think that they contribute to their child's substance abuse, therapeutic maneuvers need to be framed as the parents' helping their son or daughter, not changing themselves. Similarly, if a teenager is not willing or able to take responsibility for the chemical usage, the therapist needs to more aggressively enlist support from the parents to deal with this problem. If parents are unavailable or unwilling to provide assistance, there is poor prognosis for problem resolution.

ROLE OF THE THERAPIST

While allowing for individual personal style, the therapist adheres to the basic Bowenian stance of *observer, researcher,* and *consultant* to the family in understanding its intergenerational emotional process. The therapist should be well-grounded in systems theory and be able to communicate to family members those aspects of the theory which are of relevance to their lives.

An important goal is the development of an empathic, therapeutic relationship with the family. In the relationship, some distance is maintained by the therapist in order to avoid becoming entangled in the family's emotionality. One way this is prevented is by emphasizing the cognitive components of the family process, as opposed to the emotional components.

In order to achieve cognitive understanding of the family, the therapist assumes a researcher role by asking family members emotionally-neutral process questions. Through this approach, the family learns how its emotional process flows around issues and problems, including the teenager's substance abuse. Process questioning is accomplished in a calm, interested, and warm manner, in order to foster a safe, non-anxious environment. Humor, self-disclosure, and displacement material can be used to aid the family's understanding of the emotional process.

The goal of therapy is self-differentiation and a more adaptive level of functioning for each family member. This is accomplished by educating the family about systems, including the intergenerational transmission process. The therapist uses such teaching tools as the genogram, behavioral experiments, and questions to help family members gain intellectual understanding of the process.

A degree of self-differentiation of the therapist is important. By refusing to become triangulated, the therapist helps family members become more differentiated. The therapist does not foster emotional catharsis and transferential affect. Emotional issues that emerge toward the therapist are directly related to the family system.

KEY TECHNIQUES AND TREATMENT STRATEGIES

Application to clinical practice is based on an understanding and use of concepts inherent in the framework of this theory. This approach is not particularly technique oriented; rather, concepts of the theory of emotional functioning are applied to the specific facts of each family system. The major focus of treatment is to foster an increase in the adaptive level of functioning and differentiation of the family and its individuals.

When working with adolescent substance abuse, the authors have found certain approaches to be effective. They are:

1. Lowering the level of anxiety in the family;
2. Helping the family take a functional position;
3. Working on key nuclear family triangles; and
4. Coaching parents to work on extended family relationships.

The therapist directs the effort toward decreasing the level of anxiety in the family. This is accomplished through structuring flow of communication, content, and membership in the session.

Family members are directed to talk directly to the therapist as opposed to each other This aids in decreasing the tendency for emotionally reactive interchanges among members.

The therapist also provides direction to family interchanges outside the session. He or she advises the family to refrain from discussing toxic issues at home. Each family member is coached on taking responsibility for keeping his or her part of the emotional climate at home calm.

The genogram is also used as a tool to decrease emotionality in the family. History-taking in this fashion enables the family to gain a systemic view of the multi-generational process underlying not only the substance abuse but other family problems and issues. Members can see that they are all recipients of the same familial patterns; thus, diffusing the focus on the adolescent and his or her substance usage.

Membership is varied during the session and from session to session. It can be particularly useful to see the emotional pursuer alone to provide an outlet for discharge of anxiety. When calmer, the pursuer is more likely to listen to other family members. In addition, using this approach validates the pursuer's feelings, thereby, increasing receptivity to therapeutic suggestions. It is also important to see the adolescent alone—this builds rapport and reinforces developmental strivings toward separation from the family.

The therapist needs to coach the family in assuming a functional stance regarding the substance abuse. The therapist's focus and the family's position will take different directions depending on the severity of chemical usage.

The substance abuse may be so severe that it interferes with family therapy sessions. This is seen when the teenager comes to treatment intoxicated and experiences other intense negative consequences of usage.

Here, the primary focus is to get the teenager into an appropriate substance abuse treatment program. Family members are coached on taking a functional and responsible position to accomplish this goal. Parents are counseled to delineate the behaviors they will tolerate and communicate this delineation clearly to their teenager. They may even have to take the initiative in getting their child involved in treatment. However, the optimum goal is to have the adolescent recognize the need for a treatment program and be involved in planning entry.

At this point, the immediate family situation is the therapeutic focus. Understandably, it is unproductive to connect the intergenerational family process to current treatment planning.

Family involvement should continue while the adolescent receives substance abuse treatment. If the adolescent is unable to attend family sessions, his or her interests are supported in family therapy and this therapeutic position is conveyed to the teenager. When program staff permit, the adolescent's involvement in sessions is strongly recommended.

Family members are required to be routinely involved in the treatment program. In order to foster coordination of treatment and to avoid triangulation, the therapist maintains communication with program personnel.

If the substance abuse is not severe, primary treatment efforts do not focus on this issue. However, adequate attention must be given to the adolescent's usage of chemicals, and this behavior is monitored throughout treatment. The major aim is to unravel the process around the teenager's substance abuse and other issues in the family system. This approach serves to accomplish an important goal, that is, decreasing focus on the presenting symptom.

Clinical emphasis is placed on the key triangles in the family. Here, the goal is to help the family decrease the automatic tendency to form triangles for conflict avoidance. Openness and equally close relationships among family members are fostered in times of calm and stress.

The therapist identifies the active triangles, including the primary parental triangle. Then, the emotional processes around these triangles are illuminated. In this way, the therapist gains understanding of how the triangles work, when they are most active, and who are the key players in the process. This emotional process is explicitly conveyed to the family. Members are also instructed about how their operating styles (pursuer and distancer) are displayed in triangulation.

After the family is cognizant of how triangles operate, each member is coached on how to shift his or her personal position in a triangle. Tasks are assigned giving each member an opportunity to help change the flow of emotional energy in the threesome. The father may be instructed to move toward his child; whereas, the mother may be counseled to decrease her emotional pursuit of the child and to move toward her extended family. Such efforts can increase relationship options for the individual and other nuclear and extended family members.

Another approach directed toward de-triangulation is encouraging individuals to use *I statements.* These are simple declarative statements on how one thinks and feels without assuming how others will respond. When accompanied by a balanced position (not over- or under-functioning), the use of I statements aids members in removing themselves from a triangle.

Members are asked to monitor their inner feelings when attempting to change their behaviors in a triangle. By doing so, they gain further understanding of how they use their operating styles as ways to decrease anxieties.

The family needs to have a realistic view of the outcome of efforts toward de-triangulation. Members should share the perspective that they are experimenting at different, more constructive ways of relating. They need to know that changing behavioral patterns is difficult and will not meet with automatic success. It is helpful to predict where problems may arise and to help family members develop solutions.

Often a primary parental triangle will organize as a result of the temperamental differences of participants. In order to help diffuse this process, the therapist needs to educate family members about temperament, the constitutional aspects, the different behavioral manifestations, and the surrounding family process. Then, the family needs to develop realistic expectations of its members, given their temperamental characteristics.

As a therapist unravels nuclear family triangles, other interlocking triangles are revealed. These often involve the nuclear and extended family. Consequently, the nuclear family is confronted with the opportunity to work on extended family relationships. Now, the therapist highlights how past and present familial patterns connect through interlocking triangles. Another useful therapeutic approach is reframing; whereby, family members are offered more constructive, alternative explanations for familial patterns.

Extended family work is an important component of our theoretical and clinical orientation. When there is a low level of differentiation in the intergenerational family system, a multitude of problems can occur, including adolescent chemical dependency.

Utilizing this approach, nuclear family members are coached on developing relationship with extended family members. When doing so, individuals experience emotional upset; therefore, it is helpful for family members to be seen for individual sessions in order for them to develop an awareness of these emotions.

As therapy progresses to later stages, the frequency of sessions is usually decreased considerably. Family members are aided in outlining strategies for extended family work. They experiment with carrying these plans to fruition and discuss their endeavors with the therapist.

The result of extended family work is the acquisition of increased self-focus and an increased level of differentiation. Once achieved, individuals are able to have a more functional awareness of their past and its relationship to the present, to respond to situations with less anxiety, and to make changes more freely.

THEORY OF CHANGE

Change occurs slowly in an adolescent chemically-dependent family system. Substance dependency is an extremely difficult dysfunction to correct regardless of therapeutic approach (Bowen, 1973). Thus, the therapist must have a realistic perception concerning the speed and degree of anticipated change.

The first stage of change is symptom relief (Guerin & Gordon, 1984), in this instance, the adolescent's attainment of abstinence. Symptom improvement begins to occur when the level of anxiety in the family has decreased (Roberts, 1979). Family members are able to think more clearly and they have a better understanding of their roles in the emotional process which contributed to the teenager's chemical dependency. The family has been able to organize its strength to adaptively deal with the child's problem. They have done this by taking a different and more constructive stance. For example, the father has moved closer toward his child in a nonauthoritarian and more supportive manner. Meanwhile, the mother has not attempted to sabotage the father's efforts and she has become more consistent in her parenting. The adolescent has accepted the seriousness of the substance dependency and has taken responsibility for its control. Improvements are seen in the teenager's school performance and peer relationships.

With symptom relief, the family emotional processes that have made the system vulnerable have not changed. However, the family has usually gained the ability to recognize problems and seek therapeutic help in the future, if necessary.

As opposed to symptom relief, basic change in the family system is more lasting. Basic change "occurs at the core level of the emotional problems in the family. There is an actual change in the character of underlying forces themselves" (Roberts, 1979, p. 41). The level of differentiation or baseline level of functioning of the family system has increased which is the optimal goal of this therapeutic approach.

In an adolescent chemically-dependent family, an indication of basic change in the family is its ability to see the multi-generational process underlying the chemical dependency. Parents are willing to move into their respective extended families to change self and patterns which have fostered the substance dependency. Their entries into the multi-generational system have become natural and are not fraught with anxiety.

Along with this basic change, the family system is resilient and naturally open to change. They have an increased ability to productively handle stressors. There is less need to form over-close or over-distant, perhaps destructive familial relationships, when faced with difficulties. Members assume responsibility for their feelings and behavior in family situations in general, not only those focused around chemical dependency.

CASE EXAMPLE

Presenting Problem

The Fisher family came to the Center for Family Learning (CFL) as the result of a referral from a school counselor who was involved with Jack, their youngest son. At the time, Jack was 16 years old and a junior in a public high school in an affluent Westchester, New York, community. Throughout his junior year, Jack's grades had markedly deteriorated and he was in serious danger of failing three subjects for the year.

A psychological evaluation revealed that Jack was not learning disabled; rather, he possessed good intellectual ability to achieve at an average rank in his school. Jack's current emotional state included much underlying anger, depression, and strong tendencies to act out conflicts in self-defeating but nonviolent ways. His personality profile was consistent with a tendency to use alcohol and drugs to escape from family stress and to express anger.

In fact, Jack admitted to his family that he was using drugs. Jack admitted to using marijuana on a daily basis. More recently, his consumption had increased; he was smoking in the morning before school and was getting intoxicated on weekends. During weekend sprees, Jack was supplementing his marijuana abuse with beer.

History of the Nuclear Family

The nuclear family consisted of four members (see Figure 6-1). They were father, Ed (age 46), mother, Gwen (age 42), son, Donald (age 18), and son, Jack, the identified patient (age 16).

Ed presented himself as a responsible, low key, analytical, somewhat distant individual. He had a Master's degree in engineering, but had lost his job of 20 years as the result of merger consolidations in the company. When he lost his job, he did consulting part time while he searched for another full-time position. Although Ed did not express himself openly, he seemed depressed.

Gwen had been married to Ed for 20 years. She presented as a nervous woman and more of an emotional pursuer than her husband. Gwen described herself as the "peacemaker" and the one who "gets everything done." During the past year, she felt quite stressed and was experiencing tension headaches. Gwen graduated college with a Bachelor's degree in elementary education, but had not pursued a full-time career in teaching. Recently, in an effort to help ease financial strain on the family, she became a permanent substitute teacher.

Ed and Gwen described their marriage as fine. Gwen handled the day-to-day functioning of the household; Ed was more content to defer these responsibilities to his wife. Both reported they participated in major decisions affecting the family. The couple stated that they presented a united front in parenting the children.

Donald, the remaining member of the nuclear family, excelled academically. At the outset of treatment, Donald was living away from home at a New England college where he was completing his freshman year. His style was similar to his father's—he was quiet, academic, and analytical.

There had been conflict and distance between Jack and Donald. However, Jack admitted that, in some way, he missed Donald since he went away to school. Both boys had distant relationships with their father. Donald's had been nonconflictual; whereas, Jack's had been intermittently, openly conflictual. Both Jack and Donald had closer relationships with their mother. It appeared that Gwen was more involved with Jack then with Donald. Both parents agreed that Jack was the rebel in the family and had always been more emotionally expressive and behaviorally active.

Extended Family

Ed was an only child (see Figure 6-1). His parents were both alive, retired, and living in Arizona. His parents originally came from the Chicago area where their families resided for years. Their families

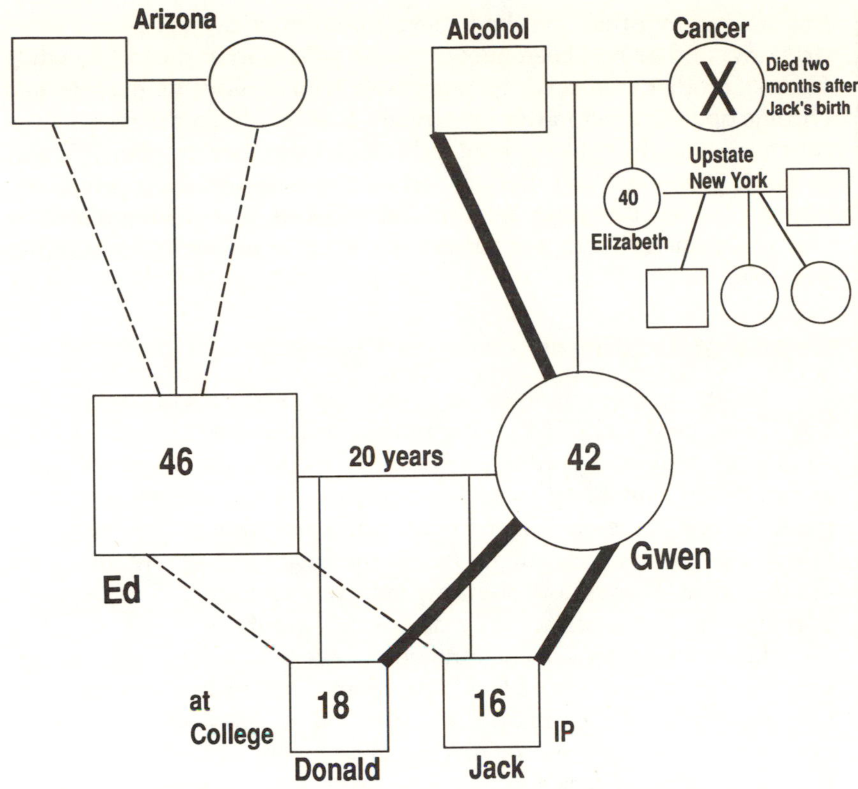

Figure 6.1 A visual representation of the extended Fisher family.

were quite socially prominent and active. Ed's relationship with his parents had been somewhat formal and distant. They visited him yearly, usually coinciding with their vacations to Europe.

Gwen, the oldest child, had a younger sister, Elizabeth, age 40, who was married with three children (see Figure 6-1). She was living in upstate New York and her children were doing well. Gwen had been the protective older sister to Elizabeth. However, their contact had been minimal over the years. At the beginning of therapy, they were seeing each other five to seven times a year.

Gwen's mother had died of cancer two months before Jack was born. Her father had been suffering from chronic alcoholism. His pattern of abuse had consisted of going on semi-annual binges, each lasting a few months. He had developed medical problems from drinking; and he had been known as the wild man in the family while Gwen's mother was covertly angry and critical. Gwen's parents had chronic open conflict in their marriage. She had been the recipient of much seemingly unwarranted criticism from her mother. Consequently, Gwen and her mother had difficulty establishing a nonconflictual mother-daughter relationship. Gwen had a long-standing close relationship with her father; she tried to help him as much as possible.

Course of Treatment

For the first few months, membership in treatment consisted of Ed, Gwen, and Jack. The configuration of membership varied from session to session. Approximately half of the sessions were with Jack alone. When Donald returned from school, he was invited to participate. On one occasion, Elizabeth attended a session with Gwen. The family was seen fairly regularly for six months; then, less regularly for another year. Throughout therapy, Jack was encouraged to continue participation in the school drug discussion group.

Ed and Gwen were encouraged to take a functional position regarding the immediacy of Jack's problem. Due to his continued involvement with drugs, his parents decided to delay allowing him to obtain a learner's permit for driving. They were counseled to accept the inevitability of Jack's failing in school. Jack took two courses in summer school—one of which he failed. Then, he modified his school schedule to address his academic failures.

Gwen was coached to move back from her involvement with Jack. She was encouraged to put extra energy into her work and her social network. Ed was coached to move toward Jack in areas other than Jack's drug abuse. This was difficult for Ed; thus, the therapist had to work with Ed by providing many concrete suggestions. One suggestion that seemed helpful was getting Ed to use his engineering skills to help Jack repair an inoperable 1969 Dodge Charger. Through this period, both parents were seen individually and conjointly to aid them in understanding their operating styles (father's distance and mother's pursuit).

Jack was given much individual time to talk about his perception of life. The therapist helped him find more functional ways of accomplishing personal goals. Jack was worried about his mother's anger at his father's distance. He was coached to resign from his job as the *emotional sponge* for his mother's emotions and to channel some of this energy toward his father. Here, part of the desired goal was to close the distance between Jack and his dad. Lastly, Jack was seen with Donald to help them discuss their differences and strengthen their sibling bonds.

As nuclear family issues were worked on, related extended family themes became clear. Particular emphasis was placed on Ed's distant relationship with his parents. Ed could see the connection between this distance and his difficulty in developing closer functional relationships with his children. He attempted to reframe his parents' distance and made some concrete efforts to decrease its intensity. However, he met with minimal success.

Gwen was coached to move closer to her sister, but in a different manner than previously. She was asked to allow Elizabeth to become an expert in their relationship by advising her (Gwen) on how to better understand her conflictual relationship with her mother. Gwen was advised to join Al-Anon to aid her understanding and coping more effectively with her father's alcoholism.

Therapy continued fairly regularly until Jack's graduation from high school. In the following fall, he joined the Navy. During the latter stages of treatment, he decided to stop using marijuana, but continued to drink alcohol without major problems. Gwen continued to attend Al-Anon and had periodic individual sessions with the therapist. Ed obtained another job. He continued to regularly write to his parents. Donald graduated from college and has been at home for a while. The 1969 Dodge Charger has been running well and is under Ed's care until Jack is discharged from the Navy.

LIMITATIONS OF THE APPROACH

Families fall along a continuum according to functioning, ranging from adaptive and well-organized to chaotic and disorganized. Similar to other forms of psychotherapy, this approach is most successful with families at the functional end of the continuum and most limited with families at the dysfunctional end of the continuum.

There are some characteristics of disorganized and chaotic families which seriously limit the effectiveness of this approach. In a chaotic family, it is difficult to outline key triangles and their surrounding process. Sherman (1984) has described the primary parental triangle in a chaotic family as "flip-flopping" (p. 33). Here, mother and father are constantly changing positions around the same emotional issue. When a dysfunctional pattern is constantly changing, it is difficult to devise a treatment plan.

A poor prognosis is also evident when family members are unable to achieve self-focus. Family projection is so intense that individuals are unable to see their parts in the process.

At times, the more functional non-abuser in the family is unable to see the process behind the abuse of the identified patient. On the other hand, the more functional member may understand the process surrounding the abuse but refuse to take responsibility for his or her contribution to its occurrence. This situation often involves adults who refuse to parent their adolescent and who expect the therapist to assume total responsibility for change.

Another serious limiting factor is present when nuclear families are isolated from the extended family and other networks. Consequently, there are limited relationship options posing difficulties in attempts at de-triangulation. These individuals try to form overdependent attachments to the therapist in lieu of real-life relationships.

Another serious limitation exists when the adolescent substance abuser is unable to connect with inner feelings. In this case, the teenage chemical abuser generally has a meager awareness of his or her emotions and cannot understand the relationship between substance usage and personal feeling state.

A poor prognosis exists when there are multiple substance abusers in a family. This is especially true if parents are abusers who are not taking responsibility for their behavior. A similar scenario is present when family members are involved with other destructive processes, such as physical abuse and compulsive gambling.

A final situation that limits the effectiveness of this approach is a family that intensely harbors a powerful and destructive secret. If clinical efforts cannot surface the underlying issue, therapy is invalidated. Sexual abuse, particularly incest, is a prime example of such a family secret.

EFFECTIVENESS OF THIS APPROACH

Presently, the major support for the effectiveness of this approach lies in testimony from individuals who have applied the theory to their families and who have claimed it produced positive results. These reports suggest that the theory is internally consistent and relevant to the complexity and richness of real-life situations.

A second source of information on the effectiveness of this approach comes from clinical reports. Noone (1981) applied this theoretical orientation in seven years of clinical work with drug abusers and their families. He concluded that drug abuse by an individual is directly related to the family emotional process. Change in the abusive behavior is indicative of change in the emotional process. Noone admitted that his observations have been affected by his theoretical perspective. However, he added that his experience with chemically-dependent families led him to choose this approach. In the final analysis, this may bear testimony to the elegance of the theory, rather than the effectiveness of treatment techniques.

It is clear that there is a serious lack of empirical research of this approach utilizing process or outcome measures. Using any systemic model, one is beset with problems in instrumentation, research design, and data analysis. These research dilemmas are just beginning to be addressed.

Moreover, there are some inherent aspects of this theoretical approach which make meaningful research particularly difficult. First, the clinical goal is global, that is, differentiation. This is an illusive concept that is extremely difficult to operationalize for research purposes. Bowen, himself, has little faith in this being accomplished.

Second, this approach is not based on static membership in sessions. An attempt is made to engage all family members, particularly the identified patient. If the identified patient is extremely unmotivated, work is continued with the more functional members of the family system. They are better able to de-triangulate; therefore, they have the most leverage for changing the system. This approach to membership makes it more difficult to utilize evaluative research methods; especially if the outcome measure is the substance abuse pattern of the adolescent. The frequency of sessions (determined by therapist and family), the role of the therapist (consultant to the family), and the open-ended nature of the therapy (periodic contact often lasting several years) makes it difficult to concretize the effectiveness of this approach.

ROLE OF ADJUNCTIVE THERAPIES AND SELF-HELP GROUPS

In our approach to chemical dependency, adjunctive therapeutic modalities are often utilized. These include self-help groups and multi-family or substance abuse therapy groups.

In general, we support the use of self-help groups for adolescent chemical dependency. The emotional support provided helps to lower the level of anxiety in the family. These groups support a major goal of our clinical approach, that is, taking responsibility for changing self, whether it be through achievement of abstinence and/or a more functional relationship.

On the other hand, involvement in self-help substance abuse groups can have negative consequences. The chemically-dependent teenager and/or the family members and friends may become so intensely involved in the group that relationships suffer. A triangular process can evolve where the self-help group takes the position in the family that was originally held by the substance abuse (Guerin, 1977). Consequently, the emotional distance in the family remains the same or increases. In therapy, the family has to be cautioned about the possibility of this occurrence.

This clinical approach does not particularly utilize multi-family or substance abuse therapy groups. Support is given for family involvement in groups consistent with our theoretical approach. If a group's focus is in direct contradiction to this orientation, this must be addressed with all those concerned including treatment providers, the adolescent substance abuser, and his or her family members.

REFERENCES

American Psychiatric Association. (1980). *DSM-III diagnostic and statistical manual of mental disorders* (3rd ed.). Washington, DC.

American Psychiatric Association. (1987). *DSM-III-R diagnostic and statistical manual of mental disorders* (3rd ed., rev.). Washington, DC.

Bowen, M. (1973). Alcoholism. *The Family, 1,*(1), 18–25.

Chabot, D. R. (1984). Commentary. *The Family, 12*(1), 47.

Collins, A. C. (1985). Inheriting addictions: A genetic perspective with emphasis on alcohol and nicotine. In H. B. Milkman & H. J. Shaffer (eds.), *The addictions: Multidisciplinary perspectives and treatments.* Lexington, MA: Lexington Books, pp. 3–10.

Cotton, N. (1979). The familial incidence of alcoholism: A review. *Journal of Studies on Alcohol, 40,* 89–116.

Donovan, J. E., & Jessor, R. (1978). Adolescent problem drinking: Psychosocial correlates in a national sample study. *Journal of Studies on Alcohol, 39*(9), 1506–1524.

Donovan, J. E., & Jessor, R. (1983). Problem drinking and the dimension of involvement with drugs: A Guttman scale analysis. *American Journal of Public Health, 73*(5), 543–552.

Finley, B. G. (1983). The family and substance abuse. In G. Bennett, C. Vourakis, & D. S. Woolf (eds.), *Substance abuse: Pharmacologic, developmental, and clinical perspectives.* New York: John Wiley & Sons, pp. 119–134.

Fogarty, T. E. (1978). The individual and the family. *The Family, 6*(1), 3–8.

Guerin, Jr., P. J. (1977). A systems view of the alcoholic family. *The Family, 4*(1), 29–36.

Guerin, Jr., P. J. (1978). Bowen—The man and his theory. *The Family, 6*(1), 20–24.

Guerin, Jr., P. J. (1976). Family therapy: The first twenty-five years. In P. J. Guerin Jr. (ed.), *Family therapy: Theory and practice.* New York: Gardner, pp. 2–22.

Guerin, Jr., P. J., Fay, L. F., Burden, S. L., & Kautto, J. G. (1987). *The evaluation and treatment of marital conflict: A four-stage approach.* New York: Basic Books.

Guerin, Jr., P. J. & Gordon, E. M. (1984). Trees, triangles and temperament in the child-centered family. In C. Fishman & B. Rosman (eds.), *Evolving models for family change: A volume in honor of Salvador Minuchin.* New York: Guilford, pp. 158–159.

Guerin, Jr., P. J. & Pendagast, E. G. (1976). Evaluation of family system and genogram. In P. J. Guerin, Jr. (ed.), *Family therapy: Theory and practice.* New York: Gardner, pp. 450–463.

Kerr, M. E. (1981). Family systems theory and therapy. (1981). In A. S. Gurman & D. P. Kniskern (eds.), *Handbook of family therapy.* New York: Brunner/Mazel, pp. 226–264.

Leveton, E. (1984). *Adolescent crisis: Family counselling approaches.* New York: Springer.

Niven, R. G. (1986). Adolescent drug abuse. *Hospital and Community Psychiatry, 37*(6), 596–607.

Noone, R. J. (1981). Observations on drug abuse and the family. *The Family, 9*(1), 46–52.

Pandina, R. J. & Schuele, J. A. (1983). Psychological correlates of alcohol and drug use of adolescent students and adolescents in treatment. *Journal of Studies on Alcohol, 44,* 950–973.

Pandina, R. J., White, H. R., & Yorke, J. (1981). Estimation of substance use involvement: Theoretical considerations and empirical findings. *The International Journal of the Addictions, 16,* 1–24.

Roberts, R. (1979). Two distinct approaches to family therapy: The ideas of Murray Bowen and Jay Haley. *The Family, 6*(2), 37–45.

Sherman, C. O. (1982). The delinquent family system and therapist interaction. *The Family, 10*(1), 49–56.

Sherman, C. O. (1984). The delinquent family system: Part II: *The Family, 12*(1), 33–40.

Smith, D. E., Milkman, H. B., & Sunderwirth, S. G. (1985). Addictive disease: Concept or controversy. In H. B. Milkman & H. J. Shaffer (eds.), *The addictions: Multidisciplinary perspectives and treatments. Lexington MA:*Lexington Books, 145–159.

PART 2
Expanding the Limits

With the increasing popularity of second-order cybernetic thinking in the family therapy field, more family therapists are moving away from viewing themselves as being separate from the family unit they are treating. The problem system is being expanded to include the following: the treatment team, the client family, extended family members, friends of the family, representatives of larger helping systems, the context in which family therapy occurs, and so forth. Similar to the expansion of the problem system, family therapists are also beginning to recognize the need for therapeutic flexibility through family therapy model shifting and integration to better meet the needs of their client families.

All of the chapters in this section touch on the themes of second-order thinking and family therapist-treatment team flexibility in a variety of clinical settings. In Chapter Seven, Durrant and Coles present their *Contextual Residential Care* model which is heavily based on the innovative therapeutic work of Michael White. This systemically-oriented residential treatment model provides clinicians with several cutting edge ideas for fostering family-therapeutic team collaboration, for actively involving parents in the therapeutic milieu, and provides many creative strategies for empowering families to overcome their oppressive presenting problems.

Harlene Anderson, in Chapter Eight, presents a highly respectful and innovative therapeutic approach for working with complex family-multiple helper problem systems. "Problems generate systems, rather than systems create problems," is one of the important premises that Anderson discusses in her chapter.

In Chapter Nine, Michael Fox presents his *Strategic-Inpatient* model which integrates the best elements of several strategic therapy approaches. Similar to the chapter by Durrant and Coles, Fox's inpatient family therapy approach strives for family-treatment team collaboration and active parental involvement in all aspects of treatment planning and decision making.

Chapter Ten, "Network Therapy: A Case Study," exposes clinicians to the social network family therapy approach. The chapter is built around a life-threatening case situation involving suicidal behavior and alcohol abuse.

Dario Lussardi and Dusty Miller, in Chapter Eleven, provide an indepth overview of the *Reflecting Team* model which was developed by the Norwegian psychiatrist Tom Andersen. Similar to Anderson's chapter, the Reflecting Team approach is quite effective with "stuck" cases in which client families are involved with multiple helpers and there are family secrets.

In Chapter Twelve, Todd and Selekman present their brief integrative family therapy approach which incorporates the best elements of many of the therapeutic approaches discussed in this book. The authors offer invaluable guidelines for intervention design, selection, and implementation.

7

Michael White's Cybernetic Approach

MICHAEL DURRANT
Director, Eastwood Family Therapy Centre
Epping. New South Wales AUSTRALIA

DON COLES
Coordinator, Youth Care
Care Force Children's and Youth Services
Ashfield. New South Wales AUSTRALIA

HISTORICAL ROOTS OF THE MODEL

Michael White is a family therapist in Adelaide, South Australia, who has been recognised throughout Australia and New Zealand for his original contribution to Australian family therapy over the last ten years. Family therapy in Australia relied heavily on imported ideas during its formative stages. There have been, and continue to be, therapists who have built upon the ideas of Virginia Satir, others who have used the structural and strategic approaches of Minuchin and Haley, and others who have employed the approach of the Milan Associates. Therapists *down under* have applied their own unique interpretations of these approaches and have managed to impart an Australian flavour to their use of these concepts. However, it is Michael White who has developed a framework for therapy that is unique.

Whilst his work has been published in Australia and overseas since 1983, it was the publication of his "Negative Explanation, Restraint and

Double Description" paper in *Family Process* (1986a), and Munro's recent paper (1987), which contrasts White's approach with other systemic approaches, that signified the status of White's ideas as an identifiable school of family therapy.

White had a background in structural/strategic family therapy and employed this approach within a hospital child psychiatry setting. His work with anorexic young women and their families prompted him to consider in more detail the kinds of belief systems that operate to perpetuate problem behaviour, and the presentation of this work at the First Australian Family Therapy Conference in 1980, and its subsequent publication (1983), represented his departure from the structural/strategic focus on the problem and sequences of behaviour associated with it to a concern with the underlying (and, in this case, transgenerational) processes of cognition.

White said that it was in 1980 and 1981 that he "began to take Bateson more seriously and develop my own reading of him" (1988). Deciding that he would not be restrained by others' interpretations of Bateson, he rediscovered Bateson's ideas about cybernetic explanation, restraint, and double description. The first manifestation of this focus was his paper on the treatment of encopresis (1984a), which introduced the notion of externalizing problems as a way of challenging restraining beliefs. Since then, White has published and taught extensively throughout Australia, New Zealand, and North America and has developed applications of his ideas to a broad range of presenting problems.

BASIC ASSUMPTIONS OF THE MODEL

The framework for understanding problems and therapy in this model is a particular application of the ideas of Gregory Bateson—how the development and behaviour of living systems may be understood in terms of *information.* The *second cybernetics* of Maruyama (1974) also provide an underpinning in his ideas about the processes that operate in interconnected living systems.

White's approach rests on Bateson's notion that, in "the world of the living" (Bateson, 1972, 1979), behaviour is a response to information and difference. Families and individuals (which also operate as information systems) select information or stimuli to be processed and acted upon. It is impossible for an individual or family to attend to and assimilate every event or piece of information which presents—that would lead to chaos. So information is selected according to *purpose;* that is, it is selected and interpreted in a way to be in keeping with the way the family sees itself (Bateson, 1972, p. 439). Information which does not fit, does not get through.

Second Cybernetics—Vicious Cycles

The family operates as a system; that is, behaviour and relationships show consistent patterns rather than being totally, randomly determined, and the behaviour of each member is influenced by, and influences, the behaviour of every other member.

Problems develop as the inevitable and natural outcome of vicious cycles. Any one of a number of random events, stresses, mistakes, or chance occurrences may be sufficient to set up such a vicious cycle. In approaching problems of adolescence, the pressures of developmental stages or typical adolescent experimentation may often be seen as events that trigger escalating patterns within a family. Members of the family will interpret events in particular ways and respond accordingly. Their responses will tend to have the effect of confirming the way the initial event was interpreted and so make it more likely that it will be seen the same way again. So the same type of response becomes more probable. As the family develops through time, the effects of any such events become amplified by positive feedback through the system, and a pattern of interaction develops and spirals.

The families we see are stuck. They are the innocent victims of vicious cycles, chance events that have precipitated a runaway or avalanche. Small variations have been inadvertently reinforced and perpetuated. The notion that, within a particular meaning-context, the escalation of the problem has been *virtually inevitable* is crucial, since family members often think someone must have done something wrong. They either feel overwhelmed by guilt or they blame another member for doing it on purpose. Notions of guilt and purpose are crippling, since they set up their own vicious cycle of guilt, blame, anger and hopelessness.

> D.A.F. [Deviation-amplifying feedback] is a mechanism which explains how small variations in a system can (or must) become associated with large effects—how small perturbations can generate chains of events that can result in gross alterations (Wender, 1968, p. 309).

Second cybernetics provides an explanation in terms of *mutual causality.* Elements within a system influence each other. This influence will be related to the way elements make sense of each other and of each other's behaviour, that is, in response to information.

All members are victims to the oppression of the vicious cycle, which leads to despair and defeat. If unchecked, the fabric of the system will deteriorate as the cycle escalates, and it may lead to a breakdown of the system. A symptom is the sign that the escalation of the cycle is reaching a critical level. When the symptom is displayed by a child or adolescent, other relationships are affected and may be threatened. Often one parent is most defeated by the cycle, and the other parent less defeated. Their relationship may be threatened by conflict. Notions of purpose implied by terms such as "overintrusive mother" and "disengaged father" simply exacerbate guilt/blame cycles.

With some families, straightforward advice on how to do things differently may be sufficient. With most families, however, the characteristics that have allowed the vicious cycle to continue will themselves stop such advice from really "getting in." A therapist can help unstick, but only the family or individual can actually discover a new way of operating. To do so, the family must be ready for the discovery. Information is only information if it can get through and be processed.

> Information is news of a difference . . . a difference that makes a difference (Bateson, 1972, p. 453–454).

Negative Explanation and Restraints

A family comes to therapy with problems to which members are unable to find solutions. On investigation, we often find that members have tried various solutions that have proved unsuccessful and have often served to perpetuate or reinforce the problems. Despite not work- these solutions have been resorted to time and time again.

The solution becomes the problem and alternative solutions seem to be unavailable. "More of the same" is applied (Watzlawick et al., 1974).

Cybernetic explanation makes sense of this. Cybernetic explanation is negative explanation—it asks not "why are things this way?" but "what has stopped things from being different?" Members habitually apply certain solutions because they are restrained from discovering alternative solutions. Habitual solutions are uniquely determined by certain restraints. Vicious cycles of behaviour occur because only *old* information is available which inevitably leads to the same attempts at solution and the same behaviour.

Since an explanation in terms of mutual causality is not concerned with what caused what or what led to what, it is not appropriate to ask why the family is like this. Our concern is with what might be preventing or restraining the family from finding a different way.

A vicious cycle has escalated because members have been unable to see things in any other way. They have been restrained from noticing information which might have led to different responses.

The family's behaviour and organisation of information is governed by *restraints*.

> Restraints act in relation to information about difference in that they establish sensory limitations. These sensory limitations contribute to a bias or threshhold for the perception of news of difference, and thus determine the ideas that we select from nature . . . Restraints render the recipient unready to respond to certain differences or distinctions. Restraints limit the system's capacity for the trial and error searching that is necessary for the discovering of new ideas and the triggering of new responses (White, 1986a, p. 171).

These restraints might be seen as preoccupations, mental sets, or views of reality which allow information to be interpreted in terms of current system functioning. Restraints may take a number of forms. Myths about families, marriages, or relationships, traditional ways of thinking and doing handed down from previous generations, preoccupations with particular subjects, and so on, all act to prevent differences being recognised and so restrain change. Restraints prevent things from being seen differently. They prevent the system from discovering or developing in alternative ways. The restraints prevent the system from being anything but stuck.

With the problems of adolescence, beliefs about correct behaviour and beliefs about the nature of adolescent problems may restrain families from responding differently. It is often the case that parents are restrained by beliefs that their adolescent son or daughter is somehow not really responsible for his or her behaviour. They may believe that he or she is disturbed, affected by outside factors, medically or psychiatrically unwell, or suffering low self-esteem and so cannot really help his or her behaviour. Such beliefs restrain parents from responding in particular ways and may contribute to an escalating pattern of interaction.

> For the benefit of stability, they pay the price of rigidity, living, as all human beings must, in an enormously complex network of mutually supporting presuppositions . . . change will require various sorts of relaxation or contradiction within the system of presuppositions (Bateson, 1979, p. 158).

Restraints reflect the family's or individual's belief systems. They are supported by a stable network of presuppositions (we all have them) which form the *code book* against which information is construed. As a vicious cycle develops, members make sense of information in terms of these beliefs or presuppositions. They provide a bias for selection of information about difference. Responses will tend to confirm the beliefs of presuppositions, so more and more only old information will be noticed. Thus, the family is limited from being able to perceive or try alternatives.

Highly restrained systems have a high threshhold for perceiving new information. Change involves responding to new information, yet much of a therapist's advice falls short of the threshhold, does not get in, and cannot be acted upon. All communication is coded. Restraints deny a system access to the new code books. Information which does not pass the threshhold cannot be decoded. Thus, highly restrained individuals, couples, or family systems are not ready to respond to information about change. They may claim to have heard it all before; when in fact, they have never heard it.

Problems as Interactional Phenomena—Restrained Participation

Problems are seen not just as the result of individuals being caught up in vicious cycles and restrained from finding alternatives, but as *interactional phenomena* in which the interactions around the problems are determined by restrained information. In developing hypotheses for therapy, the notion of members' *participation around the problems* is crucial.

Members of the system will deal with problems in particular ways, ways that reflect how they view or make sense of the situation. Members will often persist with ways of dealing with problems that appear unsuccessful and, in fact, have often served to perpetuate or reinforce the problem. Often, the *solutions* that members have applied have become the problems.[1]

Family members habitually apply certain attempted solutions or habitually react in particular ways because they are restrained from viewing the problem differently. The habitual behaviour of *all* members is uniquely determined by their restraints and presuppositions. Since the vicious cycle of participatory behavior is determined by restraints, an investigation of behaviour around the problem and attempted solutions will provide key information for building hypotheses about restraints.

[1]The idea that previous attempted solutions become involved in the inadvertent perpetuation of problem behaviour has been elucidated by Watzlawick et al. (1974).

Example. Parents of a teenager displaying irresponsible behaviour may work hard to protect their son or daughter from the distress associated with the results of his or her behaviour. They may think that minimizing this distress will allow their child to settle down and will remove whatever upset lies behind the behaviour. Over time, they may be taking more and more responsibility for their son or daughter's behaviour, thinking that the more they do this the more likely the behaviour is to reduce. In fact, they are inadvertently perpetuating a situation in which the adolescent does not take responsibility for his or her own behaviour. That is, they are participating around the problem and the irresponsible behaviour is an interactional phenomenon.

The notion of restrained participation around the problem replaces the idea of *the function of the symptom. All* members' behaviours have roles and meanings in as much as it is all mutually determined by restraints and there is no need to impute a special meaning or intentional function to a specific *symptomatic* behaviour.

Participation around the problem reflects the nature of feedback within the system. Feedback is an essential characteristic of systems and underlies the interactional nature of behaviours and problems. Bateson suggests that feedback itself acts as a restraint (1972, p. 403) since members are unaware of the interactional nature of their situation. The notion of feedback and recursive circuits suggests that all changes at one point in the system are complementary to changes at another point. The idea of participation reflects the fact that changed behaviour (the problem) in one member is complementary to changes in behaviour (the attempted solutions) in other members, such that the pattern is perpetuated.

Family members often share individualistic, purposive constructions of their situation. Each often sees his or her own behaviour as simply reactive to the other's—that is, each blames the other. Members appear to be caught in a symmetrical escalation. Adolescents will often construct the problem in terms of their parents' and authorities' unreasonableness and restrictiveness, whilst parents may see in terms of their son or daughter's defiance of deliberateness.

It is easy for therapists to become caught in this escalation. Family members often have a covert prescription that the therapist will support their position and join them in criticizing the other, or perhaps act as referee (White, 1984b). It is easy to fall into the position of seeing some people as unreasonable and the others as oppressed. Accepting such a prescription will inevitably result in one side refusing to return to therapy. It is also easy to attempt to be a conciliator, negotiating some concessions from each side. Acceptance of this role potentially leads to endless, frustrating sessions and no real resolution.

To avoid being caught in the pattern, the therapist must concentrate on the self-perpetuating nature of the pattern in which both sides are contributing to the persistence of the behaviour.

White (1985) suggests that it is useful to think of such patterns as being complementary rather than symmetrical—there are at least two sides to every description. For example, if one party is not working very hard on the problem, it is reasonable to hypothesize that the other side is working extra hard.

The behaviour of each side can be seen as *triggering* the behaviour of the other. This is not a notion of cause. Each member has responsibility for whether or not he or she responds to the trigger (although the restraints will make particular responses more or less likely). So, a child's behaviour of not thinking for himself or herself may act as a trigger for his or her parents to do more and more of his or her thinking, but it is up to them whether or not they do so. The idea of behaviour *inviting* certain responses and those responses as *accepting invitations,* which in turn, "invite" more of the problem behaviour, can be helpful (White, 1985). Because family members are blind to the interactional or *mutually triggering* nature of the situation, it is likely that the more the child engages in behaviour that invites his or her parents to do his or her thinking for him or her, the more the parents will continue to respond in their habitual way. Conversely, the more the parents accept these invitations, the more the child will behave in his or her habitual way and the less he or she will need to practice thinking for himself or herself.

Double Description

Information is news of a difference. Information does not mean anything unless it includes a difference. Bateson uses the notion of *double description* (1979, p. 227) and discusses a number of examples of sensory processes being triggered by difference. Binocular vision, for example, is informative because of the small difference between the two images or descriptions.

News of difference (new information) is essential if the family is to discover new ideas and if new responses are to be triggered. News of difference requires a recognition of difference.

> To produce news of difference, i.e. information, there must be two entities such that the difference between them can be imminent in their mutual relationship (Bateson, 1979, p. 78).

So, the discovery of new ideas and alternative ways of responding requires that the family recognise a difference between two descriptions. The therapist establishes conditions that favour double description by developing new or alternative descriptions of events and interaction. The juxtaposition of such new descriptions against the family's old or restrained description invites them to draw distinctions and it is these distinctions that trigger discoveries.

PHILOSOPHICAL VIEWS ON ADOLESCENT CHEMICAL DEPENDENCY

All behaviours in a family system are regarded as uniquely determined by the operation of restraints. Substance-abusing behaviour is no exception. A disease or illness model of dependency implies a positive explanation that limits the possibility of alternatives. It implies that something has to be *done* to *the patient* in order to effect a *cure,* and as such is at variance with an approach that seeks to provide choice, alternatives, and responsibility.

Substance abuse is a particular sign of an interactional pattern that has escalated within the context of particular restraints. It is not that it is seen as just another behaviour problem, for second cybernetics suggests that no two vicious cycles are the same. Rather, it is a behaviour that has elicited certain responses within the context of a certain way of seeing the situation such that both the behaviour and the responses have been perpetuated.

Habituation is a phenomenon present in all persistent problems. Behaviour and responses reflect particular restraints, however the behaviour and responses also tend to reinforce the restrained way of seeing that they represent. So, interactional patterns or regularities, are examples of habituation. The more accustomed family members become to a set of presuppositions, the more restrained they are from seeing alternatives. "What happens in acclimatization is that the organism buys superficial flexibility at the price of deeper rigidity" (Bateson, 1979, p. 170).

Adolescent substance abuse *is* often associated with other or broader behaviour that is considered, unacceptable, and it is helpful to see both in the wider interactional context. In particular, the pattern that White (1985) identified as common in adolescent problems, a pattern that involves *irresponsible* behaviour serving as an invitation to *super-responsible* behaviour which in turn invites more *irresponsible* behaviour, is often a useful framework to apply. Since therapy is concerned with patterns and restraints, it is immaterial whether the therapist focuses on the drug using behaviour or some other behaviour. In terms of the process of therapy, both are effectively metaphors for the wider interaction.

When dealing with chemical dependency, of course, there may be physical habituation as well as the system's habituation to its restrained interaction. The process of this habituation or addiction may be similarly explained. The body becomes accustomed to a particular set of physiological or neurological events and, as habituation increases, alternatives become less viable. Physical addiction, then, is a particular example of a restraint that decreases the possibility of alternate responses and Bateson's comment about acclimatisation is just as relevent. In fact, both the physical addiction and the client's beliefs about his or her addiction will act as restraints. Such restraints cannot be ignored and the process of overcoming a physical addiction must be included in any description of the process of experimenting with a different lifestyle. Clients often experience hangovers or withdrawal when they begin successfully experimenting with a new direction and new forms of interaction, and the physical must be predicted as one such phenomena. As with other such effects, physical withdrawal is a sign of progress, for it only happens if the person has begun to stand up to the oppression of the problem.

ROLE OF THE THERAPIST AND TEAM

The therapist's task is to create a context for change—new meanings, new descriptions, new juxtapositions, that challenge the restraints or the stable meaning context. The therapist can introduce new ideas but only the family can experiment with them. The therapist is not presented as the person who has the answers. He or she might encourage a different way of looking at things, however the answers will be discovered by the family.

In practice, the therapeutic process is one of *co-evolution,* in which family members and therapist together develop a new description and draw distinctions. The therapist may seek to create conditions for double description, however new ideas and meanings must fit with the family's experience or they are lost.

A team may be used effectively. The team may introduce messages that serve as double descriptions when placed against those of the therapist. Moreover, since therapists and clients establish an interactional system that can become embroiled in repetitive forms of interaction, a team can assist a therapist by identifying ways in which the family may be inviting the therapist to participate with them in certain ways and supporting him or her to experiment with different ways of interacting.

KEY TECHNIQUES AND TREATMENT STRATEGIES

The aim of therapy is to identify restraints and challenge these by introducing new meanings and differences. All therapy is about drawing distinctions. This is true not only of the intervention but also of the way information is gathered and commented upon. Questioning is a process of selecting information—information can be selected in ways that promote recognition of differences.

A number of the specific strategies that are discussed are common to a variety of family therapy approaches, however the ways in which they are used and understood reflect the particular assumptions of White's approach.

Increasing Readiness for Noticing Difference

Sometimes the family or individual has already made some moves in the direction of change, but often these are unnoticed. The therapist can seize them, amplify them, put a new twist on them, and so encourage the moves to persist.

Small examples of self-control or responsibility, for example, may be discovered and highlighted. Since other family members (and the adolescent) may have been restrained from really noticing these by their ideas that control is not possible or that there are no hopeful signs, this will be news to the family and will increase their state of readiness. In this way, the therapist introduces a different explanation of something that had not been noticed as different. This small *chink* in the restrained way of viewing things may make later discoveries of difference easier.

Introducing a different construction of the problem and its development may challenge the non-circular quest for causes that often works against families being ready to discover new solutions. In some cases, a therapist may construct a new explanation in terms of a vicious cycle that has swept everyone with it. "This perspective requires that the therapist assist family members to consider the deviation-amplifying feedback context of (the problem). This sets the scene for the interruption of the vicious cycle and the introduction of a more virtuous one" (White, 1984a, p. 152). A variety of examples may be offered as potential triggers to the cycle, which has now taken on a life of its own. This explanation stands against the family's own explanation and encourages distinctions to be drawn.

The idea that a problem has taken on a life of its own, that the current mess is virtually inevitable, can be incorporated in questions that force the family to select different ideas. Questions such as "how have you all survived?", "what has stopped you from being completely overwhelmed by the problem?", "how have you all been able to maintain some control over events in the face of the overwhelming oppression of these habits in the family?" challenge linear constructions.

Externalizing Problems

Families typically have beliefs about the problem which lead to their viewing it as internal, characterological, and often involving intentionality. White (1986c) identify these beliefs as being the "dormitive explanation" that Bateson (1972) mentions as being an explanation that implies some internal state. Such beliefs restrain families from noticing information about participation. Trying to convince clients that this is a family problem is not the way to deal with this and leads to futile arguments. Externalizing the problem is one way of overcoming the restraining nature of such ideas.

Problems can be externalized as part of the development of a vicious cycle argument or as part of a discussion of relative influence. A description of the problem as an external tyrant which is dominating the entire family (including the symptomatic member) is a different description which challenges notions of internal causality. As Epston (1987) summarizes, "The person isn't the problem; the problem is the problem." It allows solutions to be framed in terms of standing up to the problem rather than working through it or coming to terms with it, and so on. Externalising the problem allows a new description of a solution that involves pitting child and parents against the problem rather than having child pitted against parents (White, 1984a, p. 153).

Michael White's *sneaky poo* programme for encopresis externalizes the symptom as something tyranising the family (White, 1984). "Temper Taming" (Durant, 1985a) is an adaptation of sneaky poo that reconstructs the problem and the family's characterological explanation of it by pitting child and family together against *The Temper.* It paves the way for a dilemma about who is to be boss. See also Durrant (1985b) for an example of the use of metaphor to externalize a problem.

In some cases, the problem may be externalized overtly and therapy framed as a struggle to fight against or stand up to it. Adolescents have responded to ideas that they and the family are under the domination of habits which are pushing them around. This is often in contrast to their protestations that they are doing their own thing or could stop if I wanted to, since they are really doing the habits' thing. One young man engaged in a fight against heroin, finding that thinking of his problem as an *external* heroin which was seeking to control his life was more helpful than his ideas about his own internal pathology or weakness.

In other cases, the externalization is more implied. Reconstructions in terms of vicious cycles, as mentioned above, imply the cycle as something external that can be viewed and challenged. The identification of particular interactional patterns can be a way of externalising something to be struggled against. White (1986b) demonstrates the externalizing of the family's trouble.

Collapsing Time

Much of what happens as a cycle develops is imperceptible and goes unnoticed. Vicious cycles are not experienced as rapid escalations, they are more like *toxic trends*. The imperceptible differences over time can be made noticeable by juxtaposing the state of things at different points in time.

The therapist can identify trends in behaviour and organization and, by collapsing time, render the cycle newsworthy. Clients are encouraged to draw distinctions between the state of things at two points in time. Time can be collapsed backwards, perhaps when historical data is being collected, to make newsworthy the insidious influence the problem has had or to draw a distinction between present problem behaviour and previous non-problem behaviour. Time may be collapsed forward to highlight the inevitable outcome of continued participation. Highlighting the state of the problem now, in five years, in ten years, and so on really shows differences. Clients can be asked to predict the consequences of their behaviour at specific times in the future. Future participation of members, can be predicted by asking what you would have to do to keep helping your son or daughter in five years time, etc.

> Things undergo drastic change, but we become accustomed to the new state of affairs before our senses can tell us that it is new. . . . It is a nontrivial matter that we are almost unaware of trends in our changes of state (Bateson 1979, pp. 108–109).

Questions that collapse time allow distinctions to be drawn about trends. Members are blind to trends that lead to their increasing participation and they almost always see the current problem and nothing else. They will tend to re-interpret history in terms of the current problem, unable to select information about differences in the past, and they will often think in terms of things staying the same, unable to select information about future development.

Collapsing time juxtaposes the state of affairs at two different points in time. Using *time oriented language* assists this process. "The terms of these descriptions can include notions of 'career,' 'lifestyle,' and 'life course.' The therapist can assist family members to map their problem onto the trend by inviting them to draw distinctions between their participation with each other around the problem in the past, present and future" (White, 1986a, p. 174). White's work with schizophrenia (1987) provides a good example of the use of time-oriented language, such as *career* and *lifestyle,* to describe patterns of participation.

Relative Influence

Information about the problem can be obtained in such a way as to obtain two differently coded descriptions by asking clients about the relative influence of themselves and the problem. See White (1986a).

The family will naturally describe the problem in terms of their own restrained beliefs and this description will often include descriptions in terms of beliefs about incompetence, personality faults, helplessness, guilt, etc. The therapist frames this as the influence the problem is having on the members' lives and can explore the extent of this influence as a way of closely understanding the extent of the problem (and the restraints reflected in this influence).

Questions such as "how much is the problem supervising your son's life?", "how much of the time does the problem stop you doing things you'd like to do?", "how much is the family dominated by this problem?", "how much influence does the problem have in the adolescent's life?" are helpful. It is also helpful to ask for a quantitative assessment of the problem's influence. This is the natural explanation for the family.

The therapist then juxtaposes a different description by asking how much influence members continue to exert in their own lives and in the life of the problem. How much have they been able to stand up to the problem's oppression, and influence their own lives? This description requires the family to work hard since they are required to select different sorts of explanations and information. The therapist frames this description as a description of the extent of the family's strength.

> Relative influence requires the establishment of two differently coded descriptions. Usually, in one of these descriptions, events are coded according to the family's network of pre-existing presuppositions, and in the other, events are coded according to the therapist's contributed premises (White, 1986a, p. 173).

A young father reported that he was completely dominated by his heroin habit and was able to recount in great detail the influence it had in his life. Persistent exploration of his own influence eventually revealed that he never used heroin on the weekends that his young son visited him. He had not noticed this factor, and gained new information from the small percentage of influence in his own life that it represented.

Relative influence is a double description. Two different descriptions of the problem are placed side-by-side so that distinctions may be drawn.

Challenging Meanings Determined by Language

Families persist with problem behaviours because they are restrained from seeing things differently in order to respond differently. The restraints—beliefs and presuppositions—are the key to why things are not different.

Words are important, since they carry the meanings we ascribe to things. The name given to a problem is determined by the restraints, and reinforces the particular way of viewing the problem. Restraints may be challenged by adopting a different name for the problem. (See Durrant, 1985b), for an example of the importance of the name or definition the family has of its problem.

The way members describe the problem may give clues about restraints. For example, "He seems to forget to come home at night," "Johnny gets very angry and he seems so unhappy," "We've come to find out why she's the way she is," "She comes home with things from shops that she hasn't paid for and we're worried about her self-esteem" (all actual client quotes).

The language substance users apply to themselves, their habits, and their subculture reflect these sorts of beliefs. Therapists may need to adopt the language to be able to create rapport, but the words themselves may get in the way of what therapists say and do. Does the language imply responsibility for their situation or inability to take responsibility? (half-addicted, I'm not really addicted, habit). Does the language mask the seriousness of the situation (a taste of heroin)?[2]

Redefining such problems and giving them different names can challenge the beliefs that help their perpetuation. Therapy with an adolescent whose problem is "a dependent, addictive personality" is notoriously difficult. Therapy with the same adolescent who is "under the

[2]We are indebted to our colleague, Gerard Menses, for alerting us to some of the beliefs reflected in the language employed by substance abusers.

influence of some habits" may be more fruitful. Similarly, it may be more helpful to define a problem as being addiction to a particular lifestyle than as addiction to a substance. Such redefinitions may be introduced as part of the externalizing process or may simply be employed by the therapist in the way he or she questions the family.

Complementary Questioning

Family members have restraining beliefs which do not allow them to select information regarding their relationships with one another and the problem. As such, their habitual ways are inevitable. Therapists who try to comment directly on the participatory nature of the interaction find that families argue, get angry, or seem not to understand.

Complementary questions (White, 1986c) are questions that encourage members to think interactionally, to generate a two-sided description of their situation. The therapist develops a reconstruction of the problem by questioning both sides of the system about their participation in the behaviour of the other side. After deriving a two-sided description, the therapist may question each side about the way they invite the other side to interact.

The questions, themselves, give information about participation, however, they also elicit specific examples of ways in which family members participate together and so provide material for further questioning or discussion.

- How good are you at inviting your parents to accept responsibility for your life?
- How good is your son or daughter at inviting you to accept responsibility for his or her life? (White, 1985)

Complementary questioning can incorporate collapsing time around future participation.

- I'm intrigued at how much you've been able to get other people to work harder on your growing up than you. What other ways could your Mum and Dad work at getting you to grow up so you don't have to?
- Do you have any ideas? What parts of Anne's growing up are there that she hasn't been able to get you to try and do for her yet? How do you think she'll try to hand them over to you so she doesn't have to face them?

Further examples of complementary questioning in therapy with adolescents are given in White (1985).

Raising Dilemmas

Information is news of a difference. Seemingly new information does not pass the threshhold because restraints render it not different. Information about change can be made newsworthy in incorporating a difference in it. The therapist raises a dilemma—you may decide to pursue a different path or you may decide to continue down the same path. This is double description. The therapist may argue for both courses of action, setting out the advantages and disadvantages of both, and leave the individual or family with the dilemma. Both pathways are presented, so the change alternative is clearly different. The therapist must not argue in favour of change, since the restraints are ready for that.

> The rationale for introducing dilemmas is often in terms that it is a device for creating a therapeutic bind. An alternative explanation of the value of raising dilemmas is that they establish conditions for double description. The therapist and family members work to establish two descriptions of their participation with each other around different careers or lifestyles. These descriptions, placed side by side, enable family members to draw new distinctions (White, 1986a, p. 174).

The dilemma can be framed in a number of ways—change versus staying the same, pursuing a career as a delinquent versus forging a career of responsibility, being boss over the temper versus letting it be boss over you, growing up versus growing down, etc. The dilemma can be mirrored by a team split—The team behind the screen thinks you may not be ready to leave your current path, but I think you are ready to try something new.

Whilst dilemmas are sometimes seemingly directed at the so-called problem member, they must be dilemmas about interaction. The dilemma involves two descriptions of the future course of the family, placed side by side, so new distinctions might be drawn. The dilemma must include the participation of family members around the problem. Thus, the form of the dilemma is that of continuing to participate with each other in habitual ways around the problem direction (to persist with the current path) vs. participating with each other in new ways around a different direction or path. The therapist may predict the sorts of participation that will be necessary should the problem direction continue and set this against predictions of the sort of participation required to successfully challenge the problem and move along a new path. A simple choice is not newsworthy and makes no difference. The dilemma must juxtapose two paths of interaction or it has little effect. In fact, a simple choice to a restrained system that cannot see alternatives may exacerbate ideas about hopelessness (See Durrant, 1986, for an illustration of the way that dilemmas, that do not really address interaction, may contribute to family and therapist stuckness.)

Questions can be posed which incorporate the idea that things can be different and present information about different paths. If complementary questions have established conditions for double description in the ways described above, dilemma questions are a natural progression.

- Do you think the old direction suits you or do you think a different direction would suit you better?
- Do you think you have been too weakened by the habits to make a comeback?
- Do you think you have been too weakened by your son or daughter's habits to make a comeback?
- Do you want to find more and more ways to invite your parents to take responsibility for your life or do you think you'll be able to practice taking responsibility for yourself?
- Do you think you'll continue to accept your son or daughter's invitations to take responsibility for his or her life or do you think you'll stand up to these invitations and invite him or her to accept responsibility for his or her own life?
- Do you think you could apply the necessary pressure on yourself to stage a fight back or do you think you would crack under the pressure?
- Do you think you'll continue growing down and getting Mum and Dad to do more and more of your thinking for you or do you think you'll decide to practice thinking for yourself and take your growing up forward?
- Do you think you'll be prepared to keep doing Frankie's thinking for him or do you think you'll decide that he needs to do his own growing up thinking?
- I wonder if you think you're ready to experiment with running your own life or if you'll decide you'd prefer to sit back and enjoy the habits running it for a while longer?
- Sitting back and allowing your fears to decide what things you can do is much easier. Do you think you'll keep on sitting back comfortably or are you thinking about standing up and deciding what you can do for yourself?

Experiments

Change involves something new, something untried. Speaking of creativity and learning, Bateson postulates that "the ongoing processes of change feed on the random" (1979, p. 57). "The system will learn and remember . . . by the playing of stochastic games called empirisism or trial and error" (1979, p. 142).

The idea of the stochastic, or trial and error, nature of change has profound implications for therapy. It implies that the therapist is not somehow privy to the truth and that the final direction a family will take is unpredictable.[3] The finding of solutions becomes an experimental process for family and therapist.

If family members are prepared to explore a new direction, one that challenges old patterns of relating, they may be invited to consider experiments that could challenge the problem lifestyle and provide information about alternatives. These are not tasks imposed from the therapist's repertoire of solutions, but opportunities for trial and error experiencing of new ways.

Members may be asked to consider sequences of behaviour that are typical of their identified restrained participation and plan particular experiments that challenge or reverse these. White sets out this form of experimenting most clearly in his consideration of marital therapy (1984b). Pressure tests (White, 1985) and the sorts of tests employed in the residential situation (Menses and Durrant, 1986) are examples of experiments that set up situations to challenge habitual interaction.[4]

Clients are advised that the results of tests will be reviewed, not as evidence of purpose or intent, but for the information they provide about the possibility of difference. They may be cautioned against experimenting too quickly and advised of the discomfort that accompanies any new ways of interacting.

Responding to Responses

If the therapist is successful in making interventions that are newsworthy, the system will respond. Freed, perhaps momentarily, from the

[3]David Epston, family therapist from Auckland, New Zealand, contrasts "therapies of degradation" and "therapies of regrading." The former, which he also calls "missionary therapies" imply that the therapist possesses the truth which is somehow imposed upon the family, whilst the latter assumes a more co-operative therapeutic process in which discoveries are made and clients are left with responsibility and choice.

[4]David Epston, with his colleague Fred Seymour, developed *honesty tests* as interactional *challenges* in the treatment of adolescent stealing. They involve prescribed activities that challenge habitual participation set within a context that both makes success more likely and allows success to be noticed. The tests described by Menses and Durrant are adaptations of this idea.

predictable restrained organization of the system, alternative ways of behaving become possible. The system may select from the many alternatives quite randomly.

> To persist, the new must be of such a sort that it will endure longer than the alternatives. What lasts longer among the ripples of the random must last longer than those ripples that last not so long (Bateson, 1979, p. 54).

The random alternative responses of the family or individual will not necessarily persist. The therapist must respond to them in a way that makes them newsworthy. The system is still restrained and the family's own responses may fall short of their threshold, that is they may not recognise them. For example, an adolescent may have controlled her use of alcohol on one or two significant occasions but her parents do not recognise this since they are still preoccupied with those occasions on which she didn't.

The therapist must continue to make things newsworthy, to make responses persist. The same sorts of techniques as those already mentioned may be used.

The dilemma of the old path vs. the new can be restated, with the observation that steps have been taken along the path of change. A decision has been made. The therapist may caution against moving too quickly or even suggest that the old path should be followed again for a while so both paths can be evaluated. Thus the initial dilemma continues to be news. Collapsing time can be used to predict the longer-term consequences of these moves toward change and the kinds of participation that will be required.

As therapy proceeds, the therapist probes, investigates and searches for even the smallest indications of change. This change is seized upon, made newsworthy, and amplified. It may be exaggerated, cause surprise or puzzlement, or be highlighted by the use of humour. The therapist's own behaviour should be newsworthy. A family expects a therapist to be enthusiastic about change or reward efforts to be different. If the therapist expresses concern about such reckless moves into a new path the family experiences this as news.

Small changes will not necessarily be noticed by members. The family needs to be encouraged to draw new distinctions and to select information about new ways of participating with each other that they may have begun to experiment with. The task in subsequent sessions, in responding to the family's responses, is again one of double description.

Restraining change and predicting relapses provide a different description of the moves the family has made. By warning against continuing in the direction of change or predicting inevitable relapses, the therapist is describing future events in terms of the conservative or no-change description and so encouraging members to draw distinctions about their departures from old ways. White (1986a) suggests that this need not be considered in terms of being a way of overcoming resistance, but as another way of drawing distinctions between the old and the new. "By taking a conservative position in relation to the radical nature of change, the therapist establishes conditions for double description" (p. 177).

The potential effects of relapses and setbacks can be averted by providing different descriptions. Relapses may be labelled as setbacks or *hiccups* in progress to change their meaning and lessen the chance of their resulting in members giving up. Symptom exacerbation may be described as the inevitable hangover that occurs when the family stops being under the influence of the problem lifestyle. Thus, when the inevitable occurs, the family has been encouraged to draw distinctions differently, make sense of the phenomenon differently, and hopefully respond differently.

Small changes are sufficient. If made newsworthy and allowed to persist a small change is sufficient to set off a positive feedback process leading to a new cycle—this time not a vicious cycle but a virtuous one.

Termination

Terminating therapy rarely poses problems, since (as the noticing of difference snowballs) families have a habit of overtaking the therapist. Often, rites of passage are useful to mark the new *context* (that is, the new way of fitting together). These are ritual celebrations such as "growing up parties," "honesty parties," "celebrations of control," and so on, and involve cakes, speeches, and perhaps the presentation of awards.[5]

THEORY OF CHANGE

To find new ways of responding, families need to be freed to see things differently. They need new information, to recognise differences not available previously. They need to be able to *draw distinctions* between behaviours and ideas. Information is news of a difference, and difference must be accentuated. So the therapist works toward new perceptions

[5]Epston has developed many creative ways of using ritual to place changes within a new context and suggested the use of parties as ways of marking the new, problem-free context. See, for example, Epston (1986).

and beliefs by developing double descriptions, new distinctions, new juxtapositions of events.

Thus, change involves new ideas or information such that new ideas will be noticed and will endure. Information involves difference—a difference in the "system of presuppositions" entails a difference in the way members punctuate their experience. That is, a difference in the connections or context.

Such new information that challenges formerly restrained ways of seeing will open the possibility of trial and error experimentation with new possibilities. Solutions will be the new ideas plucked from the random that fit for the particular clients.

Information that gets through, that is different to the current organisation of the system, will elicit a response. The response may be small, it will be random (in that it is from somewhere other than the current restrained organisation) and any such response will be a small variation in the system with the potential to set off its own cycle, this time a virtuous cycle.

CASE EXAMPLE

Jason, aged 14, was referred for the possibility of a residential placement following some long-standing family difficulties and his persistent running away and drug and alcohol abuse. Jason had recently been in two residential programmes, one an inpatient adolescent psychiatry unit and the other a wilderness-style *challenge* programme. Both had been unsuccessful, and, in desperation, his father had charged him in the courts with being "uncontrollable" and Jason was now in a secure remand facility. Jason and his father, Tony, (39), attended the interview.

First Session

Tony and Jason introduced themselves. Tony, a freelance writer, presented as an articulate and personable man. Jason appeared as a rather scruffy young man, but seemed prepared to make comments in the session.

Tony explained the difficulties involving Jason that had existed for years and said he felt that Jason had been caught in the middle of problems between himself and Jason's mother, now deceased. Tony's career involved much time away from home, and Tony and his wife

(Rebecca) had drifted apart over a number of years. When Jason was around 10-years-old, Tony began drinking heavily, leading to a complete breakdown in the marriage and Tony leaving. Three months later, Rebecca was diagnosed as suffering cancer and Tony decided to return. Tony cared for Rebecca for what he described as "a further traumatic two years" before she died. Since then, Jason had lived with Tony and Tony had been involved in a series of relationships.

Tony said a number of times that he felt Jason's present problems stemmed from his exposure to these difficulties. Tony was feeling a great deal of guilt about his part in these events and in Jason's delinquent lifestyle, and the therapist began to form the impression that Tony was accepting a lot of responsibility for the present difficulties.

Jason's behaviour had been difficult for some time, with Tony feeling he was losing any control over his son and despairing as he saw him become more and more involved with the drug culture. Jason spent time away from school staying home getting drunk and getting stoned on marijuana and a variety of pills. In the past four months, Jason had run away from home six times, leading to his two residential placements. He had run away from the first after a dispute about his continued use of alcohol and marijuana and he had been dismissed from the second for smuggling alcohol into the unit. During this time, his behaviour had become increasingly out of control. Often he would run to Kings Cross and spend up to two or three weeks involved in prostitution. These times were characterized by excessive use of alcohol and marijuana as he resorted to drugs and alcohol to alleviate his discomfort and prostituted himself to finance his supply. As things had gone from bad to worse, Tony had spent long hours looking for Jason, waiting for him at known haunts, and worrying about where he was and what he was doing.

Tony said he wanted Jason to get some "direction and purpose" in his life. He was concerned that Jason seemed happy to drift along and wanted him to learn that his actions have consequences. He was concerned about Jason's drug use, his at-risk lifestyle and he felt Jason was confused about his sexuality.

Jason initially said that he was not sure what the problems were, but volunteered that he did not get along with Tony's girlfriend. He acknowledged that he "gets sick of things and takes off," but he wasn't sure there was a problem. He did not see that his lifestyle could put himself at risk and saw his drug use as his way of coping with hassles, but agreed that his drinking had landed him in some trouble.

Further discussion confirmed the therapist's emerging hypothesis that Jason and his father had become caught in an escalating interactional pattern around giving and taking of responsibility. Over a period of months, Tony had become increasingly occupied in time and effort in trying to find a solution to these problems. These steps involved spending long hours talking with Jason, going out searching for Jason and bringing him back home when found, organizing his friends to do the same, organizing and paying for activities to keep Jason busy and to "keep him away from temptation," and expending time and effort worrying about Jason's future. Over this period of time, Jason cared less and less about his lifestyle and future, seemed less able to constructively organise himself, and increasingly relied on his father and others to bail him out.

This pattern could be seen as a mutually self-supporting system—Tony's actions were invitations to Jason to rely on Tony to take responsibility for finding solutions. Jason accepted these invitations and therefore became less able to rely on himself to find solutions. This manifested itself in an irresponsible and unconcerned lifestyle, and the resulting behaviours were invitations to Tony to take even more responsibility. Tony, vulnerable to guilt about the whole situation, felt driven to accept these invitations and so continued his efforts to take responsibility for solutions. They appeared to be unaware of these mutual invitations, but were both experiencing the bewilderment of being stuck in such a pattern.

The therapist felt that Jason's drug use could be best conceptualized as both a result of and a factor that contributed to this pattern. His alcohol consumption and marijuana use were examples of actions that specifically invited other people to take responsibility for his life, and were part of the overall lifestyle pattern. In fact, the interactional pattern showed itself very clearly at times of prolonged or heavy substance abuse. Jason's father, the police, and welfare agencies took almost total responsibility for Jason's life after particularly irresponsible episodes of drinking. The therapist decided that Jason's drug problem needed to be addressed within the overall interactional patterns in which Jason and Tony were locked.[6]

[6]As set out above, White's approach primarily provides a way of thinking about behaviour and problems which lead to a variety of possible interventions. In some cases of adolescent drug use, a more direct approach might be used by focussing directly on the drugs as something dominating the adolescent and family and seeking to draw distinctions about standing up to this influence. In this case, the therapist (Don Coles) decided to focus on the overall interaction within which the drug use was one example of escalating behaviour.

Jason and Tony, not surprisingly, were unaware of the interactional nature of the problem and saw it in terms of individual faults or deficiencies. Recognizing that they would be restrained from hearing direct comments on the trends of this pattern, the therapist asked a series of questions to raise these ideas.

"In what areas of his life has Jason got out of practice at taking responsibility for himself? How long has this trend been developing? In what ways has he become good at getting other people to assume responsibility for his life? Are there times when his actions invite others to take this responsibility? What invitations from Jason is Tony particularly vulnerable to? In what ways has Tony became caught up in accepting these invitations? How does acceptance of Jason's invitations then invite Jason to take even less responsibility."

Tony and Jason did not find these questions easy and Jason objected that they were stupid. This was not surprising, since the questions implied a radically different way of constructing events. The therapist acknowledged that maybe they had not thought about these ideas before and summarized his suggestion that Jason's behaviour, despite his assertions that it was evidence of his independence and desire to run his own life, was acting as invitations to his father and others to become more and more involved in his life, and that Tony's accepting these invitations, despite his assertions that he wanted Jason to be more responsible, was effectively inviting Jason to take less and less responsibility. They agreed to think further about the questions.

These questions were designed to suggest a new description of the problem. The questions suggested an interactional focus that removed the need for individualist explanation. Describing the problem in terms of a pattern that had gone out of control was also a way of externalizing it. The new description was in marked contrast to their own way of making sense of the situation and was a way of establishing conditions for them to draw distinctions and perhaps discover new information.

Second Session

At the next session, Jason stated that he wanted to learn to take responsibility for his own life. Tony indicated that he could see how he had become caught up in accepting Jason's invitations, and that he wanted to hand some responsibility back to Jason. The therapist cautioned them that this could be a hard path, since challenging such well-practiced patterns is fraught with difficulty. Jason was not used to the pressure of such responsibility. For example, he had lasted only two weeks in the previous placement where they had expected him to take some responsibility. Perhaps the pattern had robbed him of practice at responsibility, in which case it was not surprising that he had been unable to tolerate the programme. For Tony, challenging the pattern would require resisting feelings that he was totally responsible for Jason's behaviour and welfare.

Tony was not confident of their ability to handle things together at home at this stage, and a residential placement for Jason was offered as an opportunity for both of them to experiment with the changes needed for them to stand up to the pattern.[7] For Jason, the placement would be an opportunity to practice taking responsibility for his own life and not inviting others to become involved; and for Tony, it would be a chance to begin acting in a way that invited Jason to assume more responsibility and to practice strategies for resisting Jason's invitations.

The residential staff were described as expert responsibility trainers, and it was decided that they would arrange various responsibility tests for Jason that would put him in situations of facing the pressure of taking responsibility. These tests in the residential setting could give Jason some initial practice in the difficult task of facing responsibility and provide ideas for further practice at home. Tony agreed to meet regularly with Jason and the staff to help plan the tests and to review with Jason the progress they were both making.

Placement

During the first two weeks of placement, there was evidence of Jason's habit of inviting others to take responsibility. For example, he sometimes complained that staff were bitchy when they asked him to do normal household chores and he asked staff to intervene in his

[7]Menses and Durrant (1986) have developed an approach to residential care that incorporates the ideas of White's cybernetic therapy. *Contextual residential care* seeks to extend the idea of developing a new description of the problem by developing a new description for residential placement. Since the admission of an adolescent into a residential facility can easily exacerbate notions that the problem lies within the adolescent, the new description for the placement seeks to establish a context that focuses on problem-solving and complements the therapeutic emphasis on externalization, interaction and experimenting with new directions. The approach also employs the idea of placement being a *rite of passage,* a time for the family to move from one context or way of seeing itself to another, and relies on the anthropological insights of Epston whose work incorporates ideas from Turner & Brunner (1986) and van Gennep (1960). For specific examples of contextual residential care, see also Coles (1986) and Elms (1986).

disputes with other residents. On an occasion that he was found smoking marijuana, he claimed that he needed it because it helped him get along with other people. A staff member suggested that he may be giving responsibility to the drug for his relationships. Despite the relative abundance of activities and equipment, Jason continually complained that the place was boring and that he could not do anything to organize his time. He had a period of refusing to do anything, following his refusal to carry out a consequence imposed for walking away on an outing to a shop. Staff members recognized these invitations for them to take responsibility for finding things for Jason to do and commented on that as they resisted them. All these examples seemed consistent with some of the ways in the past he had invited others to take responsibility.

However, there were also many examples of Jason being able to take responsibility for himself in his first few weeks in the unit. Jason was able to handle a number of household chores without constant reminder, took responsibility for organizing his own vegetarian meals rather than simply complaining about the food or just giving in to the temptation to eat meat, took responsibility for his own relationships by sticking up for himself on some occasions, and showed some evidence of reliability by returning to the unit when arranged.

During this time, the staff responded to Jason's behaviour in ways that would highlight for him whether he was taking responsibility himself or inviting others to do so.[8] This was usually by means of comments or questions to him, and by following these with consequences for his behaviour. Thus, the context of placement as a place for him to experiment with responsibility was confirmed. Any small steps he took in successfully taking responsibility for himself were noted and highlighted to Jason. Not surprisingly, Jason often reacted angrily to comments about his invitations to others although staff felt he was thinking more about the comments. On the other hand, he was often surprised by comments about instances in which he had accepted responsibility for himself and appeared proud of his achievements.

[8]It should be noted that the use of the term *responsibility* in this context is not meant to imply value-judgments. That is, *responsible behaviour* is not equated with *acceptable behaviour.* The term is properly an interactional description that relates to the way Jason interacts with his father and others around his behaviour. In the residential situation, staff are careful to highlight as responsible any behaviour which shows the adolescent exercising control, making decisions or accepting consequences, even if such behaviour is also regarded as unacceptable.

Third Session (Two Weeks Later)

After reiterating the context of the residential placement, the therapist asked a series of questions aimed at eliciting information about Tony and Jason's view of progress, whilst maintaining the interactional focus of the problems: "How has Jason found the hard work of being in the unit? Has he found it hard trying to give up inviting other people to take responsibility for him? Or has he discovered some new tricks for getting the staff to accept responsibility? Has Tony been able to think about other ways in the past that Jason has invited him to take responsibility? Has Tony thought of other ways that he has accepted these invitations? What pressures on Tony will make it hard to stand up to invitations?"

Tony had obviously thought a great deal about the pattern, and it seemed that these questions and ones from the previous sessions had raised some new ideas for him. He identified more clearly that some of his own responses had resulted in Jason being protected from responsibility—for example, always going out looking for Jason when he was missing and spending a lot of time and effort organizing Jason's day for him.

After hearing from the residential worker (who was present in the session) about some of the ways Jason had faced up to responsibility, the therapist complimented both Jason and Tony on the steps they had taken. They had clearly begun to experiment with departing from the old pattern—Tony was showing Jason that he was serious about not accepting these invitations, and Jason was showing that he was prepared to begin working on taking more responsibility.

At this point, Tony said he accepted this new framework but was still concerned about why Jason's behaviour had developed the way it had. The therapist commented that their family had faced many pressures over the years, and that any of these may have acted as the trigger for the patterns in the family. Things would have been exaggerated by the separation, Tony's feelings of responsibility as a single parent, his feelings of guilt about the effects on Jason, and his desire to somehow "make up to him" would have made him particularly vulnerable to invitations to take responsibility. Similarly, the pressures outside Jason's control would have naturally meant it was more difficult for him to take responsibility, and the self-perpetuating vicious cycle was established. In this way of viewing the situation, trying to find out *why* (in terms of original *causes)* was fruitless, and would probably lead to them feeling even more stuck. In reality there were many interacting factors contributing to the situation. Using the analogy of a fire, the therapist suggested that when a blaze is established the most helpful strategy is not to look for the original place that it started, but to actively take measures to put it out. This picture made sense to Tony.

Following this, the therapist raised the possibility of Jason spending some time at home building on his practice. Tony was understandably cautious about this, but agreed that part of Jason rebuilding trust was to have opportunities at home, and suggested that Jason could come home the next weekend. After consultation with the team, the therapist warned them that they would both feel pressure to revert to the old pattern. The team suggested that Tony and Jason conduct an experiment around one issue and they agreed upon an experiment in which Tony was to think of an area where he would deliberately practice giving responsibility over to Jason and resisting any invitations for him to take responsibility by reminding, pushing, or doing it himself. He was not to tell Jason what he had decided, and Jason was to see if he could guess. It would also be an opportunity for Jason to practice taking responsibility in that particular area.[9]

The therapist cautioned them to restrict the experiment to one area only (as they may not be ready for more) and emphasized that, as this was an experiment, success or failure was not as important as the information that would be gathered from it.

Jason went home that weekend and shortly after he had returned to the unit the therapist received a phone call from Tony. Tony had given Jason the responsibility of writing down a list of the activities he could do on the weekend, but had not reminded him after the initial suggestion. Jason had guessed that this was the experiment and had managed to cope with the responsibility of completing the task. Tony commented that Jason had actually taken quite a lot of responsibility on Saturday, but then found it hard to keep this up on Sunday. The therapist expressed his interest to hear more details at the next session. Tony asked that Jason spend the next weekend at home.

In the residential setting the youthworkers continued to work hard to resist invitations from Jason for them to take responsibility for problems, and thereby continued to face Jason with his own responsibility. He naturally found this difficult, and at times attempted to avoid responsibility. However, the staff felt he was making discoveries about his own ability to face responsibility.

[9]This task was a variation of White's "Pressure tests" (White, 1985) which suggest a task or experiment well-suited to challenging an interactional pattern that revolves around invitations to give and take responsibility.

Fourth Session (Two Weeks Later)

The therapist began by reviewing the two weekends at home. Overall, Tony felt that Jason had managed to take responsibility for himself 60 percent of the time, and was clearly impressed with this. The therapist discovered that Tony had required Jason to do some jobs on the second weekend that he had not completed on the first, and Tony had waited until the jobs were done before giving him pocket money.

The therapist highlighted this as a significant example of Tony challenging the pattern—it would have been tempting to give in to feelings of sympathy for Jason and hand over the money before the tasks were done, and Tony agreed that he would probably have done that in the past. Instead he requested Jason to face the responsibilities of the job and to handle waiting for pocket money.

"How had Jason managed to take 60 percent responsibility? We would have been surprised if he had managed 20 percent." The therapist complimented them both on their actions around the experiment—this had clearly been a challenge to the pattern. Tony commented that he had been surprised that Jason had not run off, and had made it to and from home on public transport on his own. The therapist complimented Tony for resisting the temptation to give in to worries about Jason's irresponsibility and to take responsibility by collecting Jason, or by bringing him back (especially since he had found it harder to keep up responsibility on Sunday). This was interaction that would not have been noticed previously.

Tony was keen to find out about an incident at the unit that had occurred the day before, in which Jason had been missing for nine hours. The therapist asked about other times that he had been missing, and contrasted this current incident to other episodes of running away. Jason had been missing for four weeks after leaving the wilderness programme and for a number of days after being dismissed from the adolescent psychiatry centre. This contrast was another example of double description. Tony was surprised to realize that this incident was different from others in the past, and revealed his belief that Jason's running away was evidence of his impulsive nature. The therapist hypothesised that ideas about impulsiveness, which imply that Jason is not really responsible for his actions, had helped fuel the pattern by encouraging Tony to feel more responsible. He questioned the staff and Jason about the incident and concluded aloud that Jason had made a clear decision to leave yesterday without permission, and then had made a decision to return after a few hours. This was not an example of acting on impulse, and he was impressed that Jason had been able to make a sensible decision after an unwise decision. This was in marked contrast to the past, when Jason had practiced not accepting responsibility for his running away but had tried to give the responsibility to others (blaming other kids, staff, the programme, needing to get away for a drink, etc.) In addition, Jason admitted he had felt uncomfortable about returning to the unit and, yet, had stood up to these feelings, which were framed as even more evidence of his desire to face up to responsibility.

Tony expressed surprise that the youth workers had not chased Jason, nor gone looking for him, and this was discussed as their way of avoiding Jason's invitations.

In discussing the things that might get in the way of continued moves in this new direction, both agreed that Jason was most susceptible to giving away responsibility when he is bored and that Tony is susceptible to trying to occupy him to keep him out of trouble. The team commented that when Jason is bored, perhaps after he has expended a lot of energy practicing responsibility, it is easy not to have the energy to keep practicing. When things get hard, it is easy to be tricked into thinking that he's out of control, that he can't control his impulses. Jason commented that his drug use happened when he was bored. The therapist suggested that the more bored he is, the more extreme are his attempts to get other people to take responsibility for him.

Tony and Jason were congratulated on the changes they were both making, and they agreed to embark on another (more difficult) experiment at home. Together we planned the experiment, with both Tony and Jason making suggestions as follows.

1. Jason to spend five minutes each morning writing down his plans for the day.
2. He is to show them to Tony to get his comment.
3. Jason to make sure he includes in the list a time when he plans to be bored. (This was to challenge Jason's belief that boredom "just happens," that is to raise the idea that he may be able to take responsibility for doing something about boredom.)
4. If Jason plans to run away, he must put this on the list. This way it will be clear that Jason is in control of decisions rather than doing things on impulse.
5. In seven days time, both will probably need a rest from this experiment. It was suggested that Jason stays in bed and not do the things on his list, and that Tony reverts to the old pattern of taking responsibility for Jason.

The idea that old pattern is familiar and so comfortable, and can be reverted to if the pressure of the new becomes too onerous, is an example of the familiar technique of restraining clients from changing. (Watzlawick et al., 1974). White (1984b) describes prescribing more of the same as another way of providing information about difference.

Fifth Session (Two Weeks Later)

Tony and Jason had partially completed the experiment, and it was clear that the process of thinking about doing it had reinforced some new ideas about the pattern. Tony had noticed some differences in Jason—not once had Jason complained to him about boredom, Jason had shown more respect for Tony's privacy (a problem which had originally been mentioned but not dealt with specifically in sessions), and Jason was making an effort to give up cigarette smoking. Jason agreed with these moves and seemed more confident and definite in his responses in the session.

Jason brought with him the lists he had completed. They were quite comprehensive and covered most days of the last two weeks. The therapist responded to this as further evidence of a commitment to do the hard work of responsibility himself, rather than relying on his father to do it. It was interesting that Jason had scheduled time to "be lazy" and not to "be bored." The therapist commented on Jason's discovery that he could be lazy (a deliberate, responsible decision) without being bored.

Tony felt Jason now had a more positive attitude about his life, and he now felt he had 50 percent trust towards Jason. This compared to a situation in the past where he was 80 percent untrusting and the significance of this difference was discussed. It was clear that the shifts in both of them were leading to a rebuilding of trust, with Tony being more prepared to give trust, and Jason showing he was more able to handle it.

The therapist also sought to draw some distinctions around control. Both Tony and Jason agreed that in the past five weeks, Jason had gone from being 10 percent in control of his life to 50 percent in control. This 40 percent gain was highlighted as remarkable given that he had been 90 percent out of control of his life for the two years previously.

Jason and Tony agreed that they would prefer to continue working on these changes with Jason at home rather than in the unit. A similar experiment was suggested to help them consolidate the changes, to be reviewed at the next session in four weeks time.

After the formal interview, a small celebration was held to mark Jason's discharge from the residential program, and to mark the change in the context of the family's struggle against the problems. They had completed their experimentation apart, and were now going on to continue and consolidate the changes together at home This change of status is significant and needs to be marked—the celebration acts as a ritual to help all concerned to notice and believe in the changes that have occurred.

The celebration was simple but significant. The therapy team came out from behind the screen and joined in, and other staff and residents in the unit came into the room. Jason and Tony cut the cake together and distributed the pieces. The therapist made a short speech congratulating them on what they had achieved, and this was reinforced by a speech by a youth worker commenting on Jason's progress in the unit. A couple of the other adolescent residents congratulated Jason on what he had done and compared this with their own struggles. Tony then made a statement about how he had learned a lot about not stepping in and taking responsibility for Jason, and thanked the residential staff for their work with Jason. He felt that they both had made a lot of progress and had higher hopes now for Jason's future. Jason thanked the staff for their help in sorting out some of these problems.

Sixth Session (Four Weeks Later)

Tony and Jason reported that the positive changes had persisted, and that now Jason even seemed to be getting on better with Tony's girlfriend. Tony identified more areas where he felt he was giving over responsibility to Jason. At present Jason was taking responsibility for making some decisions about employment, as he was neither working nor attending school. Tony felt that Jason had taken further steps to earn back trust. He said Jason seemed to be more reliable about letting him know his movements.

The team was astonished to hear of an incident in which Jason had gone to a party but had come home at 9:30 P.M. saying that people there were getting into drinking too much. This was clear evidence of a person being able to take responsibility for making his own decisions. This was evidence of him having changed from being a slave to impulse and a slave to a drug-abusing lifestyle to being a person more in control of his own life.

After further discussions, the therapist proposed that the steps they were each taking meant that they did not need to continue therapy on a regular basis and they agreed to meet in three months for a follow-up session.

Three Months Later

Tony and Jason did not attend the scheduled interview as they were moving house. Tony telephoned to say that the situation with Jason had been progressing reasonably and that Jason had not returned to his old patterns of behaviour. He was sure that Jason was no longer using alcohol or other drugs and was no longer involved in the drug and prostitution scene. However, he expressed some concern that Jason was neither attending school nor working. Tony was adamant that his concern would not lead him into taking responsibility for this problem, and he was leaving it to Jason to do the work of looking for employment whilst staying alert for any invitations that he should rescue Jason financially.

Attempts to arrange another appointment for the two of them proved difficult, however Jason came for a final session in which the ups and downs of the last three months were reviewed. The therapist raised some questions to help him to think about the pressures that would face him over the next few months and highlighted the fact that he had not run away and was now facing the pressures of responsibility at home. Questions encouraged Jason to identify the differences between his lifestyle now and that previously, to comment on what he had learned about himself and to predict how his future would be different from the direction in which it had been heading. These discussions were intended to help Jason strengthen his emerging new view of himself and encourage him to make sense of events and behaviour in terms of responsibility and self-reliance. He agreed with the therapist that he had achieved a change of lifestyle and was encouraged to share his secret that was enabling him to keep living a life that was so different from the street life and drug-involved life that he pursued in the past.

He said that he saw obtaining work as the next step for him and it was clear that Jason was taking responsibility for thinking about this problem, was not expecting someone to arrange a job for him, and was aware of some of the pressures that would face him over the next few months.

The therapist congratulated Jason again, and asked if he would consider allowing himself to share his experiences with other young people and their families who were being dominated by lives of irresponsibility and enslavement to drugs. Jason was surprised that others might benefit from his struggles, but was happy to give his permission. His *consultant* status was in marked contrast to his view of himself at the beginning of therapy and was another way of encouraging him to draw distinctions and build on his new view of his own competence.[10]

LIMITATIONS OF THE APPROACH

The approach is one which focuses on restraints and interactions rather than on particular classes of problems. It rests upon some fundamental assumptions about how people operate in the world of the living, how information is transmitted and how behaviour responds to this. As such, the approach is potentially applicable to the broad range of human problems. In addition to the usual family therapy arenas of child and adolescent behaviour problems, White's cybernetic framework has been applied to serious psychiatric problems (Mackenzie & Gara, 1986; White, 1987), child sexual assault (Durrant, 1987), domestic violence (White, 1986d) and treatment of male incest perpetrators (Jenkins, 1987). In each of these areas, as in others, the task is to apply the essential ideas to the particular restraints operating in the particular problem situations. Of course, some situations and problems reflect stronger restrained ideas (in therapists as well as clients) than others, some clients are more difficult to engage in a co-operative process of building new descriptions than others, and some problems challenge a therapist's commitment to negative explanation more than others.

EFFECTIVENESS

White's approach has evolved over the last ten years and new ideas and refinements have been included along the way. As such, definitive studies of its effectiveness are sparse. We (with our colleague, Gerard Menses) have an abundance of anecdotal evidence of the effectiveness of the approach with so-called delinquent adolescents in the residential care context. Over a four-year period, over 300 adolescents and families have been treated and informal follow-up reveals not only an increased

[10]White and Epston have developed a number of ways to reverse the status of clients by engaging them as expert consultants. These include inviting the family to make a special videotape to record their success, paying them a fee for permission to use their story, and so on, see Epston and White (1985).

rate of families reporting resolution of the presenting problem, but also a significant decrease in the average length of residential admission (as compared to the same agency prior to adopting this approach). Other therapists who have used White's approach over a number of years have similar reports and the growth of the approach in a variety of therapy settings in Australia testifies that therapists, at least, consider it useful.

White's first paper on his approach (1983) includes data on eleven anorexic adolescents who presented in nutritional crisis. All but two showed significant improvement in terms of weight gain and psychosocial measures on follow-ups ranging from two to five years. White (1988) reports that non-systematic follow-up of more than 70 cases of encopresis treated during the development of his ideas (1984a) resulted in symptom resolution in more than 70 percent of cases.

White's ideas have been challenged and refined in his work with schizophrenic clients, particularly his work at Glenside Psychiatric Hospital, Adelaide, over a number of years. A recent study of this work (Hafner, 1987) is the closest to a formal study of effectiveness. Thirty-five chronic schizophrenic clients who were referred with their families to the family therapy unit were compared to a control group of similar size. Treatments were identical apart from family therapy. Over a two-year follow-up, the family therapy group showed a reduction in average hospital admission of 35 days to 14 days, whilst the control group showed a significant increase in the length of admissions.

Only informal or anecdotal evidence exists concerning the use of the approach with substance abusing adolescents.

ROLE OF ADJUNCTIVE THERAPIES AND SELF-HELP GROUPS

In working with alcohol and drug abusers, attention must be paid to the beliefs or ideas that such people have about themselves and their problem. These beliefs may work against users really taking responsibility for their habits, and stop them really seeing the implications of continued use. Other forms of treatment must be evaluated in terms of the beliefs or ideas that they impart. They may inadvertently perpetuate restraining ideas that reinforce problem-oriented ways of participating. For example, a programme that rests on the belief that "once an addict, always an addict" necessarily contributes to a context in which clients can never really feel like they have beaten the problem. So, even an addict who is currently not using is left with substantially the same ideas about him or herself. Instead of gaining ideas of strength, competence, and success, they are left with ideas of weakness, vulnerability, and imminent failure. Such a context inevitably leads to an increased likelihood of failure being noticed and does not contribute to ideas that foster higher self-esteem and continued control.

Treatment itself sometimes mitigates against its own effectiveness in ways similar to the participation of the family. Family members often end up taking responsibility for the addict, virtually running his or her life. Restrained by ideas that this is the only way to ensure compliance with undertakings to remain drug-free, they may protect the user from the consequences of use, perhaps through loyalty, guilt, or a belief that further pressure will only make things worse. The client gets no practice at taking responsibility for his or her own life, and so it is not surprising that he or she cannot exercise responsibility with regard to decisions about drugs. Treatment programmes and helping professionals sometimes assume the same role, expecting the client to take responsibility for his or her habit within the context of the professionals taking responsibility for everything else.

Clients simultaneously undergoing other therapies or being involved in self-help groups is often a factor in therapy seeming stuck. This may be attributed to the conflict between a therapy that seeks to encourage new meanings and new ideas about the problem and a therapy that promotes familiar ideas and participation. The new is easily lost if it is not encouraged to persist, and therapy based on different premises may discourage such persistence. That is not to say that clients should never be involved in other forms of treatment. A decision by a client to join a group that provides a context for discussing and sharing successful struggles might be applauded as a decision to continue practicing a new direction (and joining a group to learn new skills or pursue new interests that might reflect such a decision than joining a drug-oriented group). A decision to join a group that focuses on failure or allows members to share their restrained views of themselves and their problems might be seen as a decision to continue practicing old ways.

When physical detoxification is required, the effects on therapy will depend on the context in which it occurs. A therapist might wonder if a decision to *dry out* is an important step on the path of a new direction in life. This could be contrasted with a decision to dry out as yet another step on the drug merry-go-round, a way of simply slowing down physical problems before embarking on more surrender to a drug-using lifestyle. A therapist might even wonder if the client should arrange regular bookings for the detoxification unit for the next few years, probably at progressively shorter intervals. In this way, the physical treatment may be placed within a context that encourages distinctions to be drawn.

After detoxification, this step might be used to create a context that implies a dilemma around the direction the future will take from now.

REFERENCES

Bateson, G. (1972). *Steps to an ecology of mind.* NY: Ballantine Books. (Quotations from 1985, Ballantine edition).

Bateson, G. (1979). *Mind and nature: A necessary unity.* London: Wildwood House. (Quotations from 1985, Fontana edition)

Coles, D. (1986). "Taking a temper apart." *Family Therapy Case Studies, 1*(1), 35–41.

Durrant, M. (1985a). "Temper taming." *Eastwood Family Therapy Centre Monograph.*

Durrant, M. (1985b). "Bowling out fears—Test victory for double description." *Dulwich Centre Review,* 17–27. (Also *The Journal of Family Therapy,* 1987).

Durrant, M. (1986). "The therapist obsessed: A struggle to get unstuck in therapy." *Family Therapy Case Studies, 1*(2), 37–49.

Durrant, M. (1987). "Therapy with young people who have been the victims of sexual assault." *Family Therapy Case Studies, 2*(1), 57–63.

Elms, R. (1986). "To tame a temper: Cybernetic therapy and contextual residential care." *Family Therapy Case Studies, 1*(2), 51–58.

Epston, D. (1986). "Night watching: An approach to night fears." *Dulwich Centre Review,* 28–39.

Epston, D. (1987). "A reflexion." *Dulwich Centre Newsletter,* Summer, 16–17.

Epston, D. & White, M. (1985). "Consulting your consultants' consultants." *Proceedings of the Sixth Australian Family Therapy Conference,* Victoria Association of Family Therapy, Melbourne.

Hafner, J. (1987). "The Glenside Hospital Family Therapy Unit: An evaluation study." *Unpublished manuscript,* Adelaide.

Jenkins, A. (1986). "Engaging the male incest perpetrator: Practical approaches for intervention in child sexual abuse within families." *Presentation to the Seventh Australian Family Therapy Conference,* Perth, Australia.

Mackenzie, E. & Gara, A. (1986). "An uphill battle: Wrestling back responsibility in the psychiatric system." *Family Therapy Case Studies, 1*(2), 59–66.

Maruyama, M. (1974). "The second cybernetics: Deviation—amplifying mutual causative processes." *American Scientist,* 51, 164–179.

Menses, G. & Durrant, M. (1986). "Contextual residential care: Applying the principles of cybernetic therapy to the residential treatment of irresponsible adolescents and their families." *Dulwich Centre Review,* 3–13 (also *Journal Strategic & Systemic Therapies,* Summer 1987).

Munro, C. (1987). "White and the cybernetic therapies: News of difference. *Australian & New Zealand Journal of Family Therapy, 8*(4), 183–192.

Turner, V. & Bruner, E. M. (eds.), (1986). *The anthropology of experience.* Chicago: University of Illinois Press.

Van Gennep, A. (1960). *Rites of passage.* Chicago: University of Chicago Press.

Watzlawick, P., Weakland, J. H. & Fisch, R. (1974). *Change: Principles of problem formation and problem resolution.* New York: Norton.

Wender, P. H. (1968). "Vicious and virtuous cycles: The role of deviation amplifying feedback in the origin and perpetuation of behaviour." *Psychiatry,* 31, 309–324.

White, M. (1983). "Anorexia nervosa: A transgenerational systems perspective." *Family Process, 22*(3), 255–273.

White, M. (1984a). "Pseudoencopresis: From avalanche to victory, from vicious to virtuous cycles." *Family Systems Medicine, 2*(2), 150–160.

White, M. (1984b). "Marital therapy: Practical solutions to longstanding problems." *Australian Journal of Family Therapy, 5*(1), 27–43.

White, M. (1985). "Problems of Adolescence." *Proceedings of Sixth Australian Family Therapy Conference,* Melbourne, Australia.

White, M. (1986a). "Negative explanation, restraint and double description: A template for family therapy." *Family Process, 25*(2), 169–184.

White, M. (1986b). "Family escape from trouble." *Family Therapy Case Studies, 1*(1), 29–33.

White, M. (1986c). "Anorexia nervosa: A cybernetic perspective." in J. Elka-Harkary (ed.), *Eating Disorders and Family Therapy.* NY: Aspen.

White, M. (1986d). "The conjoint therapy of men who are violent and the women with whom they live." *Dulwich Centre Newsletter,* Adelaide, Australia.

White, M. (1987). "Family therapy and schizophrenia: Addressing the 'in-the-corner' lifestyle." *Dulwich Centre Newsletter,* Adelaide, Australia.

White, M. (1988). Personal communication.

8

Opening the Door for Change Through Continuing Conversations*

HARLENE ANDERSON, Ph.D.
Co-Director
Galveston Family Institute
Galveston, TX

Clinical cases in which adolescent substance abuse is an issue are multifaceted and carry the spoken or unspoken mandate—"Fix it!" while therapists are often asked, "But how?" I am not sure of the answer to that challenging question, nor am I sure that that is the question.

Today such cases represent an ever-growing number of treatment failures and mandated referrals; the ideas presented in this chapter represent one way of thinking about and working with such cases. First, I will describe a consultation with a student that stemmed from a school psychologist's alarm and concern for the student. Then, I will describe my thinking and how it informed the consultation process.

THE CANDY CASE

The school psychologist received a call from the aunt of a 16-year-old student. The aunt was upset and alarmed because her niece, Candy, had

*The work described in this paper reflects one application of an evolving clinical theory with which my colleague Harold Goolishian and I have been experimenting as we continue to search for innovative ways to work with difficult clinical situations and to describe our work. (See Goolishian & Anderson, 1987 and Anderson & Goolishian, 1988.)

I would like to thank Fran Araujo of the Wes Ros Park Family Therapy Team for her helpful comments on this chapter.

been acting crazy. She reported that Candy was "cutting her clothes with scissors," saying that "the devil was telling her to do it," and was "having temper tantrums" (cursing and throwing things) whenever anyone tried to stop her.

The psychologist learned that similar episodes had occurred with increasing frequency over the last couple of months. Recently, the aunt had become concerned that her eight-year-old daughter and the other children in the family were being affected by Candy's outbursts and the family commotion associated with the outbursts. Living in the family home were Candy, Aunt Marie, her eight-year-old daughter, Uncle Bob, his wife Barbara, their two sons, ages five and eleven, and Arthur, the 73-year-old maternal grandfather. Candy's mother lived in town, but reportedly was not involved with the family. Candy's father had disappeared years earlier.

In talking with the aunt, the psychologist decided that there was no immediate danger, but that the situation merited a quick response. She offered to meet with the family within the next two days. The psychologist suggested that the aunt come in with Candy and said that it would help her to learn more about Candy if the grandfather, the uncle, and his wife could come as well.

Candy and her family were familiar to the psychologist. Although she had no personal contact with them, they were well known as one of those multiproblem families. The psychologist inquired at the main office and learned that Candy had not been attending school for the last three weeks and was failing all subjects. She also learned that Candy's cousins had poor school attendance records and that the uncle's oldest son was frequently in the nurse's office with stomachaches and headaches.

The next day the aunt, Candy, the grandfather, and the uncle and his wife came for the appointment. The grandfather introduced himself and the others. "I'm Arthur," he said, "head of the clan; this is my son, Bob. Marie and Candy, here, are my daughters." During the meeting, the psychologist learned the family members' views about what was going on with Candy: The grandfather thought that she was "just like her mother and Uncle Bob," both of whom had had these kinds of "fits" and had done "stupid things" when they were growing up. Candy, too, would grow out of this, he thought. Aunt Marie, who recently had moved back to the family home because of divorce, felt that Candy had always had problems; she believed strongly that Candy's problems were related to her abandonment by her mother at an early age. Marie said that things had become worse since the grandmother died a year ago and since Candy had started hanging out with her boyfriend and his friends, who were rumored to be involved with drugs. Uncle Bob was most concerned about her poor school attendance and performance; his wife thought that Candy needed discipline and clarification as to who was really responsible for her. When the psychologist asked about Candy's use and access to drugs and alcohol, the grandfather said that he used to be an alcoholic but had "licked it." Uncle Bob said that he drank a little. Neither thought that Candy was drinking or using drugs. Both aunts, however, were worried that Candy was involved with drugs because it was rumored that her boyfriend was a drug user.

It was also learned that two days earlier, Candy and her boyfriend had been questioned by juvenile authorities on the suspicion that they were involved with other youths who had been burning crosses in neighborhood yards and then calling the fire department to report the fires claiming that the devil started them. Candy consistently denied the use of drugs and said that the scissors incidents were "no big deal, besides," she added, "life is boring." When the psychologist asked to whom Candy felt responsible, she replied, "I have three mothers—Aunt Marie, Aunt Barbara, and my real mother."

The school psychologist was worried and puzzled about Candy. What was the problem? Was it a psychological problem related to the family situation? Was it drugs? Was it a discipline problem? Was it the influence of the boyfriend? The psychologist suggested that she meet alone with Candy the next day and meet with the family again after that. She also obtained permission to call juvenile authorities to learn what information they had about Candy's involvement with the cross burnings. The juvenile officer who investigated the case reported that they had not officially opened a record on Candy, but were investigating her boyfriend for the cross burnings and the suspicion of burglary.

In the individual meeting, Candy confessed that she and her boyfriend had been involved in the cross burnings, but said they did it for excitement and did not see what all the fuss was about. The psychologist also learned that Candy's mother called her almost daily, but that the rest of the family tried to prevent her from seeing her mother because they thought her mother was an alcoholic, therefore, a bad influence on Candy. She learned further that Candy frequently hitchhiked and picked up men at shopping malls. Candy also said that she thought both her grandfather and her Uncle Bob drank too much. Once again she denied drinking or using drugs. The psychologist became alarmed (remembering the scissors events) when Candy pulled a camera flashbulb from her pocket during the meeting and chewed on it until the glass broke. The psychologist believed that these *impulsive behaviors* suggested severe emotional difficulties associated either with drugs or with the family situation. The psychologist was anxious to meet with the family on the following day.

Candy and Aunt Marie came for the next family meeting. Aunt Marie restated her belief that Candy needed intensive psychological help; she felt that Candy was in an unstable family environment which could not provide what was needed. She believed that Grandfather Arthur, although he meant well, was getting too old to handle Candy; Bob and Barbara had their own problems; and Candy's mother, because of her drinking problem, was of no help at all. Marie was particularly upset because she felt that Candy did not appreciate how much love and concern she had shown her. Candy, on the other hand, felt that things had gone all right until Marie moved in and "tried to take over the house." Most of the conversation centered around the multiple mother roles and who was responsible for Candy. The psychologist asked if it would be possible for Candy's mother to join them for a family session. The aunt replied, "If she's sober."

The next morning the psychologist received a call from Aunt Marie, saying that Candy had one of her temper tantrums the previous night and later was found in her bedroom, picking her bleeding arm with a piece of glass. Aunt Marie insisted that the psychologist find some immediate help for Candy before the situation went out of control. The school psychologist, even more aware of the seriousness of the problem, asked the school's crisis team for a consultation.

The crisis team believed that the situation was grave enough to warrant an inpatient evaluation of Candy's psychological status and suspected drug use. The psychologist called Aunt Marie to discuss the recommendation. Aunt Marie agreed with the idea of hospitalization, but said that the grandfather and the uncle did not agree; she had not talked with Candy's mother. The psychologist said she felt that Candy was self-destructive and could have been committed for evaluation on that basis. She was concerned about Candy's safety and, yet, hoped to establish a working alliance with the family, so she chose not to pursue hospitalization, but scheduled a family meeting for the following day. She insisted that everyone attend.

Candy, her mother, and Aunt Marie arrived for the meeting. Candy's mother held firm to the idea that there was nothing wrong with Candy except that "she has been spoiled by everyone" and that "she has a mouth." She did not think drugs were a problem, but would not have been surprised if that was the case because Candy "has no supervision in that house." The mother, still Candy's legal guardian, could see no need for an inpatient evaluation. The psychologist urged strongly that the grandfather, uncle, and his wife join the others in the next family meeting because the psychologist said she believed that the adults in the family needed to develop a consistent plan of supervision for Candy and that the effects of the family alcohol problem with regard to Candy's recent problems needed to be addressed. She said she also felt that it was "sad that Candy did not have anyone in the family to attach to" and that "family meetings might provide an avenue in which Candy could feel more bonded to the family."

Aunt Marie arrived alone and reiterated that grandfather, Uncle Bob, and Aunt Barbara had their own problems. Aunt Marie was still extremely worried because Candy was pulling the same "stunts" again and had run away to her boyfriend's house. Aunt Marie demanded hospitalization and said that Candy could not return home even if she wanted to because her behavior was disruptive to the household, particularly upsetting the grandfather and the other children. The psychologist felt that the situation had deteriorated and that the family was not committed to therapy; she conferred with the crisis team again. Frustrated and overwhelmed, the crisis team recommended a consultation with the author.

After listening to the details of the case that the psychologist explained, the consultant (author) suggested that because it was such a complicated case, perhaps *we* need all the input we can get. The consultant, acknowledging that schedules might not permit this luxury, asked whether it would be possible to hold a meeting that would include the school psychologist, the crisis team, the school nurse, and any teachers involved with Candy and the other three children in the house. The consultant also suggested that the school psychologist invite anyone else whom she thought would be helpful.

Establishing Space for Familiar and Fresh Ideas: Beginning a Conversation

Twelve people attended the initial consultation meeting: the psychologist, three crisis team members, the school nurse, two guidance counselors, and five teachers (representing elementary, middle, and secondary schools). After expressing her appreciation, the consultant summarized what she knew about the case. She then said that it would be helpful to hear everyone's ideas about the case and asked attendees to contribute in the following format.

The consultant instructed the attendees to divide into three groups (preferably composed of those who worked together least) to discuss the dilemma(s) or problem(s) they thought this case presented. She also asked one person in each group to participate voluntarily as a silent listener and to listen *as if* he or she were a family member. The listeners could choose to listen as any family member and were asked not to reveal their chosen identities until a given time.

The groups then met for 15 minutes. As they shared their ideas about Candy, the other children, the family, and the school, the consultant wrote the ideas on the blackboard. (The listeners were asked to continue to listen.) As the consultant collected the ideas (multiple and divergent concerns, problem definitions, and solutions) she sorted them by themes and listed them as questions. The following themes and questions emerged:

1. **Legal and safety issues for Candy.** If she is not allowed back home, should the school report the family to child welfare? If she's at her boyfriend's house isn't she at greater risk for legal and drug-related problems? If the family cannot induce her to go to school, how can they persuade her to go to therapy? What drug programs might be available in the community other than inpatient programs? Should the juvenile court be involved, and could the court mandate inpatient treatment?

2. **The school's responsibility in this kind of situation.** Is this problem too severe to expect the school to handle? Should the psychologist work harder to find a hospital or residential placement? Should the school put so much effort into a student who has, for all purposes, dropped out of school? Wasn't it the school's responsibility to develop a curriculum for Candy that would increase the likelihood that she would attend school? Doesn't the school and its teachers have an ethical responsibility to children in families like this? Do schools have the capacity to deal with alcohol and drug abuse? Should this be the responsibility of the family and the large community?

3. **The possible effect of a school on such a chaotic, multiproblem family.** Should the school conduct family therapy? How could the school make a difference? How could the school justify spending so much time and effort with this one family when there are dozens of others just like it? What would happen to the family when the grandfather died? How could the family resolve its members' roles? What could be done about the transgenerational alcohol and drug problems? What expectations are realistic? If the school doesn't help Candy, who will?

4. **The other children.** What about the emotional stability of the 11-year-old boy? The absenteeism of the 11- and five-year-olds? Weren't the other children following in the footsteps of the family? (Someone remembered that Candy's mother had been a school problem and a drop-out.) Because this family has a history of substance abuse, aren't the other children at risk?

5. **Burnout with this and other similar difficult, chronic situa-**

tions. How can professionals maintain any personal and professional energy in the face of hopelessness? Where can teachers turn for support? How can teachers be expected to do their job in the classroom when children have serious problems that block learning? What happens when teachers must depend on counseling staff or public agencies to remove these obstacles to learning?

Continuing the Conversation

The consultant showed enthusiastic interest in the participants' ideas and was careful not to favor any one idea over another. She posed more questions, which helped her appreciate and understand the participants' worries and thoughts; these questions invited speculation and a variety of answers rather than any specific answer. For example, she asked, "If you could implement the ideal solution (to selected problems) without any obstacle, what might it be?" The consultant did not seek facts or move in any direction that might risk premature closure of any idea; she appreciated that different people had different experiences with members of this family under similar as well as diverse circumstances.

As discrepant and sometimes competing and polarized ideas emerged, the consultant showed a tolerance for each idea and wondered aloud about them. She sought multiple opinions from various angles. For example, in response to the burnout issue and with the knowledge that one teacher was soon to retire, she invited him to give his advice, based on his years of experience, as to how professionals could maintain the personal energy necessary to do our job and keep a sense of self-respect. How was this teacher able to "hang in there" so many years? (His attendance at the consultation meeting showed concern and commitment.)

The consultant's continued curiosity and restraint from judging, facilitated further discussion which evolved into a mutual puzzlement and inquiry about the case. The focus of the discussion broadened to include multiple systems and contexts—the family, its individual members, the school, and the community. Predominant ideas, opinions, and biases began to shift and blur. Now the consultant was no longer the expert to whom the questions were addressed and from whom answers were expected; all the participants became collaborators in examining the many facets and aspects of the case.

One Conversation Leads to Another . . . and Another

After this process, the voluntary listeners, who had chosen to listen as Candy, Aunt Marie, and the mother, were asked to describe their experiences of "being talked about." Each listener was filled with responses. As they spoke, the consultant asked questions to help herself and the others understand the listeners' experiences more clearly. She summarized the statements each listener had heard that they reported made them feel understood, respected, and valued—statements that might spark engagement in a conversation. She considered those statements that made them feel misunderstood, blamed, angry, and defensive—statements that might lead to actions that could appear to signal an uncooperative attitude, denial, or resistance; that is, statements that might close-down conversation.

The *voices* of the family members prompted other thoughts and questions. Everyone began to talk back and forth, criss-crossing ideas. People were talking *with* rather than *to* each other. Participants began to have a greater appreciation of the complex, multifaceted nature of the situation. They no longer thought of this family "as just another one of those families," but now were interested in learning more about all the children and understanding more about this family's unique struggle. Participants were reconstructing their original ideas and questions, defining different problems, and providing their own answers.

Hopelessness turned into gentle excitement. Frustration and a linear view of the problem (placing blame, feeling blame) gave way to more complex, more expanded outlooks. After all, they concluded, probably they would encounter generations of students from this family. Even if the participants could not help Candy, maybe they could help prevent problems with the other children and address those concerns that were already developing.

As the group members talked together, sharing their thoughts and feelings about the family situation and their roles, the psychologist expressed a sense of relief. Somehow, the case seemed more workable. Hearing her colleagues' ideas and the family's imagined perspectives gave the psychologist a better grasp of the situation. The others agreed. Yet, they did not have an answer; if anything they had more questions, but somehow answers seemed more forthcoming. Although in some ways the problems now seemed more complicated, paradoxically, they also seemed more manageable. One crisis team member said that rather than looking like one big, looming problem, it now looked more like many big and some not-so-big problems.

The participants began to sort out what they were dealing with and what to think in terms of multiple problems, goals, and strategies for reaching those goals. They also developed an awareness of timing and pacing. Maybe some goals could be tackled simultaneously, while some might have to be approached in a step-by-step fashion. What is *our* next step?, the consultant wondered as she summarized the latest questions.

Could they begin to explore curriculum for the summer and fall for both Candy and the other children? Which family member did it make the most sense to work with, to be in conversation with? How could team members address the problems better as each family member saw them? Could Candy be engaged in individual therapy? Would it make sense to try to see Candy and her boyfriend together? Were there any nonresidential drug treatment programs in the community available for Candy? (They had not determined whether Candy was involved with drugs, but they were certain that she was at risk.) Who was in the best position to befriend and influence Candy? What kind of pressure could the school district exert when it deemed a student in need of hospital evaluation or treatment and when the parents did not?

The consultant's aim was not to collect more data, to arrive at more accurate descriptions of the family, or to develop more useful definitions of the problem; nor was it to encourage, manipulate, or steer the group toward a particular solution or outcome. The consultant gave no indication that she was searching for any right or particular answer. She sought to create a context that invited people to contribute ideas jointly and to engage in mutual concern and inquiry. She wished to generate and preserve multiple ideas rather than seeking synthesis or consensus. Differences and uncertainties were appreciated; questions were the starting points for generating and clarifying. Through this process, the consultant began a conversation that created an opportunity for further conversations.

The Next Conversation

Two months later, the consultant contacted the school psychologist for a follow-up consultation. The school psychologist reported that the situation with Candy had changed slightly. Candy was not at home permanently, but sometimes she lived at home and at other times she stayed at different friends' homes. Candy did keep in touch with Aunt Marie, however, always letting her aunt know where she was. In addition, Candy had been working for six weeks at a donut shop. Uncle Bob and his family had moved to an apartment of their own, while Aunt Marie had decided to stay in the family home. Candy had completed a 30-day drug education program sponsored by the Juvenile Court, and had tested drug-free at the beginning and end of the program.

The psychologist was still concerned with Candy's emotional fragility, but felt that Candy was less impulsive than in the past. The psychologist was not optimistic that Candy would return to regular school in the fall, but the psychologist planned to investigate the possibility of a vocational program for Candy. The psychologist believed that the other children's teachers were continuing to keep in touch with each other and were sharing their concerns. The school psychologist, herself, was busy planning a new program that had been approved by the Board of Education in which she would offer substance abuse training for teachers in the district. She planned to incorporate substance abuse education and awareness, not only as part of the health and physical education curriculum, but also as an experiential part of other courses. In the social sciences, for example, students would write essays and do projects on issues such as the effects of substance abuse on industry, the economy, and the family.

THE EVOLVING CLINICAL THEORY THAT INFORMS THIS WORK

This consultation process draws on the philosophical notions of constructivism (a subject-dependent construction of reality and knowledge), hermeneutics (methods of interpretation), and linguistic domains (communication as behavior and as a generative process in a language domain) (Braten, 1987; von Foerster, 1981; Gadamer, 1975; von Glasersfeld, 1986; Maturana & Varela, 1987; Rorty, 1979; Wachterhauser, 1986; Watzlawick, 1984). These philosophical notions have significant implications for the concepts of the therapy system, the therapeutic process, and the therapist's role. These ideas influence a movement from thinking of human systems as social systems to regarding them as communicating or meaning-generating systems (Goolishian & Anderson, 1987; Anderson & Goolishian, 1988). That is, communication is not considered a product of social organization; rather social organization is considered a product of communication. Stated differently, social organization, including structure and role, stems from social communication—from language interaction. Hence, human systems are communicative or linguistic systems in which communication has relevance.

On the basis of this perspective, human systems are communicative or linguistic systems, the systems that therapists work with in therapy or consultation are considered as one kind of linguistic system, or what have been called elsewhere problem-determined systems (Anderson, Goolishian & Winderman, 1986) and problem-organizing, problem dissolving systems (POPD systems) (Anderson & Goolishian, 1988; Goolishian & Anderson, 1987). The individuals within the problem context constitute a social action system defined on the basis of communicative interaction. The system to be treated includes those who are in a *languaged* context concerning a problem. A POPD system is a system for which communication has relevance. The relevance is the problem; thus, the system is distinguished by the problem, rather than distinguishing the problem. It is a social system that is organized around *languaging* about issues that are considered problematic by those who constitute the system. Because such a system exists in language, familiar, social organization boundaries punctuated by social structure and role, such as individual, couple, family, or larger system, do not apply. Those who are in relevant communication with one another at any point in time can belong to any of the systems listed or any combinations of them. That is, the problem system can be a single or a multiperson system. The difference is that the membership of the system is defined by communicative action occurring between and among those persons concerned or alarmed about a problem; it is not defined by persons joined together by social organization boundaries.

In the Candy Case, the school psychologist requested a consultation on the family. While responding to the request, the consultant was not listening for data about the family and the school, nor information that would lead to a formulation or hypothesis about the problem. Instead, she wished to form an idea about who was concerned or alarmed and about what, and who was talking with whom. On the basis of the initial conversation with the school psychologist, the problem-organizing, problem-dissolving system seemed to include the family members, the school psychologist, the crisis team, the school nurse, possibly a few teachers, and now the consultant, herself. She did not regard the membership of the POPD system as including systems defined by social organization, each encircled by another in a hierarchical or layered fashion, such as Candy encircled by the family, the family encircled by the school, nor the school encircled by the larger community. Instead, she conceptualized the problem-organizing, problem-dissolving system as horizontal consisting of several persons with multiple problems in varying degrees, some similar to one another's, and some not.

Once a problem system has made contact with a therapist, a consultant, or any other helper, those persons are considered part of the problem-organizing, problem-dissolving system. Because a problem system is conceptualized as nonhierarchical, its process is collaborative. As an equal participant in a collaborative process, the therapist moves away from a position of knowing, diagnosing, and healing, and away from nonarbitrary problem-defining and problem-solving. Rather, the therapist moves to a position that promotes a shared problem defining and solving process. In other words, all exploration of the problem(s) and its solution(s) becomes mutual.

Therefore, a therapist (or, for example, the consultant in the Candy Case) considers herself a member of the problem system as soon as she finds herself in conversation with any member of that system. When conversation begins, in this case with the telephone call requesting the consultation, the consultant becomes actively involved in defining and solving the problem(s). From this viewpoint, the consultant is not an expert (for example, on families, substance abuse, or any other social system or problem), who solves problems from a metaposition. Rather, the consultant's expertise, talents, and skills are in those of beginning and sustaining a dialogical conversation. The therapist's role is *to create a space* in which the therapeutic process can occur and *to facilitate that process* (Anderson & Goolishian, 1988; Goolishian & Anderson, 1987).

The therapeutic process, the activity of the problem-organizing, problem-dissolving system, is regarded as a *therapeutic conversation,* namely a dialogical conversation in which people are talking *with* and listening *to* others. This process is a mutual sharing and exploring of familiar understandings; it is a collaborative effort that permits new ways to talk and think about the problem and its solution. The desired outcome of the therapeutic conversation is to solve the problem and to dissolve the problem-organizing, problem-dissolving system. The therapist does not pursue preconceived ideas about any particular outcome or solution; he or she is interested only in creating an environment in which dialogical exchange(s) can be initiated and sustained, and through which the need for conversations with a therapist or a consultant disappears.

Who should be in conversation with whom and when? This question is answered step by step; each conversation and its membership informs the next. In the Candy Case, for example, the consultant suggested that she meet (to continue the conversation she had begun with the school psychologist) with any of the following persons who would be available: the psychologist, the crisis team members, the school nurse, and teachers of the other children. Her manner and tone showed an interest in and a respect for the psychologist and her colleagues' concerns. She did not want to indicate in any way that she thought (and she did not think) that any of them was the problem and needed to be "fixed." She was, however, open to any hesitancy, disagreement, or suggestion from the school psychologist about who should attend this meeting. This openness is part of a position of mutuality and modesty, of showing interest in and respect for and about people and their ideas. It is part of the co-construction of a therapeutic process, a therapeutic reality that is opening and expanding and allows room for multiple, familiar views and unexplored possibilities.

In the Candy Case, the consultant continued to show her genuine interest in and value for others' ideas as she learned nonselectively about all the participants' ideas. Various methods such as using the blackboard and listening *as if* facilitated this position. The use of the blackboard not only helps one's memory, but is a way to explore visually and to shuffle familiar information and predominant perspectives. It also shows the consultant's seriousness regarding the others' dilemmas.

Listening *as if* helps participants to move away from being experts on knowing any member of the problem system, whether a family member or a colleague. That is, it helps them move out of observer-independent thinking ruts (which often are accusing and disapproving) and to move toward sensitivity and curiosity about how each family member understands the problem and imagines the solution.

In the Candy Case a dialogical conversation developed between the consultant and the participants and among the participants. This kind of process also allows participants to initiate dialogical conversations within their own heads. When problems seem overwhelming and attempted solutions have been unsuccessful, the hindrance can be that one is in a thinking rut because an idea or a group of ideas dominate thinking and conversation. Therefore, conversation becomes a static rather than a dynamic process. The consultant in the Candy Case was interested in establishing a dynamic conversation, inviting others to take part, and succeeding in the invitation. A partnership conversation was created, and the need for further consultation disappeared.

CONCLUSION

How one treats adolescent drug abuse is a complicated question that involves individual, family, community, and political parameters. We are all familiar with situations like the Candy Case that present knotty clinical and life issues to us as professionals. Such cases push the limits of our theory and practice. They demand our creativity. These cases are filled with pitfalls: It is hard to move outside our familiar ideas when they are not working; it is seductive to listen to our own voice rather than to another's; it is easy to have premature knowledge and tempting to exclude the expertise of other people. The approach described in this chapter has helped me avoid or at least minimize some of these pitfalls as well as others that I believe interfere with clinical creativity. Such pitfalls can prevent professionals from tapping the innovativeness and strengths of those who come to us for help.

Even so, questions arise about the limitations of this approach. In the Candy Case, for example, did the approach address what has been described as the transgenerational substance abuse problem and the chaotic family situation? Does this approach limit the therapist's or the consultant's ability to use acquired professional expertise and experience? Won't people who seek therapy and consultation be upset when the therapist does not provide solutions? Isn't this approach merely old wine in new bottles? These questions remain worthy of further exploration.

REFERENCES

Anderson, H. & Goolishian, H. (1988). Human systems as linguistic systems: Some preliminary and evolving ideas about the implications for clinical theory. *Family Process,* 27(4), 371–395.

Anderson, H., Goolishian, H., Pulliam, G., & Winderman, L. (1986). The Galveston Family Institute: Some personal and historical perspectives. In Don Efron (ed.). *Journeys: Expansions of the Strategic and Systemic Therapies.* New York: Brunner/Mazel.

Braten, S. (1987). Paradigms of autonomy: Dialogical or monological? In G. Teubner (ed.), *Autopoiesis in Law and Society.* New York: EUI.

von Foerster, H. (1981). *Observing Systems.* Seaside, CA: Intersystems Publications.

Gadamer, H. (1975). *Truth and Method.* New York: Seabury Press.

Goolishian, H. & Anderson, H. (1987). Language systems and therapy: An evolving idea. *Psychotherapy.* 24, 529–538.

von Glasersfeld, E. (1986). Steps in the constructions of "others" and reality: A study in self-regulation. In R. Trapp (ed.), *Power, Autonomy Utopia: Toward Complex Systems.* New York: Plenum Press.

Maturana, H. & Varela, F. (1987). *The Tree of Knowledge.* Boston: New Science Library, Shambhala Publications.

Rorty R. (1979). *Philosophy and the Mirror of Nature.* Princeton, NJ: Princeton University Press.

Wachterhauser, B. R. (1986). *Hermeneutics and Modern Philosophy.* Albany: State University of New York Press.

Watzlawick, P. (1984). *The Invented Reality.* New York: Norton.

9

Strategic Inpatient Family Therapy with Adolescent Substance Abusers

The Fox System

MICHAEL R. FOX, M.D.
Assistant Clinical Professor of Psychiatry
John Hopkins University
Baltimore, MD

INTRODUCTION

The treatment of any chronically, disturbing behavior, especially substance abuse, requires several systems to be effectively addressed simultaneously—the disturbing person, his or her family and the medical context and/or social control agencies with which they frequently interface.

This chapter discusses an approach that seeks to empower family members, institutions, therapists, physicians and social control agents. Since 1978, this approach has been used in traditional psychiatric units in two general hospitals, two university hospitals, a state hospital, and a state adolescent residential center. The effect has been to minimize the negative systemic effects of hospitalization, residential treatment, and medication on the family system that frequently hinder change, while simultaneously enhancing collaboration between all involved. Though never used before in a chemical dependency unit, I see no reason why it should not be as effective.

This is the right approach for me, but may not be the right approach for you. There are many *right ways* to an effective solution. It is a structure, a therapeutic process, within which any theoretical framework can function.

Until now, Strategic Therapy and inpatient treatment have been usually considered incongruent because of the noncontextual focus on the hospitalized family member (HFM). The authority struggles between non-hospitalized family members (NHFM), the disturbing person, the staff, the therapist, and the physician often lead to little systemic change with the therapist frequently losing the struggle. Family therapy is traditionally used as an adjunct to the individual treatment, for example, to obtain history, educate, keep a hesitant patient in the institution, and frequently to blame families when conflicts arise in treatment.

This approach creates an alternative to traditional inpatient treatment by changing the decision-making process. It transfers complete authority in decision making to the responsibly acting NHFM and incorporates the entire family system into the treatment system. It is derived from Strategic Therapy principles and social learning strategies as outlined by Haley, Madanes, Watzlawick, Weakland, Fisch, de Shazer, Stuart, and others. My interpretation of their work, however, should not be construed as representing their thoughts.

PRINCIPLES OF THE FOX SYSTEM

Strategic Therapy is commonly assumed to constitute a theory of causality. In fact, it forms a theory of change, a conceptualization of problem definition and resolution (Haley, 1963, 1976, 1980; Watzlawick et al., 1974; Fisch et al., 1982). It is a theory of *how* to go about changing a problem once it has become a problem, not a theory of *what* caused the problem to become a problem. It focuses upon solutions, rather than causes (de Shazer, 1985).

By avoiding the medical context, many before me have tried to promote change by reframing the behavior away from the *illness metaphor.* The Fox System finds it more successful to accept the illness definition when used by the family and the systems surrounding them. Instead, it works through changing *how* solutions deemed appropriate by the family, society, and the medical context are carried out (mandatory treatment, incarceration, medication, and institutionalization).

Solutions are derived from a process of decision making within the family and surrounding the treatment system. If we view unsuccessful solutions as the result of a habituated decision-making process involving everyone concerned, then therapy must inevitably focus on changing the decision-making process of the entire system. We must focus on changing *how* everyone goes about deciding *what* is done to change the disturbing behavior, in order to not just develop different solutions, but also different ways of deciding those different solutions. Thus, and especially in abusive situations, we should ultimately look at how power is distributed and how that distribution effects the decision-making process and the attempted solutions.

Regardless of other obvious social, biological, and psychological factors, the Fox System assumes that the task of changing a problem must consider issues of power distribution (Bepko & Krestan, 1985). All seemingly unsolvable problems and their previous ineffective solutions can be seen as a disorder of power. Others have pointed out how power is accrued within the context of a person's meaningful relationships as a result of having a difficulty or illness (Haley, 1976, 1980; Madanes, 1981, 1984). However, few have addressed how to neutralize the covert power accrued by the patient when medication, institutionalization, and social control agents are used.

Traditionally, the disturbing person's problems have been seen as exclusively derived from the biogenetic and/or socially-learned context of the individual or family. This approach also views the disturbing person's symptoms as resulting from perceiving himself or herself as lacking the necessary influence to effect a change in those relationships that are presently disturbing. Frequently, he or she responds with coercive behavior that is injurious to self or others. Of course, other family members are simultaneously experiencing the same frustration with the disturbing person, feeling similarly disempowered and acting coercively towards him or her.

The question is, "Can symptoms, behavior, and ineffective solutions be viewed as an outgrowth, an expression, of everyone perceiving themselves to be powerless in overtly influencing the disturbing person, while simultaneously discovering the covert power his or her symptoms afford him or her vis-a-vis other family members?"

Using this premise, everyone in the family will feel powerless. Eventually someone will approach experts, often within the medical context, whom he or she assumes are powerful enough to effect change. All too frequently, the medical context soon begins experiencing the same frustration with the inability to change or maintain a change in the disturbing person. Eventually the medical experts experience disempowerment themselves. Regardless of where treatment occurs, the total treatment system is frequently disempowered from effectively helping, and often in the face of effective treatments. This is the issue that must be addressed if further advances are to be made in treating violent, drug-addicted, and/or mentally ill individuals and their families.

Systems thinking assumes that power is a property of the total system, not of individuals. The power to change or to maintain a problem, does not lie within individuals, whether they be family members, physicians, therapists, social control agents, staff, or institutions. Instead, the power lies in *how* individuals relate to each other, not just in *what* they do. It lies in the rules governing the process of decision making.

It is important as agents of change, to recognize that we have absolutely and unequivocally no power. That is, no direct power to create change. If we think we do, we are fooling ourselves and becoming part of the problem. In order to effect change, we must accept that we accrue power only to the extent it is given to us by those we are attempting to help, such as the disturbing person, family members, and those professionals, agents of social control, and institutions brought into the problem by the family—all those to whom we are answerable and who have hired us to help them. We must arrange a situation where everyone involved allows us to disempower the disturbing person and empower the others involved by organizing a congruent hierarchy that respects everyone's societal role responsibilities and the situation at hand.

In previously unsuccessful cases, we can change the situation only by facilitating all those involved to do something different. Doing something different means facilitating a different solution or facilitating an infrequently used, but effective solution to be used more consistently (de Shazer, 1985). *We can also change the situation by facilitating a different decision-making process.*

Family system theory has previously focused on changing only one decision-making aspect of the disturbing person's context—that employed by family members. Since we do not have the power to change what institutions do, an alternative solution is to change how institutions attempt to help. We must not only help families interact differently with medical and social institutions, but we must change how institutions do what they do. More specifically, we must change how they decide what they do, in a way that changes the traditional power distribution.

Treatment can be simplistically divided into process and content. The content is what we do, such as specific advice, strategic interventions, hospitalization, incarceration, medications, and so on. The process is how we arrive at what we eventually do. Whether we wish to admit it or not, the disturbing person, his or her family, the therapist, the physician, the institutional staff, and the societal control agents are always overtly and covertly involved in the process of our decision making. It is this decision-making process which leads to the solutions we apply, often habitually and unsuccessfully.

Frequently, physicians and therapists only minimally consider the present and future systemic effects of their decision making on the family. As a result, the family's experience of powerlessness prior to their disturbing member's treatment, is replicated in the treatment. As a result, families are predominately left with only covert influence in the treatment decision-making process.

One way of counteracting this process is to *empower* family members by giving them *real* authority, not the illusion of empowerment as usually discussed. Therapists must give up thinking that their control over what treatment will be done, is equivalent to the power to change. They must give the family control over the treatment and the termination of treatment. Therapists must give up their illusion of power and disempower themselves as experts. In order to empower families—who had the power in the first place—we must give them the authority.

The Fox System focuses on changing the process of the treatment decision making, such that all involved are empowered in an overt and different fashion from traditional approaches. Since it is impossible at this time to ignore or change what traditional therapeutic and medical contexts do, I prefer a method of changing how physicians and therapists do what they do. Rather than changing the content of what they do, I change the process of decision making leading to what they and the family do as a team.

EMPOWERMENT THROUGH DISEMPOWERING THE THERAPIST

Keep in mind, the task of a therapist is to construct a situation where responsible family members take charge of changing the disturbing member's behavior (Haley, 1976, 1980). Therapy should, then, respectfully empower all involved by laying a foundation for new roles and responsibilities that are not based upon gender role ascriptions. However, empowerment is a principle usually applied only to family members. Rarely is it applied to the therapist and treatment team as well.

Empowerment requires a therapist to help an individual, family, or a group (including the treatment team) to assume or reclaim control over the process of what is or will be happening to them and what they do. It focuses upon actualizing their capacity to function on their own behalf, a focus rarely pursued vigorously in working with chronic populations, especially those with dual diagnoses. An empowering approach is based upon the following.

- Having a positive expectant attitude toward the disturbing person, his or her family members, and everyone on the treatment team.
- Determining what everyone indicates are their needs.
- Focusing on everyone's strengths, rather than limitations.
- Accepting all family members as resources for enriching the process of change.
- Allowing family members to play a leadership role in the treatment process, by giving them active decision-making authority.

The Fox System takes empowerment a step further by including the therapist and the treatment context as well. It attempts to empower all elements of the disempowered—the disturbing person, his or her family members, social control agents, institution staff, physician, and therapist—by changing how the treatment context makes and implements decisions.

Keeping in mind that power, and therefore, empowerment and disempowerment are always relative to each other. The Fox System primarily empowers disturbing persons and their family members by disempowering the therapist and the treatment context, vis-a-vis the responsibly acting family members. The disempowerment is an acknowledgment of the illusory nature of the treatment team's power, giving up that misperception, and giving family members overt authority over treatment decisions. Before elaborating, let me discuss the hypotheses underlying this approach.

HALEY AND MADANES' CONTRIBUTIONS

Haley maintains that a therapist is required to move in small steps from requests for mutually agreed upon voluntary moves on the part of family members, to requests that family members had previously perceived as being outside their context of what an acceptable reality is. This continues until the mutually agreed upon changes have been accomplished. Haley (1963) hypothesized that relationships can be divided into three categories—complementary, symmetrical, and meta-complementary.

Whenever we tell family members what to do, they must either accept our request or reject it. If they accept, then the relationship is mutually defined by all involved as being complementary. That is, we are in a one-up position vis-a-vis the family members who have agreed to do what we asked.

When family members respond negatively, or not at all, the relationship could be defined as symmetrical, but certainly not a resistant relationship. Another perspective could be that the family has defined the relationship as one in which therapists are in a one-down, inferior position in a complementary relationship vis-a-vis the family, while the family is in the one-up, superior position by virtue of refusing to, or being unable to, comply with our request.

This is the scenario Madanes (1984) describes in her theory of "simultaneously incongruent hierarchies." Limiting herself to a parent-child situation, she states that when a child becomes ill or behaviorally disturbing, simultaneously incongruent hierarchies are established. The parents, by virtue of being parents, are in a superior position with respect to their child; for it is the parents who are responsible for taking care of and providing for the child. This is especially true when the child is ill or emotionally upset. As the parents desperately struggle to help their child overcome his or her problems, the child, by virtue of his inability or unwillingness to change in ways they wish, can be seen as simultaneously defeating his or her parent's attempts to help.

Thus, the simultaneously incongruent hierarchies are created. On one hand, the child is in a one-down position vis-a-vis the parents in a complementary relationship, while simultaneously the child is one-up vis-a-vis the parents by virtue of the lack of change.

The only other way this scenario can be explained is by the illness metaphor, for example, parents can't help because the child's problem is a disease beyond their sphere of influence. It may also be beyond the influence of the therapeutic medical context, given its present way of helping. Perhaps a change in the methods of helping or a change in the power distribution of decision making within the treatment context will create the difference that will make a difference.

Previously Madanes' theory has not been clearly applied to the relationship between a patient and his or her doctor in a traditional medical setting nor to the disturbing person, his or her family members, therapist, and the involved social control agents. But if systems thinking applies, and given the acknowledged fact that all involved frequently experience failure the same as parents, then any unit in the system can be placed in either the parent's or child's position in this schema. A therapist or physician can be in a one-up complementary position relative to the disturbing child and his or her family members by virtue of his or her being an expert in charge and accepting a fee—simultaneously being one-down by virtue of failing to maintain consistent change in the child or family members who are unable or unwilling to consistently do what the doctor or therapist asks.

I have great empathy with families victimized by violence, substance abuse, and/or mental illness. There are often powerful forces outside the family's control that influence the range of choices available, even in a treatment setting. However, despite these forces, family members often do have choices available on which they do not act.

The process of simultaneously incongruent hierarchies is covertly taking place in all treatment situations, but almost always denied by all involved. Whenever any family member acts as if he or she is more helpless and powerless than he or she is; or he or she actually is that helpless and powerless; or when he or she is forced by circumstances, or allow someone else to take charge, then in effect, that family member is also covertly taking charge of the therapeutic relationship on a meta-complementary level.

There are always good reasons for family members or staff to not complete a request. But whenever they do not, they are, in effect and usually outside their awareness, taking charge of the treatment process while denying it. The therapist then acts as if he or she is in charge of the treatment process when in effect he or she is not, thereby completing the simultaneously incongruent hierarchies. It creates an illusion that the expert is in charge, when in fact the expert is not because of his or her helplessness and failure to effect a consistent change in the situation. Within the context of such a meta-complementary relationship with its simultaneous incongruent hierarchies, the family is in charge of the change process.

THE FOX SYSTEM SOLUTION

If the meta-complementary nature of the treatment context goes unrecognized, then multiple, simultaneously incongruent hierarchies will create a therapeutic impasse. This impasse requires a therapist to construct a meta-complementary solution. Whether they like it or not, whether they are aware of it or not, once a family accepts a meta-complementary solution, they become more vulnerable to incorporating alternative perspectives previously considered outside their context of acceptable reality. They begin to doubt rigidly held perceptions and attributions of meaning. As a result, family members are more open to new solutions based upon a reframed set of premises. Thus, they become more willing to do directives they would have previously refused (Haley, 1976).

One way of creating such a meta-complementary solution, is to tell the responsibly-acting family members the following.

> I will agree to do whatever you as a family decides must be done to help your child, as long as you allow me to prescribe *how* you will decide *what* you and I will do in treating your child. I will keep this agreement, regardless of what your decisions are, as long as it is made according to the method I prescribe and does not expose anyone involved to grave risk of harm or liability.

Once this agreement is reached, the therapist must be able to follow through—do it and deliver. This is not an engaging strategy, but rather an acknowledgment that a therapist has no direct power and is delegating whatever authority he or she has. As a result, family members are engaged differently—more hopeful, enthusiastic. They no longer fight with the therapist, except to test the authority the therapist gave them. Once they realize the therapist's commitment and his or her support of even an outrageous but doable decision, they back off and become more reasonable.

One reason people act so irresponsibly and out of control is because they often have no way of expressing responsible control. If given a mechanism to express responsible control, they act more responsible and in control. However, in order to get this opportunity, the family must incorporate the therapist into their system. They must allow him or her the authority to prescribe how they will make and implement decisions in exchange for the therapist giving them authority to tell him or her what he or she and the treatment context will do.

The responsible NHFM are given authority to make all treatment decisions, including milieu expectations and consequences, medications, privilege level criteria, discharge criteria, and behavioral plans during home visits and after discharge. They have the decision-making authority, while the therapist maintains the medical, legal responsibility for all their decisions. Their authority is changed only when the NHFM act consistently or grossly irresponsible, which in my experience has never happened.

The therapist, physician, and staff function only as consultants to the family. In the purist sense of the word, they can only advise the family on alternatives available, on the comparative assets and liabilities of each alternative and on their right to not make a decision. They can never veto family decisions, as long as they are within the agreement. They are also responsible for implementing and enforcing the NHFM's plan, exactly as defined by the decision-making parent, without deviation.

With the NHFM making all decisions, they have an opportunity to practice new patterns of influencing the HFM's behavior with maximal support from the staff in a controlled institutional setting. Those new patterns of decision making and enforcement that have influenced the HFM in treatment, can then be put into practice during family visits, home passes, and after discharge. Thus, what is done in treatment is always congruent with what will be done by the family after discharge, because how decisions are made during the admission remains congruent with how they will be made after discharge.

PLACING PARENTS IN CHARGE DIFFERENTLY

Now the therapist must decide how the family will make their decisions and enforce them, such that it is different. The prescription must be based on an assessment of the adolescent's developmental needs and the cyclical interactional sequences surrounding the family's previous problem-solving attempts, such as their habituated decision-making process. How do they make their decisions about what they do, which have proven so ineffective?

Out of frustration with the traditional mutual consensus decision-making process and the sexist vulnerabilities of putting one parent in charge and the other on vacation, I developed a prescriptive process derived in part from Stuart's (1980) five levels of decision making.

Contrary to public myth, parents rarely make and enforce decisions by mutual consensus. Usually responsibility is divided. One parent, more so than the other, has responsibility for making the rules, while the other parent has more responsibility for enforcing those rules. It is crucial that both parents be experienced as co-equal authorities, for instance, co-equal to each other and not with the therapist who is one-down in this approach.

Therefore, if we agree that therapy should be as congruent as possible with what is normally done, it seems appropriate to divide parental decision making into *rule-making* and *rule enforcement*. The Fox System puts one parent in charge of making all final decisions regarding rules and decisions in treatment, but they can do so only after obtaining input from the disturbing child, other family members, staff, and therapist. The other parent is responsible for monitoring behavior and making final decisions on enforcing the rule-making parent's behavioral plan. Thus, both are experienced by the child as having different functions, yet co-equal to each other in authority.

The decision of who will be placed in charge of which role should not be based upon stereotypic gender role ascriptions. It should allow each parent an opportunity to develop a different role interaction with the child and participate differently in problem solving, based upon what change is needed in the cyclical sequences of interactions during the parental problem solving.

How do I determine which parent does what function? Both parents usually feel powerless, but usually one more overtly than the other. Usually one is more emotionally escalating, active, loud, intrusively attempting to do something, and is openly critical of the child, while the other is more quieting, withdrawing, empathic, and tends to talk as a way of helping.

Usually both parents reciprocally respond in a symmetrical escalation, each parent believing their approach is necessary to counteract the other and each feeling defeated by the other's refusal to change. All the while, the child is in effect defeating both. It's a no win game, almost without end.

This approach arranges for the actively escalating parent, who is doing too much and experienced negatively by all others, to do less and become more positively involved with the child; while the passively escalating parent becomes more engaged in limit setting and less sympathetic with the child. To accomplish this, the actively escalating parent is placed in charge of making all decisions regarding rules and treatment plans, while the passively escalating parent is placed in charge of implementing the plan, monitoring all behavior, and enforcing the consequences. The actively escalating and now decision-making parent is free to develop a more positive relationship with the child.

The staff must always follow the decision-making parent's plan. If staff thinks a rule needs to be changed, they must address their concern to the actively escalating, now rule-making parent who can legitimately accept, modify, or reject their consultation.

Similarly, the passively escalating, now implementing parent is the person whom the staff addresses whenever they have a question as to whether the child has violated the contract or which consequence a behavior warrants. Even if they disagree with the implementing parent's judgement, the staff must enforce the decision.

The HFM must experience the actively escalating parent being completely and overtly supported by the passively escalating parent and treatment context, who are enforcing the rule-making parent's rules. In effect, this dynamically and structurally creates a reverse of what is suspected to have covertly occurred at home prior to treatment.

In this approach, the previously out-of-control parent usually regains control, cooperates, and becomes a more nurturing parent once he or she experiences himself or herself as having influence. Similarly, when the quieting parent discovers that his or her partner is changing, becoming more available and less threatening, it is not surprising when the quieting parent becomes more actively involved in the disciplining.

DEALING WITH VIOLENCE

Physical loss of control or a fear of loss of control is always an issue in families with an abusing member. Change cannot take place in an atmosphere controlled by violence or intimidation. Effective treatment requires the development of a *no-violence contract* which does not disempower the process of change or the therapist.

The Fox System allows a therapist to maintain a one-up, meta-complementary position vis-a-vis the family. While prescribing the process of how violence will be dealt with, the family members are in charge of what they do. The therapist's allegiance is to nonviolent solutions and the meta-complementary prescription, not to any particular family member who may have been predetermined as in need of protection. The therapist maintains a meta-complementary position by taking sides, not against any family member, but against the use of violence as a solution to family conflict, while holding all members accountable for changing the decision-making process leading to the violent solution.

In the first sessions, whether a history of violence is obtained or not, the therapist informs all members they must deal with any future act of violence by any one as an act of criminality and not as an involuntary act or an act of mental illness. This agreement must be kept regardless of the situation, even if there is evidence of mental illness or intoxication at the time. There are no exceptions! The therapist agrees to continue treating them only if the persons threatened or hit, or whose personal property was damaged files charges. Family members must go to a safe location, keep previous contract commitments with other family members, keep their next appointment and follow through with court appearances, even if the situation has improved by that time.

Either the violence is treated as an act of criminality or the therapist terminates therapy. A therapist can not participate in a violent violation of the hierarchical relationship between a family and society.

WORKING WITH 12-STEP PROGRAMS

In developing this approach, I unknowingly followed the wisdom of AA and other 12-step programs. In every case involving substance abuse and other co-dependent behavior, the therapist politely and insistently encourages attendance until they go. In severe or persistent abuse cases, the therapist accepts the case only on the contingency that all family members attend an appropriate 12-step program. The approach has been used in cases where one or more family members, other than the HFM, were actively abusing substances. Abusing substances does not disqualify a parent from being assigned either role, however.

Regarding the controversy over whether substance abuse is a disease or disordered behavior a therapist should maintain a meta-complementary position by having enough flexibility to work with either model and accepting the definition given by the family and treatment context.

MISCELLANEOUS CONSIDERATIONS

This approach is not done with a team. Only one person is ultimately responsible for monitoring everyone else's behavior and maintaining their assigned responsibilities—the therapist in charge of the treatment process. Therapy is kept very straightforward with little paradoxical work. Follow-up outpatient therapy is best done by the inpatient therapist, since it maintains congruity in treatment.

Attendance in adolescent group therapy, family therapy meetings, multi-family groups, and mandatory visitations are part of the prescription requirement. Every HFM must receive a complete neuro-psychiatric and medical evaluation to rule out treatable conditions that could hinder change. Medication use must be approved by the decision-making parent.

Probation officers, protective services workers, school officials, and so on are brought into the sessions whenever appropriate; they are treated according to their hierarchical position as defined by society.

CASE EXAMPLE

The following case example demonstrates how the approach is utilized in pre-admission sessions, through the vicissitudes of treatment storms and in a severe relapse post-hospitalization.

Larry was an 18-year-old, poly-substance abuser whose treatment began while he was in jail. The first session began with the following comments from his parents.

> He was such a good boy. I don't understand what happened, he keeps going off every few months. He lies about everything, and believes it! We came to the stark reality there was something wrong with him three years ago. Eventually, he quit school and worked intermittently, finally being fired for stealing. He set fire to the staircase and things started to be missing from the house. He stole $6000 cash and $15,000 in jewelry. We eventually confronted him when he stole his mother's wedding band.

Only after stealing a car, which his parents covered for, did the family enter therapy and beginning work with NA and Nar-Anon. Six months later, the family's hopes were dashed when theft charges were filed by Larry's roommate. The father lost verbal and physical control as usual and announced, "I'm finished" and disowned Larry. While the mother agreed, she related that, "It was only half-heartedly, because I'm still his mother. I paid off the roommate as usual. It wasn't that much." In fact, prior to consulting me, charges against Larry had never been filed and followed through.

While the family continued in Nar-Anon, Larry moved to West Virginia with family members. There was allegedly no contact from the parents, except for his mother's weekly secret phone call. Suddenly, a few months later, he decided to leave with a stolen motorcycle he couldn't start and was charged with breaking and entering and grand theft.

The parents frantically wanted treatment by a psychiatrist, since Larry's problems were obviously over the head of their previous non-MD therapist. "He's sick and needs to be in an institution for a long time." After discussing the hospitalization process, I placed the father in charge of all decisions and the mother in charge of enforcing.

I agreed to a hospital admission only after Larry, significant family members, and friends had signed a contract that stipulated harsh steps to be taken if Larry again slipped into any criminal behavior, refused to sign the contract, or was non-compliant in the future. It clearly stated "the family would assist Larry in avoiding responsibility for his criminal behavior one last time in order to facilitate a last therapeutic attempt to help him." If it failed, he was on his own and no one would assist him until he had demonstrated he was drug-free for 12 months outside an institution.

If Larry refused to sign the contract, his parents committed to doing the following: Mother, with emotional support from father, was to obtain explicit and detailed instructions from Larry as to how he wished to be buried in the future, since they and I were convinced he was on the road to self destruction. Larry signed the contract and was admitted.

Three weeks after admission, with the father making the final decisions on Larry's treatment plan, Larry became depressed and angry about his parents previous lack of consistent expectations. The mother also became profoundly depressed which prompted the father's attempt to cancel a therapy session and request a premature home visit. When I pointed out that his request was in violation of our agreement and his own behavior contract, as well as being unwise in light of the previous pattern. He changed his mind.

Had the father persisted, I would have reminded him that we had agreed that I was in charge of *how* therapy is done, while he decide *what* will be done. This includes, required family therapy attendance and adherence to the contract once it was developed. If they had wished to void the contract, I would have empathically understood and made arrangements to discharge or transfer Larry to another facility which would, of course, not treat him the same way. The thought of losing such control over the treatment process usually stops families from violating the contract.

While Larry progressed through his father's plan, family therapy focused on transgenerational issues. Individual therapy *coached* Larry on strategies to effectively ask for what he wants from family members, to deal with their inconsistency, and to manage conflict.

As discharge approached and home behavior plans were being developed, the father abruptly announced that he was cancelling the next appointment and taking his wife to Las Vegas for a long weekend since Larry would be home in two weeks anyway. In effect, this would eliminate a home visit and/or leave Larry unsupervised, both in violation of our contract. I privately reminded the father of the contract as outlined above and my desire to keep working with them. In anger, he cancelled the trip at considerable expense.

The next session focused on Larry's 16-year-old sister. For months, the mother had secretly allowed her to be alone in her bedroom with a boyfriend against father's wishes. Larry was appropriately helpful during parental arguments over the sister's behavior plan. Three hours later, staff found Larry "making out" with a seductive female patient. Mother, for the first time, had to make a decision and implement a consequence, forcing Larry to restart treatment at the beginning privilege level. Six weeks later, he successfully completed the program with renewed determination.

The family massively denied the possibility of any further problems after discharge. After three months, treatment was recessed with a provision that the contract would remain in place for the rest of Larry's life, that urine testing must continue for at least one year with clean results, and the family must continue NA and Nar-Anon.

Eighteen months later, the family returned. Larry was again using drugs, had fraudulently used his mother's credit card, and had an assault and battery charge pending. The dialogue and family solutions were the same, as if the previous months of treatment had not happened. After empathically listening to everyone's position and without blame, I simply reviewed the original contract, the lack of compliance, and reminded them that the contract had been the only successful intervention ever done. After great turmoil, the father decided that Larry must enter an appropriate chemical dependence treatment center, leave home, and leave his father's employment. Father insisted that mother call the credit card company, change her previous report of the card having been stolen, and file a fraud charge against Larry.

All the above were done. Larry underwent a severe transformation experience at the treatment center during his seven-week treatment. Six months later, he is working, living with his girlfriend, and working the AA program.

TREATMENT OUTCOME RESULTS

A total of 15 adolescents were admitted to a private practice, general psychiatric ward between 1979 and 1985. There were six females and nine males, with 13 percent age 13, 47 percent age 15, 13 percent age 16, and 27 percent age 17.

Eight families were upper-middle class, five were working class, and two were low income. Seven patients had biological parents, six had stepparents and two came from single-parent families. All parenting figures living in the adolescents' homes were required to be involved. Separated biological parents were crucial to the outcome in four cases, while extended family members, especially grandparents, were crucial in six cases.

All patients had severely dysfunctional interaction with their families. Using traditional criteria, two out of three adolescents would have been quickly referred for residential treatment. Sixty percent had physically assaulted a parent and/or run away repeatedly. Substance abuse was the primary diagnosis in all but two patients, they lived with parents struggling with substance abuse and co-dependency. One-third of the families had an overtly alcohol addicted parent. The incident of physical and sexual abuse, suicidal ideation, psychotic ideation, and other severe manifestations of child psychopathology approximated those found in symptom surveys of residential programs. Four patients had previous psychiatric hospitalization.

In the era of cost-containment, a successful treatment must be not only helpful, but also cost-effective over the entire life of the disturbing person. A successful treatment interrupts patterns that contribute to expense. It must prevent or reduce reliance on hospitalization, medication, and incarceration, which so often become addictive solutions repeatedly applied by family and treatment contexts. Treatment must facilitate family members remaining supportive and helping the disturbing person to remain drug-free, working, or attending school. Treatment does not guarantee a happy family life.

Follow-up has been done by periodic telephone contact with at least one parent. The last follow-up in October 1987, revealed the patients were on an average of 48 months post-hospital discharge, with the range being from 27 months to eight years.

Thirteen patients (87 percent) were never rehospitalized or incarcerated. One patient was incarcerated by his mother as part of the discharge plan and another was readmitted for drug-abuse treatment.

At the time of discharge, all patients had a tenuous but quite satisfactory relationship with their families. On follow-up, most parents reported varying degrees of disappointment with their children's lives and final outcomes. However, 10 (67 percent) described acceptable relationships with their children and appreciation of the approach. One patient is successfully working and raising her own family, but estranged from her family. Three patients are now abusing substances, however, the families credit the approach for giving them the tools to disengage. One patient has continuing psychiatric difficulties.

All patients were previously failing school and truant. Ten patients (67 percent) had severe and often undiagnosed learning disabilities. Presently, six patients (40 percent) attend or have graduated high school. The remaining nine patients are working.

Six patients had previous therapy with me, varying from 1 to 32 hours and averaging six hours. The length of hospitalization ranged from 30 to 112 days, with an average of 65 days. Each patient received an average of 28 hours therapy. Follow-up therapy varied from 2 to 13 hours, with an average of seven hours. Thus, the average total hours of therapy was 41 hours.

In summary, 11 cases (73 percent) are considered successful four years post-hospital discharge. The remainder were unequivocally unsuccessful. The pattern of re-institutionalization as a solution was broken in all but two cases (87 percent). Residential placement was avoided.

CONCLUSION

Interestingly, all the disadvantages to the Fox System are significant advantages to quality individualized patient care. The only limitation of the approach is arranging for a treatment context to support the approach.

Advantages to the staff include more quality and less conflicted contact with all family members, more interstaff reporting, decreased staff splitting, and increased ability to function therapeutically, rather than as agents of social control. The therapist must more frequently consult everyone, which allows him or her to track each person's role responsibility and the change process, thereby interrupting homeostatic maneuvers. The therapist cannot be caught in a split as long as he or she keeps his or her role responsibility of referring all judgment calls to the enforcing parent.

The NHFM are greatly inconvenienced by frequent family sessions, telephone calls asking for clarification, and working hard on home visits. However, they also perceive themselves being wholeheartedly and enthusiastically supported by the therapist and staff, as compared with previous treatment experiences where they perceived themselves as being blamed, humiliated, and seen as incompetent. In this approach, they are seen as more competent than the staff. They best know the HFM, the context of their family, and the changes needed, as well as, possess the power to change.

My experience demonstrates that simply giving appropriate authority and control in an overt and differently organized fashion to the family, mellows even the most difficult family members and staff. As a result, therapeutic impasses are more easily overcome and collaboration enhanced. Thus, the Fox System creates a simultaneously incongruent therapeutic hierarchy, which is the reverse of Madanes' construct.

Experiencing powerlessness is mentally and physically painful. The most hopeless engendering situation anyone can experience is when one experiences themselves as having no influence in an important relationship and then feels blamed for that lack of influence. This approach counteracts that experience. The NHFM remains engaged with a renewed sense of hope and success. No family has ever refused treatment based upon this approach. All families, even those I failed, described the hospitalization process as a positive experience. None felt blamed or alienated.

We all have specific biogenetic vulnerabilities. For some of us, they will express themselves in ways which leave us more socially vulnerable, in others they will be expressed in more physical ways, and still others in some combination. For all of us, the vulnerabilities will eventually be expressed. More importantly, when they are expressed, they will have powerful influences, not just upon ourselves, but also on our family members and those professionals attempting to help us.

Since it is the family who is most affected by professional decisions, they should have control over what they and the professionals eventually do. This is especially applicable, since they have covert control over the decisions anyway. So, why not overtly arrange such a situation to begin with?

REFERENCES

Bepko, C. & Krestan, J. (1985). *The responsibility trap.* New York: Free Press.

de Shazer, S. (1985). *Keys to solution in brief therapy.* New York: W. W. Norton.

Fisch, R., Weakland, J. H., & Segal, L. (1982). *The tactics of change.* San Francisco, CA: Jossey-Bass.

Fox, M. R. (1985). *The Fox system.* Unpublished manuscript.

Haley, J. (1963). *Strategies of psychotherapy.* New York: Grune & Stratton.

Haley, J. (1976). *Problem solving therapy.* San Francisco, CA: Jossey-Bass.

Haley, J. (1980). *Leaving home.* New York: McGraw-Hill.

Madanes, C. (1981). *Strategic family therapy.* San Francisco, CA: Jossey-Bass.

Madanes, C. (1984). *Behind the one-way mirror.* San Francisco, CA: Jossey-Bass.

Stuart, R. (1980). *Helping couples change.* New York: Guilford.

Subby, R. (1987). *Lost in the shuffle.* Pompano Beach, FL: Health Communications, Inc.

Watzlawick, P., Weakland, J. H., Fisch, R. (1974). *Change.* New York: W. W. Norton.

10

Network Therapy
A Case Study

ELIZABETH HEMLEY van der VELDEN, Drs.
Co-Director

LARRY L. RUHF, Ed.D.
Co-Director

KATHRYN R. KAMINSKY, R.N., M.A.
Network Therapist
The Network Therapy Team at Mt. Tom Institute for Human Services, Inc., Holyoke, MA

OVERVIEW OF MODEL

Historical Roots

As adolescent substance abuse has become a major and pervasive social problem, many current treatment models have embraced a family systems view of both the etiology and resolution of the problem. Concurrent with the rise of family therapy as a major mode of intervention for young drug abusers, a broader ecosystemic form of intervention, network therapy, has been evolving through contemporary clinical practice as a viable intervention for the treatment of adolescent substance abuse.

Network therapy was originated by Speck and Attneave (1973) who found that by gathering the entire social network of a psychiatrically disturbed client and his or her family at the moment of crisis, major positive shifts in the functionality of the client and family took place as a consequence of increased sharing of emotions, understanding, support, and creative problem-solving by the social network system. A social network can be defined, generally, as consisting of those important people who are connected to the client and members of his or her family through friendship, neighborhood, work, religious association, extended family, and service providers who are involved with the problem. In essence, the social network is the defined social community of a family.

The concept of convening a small natural community to help deal with a person's emotional problems has come down through the ages as a way in which many tribal and religious communities took responsibility to help their own members. These tribal and religious communities saw the emotional difficulties of the suffering one and his or her family as its own problem and sought to relieve the community problem by involving everyone in the healing process. Speck and Attneave properly perceived the lack of community/network involvement as part of the reason people could not move forward, and individual families felt desperately stuck trying to cope with a mentally ill member. Much of their work centered around retribalizing and knitting together a working community or network to help deal with the many problems and issues that arise in the families of the mentally ill.

There have been numerous clinicians who have taken the concepts of network therapy and utilized this intervention model to deal with such problems as psychiatric emergencies, chronic mental illness, adolescent behavior problems, suicide, and substance abuse. Experimentation with the clinical application of network therapy for a variety of psychological problems has been attempted by Garrison (1974), Rueveni (1979), Beels (1981), Kliman and Trimble (1983) and Halevy-Martini et al. (1984). All of these subsequent pioneers in the development of network therapy have put forth various theoretical models and concepts to explain the form and process of network therapy meetings. Common to all of this work is the idea of gathering a social network together at a time of desperation to help intervene in a serious emotional problem, lend support to the client and family to renew energy and support, and to change the way in which the problem is being perceived and handled.

Assumptions of the Network Model

Assumptions of network therapy models have been discussed extensively by many proponents of this approach, including Speck and Attneave (1973), Rueveni (1979), and Halevy-Martini et al. (1984). The underlying epistomology common to all models is ecosystemic; the dysfunction of the identified client is considered to be an expression of the dysfunction of the larger context of the client's network of social relationships. Any change in any part of this larger system will necessarily lead to shifts in other parts of the system, as it recalibrates to re-establish equilibrium. There are no *best* ways to do this; there are, rather, various means to achieve this end. Therapists can approach the system at the level of the service providers (professional consultation), the individual (individual therapy), the family (family therapy), the peer group (support groups and group therapy), or at the meta-level, as in network therapy which includes representatives from as many of these realms of social connection to the individual as possible.

Based on our own experience with network therapy, more is better, up to an optimal 25 participants, and more representatives of the various realms are better. With a larger group of people present at a meeting, there are more opportunities for change to happen, and with representatives of the many realms in which an individual operates, the likelihood that the effect will generalize and be maintained is enhanced. Also, the more balanced the representation of the network is in terms of the family/nonfamily composition of the group, the more accessible the group will be to change (Hemley, et al., 1984). Family members provide the emotional intensity while non-family participants are generally less invested in the status quo, and more open to change.

That family members provide the impetus for change stems from the permanence of family ties; others may come and go in the client's network, but family members hang in for the long haul, bound to a client with special intensity. This leads to another assumption implicit in our model, namely that when one member of a family is suffering, all other members of that family suffer in varying degrees as well, either through empathic connection, deprivation of needs by the client who is too needy to reciprocate the attentions of family members, or via direct caretaking burdens being placed on those closely involved with the client. This provides another important rationale for involving the network; if all members of the family are suffering, support for each of them must come from outside the family, and members of the family's social network can be called on to provide that support.

A third assumption relates to our belief that everyone has some expertise in some area, and no one is an expert about everything. Gathering all these experts together makes it more likely, in terms of actual problem-solving, that effective solutions to difficult problems will be generated.

A fourth basic assumption regards the power of rituals; convening a client's social network is a major punctuating event and the very act of gathering such a large group of people whose common denominator is concern for and connectedness to an individual and/or family seems, in itself, to be emotionally powerful and potentially healing. When an individual and/or family opens up to its network and shares secrets and allows for the public witnessing of emotional truths like shame, anger, hurt, and forgiveness, the response of the network is usually positive and sufficient for the resolution of many difficulties.

Our assumptions about what leads adolescents to become chemically dependent parallels our views on the etiology of mental illness, and can best be described as a consideration of both environmental and biological factors. We accept the premise that people can inherit predispositions to mental illness or chemical dependency, and that these predispositions and/or some environments are more vulnerable to manifest these problems as a means of coping. Family conflict and situational crises can create enough stress for those who have these vulnerabilities so that the most accessible means of responding to difficulties is through the emergence of drug or alcohol abuse, or specific mental illnesses; either can be considered as destructive coping mechanisms. Network therapy focuses on the environmental stressors by enlisting the help of the social environment that is both contributing to the problem and potentially able to provide solutions to, or at least support around, the problems that are creating stress within the individual and family. With a chemically-dependent adolescent, substance abuse can be a statement that all is not well in the family, and as such, the individual's drug problem can be viewed as a symptom within a dysfunctional family and network. The young person's difficulty can then be seen as providing an inroad into the family or network by which difficulties in the larger system can be approached and possibly resolved.

Lastly, we share an assumption with crisis intervention theory and many approaches to treatment of substance abuse, namely that change is most likely to happen at the crisis point. Generally, in many western cultures, networks gather for ritual events like marriages and funerals. The idea of gathering for other purposes like problem solving and mobilization of support is often at variance with other norms, like self sufficiency and independence. Sometimes, however, the desperation generated by a crisis can outweigh the family's resistance to gathering its network for a novel purpose. What logically follows from this is that families will usually agree to a network intervention only if they are already in crisis and when they are in crisis, change is most likely to happen. A dilemma common to families of substance abusers is that substance abuse may be a shared norm of the family system and its larger network, and the entire system may be invested in denying that a problem exists at all. In a case like this, the signaling crisis would likely be in another area, and the network can be motivated to gather for reasons other than substance abuse, which can be approached once the group has begun the work of crisis resolution. The threat of suicide, for example, can act as the catalyst in such a system as it does in the following case.

The Therapy Process

The model we use to understand the therapeutic process of a network therapy intervention was developed by Halevy-Martini et al. (1984). It describes three stages: 1) convening the network, 2) connecting the network, and 3) shifting the locus of responsibility from the therapeutic team to the network. Through this three stage process, the goal is to achieve the network effect, which means helping the family network become a cohesive supportive, functioning group that can help the client/family and other network members during crisis by providing emotional support, understanding, and practical problem solving.

Stage 1: Convening the Network

The initial task of the network therapy team is to help the client/family identify, invite, and gather together their social network to a network meeting. At an assessment meeting, after the family agrees to a network meeting, it is stressed that a balance of family members and friends be present at the meeting to create a balance of people who can offer different levels of support and understanding, and provide new perspectives and practical resources. Each family member is instructed to invite supportive friends so that no member's position is isolated. A network meeting is often held a few weeks after the assessment to allow time for contacting and inviting members of the network. The very act of agreeing to hold a network meeting and the actual inviting of the social network to convene for the purpose of helping mark the beginning of the network effect and the therapeutic process for the family/client.

Stage 2: Connecting the Network

The designated team leader often begins the network meeting by asking the group for a song. The purpose of this is to begin to bind the group and to punctuate the beginning of an unusual experience. The leader then delivers a *network speech* in which he or she tells the group the purpose of the meeting and the need for their involvement in the problems of the family. He or she sets the emotional tone for the meeting by describing the pain, difficulties, and desperation that have led the family to convene its network for help and asks that those present be open and honest. The team attempts to focus the meeting and facilitate group cohesion by involving everyone present. Typically, we go around the room and ask people to state their name, relationship to the client, and to explain what they think needs to be addressed in the meeting.

After this "go-around," the group often spontaneously deepens its discussion of the most salient issue that emerged from the opening. People are invited to express their differing views and offer perspectives and to share their own life experiences as they relate to the issue. At times, the team may employ psychodrama and encounter techniques to work through emotional impasses. As the group shares in the expression of grief, guilt, anger, or joy, it becomes bound together and can now work in an effective, unified manner to offer emotional and practical support through the crisis period and beyond.

Stage 3: Shifting the Locus of Responsibility

Once family problems are clarified and emotions surrounding the problems are shared and understood by the group, practical problem solving can take place. Up to this point, the network therapy team plays an active and directive role. Now the responsibility for problem solving and provision of on-going emotional support is allowed to shift back to the network itself. As problems are presented again, the network strives to develop actual plans and strategies, and individuals commit themselves to dealing with particular issues. Sometimes work committees are formed during the meeting itself. More often, the actual work of resolving the family problems happens after the meeting is formally ended. When the network is well balanced, emotionally connected, and understands the complexities of the problems, it can function as an effective, therapeutic agent for the family in helping to resolve some of the persisting difficulties.

CASE EXAMPLE

Referral

The Network Team was approached about this case in March 1987, by Tom, a therapist at a local mental health agency who had worked with us in the past. Tom felt that this case was *stuck* and that the Network approach might move it along.

The client was Ann Clark, an 18-year-old, who presented with a severe eating disorder. She entered therapy in January 1986, and began to show a decrease in symptoms. However, in November 1986, her 19-year-old brother, Jason, was killed in a car accident in which he was driving while intoxicated. Her anorexia soon returned. She also became depressed and suicidal, and these feelings were exacerbated by frequent alcohol abuse. These symptoms had not lessened despite anti-depressant medication and intensive individual and family therapy.

We agreed that an assessment for a major network would be the next step. We ask therapists to present us as colleagues who work specifically with families having difficult problems. We do not call these meetings *therapy* as many of our referrals are with people already discouraged and resistant to therapy. Tom was instructed to ask the family to meet with us about issues of support, problem solving, and treatment planning. He was sure Ann's father, Robert, and his wife, Sarah, Ann's stepmother, would come to a meeting, but was less sure about Ann herself. This was not surprising as family members are often eager for the network, while the identified client is resistant. We agreed that Robert and Sarah would suffice for the assessment, but advised Tom to invite all the children.

Assessment

The assessment was held about two weeks after Tom approached us. It is best to have the meeting within a few weeks of the referral while there is still a feeling of crisis. Assessment meetings are held in our office, which is physically separate from the Mental Health Center. We find this helps clients to see us as consultants distanced from traditional treatments. One member of our team is designated as the leader, one as the co-leader, and the third as observer and notetaker. The third member gives his or her observations only toward the end of the meeting.

Robert and Sarah were the only family members to attend. Tom and Janice, Ann's individual therapist, also attended. Tom was the family therapist and Janice's supervisor.

The leader began by explaining that we knew little about the family circumstances, but that we understood that Ann was having considerable difficulty and also that there had been a recent death of another child. We explained that if one member was suffering, then everyone was. We expressed our hope to provide some help and support during those difficult times. Each person was given the opportunity to say what they felt needed to be covered in this meeting. Tom and Janice both expressed the need to get more people involved as Ann remained acutely suicidal. Robert spoke emotionally about his distress over his daughter's behavior and angrily about his ex-wife, Bonnie, and her present husband, Lou. He said that Lou was abusive to Bonnie, and that the children suffered verbal abuse from Lou and tremendous pain over their mother's position. Robert also implied that, while still married to him, Bonnie had been involved with Lou. Sarah was more moderate in her presentation. She agreed with Robert that the situation with Bonnie and Lou was difficult, but was less angry at them and more angry at Ann. Sarah worried that Ann was suicidal and abusing alcohol.

Tom had explained Network Therapy to the Clarks prior to the assessment and they agreed to a bigger meeting. We were thus able to spend less time examining the feasibility of gathering a larger group or pursuing other treatment alternatives. Many times assessment meetings provide an opportunity for consultation to the presenting therapist and bring new information that can move the case along, even if a larger network meeting is not indicated or agreed upon. The Clarks agreed to have the first meeting in their home.

In this case, all agreed that a network meeting was the next intervention of choice, so we spent the rest of the session deciding who could be involved and how. We suggested that all involved members should come to the network meeting including the family, extended family, and all the service providers. Because we feel that balance between blood and non-blood participants is crucial, we encouraged the family to include others such as friends, neighbors, work colleagues, schoolmates, and clergy. In some cases achieving balance is difficult because the family is impoverished of supports, or resistant to adding people. In these cases, we talk to the family about their fears, and share our experience about why we think larger groups are more helpful. In these cases, we might continue working with a family over time, in the hopes of building up to a major network meeting.

The Clark's had a sizeable network upon which to draw, but there were some problems about inviting Lou. Robert refused to have him in his house. We asked Robert and Sarah what they thought would happen if Lou came, and whether Bonnie would come if Lou wasn't invited. They said they believed Bonnie would come anyway. Knowing that just raising the question would result in some interesting family conversations in the coming weeks, we asked the family to reconsider. Simply agreeing to and inviting people to a Network meeting has the effect of stimulating a stagnating system. In the end, the family must decide who to invite.

Robert and Sarah wondered if Ann, herself, would come. We assured them that the purpose was to support the entire family and that it was for Ann to gauge her need to be involved. Most identified clients attend, while some stay in the house and avoid the meeting, while some don't come at all. We also asked that some friends of Jason be invited, so issues around his death could be aired. We believed that some of Ann's recent difficulty was linked to unresolved grief over his death and that this should be addressed. Robert and Sarah asked how to invite people, and were advised to say that they were having a meeting about serious problems in their family and were asking their friends to join them for support.

The Network meeting was set for one week later. Usually we like to have more time between the assessment and the Network meeting to allow for the network effect, but in this case there had been much preparation by Tom before the assessment, so we moved more rapidly. The client's home is the natural setting for the meeting. The Clark's agreed to hold it in their home since Ann lived with them.

The issue of Ann's alcohol abuse was hardly touched upon at the assessment. We felt that the immediate focus should be Ann's suicidality, as this would increase the likelihood of convening a large group. The family's substance abuse could be addressed in a timely manner at the larger meeting.

Network Meeting 1: Focus on the Risk of Suicide and Unresolved Grief

The first major Network meeting with the Clarks was held on a Wednesday evening, one week after the assessment. The meetings usually run from two-three hours, and eating and drinking during the meeting is discouraged as this distracts the group's attention. The house was in a middle-class, suburban neighborhood. When we arrived there were 24 people gathered, plus the three network therapists—it was well balanced in terms of family and friends. The group consisted of the following:

FAMILY: Ann, Robert, Sarah, Ann's brother, Sam, Sarah's son, George, Bonnie and her mother and grandmother and Robert's brother, John, for a total of nine family members.
FRIENDS: Five adult family friends and six late-adolescent family friends for a total of 11 friends.
SERVICE PROVIDERS: Janice and Tom, plus a crisis worker from the area who had dealt with the family during its many crises for a total of three members.

The leader opened the meeting by asking the group to stand and for someone to suggest a song to be sung together. Sam suggested

"Row, Row, Row Your Boat," which was sung with great gusto by the group. We expected a long, difficult meeting ahead, as the song often indicates the theme and affect level of the meeting to come ("Row, Row, Row Your Boat" is a frequent indicator of resistance and denial). The group then resettled and the leader gave an emotional opening speech about the losses in the family through divorce and death, and the pain and suffering felt by everyone in the family. He expressed the hope that during this meeting, all members would talk honestly about these difficulties so that everyone would feel less isolated and more supported. He then asked the participants to introduce themselves, explain their relation to the family, and define what they think would be important to discuss. People spoke eloquently about their concern for Ann's life, and made many connections between the possibility of her committing suicide and the reality of Jason's recent death. We asked the members to talk about Jason's death, and how it had effected each of them. At first, many mentioned only what a fine person he was, and then gradually, they began to talk about his pain. Ann spoke about the night he had been killed. He was upset and had asked her to accompany him on a trip to get beer, but she had refused. Now she felt responsible for his death and wished she were dead, too. She cried deeply as she spoke and those present began to understand her anger and suicidality in a new way. Others talked about the losses in their own lives and how they felt, coped, and expressed their own pain and guilt. A crisis worker spoke of the loss of her own brother only a few years ago and the difficulty she had in letting go of him as well as how guilty she had felt, when she began to get on with her life. Another told of an experience similar to Ann's—in which she had refused a request of a friend who met a violent death the next day—she spoke with great feeling of the sense of guilt she carried with her from that tragedy. It became clear that many people in the room were experts in living with pain, loss, and guilt and they shared these experiences with each other. Through this profound emotional sharing, the group connected, making a shift toward problem solving possible. The focus then moved back to Ann, with group members asking if she could reach out to others when she felt overwhelmed. A close friend said she wished that Ann would call her more, but explained she had a hard time with Ann's style of calling because it made it difficult for the friend to help. The discussion then opened again to the group as people talked about the uneven and unpredictable timing of recovering from a loss, and about the guilt they felt at forgetting the pain or getting support. Sarah made it clear that Ann was not the only one in pain and that Robert was also having a hard time with this. Robert then talked about getting depressed to counter pleasurable times. His brother, John, and Sarah both mentioned his excessive drinking during those times. Robert then acknowledged that he and Ann were very much alike in this way—using alcohol to obliterate pain. He stated defensively that at least he stayed home when drunk, while she went out and put herself at risk. This was the first indication of a growing willingness within the group to tackle the widespread abuse of alcohol in this system.

Toward the end of the meeting, the focus shifted to Ann's mother, Bonnie, who had been sitting quietly, chain smoking. Friends who had known both Robert and Bonnie for many years, expressed concern for her pain and isolation and for how she was managing with Jason's death. People also spoke of Ann's worry about her mother. Bonnie spoke quietly, and said that even though it had been difficult, she was doing OK, and that she had her own therapist. She did not seem to want to continue speaking and this was respected by the group. Several people offered support should she need it. Robert couldn't do that, as he remained angry, but Sarah said she could, mother to mother.

After three hours everyone was emotionally drained and we decided to end the meeting. We asked Ann and her family if they would like another meeting and they agreed they would. It was scheduled for one month from then. We suggested that Bonnie bring her therapist and anyone else she felt would be helpful, as she had an especially isolated position within this Network.

This had been a powerful meeting. Even though alcohol abuse and Bonnie's welfare were only touched upon briefly, other issues had been publicly expressed and responded to in a supportive way.

Network Meeting 2: Focus on Alcohol Abuse

The second network meeting was held one month later. The group had dwindled. Sam and the Crisis worker were unable to attend and a few of the adolescent friends were absent. The group chose to begin the meeting with another childhood song, "Twinkle, Twinkle Little Star," which again indicated possible resistance to working on difficult issues. The following were suggested as topics to discuss: In what ways was Ann doing better; how Robert deals with his sadness; and how Ann could deal with Bonnie and Lou.

We began by asking for more specifics about Ann. We wanted everyone to appreciate her gains. She was now working and going out with friends more. Her depressive episodes were less frequent and better tolerated. She was acting out less. The discussion shifted to how the rest of the family dealt with their sadness. Robert more openly acknowledged his longtime use of alcohol and said this had increased since Jason's death. Some group members noted that it seemed to be a problem in the whole family as Bonnie, Lou, Jason, and Ann also had difficulties related to alcohol. Other members in the Network talked about some of their own problems with alcohol. Some had gone to AA, while others wondered if they had problems or not.

Robert then brought up the issue of Ann's relationship with Lou and Bonnie and how much it upset him; he said he felt that often Ann's depressions were a reaction to that relationship. Ann talked of how difficult it was for her to see her mother with Lou around. He often got drunk and became physically abusive to Bonnie. Ann never knew whether to leave or to stay and protect her mother. There was some discussion about the possibility of Ann seeing Bonnie alone. At this point Bonnie took a stand. She said she was married to Lou and could manage him and would not alienate herself from him to see her children. She reminded people that she had always been capable of protecting both herself and her children. She said when he was drunk she kept the kids away, and if he got drunk during their visit, she wanted them to leave. When asked if she could protect herself, she said she, too, had left when things got dangerous. When asked if she ever felt suicidal, she said that she did, but at this point would not act on it. Some members of the group were upset that she shared these feelings with Ann while others acknowledged her right to feel them and their hope that she too was getting help, as her death would be devastating to Ann. There was then some talk about the additional loss of the former marriage between Robert and Bonnie. Some of the Network members and therapists had been divorced and were able to talk about the anguish and guilt they had felt for the pain suffered by children in divorces.

The meeting ended with a plan that Ann and Bonnie would do some work with Tom on aspects of their relationship. Ann also agreed to renew her individual therapy work with Janice (she had not gone for her own therapy for some time). The family decided that things were more stable now, but that they wanted another meeting in four months, around the time of both Jason's and Ann's birthdays as they expected to need additional support at that time.

It appeared that between the first meeting and this one, Ann had moved out of the role of the identified client. In this meeting, the family and friends talked more openly about issues that concerned Bonnie and Robert.

Network Meeting 3: Tying It Up

This meeting was much smaller than the previous two. Attending from the family were Sarah, Robert, Uncle Ray, Ann, Bonnie and Bonnie's mother and grandmother. The therapists Tom and Janice attended as did two friends, one of Bonnie's and one of Sarah's, both of whom had been very active in the previous meetings. It was possible that this smaller turnout indicated that the crisis was no longer perceived as acute. The team proceeded with the usual structure. The leader opened the network by summarizing the subjects touched on during previous meetings, and recalled the intensity and openness of those meetings. The song picked was "Freres Jaques" (Are you Sleeping, brother John) which suggested to us the possibility that the group was becoming aware of the need to wake up, and take more responsibility. The two main issues introduced to discuss were the difficult relationship between Ann and her mother (brought up by Robert and Sarah) and the planning for Ann's and Jason's birthdays.

Most of the meeting focused on the complex manner in which Ann's difficulties with Bonnie effected Robert and Sarah. It appeared that although Ann and Bonnie were still having problems around Lou, both were coping. What seemed most upsetting to the group, at this point, was that Robert continued to suffer and drink because of Ann's concerns, and how this, in turn, frustrated and angered Sarah. This was the first time that the relationship between Robert and Sarah had been discussed at a meeting and both seemed uncomfortable. Tom asked the group why they thought that Robert was so preoccupied with Bonnie and Lou, and there was a sense that Robert still had feelings about Bonnie. One of the team then asked that the individuals in the group speak to Robert "from the heart." This intervention acted as a ritual to help punctuate a position, offer support, and provide feedback. The speaker is asked to sit across from the person and give him a message "from the heart" as a statement of encouragement or support. Many people took turns sitting by Robert, acknowledging his conflicts, talking about his love and strengths, and encouraging him to deal with both his drinking and his conflicts. These were intense and powerful moments.

At the end of the meeting, some time was spent discussing plans for the upcoming birthdays of Ann and Jason. At first, the team asked the group to share how other birthdays had been spent and then everyone discussed how much should be repeated and who could handle what. Previous birthdays had been spent at a swimming and boating club and had been a whole day affair. It was decided that they would do this again, but that this year Bonnie would be included, so they could all be together to remember Jason and share with each other the mixed feelings of the day. In a way this discussion served as practice in coping with those feelings.

The family decided not to plan anymore meetings at this time that things were in place and they would call us in the future as needed. We ended the meeting by telling the Network members how impressed we had been at their tenaciousness and support of each other, and that we felt honored that they had allowed us to be a part of this process.

Review of the Case

Network therapy can best be understood as an intervention that works to get stuck systems moving again, rather than as on ongoing therapeutic modality. The goal of the therapy is to mobilize the network so that it can proceed on its own to deal with the problems that originally brought the family to convene its network, and with any subsequent problems that may have come to light during the actual network therapy process. In the case of the Clark family Network meetings, the presenting problem, Ann's suicidality, seemed to have been resolved for the time being, and an effective support system was now in place to reduce the likelihood of a reoccurrence and to protect her in case she should ever feel suicidal again.

Another gain for the family was the experience of openly grieving the death of a child and the end of a marriage. The taboo around discussing these painful subjects had been lifted, and it became possible for the social network to console and share in the family's burden of grief. Other problem areas, such as Bonnie's difficult relationship with Lou, Robert's unresolved anger at Bonnie, and especially the abuse of alcohol by several members of the family and network as a means of coping with depression and anger, were made public but not resolved. We were satisfied that the referring therapist's original goal of getting the case unstuck had been met. Our hope was that the Network, including the individual and family therapists who were members of the Clark's social network, would pursue resolution in these other areas as well, in the context of its ongoing relationship with the family.

NETWORK INTERVENTIONS AND SUBSTANCE ABUSE: CONSIDERATIONS

There are different moments in the course of a person's history with substance abuse when some kind of network intervention could be useful. Callan et al. (1975) have reported on network interventions for drug abusers in residential treatment to prepare for leaving the facility and to reinforce whatever gains were made in treatment. Logan (1983) has written about network interventions organized for the purpose of bringing resistant alcoholics to treatment. In our own work, we have held a series of smaller (up to 10 participants) network meetings to motivate a dually diagnosed (alcoholic and schizophrenic) client to seek treatment for his drinking problem.

A distinction needs to be made between client systems in which the identified client is the only substance abuser, and those in which many members of the system abuse. In the former, mobilizing the network to bring someone into treatment, as in Logan's work, would seem a relatively straightforward task, taking the usual resistances to going public into consideration. The therapy course is less clear for those systems in which many members abuse and the level of denial regarding the pervasiveness of the problem would interfere with efforts to mobilize such a group toward treatment for one of its members. In a case such as the one described, the initial focus of the network's concern is on any problematic behavior other than substance abuse. Here, the energy around which the network can mobilize is focused on relieving the other problems, and the substance abuse is approached gingerly.

The initial task of the therapy team is to engage the group. If the substance abuse is confronted prematurely, the network could be alienated and no further work with it will be possible. Ideally, the therapy team needs to wait for someone within the network, itself, to bring up the problem of substance abuse by the client and others in the system before it can be addressed. This is indeed what happened in the meetings with the Clark's network.

EVALUATION AND FOLLOW-UP

The few outcome studies involving network therapy have involved psychiatric populations (Schoenfeld et al., 1985 and 1986). The 1985 study demonstrated a significant decrease in service utilization by clients post network therapy as compared to their level of service utilization prior to network therapy. This suggests that the social networks of these clients had become more effective in meeting their needs. The 1986 study compared the number of total days of psychiatric hospitalizations for 20 clients who had participated in network therapy and 20 who had not, before and after referral to the program, with follow-up periods ranging from six months to two years. On the first criterion there were decreases for both groups, with the decrease for the participant group significantly greater (74 percent compared to 19 percent). As for total number of days of hospitalization, the participant group demonstrated a 76 percent decrease, while the comparison group demonstrated a 12 percent increase in psychiatric hospitalizations.

We have no hard follow-up data specific to network therapy with adolescent substance abusers, and the case reported here is too recent to be certain about the outcome, despite the feelings of optimism expressed by the members of the Clark Network when we terminated our work with them. Clearly, this is an area that will need further research and experimentation. It is our belief that network therapy could prove to be an effective and innovative tool in treating adolescent substance abusers, especially in those cases where more traditional treatment methods have failed, and where there is an existing supportive social network available to the client.

REFERENCES

Beels, C. (1981). "Social networks and the treatment of schizophrenics." *International Journal of Family Therapy,* 3, 310–316.

Callan, D., Garrison, J., Zerger, F (1975). "Working with the families and social networks of drug abusers." *Journal of Psychedelic Drugs, 7*(1) Jan.-March, 204–210.

Garrison, J. (1974). "Network techniques: Case studies in the screening-linking-planning conference." *Family Process, 13,* 337–353.

Halevy-Martini, J., Hemley, E., Ruhf, L., Schoenfeld, P. (1984). "Process and Strategy in Network Therapy." *Family Process, 23,* 521–533.

Hemley, E., Halevy-Martini, J., Ruhf, L., Schoenfeld, P. (1984). "Conceptual issues in network therapy." *International Journal of Family Therapy,* 6(2) Summer, 68–81.

Kuman, J., Trimble, D. "Network Therapy" in Wolman and Stricker (eds.), (1983). *The Handbook of Family and Marital Therapy,* New York and London: Plenum Press.

Logan, D. (1983). "Getting alcoholics to treatment by social network intervention." *Hospital and Community Psychiatry, 34,*(4), 390–404.

Rueveni, U., (1973). *Networking families in crisis,* New York: Pantheon.

Shoenfeld, P., Halevy-Martini, J., Hemley, E., Ruhf, L. (1985). "Network therapy: An outcome study of twelve social networks." *Journal of Community Psychology, 13,* 281–287.

Schoenfeld, P., Halevy-Martini, J., Hemley, E., Ruhf, L., (1986). "Long-term outcome of network therapy," *Hospital and Community Psychiatry, 37,*(4), 373–376.

Speck, R. V. and Attneave, C. L. (1973). *Family Networks,* New York: Pantheon.

11
A Reflecting Team Approach to Adolescent Substance Abuse

DARIO J. LUSSARDI, M.A.
Co-Director, Brattleboro Family Institute, Brattleboro, VT

DUSTY MILLER, Ed.D.
Senior Faculty, Brattleboro Family Institute, Brattleboro, VT

INTRODUCTION

We approach the problem of adolescent substance abuse from a systemic theoretical perspective, emphasizing a recent innovation known as the *Reflecting Team*. Operating within this framework provides greater therapeutic flexibility, allowing for the possibility of intervening in many ways. Within this context, we can maintain a neutral therapeutic position and assume other stances when neutrality becomes less useful.

We will begin by describing the significant issues for treatment. Our focus in this chapter is the situation of therapist-client impasse, the dilemma we face when offering treatment to clients who rarely choose to be in the role of *identified patient* either in relation to us or their families. We will discuss the developmental issues most often relevant to treating adolescents in a family context. We will also look at the problem of alcoholism when it is transmitted from generation to generation and the related predictability of family-helper conflict. A systemic contextual scheme will be outlined as we look at treatment. The reflecting team approach will be discussed indepth and we will illustrate our treatment model with a case study.

ADOLESCENTS AND THEIR FAMILIES

Adolescence is a time of great change for both the adolescent and his or her family. It can be a stage filled with confusion and ambiguity regarding what behaviors are appropriate and/or acceptable. Former rules and expectations are questioned when both new behaviors and new ideas are introduced into the family system and the parents and the adolescent begin to adjust to these changes. Familiar forms of encouragement and discipline may no longer be useful or appropriate (Lax & Lussardi, 1988).

This is a time when new behaviors and experimentation can possibly lead to more serious consequences. When children are at an earlier stage of development, their activities are usually more carefully supervised. They do not have the freedom or accessibility to the adult world that is available to most adolescents. Adolescents are exposed to new activities that can include driving, sex, alcohol, and drugs: Any or all of these activities can have potentially devastating results.

While these changes are occurring, families may be facing additional developmental transitions. These transitions may raise new problems and worries: health problems, increased dependency on the family or death of grandparents each illustrate one set of potential problems. Parents may be facing individual mid-life transitions. The accompanying changes can lead to additional stress within the family, while the family is preparing to launch its adolescent. On the other hand, dealing with the erratic moods and behaviors of the adolescent may provide a welcome distraction from these larger, sometimes overwhelming, changes facing the family.

Families who come to therapy with their adolescents are often confused and sometimes angry about their children's behavior, as are the adolescents about their parents' behavior toward them. Parents may differ with each other about what they should expect of and how to deal with their adolescents. In addition, often there is an absence of clarity regarding roles and expectations. This may derive from discrepancies experienced as coming from parents, peer groups, teachers, as well as messages from the larger cultural influences such as television and advertising (Lax & Lussardi, 1988).

There are several ways an adolescent's drinking/drug abusing problem may be viewed by the family, given the confusion of roles and rules we have so far described. The adolescent may be seen as showing the family a ritualized behavior understood by the family as coming of age. In families where excessive drinking is not the norm, this form of behavior is *not* acceptable as a statement that the adolescent is announcing a developmental shift. In families where drinking is a central organizing principle of family life (Steinglass, 1980), the adolescent drinker is offering a more acceptable communication. In either type of family, the adolescent's drinking is likely to be considered a problem when there are serious consequences, especially highway accidents and/or criminal behaviors.

When we meet a family brought to our offices because of the consequences of problem drinking, we are sensitive to the possibility that there are others in the family who share this problem. Because this is so often the situation, we will discuss the special treatment concerns raised by the occurrence of multigenerational alcoholism.

THE IMPACT OF PROBLEM DRINKING ON THE FAMILY-HELPER SYSTEM

AA and Al-Anon programs and family therapy research and treatment have looked carefully at how alcohol works within the family system. What has been often overlooked is the significance for the family-larger system relationship maintaining the multigenerational chronicity of the symptom. It is our experience that the issue of control is often central to the organization of the alcoholic family in its relationship to larger systems. Just as the alcoholic or problem drinker may appear to control another family member through out-of-control drinking, the entire family may seem to be engaged in a primary struggle to control involved therapists through a parallel process.

Just as the adolescent may be communicating something about himself or herself through his or her substance abuse to his or her family and social network, so it may be that families perpetuate problem drinking as a form of metaphoric communication about themselves in relation to the outside world. The identity as a drinking family may be punctuated as simply an ethnic identity (We're Irish . . .) or may be given a more complex punctuation. This communication pertains to myths and rules concerned with maintaining control in the family's relations with outsiders.

While the family may appear to be seeking help from the larger helping system, particularly with regard to the adolescent's substance abuse, it may be simultaneously attempting to control and/or extrude the very same system. For example, the family may be issuing an invitation to the larger system, while simultaneously organizing to conceal a family secret which is intricately connected to, or obscured by, the drinking/drug abusing behavior.

Learning what the primary family rules and myths appear to be both about outsiders/helpers and about drinking, may be a key to translating what has been labelled as the family's *resistance* (i.e., maintaining their organization around symptomatic drinking). The substance abuser's attempts to get help may involve a confusion of levels of meaning in the messages given to the helpers.

Through the use of more indirect forms of communication (metaphors, circular questions, reflecting team conversation), it may be possible to better understand the confusion of meaning and to respond to clinical interventions that will less likely violate or threaten the family's rules and myths. The therapist or counselor is himself or herself a larger system representative. Thus, if the family says to the therapist, in essence, "we are doomed to chronic symptomatic cries for help but we are also doomed never to be helped," family members are describing to the therapist their historical pattern of interaction with larger systems and simultaneously, are engaging in the very behavior they are describing. Any direct response to this may put the therapist in a double bind. Either trying to help or refusing to try to help puts the family-helper system into the same stuck pattern where it has been before.

If, instead, the relationship is addressed more indirectly through a conversation about levels of meaning in family-helper communication, an atmosphere may be created which feels new and different to both the family and the helpers. To be able, through metaphoric and exploratory communication, to *meta comment* on the client-therapist relationship, while simultaneously engaging in, may provide a new atmosphere in which change can more likely occur.

Acknowledging the sociocultural factors involved in the family's organization around problem drinking is essential to understanding what the family is saying about its relationship to larger systems. If the family is part of a religious context, for example, in which the confession of sins has a cyclical pattern, it would be important to understand how helpers are both involved in the family's problems and also dismissed from them. A family in which work is a singly significant value may be communicating something quite different in its organization around drinking than a family where the system is viewed with contempt. In the latter, maintaining control in relation to the outside world may be specifically communicated by refusing to change or by doing nothing.

In a family where alcoholism has not been a problem for two or more generations, the complexity of the client-helper relationship may be quite different or much the same as the situation just described. The adolescent's drinking behavior may be more openly targeted by the family as a problem, while other aspects of the larger systemic problem may go unnoticed. In a case like this, the family members involved in therapy because of the adolescent may indicate that it is up to the therapist to *fix* the identified patient. Isolated instances of problem drinking may be cited as peripheral to the family's history, but the message is clear: We are *not* a family inflicted with the problem of alcoholism; therefore our child's drinking is not a problem we can relate to, so it's up to the experts to fix.

This alternative situation may present similar problems for the therapist. Both types of families find it threatening or forbidden to talk about the drinking problem openly as part of their family story. When the therapist or counselor tries to connect the adolescent's substance abuse with the family's whole pattern of relationships, rules and myths, the family reacts against this intrusive idea.

Sometimes the adolescent's drinking or drug problem seems to be a vehicle for preparing to separate and leave the family. It can be seen as a kind of separation communication and a communication about other family problems. It is an unusual adolescent who can openly state either of these messages. Generally, the adolescent is not interested in analyzing the possible meanings of the message when confronted by family and helpers with the issue of his or her drinking. When this lack of interest on the part of the adolescent reverberates through the whole family system, the helper faces a familiar, but difficult challenge.

In describing how we use a systemic approach, through the format of the reflecting team, we emphasize the development of a genuine conversation between the family and the larger helping system. We advocate saving the necessary directness of confrontation and education for a time in treatment when the family, including the adolescent drinker, feel comfortable enough with the therapist to begin to tell the real story. This story includes genuine descriptions of the multiple meanings the drinking has for everyone involved in the current problem. There is also a more full and open communication about the meaning of *talking about* secrets, sources of shame and connected defiance, and historical patterns of struggles for control both within the family and between family and outsiders.

In the following treatment description, we will focus on how the reflecting team works and then illustrate how we most likely use this treatment format in working with adolescent substance abusers.

REFLECTING TEAM—HISTORY AND ASSUMPTIONS

The Reflecting Team Model was first developed by Norwegian psychiatrist Tom Andersen and his colleagues at the Tromso University, Institute for Community Medicine. Rooted in the principles of second order cybernetics and the new epistemology, this model is an expansion of the systemic approach developed by the Milan Associates (Palazzoli, et al., 1978; Campbell & Draper, 1985; Boscolo, et al., 1987). Having been influenced by the Milan Associates as well as the ideas of Bateson, Maturana, von Foerster and others concerned with the science of *observing systems*, this approach maintains several assumptions.

One important assumption is that a stuck system (for example, a family with a troubled adolescent) needs "new ideas" (Andersen, 1987) in order to broaden its perspective and understanding so that change can occur. This belief is coupled with the idea developed by the Mental Research Institute (Watzlawick et al., 1974) that problems are maintained by the repeating sameness of ideas and behaviors.

We also believe that there is a recursive relationship between beliefs and behavior. That is, people act in accordance to their belief systems. As beliefs change, behaviors will also be modified.

Another important assumption maintains the notion that there exists no objective reality or truth. Rather, we each formulate our own versions or pictures of reality by the distinctions we draw based upon our experiences and beliefs in comparison to others. Therefore, an important task of the clinician is to discover the assumptions, beliefs, and pictures held by our clients (as best we can) in order to generate new distinctions and alternative realities which may introduce the "difference which makes a difference" (Bateson, 1979).

Related to this, the therapist is a participant in the construction of the therapy system's reality (von Foerster, 1981). His or her own impressions may not necessarily be the truth but may fit the system to the extent that the impressions are accepted (von Glasersfeld, 1984).

Another important assumption has to do with positive connotation which was developed within the Milan systemic framework. Within this framework, it is assumed that it is difficult (if not impossible) for people to "leave the field" or change under a negative connotation (Hoffman, 1986, Boscolo et al., 1987).

THE REFLECTING TEAM METHOD

Guided by these assumptions, the reflecting team observes the interview or discussion between the therapist and family, forming ideas and impressions based on the developing picture. At some point during the interview, the therapist will ask for the ideas of the team. The team then enters the room as the family and therapist go behind the mirror to listen to the team discuss their thoughts, questions, and impressions. The team and family (along with the therapist) then switch places again and the family is asked about those elements of the teams discussion that struck them in a particular way. This format establishes a recursive process between the team and the family-therapist system which creates a changing/unfolding story. The story begins with a version held by the family, it is then reflected back by the team (with new punctuations), and heard by the family—from a new position—behind the mirror, listening, and then responding again. This process provides many versions of a standstill, stuck situation, and changes it to a fluid, moving picture with alternative descriptions, explanations, and new possibilities for meanings and behaviors.

The changing of positions between the team and the family can occur more than once and can be accomplished in many different ways with various numbers of therapists. It can also be accomplished without a one way mirror. Two therapists can have a conversation in front of the family and in the same room. (See Andersen, 1987, for a description of working guidelines.)

What seems to be of utmost importance in this recursive process is the experience of unfolding the picture from different (meta) positions. New perspectives and punctuations are offered within a positive frame of reference. It should be noted that this does not mean that the team or therapist would positively connote harmful or dangerous behaviors such as abuse. Rather, this notion concerns tapping into a person or system's strengths, resources, positive attributes, and good intentions as fuel for change.

One of the more radical differences this method introduced has been to bring the therapy team out from behind the one way mirror to "reflect," spontaneously, their impressions of the conversation which has taken place between the therapist and family. In effect, this method has eliminated the secret collaborations undertaken by teams working within the traditional Milan style. This change allows team members to present their thoughts in ways enabling the family to hear those ideas within a positive frame. This also places the team at the same hierarchical level as the family as they literally trade places and share in the experience of being observed and watched. Although it was never the intention of the Milan method, the hidden team was often perceived as a higher power, conspiring against the family and sometimes the therapist. The reflecting team approach creates a context in which all members (team, family, and therapist) are engaged in an exploration for new meanings and alternative behaviors.

FAMILIES WITH ADOLESCENT SUBSTANCE ABUSERS

When working with families in which adolescent substance abuse is a problem, we tend not to assume that one particular approach or perspective is best for every family. In keeping with the reflecting team approach, we prefer to discover what the families' views and beliefs are about the problem. However, we also hold in our minds that which we have learned from our experience. Although we do not take on an expert position, we do maintain our knowledge and expertise.

In so doing, we attempt to determine each family's views and history with helping systems as well as exploring the history of the idea of coming for therapy. In a case where the family is sent by the court or other agency, we explore the family's thoughts about the referring person's reasons for requiring therapy. If the family is vague or confused, we often find it necessary to include the referring persons to get their perspectives. As much as possible, we try to give this responsibility to the family.

In gathering the system's perspectives, we are also interested in the history of difficulties including past generations. We are also curious about other difficulties and transitions occurring in the family. Having obtained perspectives, which could range from bad friends to bad genes, and given this particular problem, we explore whether other members in the family, either present or past, had similar difficulties. By assuming this position, we are open to seeing the expression of substance abuse as a metaphor for other problems—as a symptom of a life stage transition as well as a disease.

In our work with families where issues of control and secrecy are more dominant, we have found the model of the reflecting team especially valuable. For example, when the secret of parental drinking is central to the family members resistance to treatment, the team may offer the following speculations.

- "I wonder if at some time in the past, members of this family were worried about someone else (besides the adolescent) in the family . . ."
- "It could be that even though everyone was worried about someone else, it might be considered disloyal to talk about these worries outside the family . . ."
- "Perhaps it is only the women in this family who have the job of worrying? If this is so, how do the men do their part in protecting the family?"

When such speculations are offered in the presence of the family, space is often provided to talk about worrying, secrets, and issues of loyalty and protection The maintenance of denial around family drinking problems may continue on an overt level, but tends to begin to move upward on the meta level of communication.

The reflecting team method also broadens the possibilities for discussion of the family's potentially difficult history of involvement with the larger professional system. Because the interviewing therapist may be putting the family in a difficult position by asking them how they view helping professionals, direct, honest responses are not always forthcoming. The reflecting team, on the other hand, can address a range of possible issues related to sensitive subjects. Questions and reflections might include the following.

- "It could be that in Mr. _______'s family, it was considered very shameful to talk about illness . . ."
- "Maybe it is difficult for John to talk about his pot smoking here because Mr. _______ and Mrs. _______ disagree on whether it is his problem or only a problem in the mind of his probation officer . . ."
- "I wonder if Mrs. _______ would be more comfortable talking about her son's problem to her priest or to her family doctor? Would her mother have talked about a problem like this to anyone at all? Maybe her sister or her mother?"

Responses to such questions and speculations often help us to understand more about the beliefs within the family as to how serious the adolescent's problem is, how each family member feels about talking about it in therapy, and whether there is one person in particular who is interested in seeking help.

One benefit of this approach is that regardless of the families explanations, the team and therapist can offer other possible explanations. This allows the reflecting team to maintain flexibility and maneuverability, allowing for a broad range of expression and intervention. Within this range, the therapist and team are free to be confused, to express concern, and/or take a stronger position when safety becomes a factor.

It is the movement from one explanation to many, which allows information, new meanings, and the possibility for new behavior to occur. The way the family receives this information is also significant. Listening to a version of their story, as understood by a team of therapists, from behind a one-way mirror can make the story seem bigger than life. The effect may be similar to the phenomenon of watching a movie on a big screen, in which characters and their problems seem more dramatic. Even tough, acting out adolescents who are not interested in therapy are often glued to the mirror listening to the unfolding story magnified by the context. We have observed many dramatic shifts after a family has experienced this method.

CASE EXAMPLE

Mrs. B and her 17-year-old son, Don, were referred for family therapy by a juvenile offenders' program; Don was arrested on a larceny charge after he had been drinking and was given the choice of (a) going to therapy, doing community service, and paying a restitution fee, or (b) going to court. Don had a previous juvenile conviction for a similar offense and chose option a.

When Mrs. B and Don first came to see us, Mrs. B mentioned that she had seen another therapist at our agency previously, for her own individual therapy. She appeared to be in some distress as she mentioned this, saying it was difficult to be back in our building. A superficial inquiry about the previous therapy gave us little understanding of what the therapy had been for, whether or not it had been useful, and why it had ended.

Mrs. B was less engaging, initially, than Don who presented as charmingly contrite about his offense, hopeful that therapy would be useful, and adamant that he was responsible for his wrong-doings—not his mother or anyone else in the family. He seemed worried that the mandate of family therapy meant that both the court and our team would somehow consider his mother was to blame. His mother also shared her concern that she would be viewed as a bad parent as a result of her son's difficulties.

Mrs. B presented as a worried, financially overwhelmed single parent: Besides Don, she was also raising two younger children. She lived upstairs from her parents, but described them as needing to be protected from her family's problems due to their age. She received minimal help from the children's father who lived a considerable distance from the family.

Despite Don's eagerness to take responsibility for his stealing escapade, he was far from an easy client to work with because of his consistent minimizing of other problems in the family including his drinking and the seriousness of several previous criminal episodes. His mother also did not seem interested in exploring the ramifications of his criminal behavior or his potential drinking problem.

Given this picture, we thought it might be important to understand more about their history of involvement with the larger professional system. While one of us remained in the primary role of interviewer, the other interjected reflections periodically throughout the sessions concerning the troubled relationship the Bs indeed seemed to have with the police, previous therapists, the court system, and the school system. It was quite clear that not only did Mrs. B and her son find the larger helping system uniformly either intrusive or indifferent to their real needs, but this view was shared by her parents as well.

Mother and son described for us an event in which the police were portrayed as behaving like the Gestapo: They had arrived uninvited and insisted on searching the grandparents' barn for stolen property, terrorizing the frail, elderly grandparents and the entire family. What Mrs. B and Don chose to omit from the story was that, in fact, there had been a number of valuable stolen items in the barn and that the police had reason to know what they would find there. We did not challenge or confront this, instead we speculated about how, if this was a family which was intruded upon and violated, coming to therapy may be viewed as more intrusion.

We remained as flexible in our initial inquiries and reflections as we could be, managing to sympathize with the difficulties of single parenting, having the family privacy invaded, and being disappointed in previous attempts to get help through therapy. We also praised Don with great regularity for his loyalty to his mother, and how much his history revealed a consistent desire to support her in every way a son could. This was genuine commentary on our part: It was evident that Don was loyal to his mother and that she turned to him more as a friend/lover than a child.

Another significant piece of Don's self-description was his belief that men keep their feelings, pain, worry, and so on, to themselves; women are the only ones who talk about these things. He had a strong sense of identification with his grandfather; despite his desire to be gracious towards us, he was quite expressive in sharing his grandfather's lack of faith in therapy. His mother confirmed this, but began to separate herself by declaring herself more of a believer in therapy and having some concerns. Don remained adamant that there was nothing to talk about and that what he had done was history.

We adjusted our format to this information by agreeing that therapists couldn't, of course, force anyone to participate in therapeutic conversation. Therefore, we suggested that it might be more useful to continue our sessions in a different way. The women (Dusty and Mrs. B) could discuss Mrs. B's concerns, and the men (Dario and Don) could have brief reflections through conversations with each other about the women's conversation. Dusty and Dario would also occasionally reflect in front of the two of them. Both Don and his mother embraced this format with surprising enthusiasm.

Quite quickly it became apparent that Mrs. B was still grieving and angry about the past therapy which, from her viewpoint, had been terminated abruptly because her insurance ran out and she was no longer able to pay. As Dusty and Mrs. B continued their conversation, other concerns began to emerge. She was worried about many of Don's behaviors; in particular, she was concerned about his inability to maintain his responsibilities and consider his difficulties seriously. Mrs. B explained that it was hard for her to express her concerns to her son directly.

The conversation became confusing about where the boundaries of emotional closeness actually were. We wondered if perhaps therapy ended for members of this family when things became too close for comfort, or when family secrets were about to be revealed? Within the brief discussion between Dario and Don, it was revealed that Don's father also was viewed as irresponsible and that he drank regularly. It was revealed that Don had been planning to live with his father while he attended college. Later, the two therapists reflected in front of the mother and son about the consequences there might be if Don continued to neglect his responsibilities. Would his planned departure to college be postponed? Would this be some type of expression of loyalty to his family? What concerns would his mother have if this were to occur? If Don departed as planned, what continuing concerns would his mother have?

In one session we changed our format: Dario happened to be out sick, so Dusty met with Mrs. B and Don alone. Mrs. B was unusually tearful and expressed suicidal thoughts and feelings of profound helplessness. The precipitant seemed to be a combination of financial worries and the recent loss of a close female friend who had moved away. Don withdrew verbally and emotionally, stating only that he believed, like his grandfather, that you just had to "bite the bullet" and get on with life. Dusty suggested that Don was, in fact, in considerable pain himself because he probably wanted to help his mother, but could not. This provoked a sudden revelation for him about the funeral of a cousin his age who had committed suicide the year before. "No one," Don said, "had understood the extent of his pain and why he could not force himself to go to the funeral."

Given the amount of emotional expression from Mrs. B, the next session was arranged for Dusty and Mrs. B to meet alone. Mrs. B told an extremely anguished story that day of extraordinary family trauma and denial in which it emerged that she was, in fact, going strongly against the family rules about expressing grief, any other emotions, or talking about traumatic or distressing realities. She began to acknowledge that there had been considerable drinking in the family and that she was concerned about her son, Don, despite her early stance of minimizing and denial.

At this point, the therapeutic relationship had shifted from frank mistrust for all concerned, to the beginning of a more genuine collaboration. Mrs. B was able to talk more openly about her financial worries and loneliness, the changes anticipated by everyone as Don drew closer to the "leaving home" stage of life, and the multigenerational ambivalence about seeking help outside the family. Don's revelation about his cousin also began to erode the picture that all was well with him. Not having had much contact with Don's father, Mrs. B was unsure if he was actively drinking and, therefore, was uncertain if this would be the best place for Don to be while at college.

It was now possible to address the problem of alcohol abuse much more directly. Don and his mother had listened to our questions, observations, and had gathered enough information about us to make it safer for them to talk with us about areas of shame including alcohol use and abuse.

At this point, it was now possible for us to be more direct about our concerns: We were able to tell Mrs B and Don how much we wondered about how to talk about drinking in an *open* rather than *closed* conversation. It had also become possible to suggest that abstinence from alcohol for a specific period of time might allow Don—or any other family member who might be worried about his or her drinking—to test how far the potential addiction had progressed. Now, we also could offer the family our suggestions about exploring the possibilities of joining a peer support group such as AA or Al-Anon.

We think that it is often worthwhile to spend slow, careful time learning the adolescent and family's beliefs and fears about substance abuse, therapy, and sharing of secrets. When this work has been done successfully, the relationship developed between client and therapist is strong and safe enough to allow more effective communication about substance abuse. It is only after doing this careful work in the Reflecting Team Model that we feel comfortable with more confrontational and educational stages of treatment.

CONCLUSION

In this chapter, we have described the problem of adolescent substance abuse using several contexts. At one level, we have suggested that the developmental issues of the family with an abusing adolescent are significant for the therapist to understand, especially when the norm is for adolescence to present only one of several major transitional events the family may be experiencing. We have also looked at substance abuse and what this means for families in relation to the larger helping system. We have focused on issues of control and shame as central for both individual and family treatment consideration.

Because adolescent clients and their often angry and defensive families present major therapeutic challenges, we have described a new treatment model which we are finding unusually effective. The Reflecting Team Model allows for greater possibilities in engaging resistant clients and their families. In examining the average length of therapy over the past two years, we found that we are averaging between seven to eight sessions per client system. These figures include one shots as well as longer term cases. Because the model is still new to us, we cannot compare how it measures next to more established, traditional approaches to treating the adolescent substance abuser. We are hopeful, however, that it has already begun to help us in getting closer to the kind of genuine conversation we believe is necessary for change to take place in the client-helper relationship.

REFERENCES

Andersen, T. (1987). The reflecting team: Dialogue and meta-dialogue in clinical work. *Family Process, 26*(4), 415–428.

Bateson, G. (1979). *Mind in nature: A necessary unity.* New York: Ballantine.

Boscolo, L., Cecchin, G., Hoffman, L., & Penn, P. (1987) *Milan Systemic Family Therapy: Conversations in Theory and Practice.* New York: Basic Books.

Campbell, D. & Draper, R. (eds.) (1985) *Applications of Systemic Family Therapy: The Milan Approach.* London: Grune & Stratton.

von Foerster, H. (1981) *Observing Systems.* Seaside, CA.

von Glasersfeld, E. (1984). An Introduction to radical constructivism. In P. Watzlawick (ed.), *The Invented Reality.* New York: W. W. Norton.

Hoffman, L. (1986). Beyond power and control. *Family Systems Medicine, 3:* 381–396.

Lax, W. & Lussardi, D. (1988) The use of rituals in families with adolescents. In E. Imber-Black, J. Roberts, & R. Whiting, (eds.), *Rituals in Families and Family Therapy.* New York: W. W. Norton.

Maturana, H., & Varela, F. (1987) *The Tree of Knowledge: The Biological Roots of Human Understanding.* Boston: Shambala Publications.

Miller, Dusty. (1983) Outlaws and invaders: The adaptive function of alcohol abuse in the family-helper supra system. *Journal of Strategic and Systemic Therapies,* 2(3): 15–27.

Quinn, W. H., Newfield, N. A., & Protinsky, H. O. (1985). Rites of passage in families with adolescents. *Family Process, 24*(1): 101–111.

Palazzoli, M. S., Boscolo, L., Cecchin, G., & Prata, G. (1978). *Paradox and Counterparadox.* New York: Aronson.

Palazzoli, M. S., Boscolo, L., Cecchin, G. & Prata, G. (1980) The problem of the referring person. *Journal of Marital and Family Therapy, 6:* 3–9.

Steinglass, P. (1980) A life history model of the alcoholic family. *Family Process 19:* 211–226.

Watzlawick, P., Weakland, J., & Fisch, R. (1974). Change: Principles of problem formation and problem resolution. New York: W. W. Norton.

12

Beyond Structural-Strategic Family Therapy

Integrating Other Brief Systemic Therapies

THOMAS C. TODD, Ph.D.
Chief Psychologist, Forest Hospital, Des Plaines, IL

MATTHEW D. SELEKMAN, M.S.W.
Family Therapy Supervisor
Des Plaines Valley Community Center, Summit, IL

HISTORICAL ANTECEDENTS

The present model, which we consider a major elaboration of the structural-strategic model of family therapy, still owes a considerable debt to the pioneering work of Stanton and Todd and their colleagues at the Philadelphia Child Guidance Clinic. Not surprisingly, that work, in turn, had been influenced by both Haley and Minuchin.

Haley, who was a consultant to the Stanton and Todd project, helped to shape the stages and goals of the therapeutic program. (See Haley, 1980, for further elaboration of these ideas.) Haley placed particular emphasis on keeping the early stages of therapy focused on the presenting problem, rather than being diverted onto other issues in the family. The therapist's job was typically seen as uniting parents to correct the family hierarchy, rather than encouraging marital squabbles.

The primary goals of therapy were seen as consistently relating to the primary problem of substance abuse. Other family problems were acceptable if clearly related to the presenting problem. Haley also emphasized that therapy rarely can proceed directly to the desired goal, but instead might need to go through a transitional stage first. (The classic example is putting a peripheral parent fully in charge, with the eventual goal being an equal parental balance of power.)

Minuchin's contribution was seen most clearly in intervention techniques (Minuchin, 1974; Minuchin & Fishman, 1980). In the Stanton and Todd project, the therapists frequently relied on typical structural techniques such as joining, enactment, intensifying, and restructuring.

The work of Stanton and Todd and their staff, which culminated in *The Family Therapy of Drug Abuse and Drug Addiction* (Stanton, Todd, & Associates, 1982), developed a specific program that went well beyond the basics of structural and strategic (*a la* Haley) therapy. Most notable was their emphasis on techniques for engaging substance abusers and their families (Stanton & Todd, 1981) and their emphasis on "noble ascriptions" regarding the role of the substance abuser in the family. Specific modifications for work with adolescent substance abusers were described by Fishman et al. (1982).

KEY ASSUMPTIONS

The basic assumptions of the structural-strategic model have been articulated elsewhere (Stanton and Todd, 1982) and will not be repeated here. For the purposes of this chapter, we wish to highlight those assumptions that facilitate the integration of other brief systemic therapies with the structural-strategic model.

As will be seen later in this chapter, our integrated model incorporates elements and techniques from a number of other models. Most notably these include the solution-focused model (de Shazer 1985, 1988; Berg & Gallagher, this volume), Michael White's cybernetic-systemic model (White, 1985, 1987, 1988; Durrant & Coles, this volume), the Milan systemic model, and the strategic approach of Madanes (1981, 1984).

We have identified several common assumptions that characterize to varying degrees all of these approaches. (See Table 12.1 for summary.) It is this set of assumptions that make these models relatively compatible.

All of these models are almost completely ahistorical, emphasizing present interaction and looking toward the future. The change process is seen as built on small changes, achieved by activating or accessing strengths, rather than dwelling on pathology.

These approaches are highly pragmatic. The therapist plays an ac-

TABLE 12.1 Key Assumptions Common to Elements of the Todd and Selekman Integrative Model.

Empahsis on present and future, not past
Little emphasis on insight; positive reframing used instead
Interpersonal changes will result in improvement
Small changes are crucial
Build on strengths
Pragmatic—emphasis on what works
Keep it simple; untangle the web of helpers
Therapy is relatively short-term
Therapist plays active role
Solution is unique to each family

tive role in seeking to discover what works, developing a solution that is unique to the particular family and case. As this happens, the therapist will phase out, assuming that the family can cope without long-term therapy.

It should be noted that the models mentioned in this section do have important differences. Differences on a pragmatic and technical level will be addressed in the section on intervention selection in this chapter. More basic theoretical differences will be discussed in the final chapter of this volume.

Philosophical Position on Adolescent Chemical Dependency

Although the disease model of chemical dependency treatment (education plus AA or NA) is quite popular today. There is very little, if any, empirical evidence for its effectiveness with adolescent substance abusers. These youth are frequently given such diagnostic labels as *chemically dependent, drug addicted,* or *alcoholic.* It is our concern that often these diagnostic labels may do more harm than good for these young people who are grappling with the normal developmental tasks of identity formation and individuation from their families (Ellis, 1986). The chemical dependence label implies that the adolescent has a disease or illness that is lifelong and incurable. The disease-oriented therapist will view the site of pathology as within the adolescent, with little consideration for the social contexts in which the substance-abusing behavior occurs.

Ethnographic and longitudinal studies with adolescent drug abusers have repeatedly demonstrated that the chemical dependence label is not accepted by adolescents because it clashes with the norms and values of the adolescent's social world (Glassner & Loughlin, 1987; Glassner, Carpenter, & Berg, 1986). Adolescent drug abusers value self-control of their drug use, detest such labels as alcoholic, drug addict, and burnout, and typically expect that they will drastically reduce or totally eliminate chemical use when they reach adulthood (Glassner & Loughlin, 1987). This belief is justified in many cases when even adolescents with high levels of drug usage do not exhibit chemical dependency in adulthood.

In our clinical work with adolescent substance abusers, we avoid applying a permanent label of addict wherever possible, especially early in treatment before we have ascertained their responses to our treatment approach. When working with adolescent substance abusers, we focus on the young person's social context, including his or her family, peer groups, and other larger helping systems. If the adolescent substance abuser displays severe physical withdrawal, we will pursue hospital detoxification and short-term hospitalization as needed. The majority of adolescent substance abusers we have treated fall into the categories of experimenter, misuser, or abuser, rather than addict. When this is the case, it is important to help the family to react appropriately, rather than overreacting and creating a self-fulfilling prophecy (Todd, 1988).

With some highly reactive parents, we may make them aware of such self-help groups as Al-Anon and Families Anonymous for additional support and guidance. Similarly, we believe that young people's AA and NA groups can be quite useful to some adolescent substance abusers who could benefit from further positive social support outside of family therapy sessions, especially those whose entire peer group are heavy users. However, we believe strongly that therapists should avoid adopting a rigid policy regarding the mandatory participation of all family members in self-help groups. We have found it more useful to conduct a differential assessment on a case-by-case basis to determine which families could benefit from participation in self-help groups. If a family member is already actively involved in a 12-Step self-help group prior to beginning family therapy and has found this helpful, we will support this client's healthy choice of coping strategies.

TECHNIQUES FOR INITIATING TREATMENT

The Relevance and Role of Family Members

Stanton and Todd (1982a) have emphasized the importance of the "non-blaming message" in the recruitment into treatment of families of drug abusers. While it is true that families of adolescent drug abusers are typically much easier to engage in treatment than those of adult heroin addicts, it is still important for the therapist to offer a rationale for the involvement of family members that is non-blaming. This message should be tailored to the particular clinical situation, and may involve any of the following elements.

1. It is always safe to stress the need for a maximum, coordinated helping effort on the part of everyone involved in the life of the substance abuser. While therapists should convey the expectation that therapy can be helpful, therapists should also make it clear that they need all the help they can get.
2. Therapists should imply beliefs that parents and other family members have a genuine desire to be helpful to the substance abuser, while also noting that, despite this desire, they may not know the best way to be helpful, or they may try to help in ways that turn out to have the unintended effect of promoting drug abuse or undermining abstinence. (This is similar to the idea of *enabling.*)
3. Similarly, the therapist should *not* imply an underlying motivation on the part of parents and family members to see the identified client fail and use drugs. Instead, it is better to imply that significant others learn to accommodate to drug use and its consequences over a period of time, and that they may be unprepared for the upsetting effects of abstinence. The analogy is made to a broken leg or physical disability—no one wants such a handicap and anyone would like to get rid of it, yet, the person having the handicap and those around the person may be unaware of the complex accommodations that have been made to the condition, which will be upset initially by a return to normalcy.

The abuser or another family member may propose some alternative basis for involvement in family therapy, such as improving communication, dealing with parental problems, or addressing problems of a sibling. The therapist should accept such contracts cautiously and regard such goals as secondary to the primary goal of reduced drug involvement. If difficulties develop with these goals, or if dealing with these goals seems to be over-stressing the abuser at an inapppropriate time in relation to the drug treatment, the therapist should always be ready to abandon or postpone the goals. (See Todd, 1988, for detailed consideration of such timing.)

Assessment and Goal-Setting

Since our therapeutic approach is goal-oriented and short-term, we move quickly to begin to negotiate achievable goals. These need to be stated in concrete behavioral terms so that goal-achievement can easily be recognized. These goals are then translated into smaller steps that can realistically be accomplished in the one-to-two weeks between sessions, so that the change process can be launched.

Therapeutic goals should relate directly or indirectly to the drug abuse. Changes in drug usage should be linked to other changes, including individual changes in the adolescent, changes in family interaction, and changes in the larger context. When such positive links can be made, symptomatic improvement is more likely to last.

In the contracting process, it is important to investigate the family's previous attempted solutions, any previous treatment experiences, and their expectations of therapy. Especially after making it clear in this way that we are interested in *their* goals and *their* expectations, rather than imposing our own, we are typically successful in developing an explicit contract concerning the goals and methodology of therapy.

The earlier Stanton and Todd (1982) model assumed that it was important to assess the function of the substance abuse in the family system and to identify those factors in the family that maintain the drug abuse. It now seems that such functional hypotheses are typically useful only in cases of chronic substance abuse where the family has adapted to the substance abuse over a long period of time. In adolescent substance use, we rarely find it necessary to begin with such hypotheses and we believe that they can hinder the change process.

As we will elaborate further in the section on techniques, we find that the majority of cases respond to our positive, change-oriented approach, but that there is a significant minority in which any straightforward efforts are doomed. In such cases, it may be useful for therapists to gather data to develop functional hypotheses. Often with these cases, it is virtually impossible to negotiate a specific contract with clear-cut goals. Instead, as will be discussed later, therapy is typically more indirect with hypotheses used to develop solution-focused prescriptions, systemic questions and feedback, and, when necessary, paradoxical interventions.

Utilizing the Basic Structural-Strategic Model

Although much of the remainder of this chapter will be devoted to our efforts to integrate new techniques and ideas with the basic structural-strategic model, remember that the basic model is still useful with a sizeable proportion of adolescent cases. The structural-strategic method is presented comprehensively in Stanton and Todd (1982), with many clinical examples in Stanton, Todd, & Associates (1982), so only a few major points will be emphasized here.

Following Haley (1976, 1980), we emphasize the importance of a correct hierarchy that has the parents clearly in charge of the family (but not, as will be emphasized later, at the expense of the adolescent). The structural-strategic therapist works actively and directively to accomplish this.

The importance of concrete and realistic goals has already been emphasized. Within the structural-strategic model, the therapist uses enactment within the session and homework tasks between sessions to help families move toward these goals.

Faced with problems of non-compliance with tasks, whether during sessions or between sessions, the therapist will use several straightforward techniques before moving beyond this model. These include intensified joining efforts, simplification of assigned tasks, and personal appeals from the therapist for more effort from family members. Usually, it is only when all of these avenues have been attempted that the structural-strategic therapist will conclude that other measures are needed (Todd, 1988).

EXPANDING THE MODEL TO INCLUDE ELEMENTS OF OTHER MODELS

Since the development of the basic structural-strategic family therapy approach (Stanton & Todd, 1982), we have become increasingly aware of its limitations in our day-to-day work with adolescent substance abusers. One major limitation of the basic structural-strategic model is the narrowness in the choice of interventions by the therapist or therapeutic team. A significant subgroup of the substance-abusing families we have treated did not respond well to our direct restructuring interventions. These families often came to us with a long history of treatment failures. In some cases, the substance abuse or alcoholism problem had developed a life of its own over three or four generations in these families. Thus, straightforward interventions had little impact on these intractable symptoms. We have also discovered that it is not always possible to engage all family members connected to the presenting problem, particularly in families with multiple chemical abusers. In order to better meet the needs of our client families and broaden our therapeutic armamentarium, we decided to expand the basic structural-strategic model to include some of the therapeutic ideas and interventions of Madanes, de Shazer, Milan, and Michael White. Now, we will briefly describe how we have incorporated the previously mentioned systemic thinkers' work in our newly expanded model.

The Work of Madanes and White

The creative therapy methods of Madanes and White have injected a playful element into our therapeutic work with adolescent substance abusers and their families. Madanes (1981, 1984) has had a major impact on our enlisting the substance abuser and his or her siblings as co-therapists (Selekman, 1987a, 1987b). In some cases, we have made strategic use of the substance abuser's peer group to help the former remain drug-free outside of therapy sessions (Selekman, 1989b). We frequently employ pretending techniques (Madanes, 1981) as a playful way to disrupt problem-maintaining sequences of interaction in the family. For example, once the problem-maintaining sequences have been identified, we may ask the substance abuser to pretend to be *high* on drugs and have family members guess whether he or she is really high or is acting. The substance abuser is instructed not to tell the family anything until the following session. Once the substance abuser has become drug-free, family members can be instructed to pretend to engage in both their old and new patterns of interacting on alternate days, in order to help the family identify differences and make distinctions.

We have found White's habit control meetings (White, 1988), externalization of the problem (White, 1985; Tomm & White, 1987; Durrant, 1985, 1987, Durrant & Coles, this volume), and various categories of cybernetic questions (see Systemic Interviewing Section) to be most useful in the context of adolescent substance abuse problems. Durrant (1985), a colleague of White's, has developed an effective method for empowering children and their families in taming temper tantrum problems. We have successfully adapted Durrant's *Temper Taming* model for substance abuse problems. After externalizing the adolescent's drug abuse problem, such as "marijuana addiction" (parent's label) to become "Pot" (the adolescent's language), the family is instructed to keep track on a daily/weekly chart the victories of the identified client and those of Pot over one another. The identified client is also instructed to write down in a notebook the various things he or she does daily to avoid being pushed around by Pot. Family members are asked to participate in specified exercise regimes together in order to be physically and mentally prepared to go to battle with Pot. At the end of designated evaluation periods, the therapist can highlight differences and have family members make distinctions between their old and new ways of interacting with one another and Pot. Therapy will be concluded with a celebration party for the family's conquest of Pot. Celebration can consist of a party, cakes, trophies, certificates, and so forth (Menses & Durrant, 1987). It has been our clinical experience that some families with long histories of treatment and chemical abuse problems tend to respond quite well to the playful and positive orientation of Michael White's cybernetic therapy approach.

Solution-Focused Therapy

The brief solution-focused therapy approach of Steve de Shazer and his colleagues (de Shazer, 1985, 1988; Lipchik, 1987a, 1987b; Weiner-Davis, de Shazer, & Gingerich, 1987; Molnar & de Shazer, 1987; Berg & Gallagher, this volume) has had a profound impact on how we view problems, on our interviewing strategies (see Systemic Interviewing Section), in goal-setting, and in the co-construction of solutions with families. We will limit our discussion to a few of the major theoretical assumptions and therapeutic interventions that have been useful in our work with adolescent substance abusers and their families. From our standpoint, de Shazer's most important contribution to the family therapy field is his immediate search for exceptions—when the presenting problem is *not* occurring. Weiner-Davis (Weiner-Davis et al., 1987) has taken this a step further by helping family members identify "pretreatment changes." According to de Shazer (1985), there are always exceptions to the rule. This de Shazer rule-of-thumb has greatly challenged our thinking about clients' problems, particularly our tendency to focus excessively on problems, rather than on what is already working for families. In the area of substance abuse problems, de Shazer (1987) has found it helpful to schedule longer time intervals between sessions for improving clients as a vote of confidence and as a method of allowing the change process to grow.

We have found the use of compliments (de Shazer, 1985) to be a highly effective engagement strategy with substance abusers and their families. Complimenting family members on their various strengths, not only can rapidly foster cooperation between family and therapist, but this interventive tool can greatly increase the likelihood of the family's following through with therapeutic tasks.

de Shazer and his colleagues have developed two therapeutic tasks that are particularly effective with adolescent substance abusers and their families: (1) Asking the substance abuser to "pay close attention to what he or she does to avoid the temptation/urge to get high or drunk" (adolescent's language) over a designated period of time; and (2) Asking parents to "do something different" in response to their adolescent's getting intoxicated, no matter how crazy, weird, or off-the-wall (de Shazer, 1985). The first intervention is an excellent relapse prevention tool. The second intervention works well with parents whose attempted solutions have become repetitive and who are willing to tap into their creative resources. This intervention can also successfully disrupt the ineffectual parental dance around the substance abuser. Some parents have discovered highly creative and effective responses to their adolescent's substance-abusing behavior, for instance, firing squirt guns at their adolescent, rather than engaging in lectures and power struggles.

Milan Techniques

The major contribution of Milan theorists to our approach has been the use of circular questions in the areas of problem-assessment and purposeful interventions. (See Systemic Interviewing section.) We also frequently utilize two of the original Milan group's classic interventions. The Odd Day/Even Day ritual (Palazzoli et al., 1978) is particularly useful for parents who have a tendency to undercut one another in their management of their adolescent's substance abusing behavior. By putting each parent exclusively in charge on alternating days, parental differences are amplified and made accessible to the therapist. The Invariant Prescription (Palazzoli et al., 1988) is effective with clinical situations in which the substance abuser and his or her siblings have disempowered their parents in the hierarchy. This pattern can be disrupted by having the parents disappear without explanation to the children (many times after taking precautions such as having the police watch the house).

Engaging the Adolescent Substance Abuser

We have found it to be most advantageous for the therapist to provide the adolescent substance abuser with ample individual session time in the early stage of family therapy in order to establish therapeutic leverage. By joining well with the adolescent substance abuser, the therapist will not lose any ground with the identified client when empowering the parents. Otherwise, this can be a particular danger early in family treatment, before the therapist has had time to support the parental subsystem. The authors have found a number of engagement techniques to be useful with adolescent substance abusers, including positive relabeling of negative behaviors, the use of metaphors, empathy, humor, therapist use of self, and familiarity with street language (Selekman, 1989b). The engagement process will occur much more rapidly with the adolescent substance abuser if the family therapist demonstrates a good grasp of the adolescent culture (e.g., music groups and teenage cult figures), as well as the street names of drugs and drug paraphernalia.

Once the therapist has developed a strong alliance with the adolescent substance abuser, the latter can be utilized as a *family systems consultant* by the therapist in gaining an inside view of the abuser's family system, such as learning about present family stressors (Selekman, 1987a, b). Since the adolescent substance abuser may be intimately involved in the parent's marital drama, the family therapist can learn about the quality of the marital relationship and possible parental chemical abuse. It is useful to explore with the adolescent substance abuser what family problems are most troublesome to him or her. A secret pact can be made between the adolescent substance abuser and the therapist regarding the latter's assuming sole responsibility for the resolution of the family and marital problems. Throughout the course of family therapy, the therapist should also convey to the adolescent substance abuser the therapist's commitment to serve as an advocate and arbitrator for the substance abuser across generational lines.

In some adolescent substance abuse cases, the parents are initially unable to bring in the identified client for family therapy. This may be due to the substance abuser's power in the hierarchy or often because an overinvolved parent is being protective of the adolescent. Although it is helpful to have all family members present in the first interview, all is not lost if the identified client fails to attend. The family therapist can take advantage of seeing the parents alone by using this time to empower the parents and explore their attempted solutions. Homework assignments can be given to the parents to help disrupt the ineffectual family interactions around the substance abuser.

We have found that novel and surprising interventions can serve as powerful motivators for engaging difficult adolescent substance abusing clients who refuse to attend family sessions. Once the parents can identify the context, the frequency, and the times in which the substance abusing behavior occurs, well-timed, surprise interventions can be employed to disrupt the drug use pattern. Families have had surprise visitors come to their homes during the times when the substance abuser gets high—a singing telegram and actors dressed up as FBI detectives. If the parents can locate drug stashes (hiding spots for drugs) in their home, the drugs can be replaced with a favorite snack or candy. It has been our experience that substance abusing behavior can be drastically altered or eliminated if any aspect of the drug use ritual is disrupted. Peele (1985) supports our position by stating that "the rituals which accompany drug use and addiction are important elements in continued use, so much so that to eliminate essential rituals can cause an addiction to lose its appeal." (p. 14) Novel, surprise interventions can be effectively employed at any stage of family therapy and can help considerably to neutralize the substance abuser's power in the family.

Systemic Interviewing

An important component of our expanded structural-strategic model is the use of circular and cybernetic questions in the areas of problem assessment, goal setting, and purposeful interventions. Our systemic interviewing methods have been strongly influenced by the Milan Associates (Palazzoli, Boscolo, Cecchin & Prata, 1980; Boscolo, Cecchin, Hoffman, & Penn, 1987; Penn, 1982, 1985; Tomm, 1987, 1988), Steve de Shazer and his colleagues (de Shazer, 1985, 1988; Lipchik, 1988a, 1988b; Lipchik & de Shazer, 1986; Nunnally, de Shazer, Lipchik, & Berg, 1986; Weiner-Davis, de Shazer & Gingerich, 1987; O'Hanlon & Weiner-Davis, 1989), and most recently, the innovative cybernetic approach of Michael White (Durrant, 1985, 1987; Tomm & White, 1987; White, 1985, 1987, 1988), For the sake of brevity, we will briefly discuss some of the major categories of questions developed by the previously mentioned family therapists, which we frequently utilize in our work with adolescent substance abusers and their families.

Lately, we have found it most advantageous to begin our systemic inquiry with families by exploring with family members whether they have noticed any pre-treatment changes (Weiner-Davis et al., 1987). Weiner-Davis and her colleagues found in their research that with at least two-thirds of their cases, differences or changes had already begun to occur with the client's presenting problem in the time period between the initial phone call to the therapist and the first appointment. This information can prove invaluable for the therapist and family, alike, in co-constructing potential solutions to the presenting problem. If the family cannot identify any pre-treatment changes, or any present differences in the problem area, we may use the Miracle Question (Berg & Gallagher, Chapter 5, this volume) to access information from family members regarding exceptions to the presenting problem. Family members are asked the following: "If you were to go home tonight and wake up tomorrow and there was a miracle, no more problems, what would be different in this family?" The Miracle Question is an excellent interventive tool for establishing treatment goals with families.

Following our exploration of pre-treatment changes and exception sequences of behavior with the family, we attempt to secure a clear statement of the problem that includes the following: "What brings you in now?"; "What would you like to change?"; asking one or more family members, "Give me a motion picture of what all family members do when X gets high or drunk?" The latter question is useful for obtaining a circular picture of the family reactions when the presenting problem occurs. This circular question provides the therapist with important information regarding family members' attempted solutions and multiple locus points for intervention. Helpful and ineffective attempted solutions are explored, including past treatment experiences. Ranking and difference questions (Palazzoli et al., 1980; Penn, 1982; Tomm, 1987, 1988) are useful for gathering information about coalitions around the presenting problem. For example, we may ask the adolescent substance abuser to rank order on a scale from one to 10 each family member in terms of their degree of concern about his or her drug use The ranking task can be expanded to include extended family members, significant others, peers, school officials, and so forth. Triadic questions (Palazzoli et al., 1980) are also helpful for assessing coalitions and differences in family relationships.

Future-oriented questions can be useful for establishing treatment goals, for escaping from therapeutic quandaries, and in the co-construction of solutions. As we mentioned earlier, the Miracle Question is not only a powerful interventive tool for goal-setting, but can also provide building blocks for constructing solutions. We have developed a variation of the Miracle Question that produces similar results in eliciting from clients where they would like to be at the end of treatment. A family member is asked, "If you were to show me a motion picture of what your family will look like when there are no more problems, what will I see?" "What will be different?" "What will you and your parents be talking about or doing together?" This detailed future-oriented inquiry can be linked to the present family situation by asking family members if any of the reported differences are already occurring. Lipchik (1988b) begins some of her sessions by asking clients the following: "How will you know you don't have to come here anymore?" We particularly like this question because it not only assists clients in identifying their goals, but it also conveys a clear message that change is inevitable. Finally, another useful interventive tool for eliciting treatment goals from clients, are scaling questions (Berg & Gallagher, Chapter 5, this volume; de Shazer, 1985; Lipchik, 1987a). Clients are asked to rate their situation on a scale of one to 10, before treatment, in the present, and where it needs to be for them to be satisfied. Scaling questions are excellent for generating exceptions and providing the family and therapist with a quantitative index of progress over the course of therapy.

Eastwood, Sweeney, and Piercy (1987) have developed a brief family therapy model for first-time, court-mandated adolescent substance abuse cases, that mainly consists of the use of future-oriented questions and problem-solving methods with the family. As the authors have pointed out, these *no problem-problem* families fail to respond to traditional family therapy approaches because of their involuntary status. Future-oriented questions are employed to enhance family problem-solving capacities and for the prevention of future involvement with the juvenile justice system.

Although we are fairly new to White's cybernetic therapy approach, we have found that his categories of cybernetic questions add an important dimension to our therapeutic repertoire. One of White's most valuable contributions to the family therapy field is his use of questions to externalize the problem outside the symptomatic family member (Durrant, 1985, 1987; Tomm & White, 1987; White, 1985). For example, we might ask a marijuana-abusing adolescent how long Pot has been pushing him or her around in relationship to school officials and parents. Other externalizing questions will be asked in such a way to convey to the family that Pot is oppressing all of them. Externalizing questions actively challenge outmoded family beliefs regarding the problem residing within the substance abuser. These questions also serve to break-up vicious guilt/blame cycles of interaction that frequently occur in substance-abusing families (Selekman, 1989a).

Complementary and raising dilemma questions (Durrant, 1987; Tomm & White, 1987; White, 1987) are effective at rapidly mobilizing familial resources, creating emotionality, and readying the family for combat as a group against the tyrannical problem. A set of complementary questions we often utilize with adolescent substance abusers and their parents, is as follows. "Do you see how Coke is putting your parents in charge of your future?" and "Do you see how Coke is taking away your daughter's future?" The following raising dilemma questions were used by one of the authors in successfully challenging a heavy alcohol-abusing adolescent to take immediate action against the four-generational reign of the Alcohol Monster over him and his family: "Will you continue to follow the family tradition of allowing the Alcohol Monster to make you a passenger in life, or do you prefer to establish a new tradition of succeeding in life?" In the above mentioned case, alcoholism was externalized into the cybernetic metaphor of Alcohol Monster (Selekman, 1989a). Cybernetic language and questions can effectively open up space for family members to entertain new ways of viewing the problem and interacting with one another.

DEALING WITH SYMPTOMATIC IMPROVEMENT AND RELAPSES

The handling of symptomatic improvement or relapse is far from simple. Changes in either direction must always be evaluated in terms of previous patterns of improvement, the stage of therapy, and the ideal stance of the therapist and other team members. Only after all of these factors have been considered can an appropriate therapeutic plan be developed.

When therapy is proceeding well and there are no mitigating circumstances, it is reasonable to expect significant improvement as early as the third or fourth session. When this improvement occurs on schedule, it is crucial to consolidate the changes and shift to interpersonal issues. To consolidate positive therapeutic change, the therapist should usually adopt a stance of guarded optimism—the changes appear desirable and real, but they may not last. Change is often three steps forward and two steps back (de Shazer, 1985). If a supervisor or team is involved, they can split on this issue: the treating therapist supports the change and takes an optimistic stance, while the team members or supervisor act more pessimistic and skeptical.

As symptomatic improvement occurs, interpersonal issues often emerge. If so, it is crucial for the therapy to begin to focus more directly on these issues. If no interpersonal issues surface, it is important for the therapist to link symptomatic improvement to interpersonal changes in the family. If the family is allowed to maintain an exclusive focus on the abuser and the possibility of a return to drug use, rather than focusing on interpersonal changes, a relapse will typically occur.

The therapist has considerable latitude in influencing the stance taken by the family when a relapse or slip occurs. At one extreme, it may be appropriate to treat an early relapse as a major crisis, mobilizing the resources of the family to meet this challenge. Usually such a relapse has already been anticipated and planned for, and the relapse is the occasion for activating this plan.

In contrast, it is often desirable to treat a relapse, occurring later in treatment, as a temporary slip rather than a permanent reversion to drug use. When the family has made solid progress, the therapist should convey the attitude that they already know how to cope with this temporary setback. Usually the relapse comes when the family is facing an interpersonal crisis, with the relapse functioning to divert attention away from the interpersonal issues. The therapist must recognize this pattern and prevent this diversion from occurring, even though it may also be necessary to deal with the relapse directly.

TECHNIQUES FOR ENDING TREATMENT

Reviewing Goals and Giving Credit for Change

Structural-strategic therapy is typically of brief duration, and with the modifications listed previously it is even briefer, usually under 10 sessions, over a period of a few months. Within the context of such brief therapy, it is particularly important for the therapist to review goals periodically and be prepared to terminate when goals have been achieved. Even when goal-achievement is less than perfect, the therapist may wish to move toward termination with the prediction that positive change can continue.

Stanton (1981) has argued that it is important for the patient and family to receive most of the credit for change. The therapist should only take credit as a facilitator or catalyst, making it clear that the family has done the real work. It is also dangerous for the abuser to get too much credit for change, since this lessens the commitment of the parents to maintaining the changes and preventing relapse. In this respect, it is important to link drug improvement to changes made in interpersonal areas.

The family should be warned in advance that life may not go smoothly and that future problems can be anticipated. It is useful to review the problem-solving skills they have learned in the course of therapy to create confidence that they can deal successfully with future problems or crises.

As termination approaches, longer intervals between sessions are appropriate. Usually the final sessions are treated more as extended follow-up visits than as therapy sessions, for instance, having the family come at monthly intervals to review progress and to insure that there has not been any slippage. If therapy has ended ahead of schedule, the family can be told that they have a few sessions in the bank, in the event that any problems develop during the follow-up period.

INTEGRATIVE PRINCIPLES

Thus far, we have presented a model that clearly has a structural-strategic foundation with other elements included as additional techniques and specific tactics. These techniques have wide applicability and can improve the effectiveness of the basic model considerably.

In this concluding section on our model, we wish to present some general guidelines for making major shifts in strategy that represent application of particular models in relatively pure form. Obviously one chapter cannot begin to develop competency in the application of other major models, particularly the solution-focused model, White's cybernetic model, and a consistently paradoxical approach. The first two models are present in more detail elsewhere in this volume. (See chapters by Berg and Gallagher and by Durrant and Coles.) For a consistently paradoxical approach, see Todd (1981) and LaForte and Todd (in press).

The guidelines presented in Table 12.2 outline the major choice points in selecting or changing strategies in a major way. The table illustrates the flow of these major treatment decisions through the course of therapy. Each principle is elaborated in more detail below.

1. If the family is in crisis (and the crisis is not chronic), use straightforward problem-oriented techniques.

When a family is in the midst of a bonafide crisis, it is in a particular malleable state and open to straightforward influences. This period of crisis tends to be self-limiting, so time is of the essence. For these reasons, this is the perfect opportunity to help the family resolve the problem by reorganizing the family in straightforward ways.

TABLE 12.2 General Guidelines in Intervention Selection in the Todd and Selekman Model.

1. If the family is in crisis (and the crisis is not chronic), use straightforward problem-oriented techniques.
2. Be alert for outside agents who may maintain the problem or define the terms for therapy. Assess customership and resolve issues such as therapeutic jurisdiction and who should attend sessions.
3. Find out enough about previous therapy to avoid repeating previously unsuccessful strategies.
4. If necessary, make considerable effort to get everyone to attend sessions.
5. If the parents are undermining each other and the adolescent is out of control, use directive, structural-strategic techniques to put the parents in charge.
6. If step 5 is necessary, ally yourself with parents, but be careful to join the problem young person and avoid unnecessary antagonism.
7. If there is no hierarchical problem (or after it is resolved), seek positive solutions directly, using the solution-focused approach.
8. If positive solutions are not readily accessible, obtain more data concerning behavioral sequences, life cycle stage, function of symptom, and consequences of change.
9. In conjunction with step 8, be prepared to split the team and use the Greek Chorus technique.
10. With a pessimistic, heavily entrenched family, externalize the problem a la White.
11. As a last resort, use a consistently paradoxical approach.
12. Regardless of the decisions made above, begin to disengage and have longer intervals between sessions in response to progress.

2. Be alert for outside agents who may maintain the problem or define the terms for therapy.

Much wasted therapeutic effort can be avoided by paying close attention to the referral process and to helpers who may already be entrenched in the situation. Adolescent chemical dependency cases often seem to involve lawyers, other therapists, probation officers, and school personnel. The chemical dependency field also seems particularly prone to politically charged debates about etiology and appropriate treatment.

2b. Assess *customership* and resolve issues such as therapeutic jurisdiction and who should attend sessions.

Assessing customership in the chemical dependency field is often complex. Adolescents are particularly likely to come to therapy under heavy legal, school, or family pressure. While we do not typically advocate a therapy focused exclusively on the individual customer, as is discussed in Statement 4, it is definitely important to identify non-customers and ascertain their availability for a more legitimate contract. It may be useful to conduct a macrosystemic assessment with the family to determine everyone who is involved in defining and attempting to solve the problem, including other helpers, friends of the family, and extended family. Based on this, the therapist should negotiate with the family regarding who should be involved in therapy sessions.

When establishing therapeutic jurisdiction, it is often a mistake to believe that a battle over therapeutic ideology is a winnable war. Instead, we tend to emphasize that in substance abuse cases there is generally plenty of work for everyone, and we attempt to achieve a peaceful coexistence.

3. Find out enough about previous therapy to avoid repeating previously unsuccessful strategies.

As mentioned earlier (see Table 12.1), our model is strategic in Haley's sense, meaning that each case merits its own unique strategy. One of the major applications of this principle involves avoiding previous strategies that were unsuccessful. (The following case example provides a dramatic example of this.) Hearing the reactions of family members to previous treatment efforts will usually provide important clues regarding therapeutic paramedics such as session attendance, the role of individual therapy, and so on. This material can provide potentially useful reframes for problematic situations and give clues regarding power struggles that can be avoided.

4. If necessary, make considerable effort to get everyone to attend sessions.

Recruiting family members to attend therapy in adolescent chemical abuse cases rarely requires the Herculean efforts described by Stanton, Todd, and Associates (1982) in their work with adult heroin addicts. Nevertheless, extra effort early in therapy to promote full attendance can pay major dividends.

As mentioned earlier, we believe that therapy can be maximally effective when all family members can be meaningfully involved. Granted, it may be possible to work only with the customer using techniques from the MRI and solution-focused models, or to put the parents in charge without ever seeing the adolescent client. When possible, however, we prefer to engage everyone, including the identified client, siblings, and both natural parents (plus new stepparents, the live-in boyfriend or girlfriend of a parent, etc.). This is the ideal situation and assumes that such efforts will not result in untoward antagonism from family members.

5. If the parents are undermining each other and the adolescent is out of control, use directive, structural-strategic techniques to put the parents in charge.

Evidence from our work, as well as three research projects which will be discussed in our chapter on research, indicates that straightforward application of structural-strategic principles can be quite effective in a large proportion of cases. Often these are families who have not had extensive previous treatment and who can be mobilized to take charge.

6. If it is necessary to put the parents in charge, ally yourself with the parents, but be careful to join the problem young person and avoid unnecessary antagonism.

Correcting the hierarchy by putting the parents in charge can be critically important, but the therapist should not achieve the alliance with the parents by antagonizing the adolescent. When the parents have not been in charge of their household, it may be difficult to have them overpower an adolescent who has taken a hard-line stance against therapy. For these reasons, it is rarely a mistake to use the techniques for engaging the adolescent described earlier in this chapter.

7. If there is no hierarchical problem (or after it is resolved), seek positive solutions directly using a solution-focused approach.

As mentioned earlier in this chapter, we have been successful in incorporating elements of de Shazer's solution-focused model. While the basic structural-strategic model is definitely strength-oriented, de Shazer's model indicates that family solutions are quite accessible and can be pursued directly.

8. If positive solutions are not readily accessible, obtain more data concerning behavioral sequences, life cycle stage, function of symptom, and consequences of change.

It is a mistake to give up the solution-focused approach too easily. Within the model, there are several additional techniques for generating solutions, including presuppositional questions and the Miracle Question discussed earlier.

If we exhaust all of these avenues, we fall back upon a more hypothesis-based approach. Fruitful areas to explore include sequences of behavior around the symptom, examining the relationship between the substance abuse behavior and life cycle issues, looking for other interpersonal functions of the symptom, and examining the potential consequences of change. These hypotheses can then be used to develop straightforward interventions within the structural-strategic model.

9. In conjunction with (8), be prepared to split the team and use Greek Chorus.

In the discussion of point 2, we alluded to the tendency for substance abuse problems to polarize helpers and family members. A related danger, therefore, is for the therapist to be overly identified with straightforward requests for change. It is rarely a mistake to find some way to incorporate a split team or Greek Chorus intervention (Papp, 1983). The primary therapist can be optimistic and take a pro-change position, but this should be offset by an emphasis on caution and restraint from change. This more pessimistic position can be attributed to the team behind the mirror, a supervisor, or the accepted wisdom in the field.

10. With a pessimistic, heavily entrenched family, externalize the problem a la Michael White.

Our dialogues with other adolescent substance abuse programs suggest that different techniques are necessary for chronic cases in which everyone feels hopeless and demoralized. We have been particularly impressed with the potential of White's model with such cases. Rather than having the family members blame the abuser or each other, the problem is externalized with the hope that family members will join together to defeat the oppressive problem.

11. As a last resort, consistently use a paradoxical approach.

As has been emphasized elsewhere (Todd, 1981), a consistently paradoxical approach should only be adopted as a last resort. While such cases are rare, they are characterized by such extreme behavior that outrageous measures seem natural. We have taken such extreme examples of parental behavior as giving a son $15,000 for drugs, driving the addicted son to the ghetto to purchase drugs and practically buying the drugs for him, and holding and dispensing heroin for the addict. Although the therapist may find it difficult to adopt a paradoxical strategy with a straight face, the therapist usually needs to ask the parents if they have really done enough, why they decided that $15,000 was their limit, and so on.

12. Regardless of the previously made decisions, begin to disengage and have longer intervals between sessions in response to progress.

Regardless of the specific strategies we have adopted at the various choice points identified, we agree with Stanton's emphasis that the family should always get its share of the credit for change (Stanton, 1981). This takes different forms with the different strategies we outlined. In the structural model, the therapist has identified strengths and helped the family to problem solve. In the solution-focused model, the family presumably has found its own solution and been complimented by the therapist. If the problem has been externalized, the family is congratulated for their victory over a previously oppressive symptom. When the approach is more paradoxical, the therapist or Greek Chorus grudgingly acknowledges that the family has done most of the hard work. Consistent with this, it seems only natural that the therapist and the therapy should gradually become less important in the life of the family. The family will do most of the work in later sessions, the sessions, themselves, will seem less significant, and the therapist will underscore this progress by scheduling sessions less frequently.

CASE EXAMPLE

The Hitchin' and Runnin' Kid

The following case illustrates the application of these general principles and shows how several of the specific techniques discussed can be combined into a coherent whole. In this case, the therapist and the team employed a combined solution-focused and cybernetic-systemic approach with the family, due to the chronicity of the presenting problem and the fact that the family had already experienced failure with the structural family therapy approach. The case demonstrates the importance of carefully assessing the family's attempted solutions, engaging the adolescent substance abuser early in treatment, and flexibility in therapist/team intervention selection.

*Bonnie Howell, age 16, was referred to the agency via the Regional Crisis Network for her long history of running away, heavy substance abuse, and police involvement. Mrs. Roberts (Mary) had called the Crisis Network for the names of agencies in town that provide family counseling for adolescents. The Roberts family had just moved to Illinois from Arizona in order for Mary's husband, James, to be available to his father who recently became confined to a wheel chair due to a chronic illness. James allegedly was the most devoted of the father's four sons. According to the crisis worker, Mary reported that Bonnie had the following problems: running away from home since age 11 (hitchhiking from Arizona to the east coast), heavy polydrug abuse on a daily basis (marijuana, alcohol, mainlining cocaine and heroin, and inhalants), chronic violation of parental rules, stealing, school failure, prostitution, street and motorcycle gang involvement, and legal problems. Mary also reported that Bonnie had a long treatment history, including family therapy, residential treatment, and incarceration in correctional facilities since age 11.

The trigger for Mary's phone call to the Crisis Network and the therapist's agency was Bonnie's most recent run away episode (Bonnie had hitchhiked from Arizona to Florida). Bonnie was apprehended by a city police department in Florida and was flown back to her parents in Illinois. After receiving the intake report, the therapist called Mary to schedule a family session.

First Session

Present in the first session were James, Mary, and Bonnie. Mr. and Mrs. Roberts were an attractive, conservative couple, while Bonnie's appearance was quite striking and provocative. She was wearing a black tank top, tightly fitting cut-off pants, considerable amounts of make-up, several earrings in one ear, and huge tattoos on both arms. Bonnie appeared to be ruggedly built and adopted an initial posture of "Don't mess with me!"

The early portion of the session was used to join with the family. The therapist explored with each parent their occupational back-

*The names and locations mentioned in this case have been changed to protect client confidentiality.

grounds and favorite pastimes. James reported that his major skill area was repairing trucks and other large machinery. He loved playing golf and going out to dinner with Mary. Mary had been an airline stewardess before being layed off. Her favorite leisure activities were reading and going for long walks with the family. The therapist joined with Bonnie around her musical tastes. Bonnie shared with the therapist that she enjoyed female rhythm and blues singers most of all—she and the therapist compared personal preferences regarding such singers.

After spending sufficient time joining with each family member, the therapist shifted gears and inquired of the family how he could be helpful to them. In an angry tone of voice, James recounted how Bonnie has been "running away from state to state for the past five years!" He also reported that Bonnie had been arrested on several occasions for "sniffing" liquid paint. Bonnie interrupted James and boasted about how she and her friends used to "break into a liquid paint plant" in order to "get high." Mary saw the running away problem as being a result of "Bonnie's chaotic upbringing." Bonnie's biological father was an alcoholic and abandoned Mary and her daughter. Mary had been married three times before meeting James. She also disclosed that she was a "recovering drug addict and alcoholic." During her "drugging days," Mary's mother virtually raised Bonnie all by herself. Bonnie had nothing to say about the presenting problems.

In an effort to externalize the running away problem, the therapist asked a series of cybernetic questions. The therapist first pointed out how the Running Away Monster had been oppressing all of them for five years! Bonnie was asked: "Do you see how this Running Away Monster puts your parents in charge of your future?" Bonnie responded with: "I don't know about that!" The parents were asked: "Do you see how this running away monster is trying to take away your daughter's future?" James responded to this question by blaming Bonnie for "not being invested" in pursing "an education and in changing." In an attempt to cut-off James's blaming, the therapist asked Bonnie if there were "any times lately" when she "snuck up on the Running Away Monster and refused to let it push her around." Bonnie reported to the therapist that a month ago, when tempted to run away, she was able to "blow-off" the urge to run and "had a smoke in the backyard" instead. Listening to Whitney Houston tapes was another solution that worked for Bonnie. In order to gain detailed information about the family process around the Running Away Monster, the therapist asked Bonnie the following question: "Are there ever any early warning signs when you sense that the running away monster is lurking around the corner?" According to Bonnie, there is a "build up of tension and fighting" that precipitates her wanting to run away.

The therapist explored with the family their attempted solutions. Mary reported to the therapist a long shopping list of treatment facilities and agencies where they had received counseling. The therapist inquired of the family what they had found both useful and unhelpful in past therapy experiences. Mary was quick to point out how her "last family therapists" had "alienated" all of them. According to Mary, these family therapists (structural family therapists from a reputable family institute) had excluded James from parenting responsibilities because of his stepfather status and his conflictual relationship with Bonnie. Mary had greatly objected to this treatment strategy, for she felt that James should have been actively involved with her as a co-parent. Bonnie "hated" the therapists because they "never wanted to hear her point of view." In terms of past parental "attempts at dethroning the Running Away Monster," the Roberts reported that they had exhausted all of their consequences and solutions for Bonnie's misbehavior. According to James, Bonnie has consistently refused to remain at home when grounded. Neither parent could identify any useful tools they had received from previous counseling experiences.

In an effort to generate some potential building blocks toward resolution, the therapist asked the Miracle Question ("If you were to go home tonight and wake up tomorrow and there was a miracle—no more problems—what would be different in this family?") This interventive question failed to produce any positive responses or specific treatment goals. It appeared that all family members perceived their present and future realities as being hopeless.

At this point in the session, the therapist met briefly alone with the parents to obtain more specific details about their attempted solutions and expectations for Bonnie. Both James and Mary reported feeling totally frustrated with trying to change Bonnie's behavior. They had tried everything from lectures to incarceration which were all to no avail. The Roberts could not think of one thing that had worked in curtailing Bonnie's running away problem. The therapist asked the parents "what one small sign of progress would look like" for Bonnie. According to Mary, there would be "no more knock down, drag out fights" when she would ask Bonnie "to do things around the house." James, on the other hand, remained global with his expectations for Bonnie, such as "not running away anymore." The parents could not agree on a goal.

The therapist spent the last 15 minutes of the session with Bonnie. He began the discussion by stressing that he had no intentions of having her locked up anywhere. Bonnie was complimented by the therapist for showing up for the session, despite the fact that "counseling was a drag" for her. The therapist discovered that the parents had lied to Bonnie about going for counseling. The therapist explored with Bonnie how he could be helpful to her, particularly how this treatment experience could be different from past therapy experiences. Bonnie firmly stated "you would listen to what I would have to say." Apparently, past family therapists would "side up" with Bonnie's parents against her. The therapist explored with Bonnie whether she had any concerns or worries about the present family situation. Bonnie disclosed that she did not get along with James because he "screams a lot and sometimes slaps me." The therapist tracked a recent sequence of interaction in which James had struck her. Bonnie was told by the therapist that he "will not tolerate or accept any physical abuse toward her." Bonnie disclosed that some of her running away incidents were directly related to her parents screaming at her. Bonnie also pointed out that sometimes she runs away "for adventure." The therapist and Bonnie discussed the latter's plans to go to school and attempt to secure a job. Bonnie agreed to "hang around for awhile" in order to get back in school and get a job.

After taking a ten-minute consultation break to meet with the team, the following message and task was presented to the Roberts.

> We are very impressed with the fact that despite your having had oodles and oodles of counseling, you are willing to give this experience with us a try. We are impressed with how all of you are survivors and have great strength in coping with all of the major changes in your lives, especially the way you all can bounce back. We are all very impressed with you, James, the way you are involved with Bonnie's struggle with the Running Away Monster. We see a lot of natural fathers who turn over parental responsibility to their wives. We are very impressed with you, Mary, for your willingness to accept responsibility for your struggles in the past, obviously you are well-versed with the fourth, fifth, and sixth steps of AA. The team was very impressed with how open and hopeful you were Bonnie, even though you didn't want to be here. You seem to want to resolve this. We are also impressed that you, Bonnie, decided to turn over a new leaf—you came back, you stayed home last night, you came here today, and you are planning to hang around for awhile. We are impressed with all of this. In order for you to give us more information about your family, between now and the next time we meet, we would like all of you to notice what's happening in your family that you want to continue to happen.

During the delivery of this intervention, each family member gave considerable verbal and nonverbal confirmation of the compliments delivered to them.

Session Two

The therapist began the session by asking the Roberts: "So what's happening that you would like to continue to have happen?" Much to the therapist's surprise, both James and Mary noticed several positive changes in Bonnie over a week's time. The parents noticed the following changes: Bonnie landed a job working on a farm, she did her household chores without any power struggles, she helped James with the yard work; there were no signs of alcohol or drug use, and no running away incidents. Bonnie noticed that her mother had initiated a "fun family walk in the woods," she did not yell once at her, and she actually got along with James. The therapist asked a series of present and future-oriented, circular questions to further amplify the differences for the family. The majority of the session time was used to secure from the family detailed descriptions of the changes. The therapist had the family compare and contrast their previous family interactions with their new dance steps. Bonnie and the therapist met briefly alone to further solidify a therapeutic alliance. The therapist decided to enlist Bonnie's services as a co-therapist. As her homework assignment, Bonnie was instructed to "do two-to-three secret surprises which would shock the hell out of her parents in a positive way." Bonnie smiled and began to think of some nice things she could do to shock her parents.

After a brief consultation break with the team, the therapist delivered the following message to the family.

> We are extremely impressed that you (the parents) noticed all of the positive changes with Bonnie: her quickly landing a job, her cooperation around the house, her completion of chores, and her helping James with the yard work. We were very impressed with Mary's family walk idea. It seems like all of you had fun together on the walk. James, we would like to compliment you on your being cautious about Bonnie's changes. (James had appeared to the team to be somewhat skeptical of his stepdaughter's changes.) We agree with the AA philosophy of "One Day at a Time." For homework, we have asked Bonnie to perform two to three positive surprises for you (the parents). What we would like you parents to do is pretend like you are Sherlock Holmes detectives and try and figure out without comparing notes what the surprises were. We will discuss your discoveries next week.

Session Three

The Roberts family came in all smiles and laughing together. The therapist inquired in a playful way about "which Sherlock Holmes detective discovered the secret surprises first?" Mary reported that Bonnie had brought her a blanket while she was laying on the couch sleeping. Mary also noticed that Bonnie had gotten out of bed in the middle of the night to stop their dogs from barking all night. James had discovered that Bonnie had cleaned his dirty car windows. The family went for a long, three mile walk. Again, Mary had initiated this enjoyable family activity. The therapist elicited details from each family member about their walk together. Apparently, James pretended he was the "boogeyman" and the women tried to ambush him. On a negative note, Bonnie and her paternal grandfather got into a major verbal dispute on one day. James had disrupted the fight and shared his wisdom with Bonnie about how to deal with his father. This kind of fatherly support was different for James and Bonnie. The therapist asked future-oriented questions to elicit from the family how they would handle future difficulties with the grandfather and their stressful situations. (Both parents were unemployed and the grandfather was being difficult with all family members.)

The therapist delivered the following message to the family after his consultation break with the team.

> We are very impressed with the Brady Bunch feel to you guys—laughter, fun, and good times! Again, Mary, you came up with the winner family activity of walking. Your three-mile walk shattered the house record! You gals are tough, trying to ambush the boogeyman. James, we were most impressed with your sharing your wisdom with Bonnie about how to deal with your father. After the fight with your grandfather, Bonnie put your wisdom into practice by remaining quiet when he and she almost locked horns on Friday again. Bonnie, we were very impressed with all of the nice caring things you did for your parents: helping out with the dogs, tucking mom in with a blanket, and cleaning your stepdad's car windows. You are also a very fast learner when it comes to dealing with grandfathers. Between now and the next time we meet we would like you to notice what is working for all of you in the family.

Fourth Session

The Roberts came into the fourth session looking as if they all had just returned from a funeral. Rather than jumping the gun too soon with inquiring about exceptions to problematic behavior, the therapist commented on the gloomy atmosphere in the room. Mary reported that she had been turned down from a job. Several fights had erupted between Bonnie, James, Mary, and the grandparents during the week. Mary pointed out that Bonnie did not cause the fights, but the grandfather was the culprit. At this point in the session, each family member disclosed one thing they did to cope with the tyrannical grandparents. James took the car out for a long spin; Mary locked herself in her bedroom and read AA-oriented books; Bonnie went to a friend's house. After discussing with the family how successful these attempted solutions were, the therapist met alone briefly with both the parents, then Bonnie.

The following message and intervention was delivered to the family after the consultation break.

> We are all very impressed with the fact that despite your rough weeks and long history of counseling, you guys did not drop out of therapy with us. The team was struck by the huge amount of stress you all were under, but instead of blaming Bonnie for all of the problems, you all came up with creative ways to cope. James went for a long spin in the car, Mary read her AA books for a spiritual fix, and Bonnie went to her friend's house. A lot of families don't know how to take time outs from one another. The team reprimanded me for not telling you last week that change is three steps forward and two steps back. Since things are so stressful, we were debating whether to give you homework or not—like noticing the signs of when things are back on the right track again or taking a vacation—you decide. Let's meet in two weeks!

Fifth Session

Two weeks later, the Roberts came in with good news about James' new job. James secured an excellent paying truck mechanic job. Mary reported that she had a second interview with an airline company which had gone well. Bonnie had an intake interview at a special day treatment school program that was part of the therapist's agency. Bonnie was quite excited about starting her new school. The family reported still having major problems with the grandparents. On several occasions, James stood up to his parents without allowing Bonnie to fight his battles for him. This was a major change for this family. In dealing with the grandparents, Mary and Bonnie took off in the family car for long rides or went to a shopping mall. The therapist highlighted differences in family interaction and coping strategies for the family.

After the consultation break with the team, the following message and intervention was delivered by the therapist.

> We are very impressed with your creativity in a stressful situation such as being able to pick up as a family and go for a long ride, or go to the shopping mall. James, we are impressed with your ability to stand up to your parents, put them in their place, and help Bonnie deal with them better. Mary, we are impressed with your helping Bonnie out by removing her from such a stressful situation and having fun after leaving the house. With crisis situations, there is usually a build up, a crisis, and a resolution. With you guys you can have a build up, a family outing, and a resolution in place of the crisis—that's another alternative! The team is blown away by your creativity and resourcefulness. Since you are doing so well, we would like to give you a three-week vacation from counseling. See you in three weeks!

Sixth Session

The Roberts came into the office all smiles and quite pleased with how things were going. Bonnie had not displayed any signs of drug use nor had run away. James was sporting a beautiful suit and looked like a male model. He had just received a raise at work. Mary landed a job with a small airline company as a ticketer. Bonnie loved her new school and all of the rowdy kids there. Although the grandparents continued to "stress out" the Roberts clan, the family came up with more effective and creative solutions to combat the tension at home, such as James and Mary went out looking at "dream houses;" the family hopped into their car and disappeared for several hours without any explanation to the grandparents (the Roberts were unaware that they were naturally carrying out Palazzoli's Invariant Prescription); James went out to a "driving range to hit a couple of buckets of golf balls;" or the family went to play put-put golf together.

The therapist delivered the following message and intervention to the Roberts after his brief consultation break.

> The team is very impressed with how creative all of you are under such tremendous stress. You went out looking for dream houses, you played put-put golf, James went to the driving range, and you blew the grandparent's minds by mysteriously driving off into the sunset for several hours. The team thinks that you, James and Mary, are two of the most creative and resourceful parents they have ever seen. Bonnie, the team is very impressed with how responsible you have been acting—doing well in school. The team thinks you are doing a great job of fighting off

> and achieving victories over the running away problem! Between now and the next time we meet, we would like you to continue doing what's working. As we believe, if it works, don't fix it. We will see you in four weeks.

Final Session

Four weeks later, Bonnie and Mary came alone to the session. James was unable to make the session due to work responsibilities. Mary shared with the therapist that they had bought one of their dream houses in a small town 50 miles west of the grandparent's house. The official moving date was six weeks down the road. The therapist and family discussed terminating due to all of their improvements. Although Bonnie was somewhat hesitant, Mary and James had agreed before this appointment to discuss discontinuing counseling. The therapist asked the twosome what they would need to do to go backwards. Both Mary and Bonnie were clearly able to make distinctions between their old family interaction and their present dance steps.

In an effort to unhook the Roberts from spending a lifetime in therapy, and to further highlight news of a difference, the family was instructed to write their official discharge summary from therapy that they would mail to all of their previous therapists. Mary came up with a list of six reasons why they should no longer be in therapy.

1. We have made it, despite all of your diagnoses!
2. You can reason with Bonnie better.
3. No more knock down, drag out fights.
4. Bonnie doesn't run away.
5. Bonnie came home on time a lot.
6. Bonnie seems to have been straight (drug-free).

After highlighting differences for the family, the therapist met briefly with Bonnie. The therapist heavily praised Bonnie for doing a fabulous job at home and at school.

The team had the following parting message for Bonnie and her mother.

> We are really impressed by the way you have been able to defy, degrade, and defeat the Running Away Monster, despite being under so much stress and turmoil. Mary, we were very impressed with your being able to identify Bonnie's many changes: You can reason better with her, no more knock down drag out fights, she hasn't run away, she has come

home on time, and she seems to have been straight. Bonnie we are very impressed with your super responsible behavior: not cutting classes, doing well in school, not breaking your curfew, and straightening out a bit. One team member thinks that since you and I get along so well that you will try and develop a problem in order to get back in family counseling. I was really flattered by that, but give you more credit than she does. Things will not always be a bed of roses, but we are convinced you guys know what to do in dealing with life's challenges. Before wishing you good luck, I would like to reward you, Bonnie, with this certificate for successfully taming a Running Away Monster. Good luck with everything!

Follow-up

Follow-up phone calls were made to the Roberts at six, 12, and 24 months to assess treatment outcome. The therapist discovered from Mary on all three occasions that Bonnie "had not run away" and that she continued to "do well in school." Mary reported that she had not noticed any signs of drug use on Bonnie's behalf. Much to the therapist's surprise, the family had sent four copies of their discharge summary from therapy to four of their past therapists.

CONCLUSION

Bonnie's case best exemplifies our present thinking on family therapy with adolescent substance abusers. As the reader can clearly see, we place a high priority on therapist/team flexibility in the areas of intervention selection and of shifting models when deemed necessary. It was clear to us in the initial session that a pure structural-strategic approach with Bonnie's family was destined to fail. Furthermore, if the therapist had failed to engage Bonnie early in treatment through the use of individual session time, the latter would have most likely run away. Thus, we abandoned the structural-strategic model altogether, and instead, utilized a combined solution-focused and cybernetic-systemic approach that capitalized on family member's strengths to co-create a context for change.

REFERENCES

Boscolo, L., Cecchin, G., Hoffman, L., & Penn, P. (1987) *Milan systemic family therapy: Conversation in theory and practice.* New York: Basic Books.

de Shazer, S. (1985). *Keys to Solution in Brief Therapy.* New York: W. W. Norton.

de Shazer, S. (1987, July). *Brief Treatment of Alcohol and Drug Abuse: An Alternative that Works*. Three-day workshop at the Brief Family Therapy Center, Milwaukee, WI.

de Shazer, I. (1988) *Clues: Investigating solutions in brief therapy.* New York: W. W. Norton.

de Shazer, S., Berg, I., Lipchik, E., Nunally, E., Molnar, A., Gingerich, W., & Weiner-Davis, M., (1986) Brief Therapy: Focused solution development. *Family Process, 25,* 207–222.

Durrant, M. (1985) *Temper taming.* Unpublished manuscript.

Durrant, M. (1987) *Foundations of systemic/cybernetic family therapy.* Unpublished manuscript.

Eastwood, M., Sweeney, D., & Piercy, F. (1987). The "no-problem problem": A family therapy approach for certain first-time adolescent substance abusers. *Family Relations, 36,* 125–128.

Ellis, D. C. (1986). *Growing up stoned: Coming to terms with teenage drug abuse in modern America.* Pompano Beach, FL: Health Communications.

Fishman, H. C., Stanton, M. D., & Rosman, B. L. (1982). Treating families of adolescent drug abusers. In M. D. Stanton, & T. C. Todd, & Associates, *The family therapy of drug abuse and addiction.* New York: Guilford Press.

Glassner, B., Carpenter, C., & Berg, B. (1986) Marijuana in the lives of adolescents. In G. Beschner & A. S. Friedman (eds.), *Teen drug use.* Lexington, MA: Lexington.

Glassner, B., & Loughlin, J. (1987) *Drugs in Adolescent Worlds: Burnouts to Straight.* New York. St. Martens Press.

Haley, J. (1980) *Leaving home: Therapy with disturbed young people.* New York: McGraw-Hill.

Lipchik, E. (1987a) *Interviewing.* Rockville: Aspen.

Lipchik, E. (1987b, February) *Systemic Interviewing.* One-Day Workshop at McHenry County Youth Service Bureau, Woodstock, IL.

Lipchik, E. & de Shazer, S. (1986). The purposeful interview. *Journal of Strategic and Systemic Therapies, 5,* (1), 88–99.

Madanes, C. (1981). *Strategic family therapy.* San Francisco: Jossey-Bass.

Madanes, C. (1984). *Behind the one-way mirror: Advances in the practice of strategic therapy.* San Francisco: Jossey-Bass.

Menses, G., & Durrant, M. (1986) Contextual residential care: The applications of the principles of cybernetic therapy to the residential treatment of irresponsible adolescents and their families. *Dulwich Centre Review,* 3–13.

Minuchin, S. (1974) *Families and family therapy.* Cambridge, MA: Harvard University Press.

Minuchin, S. & Fishman, H. C. (1980) *Family therapy techniques.* Cambridge, MA: Harvard University Press.

Molnar, A. & de Shazer, S. (1987). Solution-focused therapy: Toward the identification of therapeutic tasks. *Journal of Marital and Family Therapy, 13*(4), 359–363.

O'Hanlon, W. & Weiner-Davis, M. (1989) *In search of solutions A new direction in psychotherapy,* New York: Norton.

Palazzoli, M. S., Boscolo, L., Cecchin, G., & Prata, G. (1978) A ritualistic prescription in family therapy: Odd days and even days. *Journal of Marriage and Family Counseling. 4* (3), 3–8.

Palazzoli, M. S., Boscolo, L., Cecchin, G., & Prata, G. (1980) Hypothesizing—Circularity—Neutrality: Three guidelines for the conductor of the session. *Family Process, 19* (1), 3–12.

Palazzoli, M.S., Cirillo, S., Selvini, M., & Sorrentino, A. M. (1988) *Family Games.* New York: W. W. Norton.

Papp, P. (1983). *The process of change.* New York: Guilford.

Peele, S. (1985) *The meaning of addiction.* Lexington, MA: Lexington.

Penn, P. (1982) Circular questioning. *Family Process, 21*(3), 267–280.

Penn, P. (1985) Feed-forward: Future questions, future maps. *Family Process, 24*(3) 299–310.

Selekman, M. D. (1987a). Ally or foe? Strategic use of the adolescent substance abuser in family therapy. *Journal of Strategic and Systemic Therapies, 6*(4), 12–16.

Selekman, M. D. (1987b). Conquering a chemical monster: A case of adolescent substance abuse. *Family Therapy Case Studies, 2*(1), 51–57.

Selekman, M. D. (1989a). Taming chemical monsters: Cybernetic-systemic therapy with adolescent substance abusers. *Journal of Strategic and Systemic Therapies, 8*(3), 5–9.

Selekman, M. D. (1989b). Engaging adolescent substance abusers in family therapy. *Family Therapy Case Studies, 4*(1), 67–74.

Stanton, M. D. (1981). An integrated structural/strategic approach to family therapy. *Journal of Marital and Family Therapy, 7,* 427–439.

Stanton, M. D. & Todd, T. C. (1981). Engaging "resistant" families in treatment: principles and techniques in recruitment. *Family Process, 20,* 261–280.

Stanton, M. D. & Todd, T. C. (1982). The conceptual model. In M. D. Stanton, T. C. Todd, & Associates, (1982). *The family therapy of drug abuse and drug addiction.* New York: Guilford.

Stanton, M. D., & Todd, T. C., & Associates. (1982). *The family therapy of drug abuse and drug addiction.* New York: Guilford.

Todd, T. C. (1981). Paradoxical prescriptions: applications of consistent paradox using a strategic team. *Journal of Strategic and Systemic Therapies, 1*(1), 28–44.

Todd, T. C. (1988). Developmental cycles and substance abuse. In C. J. Falicov (ed.), *Family transitions: Continuity and change over the life cycle.* New York: Guilford.

Tomm, K. (1987). Interventive interviewing: Part II. Reflexive questioning as a means to enable self-healing. *Family Process, 26,* 167–183.

Tomm, K. (1988). Interventive interviewing: Part III. Intending to ask lineal, circular, strategic, or reflexive questions. *Family Process, 27*(1), 1–15.

Tomm, K. & White, M. (1987, October). *Externalizing problems and internalizing directional choices.* Training Institute presented at the Annual Conference of the American Association for Marriage and Family Therapy, Chicago, IL.

Weiner-Davis, M., de Shazer, S., & Gingerich, W. J. (1987). Using pretreatment change to construct a therapeutic solution: A clinical note. *Journal of Marital and Family Therapy, 13*(4), 359–363.

White, M. (1985). Fear busting and monster taming: An approach to the fears of young children. *Dulwich Centre Review,* 29–33.

White, M. (1987). Family therapy and schizophrenia: Addressing the in-the-corner lifestyle. *Dulwich Centre Newsletter,* 14–21.

White, M. (1988). Anorexia nervosa: A cybernetic perspective. In J. E. Harkaway (ed.), *Eating disorders.* Rockville: Aspen.

PART 3
Research and Integration

To date, little family treatment outcome research has been conducted with adolescent substance abusers in the addictions or family therapy fields. Recently, however, the National Institute On Drug Abuse funded three major family treatment outcome research projects with adolescent substance abusers at Texas Tech University, Purdue University, and the University of California, San Francisco. This section of the book will compare and contrast some of the preliminary results of these three studies and an Italian research project involving adolescent and young adult substance abusers. The implications of these research findings for informing clinical practices with adolescent substance abusers and their families will be discussed.

Newfield, Kuehl, Joanning, and Quinn in Chapter 13 present their unique family ethnographic research approach which was utilized in their family treatment outcome study at Texas Tech University. This anthropological research interviewing method appears to capture best the family members' perceptions of their family therapy experience at follow-up.

In Chapter 14, Selekman and Todd provide an overview and comparative analysis of the National Institute On Drug Abuse studies with an important Italian research project. A common theme that runs through all four of these research projects is that no one family therapy approach works best with all adolescent substance abuse cases, that model shifting and integration may be necessary in different case situations.

13

We Can Tell You About "Psychos" and "Shrinks"

An Ethnography of the Family Therapy of Adolescent Drug Abuse*

NEAL A. NEWFIELD, Ph.D.
Assistant Professor
Department of Behavioral Medicine and Psychiatry
West Virginia University, Morgantown, WV

HARVEY P. JOANNING, Ph.D.
Associate Professor
Department of Family Environment
Iowa State University, Ames, IA

BRUCE P. KUEHL, Ph.D.
Marital and Family Therapist
Community Mental Health Services, Inc.,
Rhinelander, WI

WILLIAM H. QUINN, Ph.D.
Associate Professor
Department of Child and Family Development
University of Georgia, Athens, GA

Since the beginning of the twentieth century, the sine qua non of good research has been the hypothetical deductive method in combination with the principles of experimental design. Yet the more reduced, mea-

*This research is funded by a grant from the National Institute on Drug Abuse; grant number R01 DA 03733-01. The authors would like to thank the *Alcoholism Treatment Quarterly* and the *Journal of Family Psychology* for allowing material being prepared for publication in their journals to be reproduced here (see Newfield, Kuehl, Joanning, & Quinn, in press, and Kuehl, Newfield & Joanning, in press).

surable, and clear cut the variables, the better control we have of contextual influences, the less we are able to generalize the findings to the empirical world. At times we are like drunks looking for lost keys under the street lamp. We did not drop the keys there, but the light is so much better for looking.

In family therapy, with few exceptions, all of what we know about psychosomatic illness, schizophrenia, drug abuse, or families with any symptomatic member comes from therapist observations within the context of therapy. This situation is similar to the study of primates in the second half of the last century. Proper English gentlemen would go to the zoo and observe the monkey cages making observations concerning primate behavior that would later not stand up to observations in the wild. Our understanding of families and family therapy is from the perspective of the jailer who is studying the animals captive in his or her office or hospital.

Once you apply this lens to the field of family therapy, a whole series of fresh questions are generated. What are the naturally occurring therapeutic transactions that occur in an individual's context stemming the course of addiction, how is it that one person can stop taking heroin or cocaine after years of use without professional intervention and, yet, others continue using till death? Those who do not use drugs but live in a subculture of use and abuse, what maintains their beliefs and behavior? Is the behavior of drug abusers and their families in anyway similar at home and in the office? How much of their response is context dependent? What do our *captives* think of family therapy, do they find our behavior odd, and how do they make sense of our machinations? It is this last question that prompted this ethnography of the family therapy of adolescent drug abuse.

Ethnography is that branch of anthropology concerned with describing individual cultures or aspects of cultures in a noninterpretive manner. According to Malinowski, one of the founders of modern ethnography, the goal of ethnography is to "grasp the native's point of view, his relationship to life, to realize his visions of his world." (1961, first printing 1922). While there are a limited number of ethnographies addressing what it is like to live in the totally institutionalized environment of an asylum (Goffman, 1961), in a psychiatric hospital (Caudill, 1958), with a schizophrenic family (Henry, 1961), and how to make a living being "crazy" as part of a community treatment program (Estroff, 1981), there are no ethnographies of either individual or family therapy based on the client's recounting of the experience. This is true despite the fact that psychotherapy, family therapy, marriage counseling, and various other forms of therapy and counseling are relatively common experiences in Western society.

Most of what is written and discussed about a client's experience of therapy comes from the perceptions and impressions of practitioners, researchers, and theoreticians (Kruger, 1986; Fessler 1983). Keeney and Ross (1985) refer to their work in *Mind and Therapy* as a "cybernetic ethnography," however, this work is an ethnography about how practitioners conceptualize therapy rather than about the way clients conceptualize it. Although Napier and Whitaker (1978) in *The Family Crucible* come close to writing an ethnography of family therapy, it too is from the perspective of therapists, not clients. Tyler and Tyler (1985) have written an ethnographic account of being a trainee in family therapy. They state that the greatest challenge for the trainee lies not in trying to understand the clients, but in seeking to understand the supervisors with all their obscurities and jargon.

Studies that document the therapeutic experiences as told by the client are essential from a constructivist-based cybernetic orientation. The doctrine of constructivism asserts that we construct or invent reality rather than discover it. "Representation of the world like the world itself, is the work of man; they describe it from their own point of view, which they confuse with truth" (De Beauvoir, 1952). Objectivity or the properties of the observer not entering the descriptions of what is observed (Von Foerster, 1974) is impossible. This is in contrast to logical positivist assumptions, such as quantification and objectivity upon which most science is based. Logical positivism supports the idea that perceptions can be objective and accurate templates of reality. Cybernetics in Greek means steersman and is the "science of control and communications in the animal and the machine." It is concerned with information and communication as control in effective organizations (Von Foerster, 1974, pp. 2-4). Where interpersonal problems exist, there is a problem with information and communication and a reality may be constructed that sustains ineffective organizations with resulting problems.

Within a constructivist-based cybernetic orientation, clients are conceptualized as autonomous subsystems that are part of a larger therapeutic system consisting of the interacting meaning systems of the client(s), therapist(s), and any therapeutic team or supervisor(s) that might be involved. The client(s) + therapist(s) + therapeutic team + supervisor(s) are caught as if in an invisible web, every movement in each creating a stirring in the other. Within this web of meanings, all who are caught co-create the therapeutic system for change. The unspoken assumption in nearly all psychotherapy approaches is that therapy is something the therapist administers and the client passively and willingly receives (Kruger, 1986). However, the feedback of information from the client subsystem to the larger therapeutic system is fundamental and necessary for the overall therapeutic system to establish and effectively accomplish mutual goals. A qualitative ethnographic investigation into the client's experience and perceptions of therapy can challenge the way the therapist typically thinks about and implements interventions.

While the purpose of a quantitative approach is to "generate knowledge that is determinant and empirical with finite relationships between facts and objective reality" (Leininger, 1985, p. 7), modern qualitative analysis uses neither an experimental design nor maintains a fixed posture of inquiry once research begins. This difference reflects the fact that qualitative investigations are not concerned with first constructing hypotheses based on previous research and then testing them on informants, nor are the investigations concerned with studying independent variables holding all things constant. Rather than starting with a theory and hypotheses, this approach generates its own, "bootstrap" fashion (Agar, 1980). The ethnographer looks to the people who are conceptualized as his or her *teachers* or *informants* (rather than *subjects)* to highlight the important considerations of a given area of study (Leininger, 1985). However, as with most quantitative research, much of modern qualitative research is conducted within a logical positivist and realist paradigm (Marcus & Fischer, 1986). Approached this way, reality is conceptualized as primarily external to the self and verifiable through the use of logically sound and objectively verifiable methodologies (Lynch-Sauer, 1985). Through proper methodology, many modern ethnographers believe that the uncovering of an objective, discoverable reality is possible.

In contrast, postmodern or what is occasionally called *antifoundationalist qualitative research* (Clifford & Marcus, 1986; Marcus & Fischer, 1986) asserts that there is *no* position from which an investigator can neutrally observe a phenomenon. All social science statements are conceptualized as partial truths (Clifford, 1986), manufactured and autobiographical in that an event described is part of the investigator's past experience (Fabian, 1983). What must be given up is the doctrine of "immaculate perception" (Sass, 1986). In the final analysis there are no neutral observers and no way of experiencing reality directly, nor is there ever a complete or final accounting of a phenomenon (Tyler, 1986). This approach is more consistent with radical constructivism and the cybernetics of observing human systems than approaches conceptualized with a realist and logical positivist paradigm. Our biology prevents us from ever having the ability to be objective (Simon, 1985; Varela, 1986). As such, each person is alone with his or her own construction of reality (Von Glasersfeld, 1986).

Steier (1985) argues persuasively for a cybernetic methodology of family therapy research that relies heavily on an ethnographic approach as a means of examining how therapeutic change is constructed from the client's perception. Using an ethnographic approach can be consistent with conceptualizing families as autonomous systems with a set of constant relations that form their identity and with a circularity of internal transactions that are structurally coupled or linked with the environment. As such, the purpose of this study is to provide feedback to therapists and others involved with therapy regarding clients' experiences of family therapy through the analysis of ethnographic interviews conducted with the clients.

METHODOLOGY

Context

This investigation is nested within a four-year National Institute on Drug Abuse outcome study testing the effectiveness of structural/strategic family therapy, family drug education, and traditional group psychotherapy in the treatment of adolescent drug abuse (Joanning et al., 1984). For an elaboration of the treatment model used in the family therapy conditions see: Quinn, Kuehl, Thomas, Joanning, & Newfield, in press, and Quinn et al., 1988. Therapists in the family therapy treatment condition were male graduate students working on their doctorate degrees in marriage and family therapy in a program accredited by the American Association for Marriage and Family Therapy.

The present study is concerned primarily with constructing an initial ethnographic account of the family therapy treatment condition as discussed by the family members that participated. As such, this is a mini-ethnography. This study is not concerned with documenting and analyzing the broad range of lifeways of a group of people (an undertaking that could require years; Leininger, 1985, p. 35). Rather, this study is limited to a discussion of the clients' construction of the therapy experience around focused domains of inquiry.

Informants

The informants were residents of Lubbock, Texas, a midsize city in Southwest United States. The study was based on an opportunistic sample. In opportunistic sampling the ethnographer selects whatever informants are available and may reward him or her with relevant information (Honigman, 1970). The sample consisted of 12 families who were interviewed for a total of 76 hours, including 12 mothers ranging in age from 31 to 49 years (x = 40), 8 fathers ranging in age from 36 to 54 years (x = 43), and 17 adolescents (10 males, 7 females) ranging in age from 10 to 22 years (x = 16). The informants were predominantly white, middle class, and attended an average of 10 therapy sessions (range = 6 to 16). The bulk of the interviews were conducted by the first authors in the homes of the informants.

Opportunistic sampling was judged appropriate since this study is not designed to answer questions such as "how much" and "how often," but instead is focused on developing answers to such qualitative questions as: what does occur, what are its implications, and how are different occurrences linked to each other. Opportunistic sampling is sufficient for the needs of investigators who are primarily concerned with documenting patterns of behavior that occur and recur in varying sets of social relations (Mead, 1953).

Ethnographic Construction

The informants were contacted by phone upon completion of family therapy. Interviews took place in the families' homes (with a few minor exceptions) in an effort to gain the clients' cooperation and create a context in which the families could teach the ethnographers about their experiences in therapy. The interviews began with the following explanation: "We want to chronicle for other families and for people who work with families what your experience at Texas Tech was like so that these people can benefit from what you have learned." A written consent form was also signed by the family elaborating on the orally presented statement. All interviews with families were audiotaped and transcribed into hard text. Interviews were usually 90 minutes in length and most families were interviewed two or more times.

The ethnographic interviews were conducted and the text analyzed according to the Developmental Research Sequences (DRS) of Spradely (1979). When using the DRS, both questions and answers are elicited as much as possible from the informant. Initial questioning is analogous to presenting a Rorschach inkblot to a subject. At first, only general questions are asked; then, the categories in the initial responses are used to ask further descriptive questions. For example, instead of asking an informant what she or he thought about "family therapy," in which case a distinction would have been drawn by the interview that the informant might not have considered, less structured questions were asked, such as: "If another family came to you and said, 'we are going to go out to the University to do what you did, could you give us a tour of what it is going to be like?' What would you say to them?" A question such as this would then be expanded upon using information and terms from the informant's first response.

The texts of all interviews were subject to domain analysis as specified by the DRS. A *domain* is defined as an informant-expressed relationship between a folk (native) category designated by a cover term and a number of other categories included under the cover term. The cover term and the included term are paired together through a semantic relationship. For example, one family used the term "Psychos" as a cover term for "shrinks, psychologists, and counselors." Psychologists (included term), are a kind of (semantic relationship of inclusion), Psychos (cover term). All the terms included under the cover term have at least one characteristic in common: They are a "kind of Psycho." There are approximately 13 universal semantic relationships that are found in virtually all cultures. Spradley (1979, p. 111) has identified nine in particular that he has found useful. These semantic relationships are:

- Inclusion—X is a kind of Y;
- Spatial—X is a place or a part in Y;
- Cause-effect—X is a result or cause of Y;
- Rationale—X is a reason for doing Y;
- Location for action—X is a place for doing Y;
- Function—X is used for Y;
- Means-end—X is a way to do Y;
- Sequence—X is a step or a stage in Y; and
- Attribution—X is an attribute or a characteristic of Y.

Included terms form an array of symbols under the cover term of a domain. A *domain* constitutes the set of total meanings of its included terms. *Domain analysis* is an ethnosemantic method that is designed to discern how people classify their experience through the terminology they use to talk about it (Sturdevant, 1972). It is a basic assumption of this method that dimensions of meaning in cultural experience can be developed through the study of language (Frake, 1962). Constructing a list of domains results in the delineation of areas of cultural meaning a client might draw.

Structural questions are used to verify the existence of different domains and to elicit additional included terms under the cover terms of domains. For example, "Are there different types of psychos?"—"Yes" (verification). "Are social workers a kind of psycho?"—"Yes, (verification) they are not very good at counseling but I guess you could say they are Psychos" (a new included term has been elicited).

Taxonomic and componential analysis can be performed for domains that are central to an informant's experiences of health, family problems, drug abuse and therapy, and those domains that are of theoretical import to the investigators. Taxonomic analysis differs from domain analysis in that it attempts to show the relationship between included terms in a domain by establishing a hierarchy of levels, with each term included at one level, included under only one included term at the next highest level. Taxonomic analysis is used to examine the subsets of relationships within the array of included terms in a domain. In taxonomic analysis, included terms are classified based on only one semantic dimension. A two-level taxonomy is little different than a domain. Taxonomic analysis attempts to examine the subsets of relationships within the array of included terms in a domain.

While taxonomic analysis partitions included terms into levels of subsets based on only one semantic relationship, analysis can be taken an additional step. Componential analysis attempts to understand how a system of symbols related to each other on multiple dimensions of contrast (see Table 13.1). These dimensions of contrast form a paradigm for defining the included terms based on the attributes that differentiate the members of the contrast set.

Lastly, cultural themes may be developed. The relationship between domains is examined for a gestalten or organizing principle between them.

TABLE 13.1 Paradigm for Kinds of "Psychos" and "Shrinks"

	Dimensions of Contrast				
	1	*2*	*3*	*4*	*5*
Professions					
Pastors	High	Low	Low	Low	NA
Counselors	Moderate High	High	Low	Moderate	NA
Psychologists	Moderate	Low	High	High	Moderate
Psychiatrists	Low	Low	Moderate	High	High
Social Workers	Low	Low	Low	Low	NA

*Key
1. Caring
2. Life Experience
3. Technical expertise in Therapy
4. The Ability to Address Serious Problems
5. The Ability to Dispense Medication

Striking similarities exist between the steps necessary in constructing an ethnography and the formulation of a substantive grounded theory following the guidelines of Glasser and Strauss (1967). The heart of *grounded theory* is the constant comparative method. Each incident in the data is coded into categories. Categories become the conceptual elements of the theory. Each category in turn consists of properties that are the conceptual elements of a category. Different incidents in the data are examined in terms of the categories that are emerging for the purpose of enriching the categories. Theoretical saturation occurs when additional data does not expand the properties of a category. Low level categories generally emerge quickly while higher level categories or what Glasser and Strauss call "overriding and integrating, conceptualizations—and the properties that elaborate them" (1967, p. 36) usually emerge later. Loosely substituting the word domain for categories, grounded theory construction begins to resemble the DRS and the construction of ethnographies. Domains, with their included terms or properties emerge first. Then taxonomies that are subsumed under other taxonomies and still later, paradigms or what in grounded theory would be called overriding conceptualizations and their properties are constructed. Lastly, themes are developed or hypothesized relationships between the categories are created. The more general steps for creating a grounded theory along with the specific techniques of the DRS served as useful guidelines for the construction of this ethnography and we often shuttled between the two methods.

Validation is an important process in the structure of ethnographic construction. The domain and componential analysis reported here were subject to validation both with and between informants until a common description of the experience of informants going through the family therapy condition was established. This is not to claim that this study is objective or generalizable to other populations. From a constructivist perspective, a researcher creates descriptions of reality rather than discovering them.

The analysis of a single interview in this study could easily result in the identification of 40 new domains, yet all domains are not given equal attention. How is it that some domains are selected for elaboration and development, while others are ignored?

Domains emerge from the creative interactions between the ethnographer, the traditions of ethnography, the informants being interviewed, and the audience for whom the ethnography is being prepared. These three elements limit, but do not determine the final project. The meaning systems of people are not discovered through ethnography, but are generated like any substantive theory (Glasser & Strauss, 1967). The ethnography produced is neither subjective or objective, but rather interpretive (Agar, 1986, p. 19). Ethnographies are attempts to bridge the meaning world of a people with that of a professional audience through the meaning world of the ethnographer, as such, ethnographies are "actively situated between powerful systems of meaning" (Clifford, 1986, p. 2). The domains presented in this chapter: 1) expectations of counseling, 2) types of psychos and shrinks, 3) the setting, 4) individual versus family therapy, 5) characteristics of the counselor, 6) adolescent bullshitting, and 7) how counseling progresses, were selected because the information elicited was inconsistent with what the families were expected to say about therapy based on the authors' experiences as therapists, supervisors, and teachers. It is this breakdown in logical integration, consistency, and intelligibility or what is often called coherence between cultures, that the ethnographic research method is designed to address (Agar, 1986). In this case, the breakdown appears between the cultures of therapists and clients. For a discussion of some additional domains see Kuehl (1986).

RESULTS[1]

Domain: Expectations of Counseling

Expectations of counseling was one of the first domains to emerge. Although clients' expectations involved various included terms, there was a general expectation among both the parents and the adolescents that therapy was going to be quite somber: "suits, vests, no jokes, no giggling, just very straight." At least one individual gave consideration to the possibility of being put on a couch, and another came prepared to remain at the clinic indefinitely. Adolescents seemed to have the most idiosyncratic expectations of therapy; many of these seemed to have been influenced by what they had seen on television. One adolescent informed the ethnographers that he half expected his therapist to behave similar to television comedian Bob Newhart in his psychologist role, but not be nearly as funny. Both adolescents and their parents expected that "drilling or questioning" was going to be part of the therapy process and that the focus of this questioning was going to be on the adolescent and his or her drug use.

ADOLESCENT: I didn't know, I thought maybe it would be like television where they show people shouting at you, stuff like that. We

[1]Quotes from informants are minimally edited for readability.

went in a little room and I thought 'wait a minute, what are we going to do?'

ADOLESCENT: I thought I was going to have to answer a lot of questions I was not sure how to answer. I thought they would ask every detail about everything, where I had done it and with whom, and all that. I thought I was going to have to go through it all over again: I was going to have to sit there and answer all the questions and I'd be the only one that they'd talk to.

While parents expected that their children were going to be questioned in safe, neutral environments, they also expected that they were going to get some clear answers and quick results from the therapist. They approached these family therapists in the same manner they would approach a physician for treatment. However, what the informant experienced was that when they asked a question about how to solve the problem the therapist in many instances turned the question around by using such maneuvers as asking the client what he or she thought the answer should be? Such maneuvers sometimes seemed like ludicrous game playing to desperate parents seeking answers from an expert who has years of education and experience dealing with these problems, and who often had a group of experts with which to consult behind a mirror.

MOTHER: I guess this was something I had in mind when I came to the counseling sessions, to be able to find something tangible, some kind of an answer to the situation. What we found was people as yourself to field the questions and throw them right back at us, and possibly put a new wrinkle to them and make us think about it and not have ever given us any kind of an answer. This was a cop-out for us because we were at our wits' end as far as frustration and as far as what we thought we should or should not, or could or could not do, and we were frightened of whatever the future may be.

On the other hand, some informants stated that they experienced such maneuvering as the therapist's way of developing or bringing out thought and feeling so as to lead the clients to formulate their own answers.

MOTHER: A good counselor can sit and listen and then ask you just the right thing that makes the lightbulb go off. It just sets you off on the train of thought he wants you to go on. His questions helped me to talk about and see things I hadn't thought about before. Sometimes I got the feeling he was always two or three steps ahead of me, like he had it figured out and now he was going to help me figure it out.

Domain: Types of Psychos and Shrinks

The second domain to emerge is related to the distinctions clients make regarding where to seek help. For the most part, the distinctions clients drew appeared to be quite different from those a therapist might expect.

Clients used the term *counselor* most often. The term was used by some informants as a generic term to indicate any individual who works with people and gives advice. The term was used by other informants to refer to a narrow field in which one has some personal experience, less education than other titles, and perhaps a student status somewhat like an intern. For example, family members often referred to the graduate student with whom they were working as counselors and assumed that these counselors upon graduation would become *psychologists*. This perception persisted despite the fact that the graduate students were careful to identify themselves as marriage and family therapists, and that the program is not taught out of psychology, but in the College of Home Economics. The members of only one family referred to their experience at Texas Tech University as "family therapy." It was usually referred to as "meeting, group, group psychology, or counseling."

MOTHER: There's all kinds of counseling, isn't there? I know there is some for abused children, there's some for battered wives, I am sure there must be some for addicts and alcoholics.

ETHNOGRAPHER: Is a psychologist a type of counselor or is a psychologist different from a counselor?

MOTHER: He is a counselor. There is no difference between a psychologist and a counselor.

ETHNOGRAPHER: Would a psychiatrist be a type of counselor or would a psychiatrist be different?

MOTHER: I think they are missing a few things, you know. It is easier to just give people some drugs and get them addicted, than it is to really help a person. A psychologist will come near people, they don't prescribe drugs that much, they do more counseling. A psychiatrist gives people drugs to get them off their back.

ETHNOGRAPHER: Would a counselor prescribe drugs?

MOTHER: Just a counselor can't prescribe drugs, they don't have a license to do so . . . most psychologists will not use drugs the majority of them . . . I think they [psychologists] are licensed to give medication . . . I think it is the lower classes of drugs . . . I don't know the classes any more . . . I think psychologists just have the first three levels . . . What is it, a four year program for a counselor, just a college degree, and a psychologist is a Ph.D. . . . and a psychiatrist has to go the eight years to med school.

ETHNOGRAPHER: Are social workers counselors?

MOTHER: I think social workers don't really have close contact with their clients. They don't really care. They lay it on the line, what they can do to help and that is it. They lay it on the line, what they can do, you know, they really don't take a personal interest ever. I would hope a psychologist would care whether that person went ahead and killed himself or not. It is not just a client, it is not just a paying customer.

Most referrals to family counseling are self-referrals. This means that each family must draw distinctions concerning when it is appropriate to refer to pastors, counselors, psychologists, social workers, family therapists, psychiatrists, or whatever other categories of treatment providers they distinguish. From the vantage points of these disciplines, each has distinctive areas of knowledge. The definitions of these different disciplines held by family members, if the definitions exist at all (family therapy did not seem to exist as a profession), are often at considerable variance with the definitions held by the different professions.

Componential analysis was employed in order to organize the distinctions drawn by family members into a semantic paradigm of mental health care providers. The bulk of family members opinions could be characterized as falling along five semantic dimensions. These dimensions are: 1) caring, 2) life experience, 3) technical expertise in counseling, 4) the ability to address serious problems, and 5) the capacity to dispense medication. Pastors were considered naive in life experiences, low in technical expertise, lacking the ability to address serious problems, and unable to dispense medication, but were ranked high in caring. Counselors were moderately high in caring, experienced since "they had been there," but low in therapy skills and only moderately able to address serious problems due to their lack of professional education; like pastors they were unable to dispense medication. Psychologists, because of their education, had the ability to address serious problems, were counseling experts, and able to dispense moderate amounts of medication, but since working with people was "just a job" they were only moderate in caring, and rated low in experience since most of what they knew "came from books." Psychiatrists were described as caring very little about the people they worked with, naive in terms of life experiences, but able to deal with serious problems when hospitalization was necessary, could dispense medications, and had moderate counseling skills. Social workers were thought of primarily as bureaucrats and rated low across all the semantic dimensions mentioned.

The reader is cautioned that no set of generalizations should be used to steal the voice of the client. These distinctions are presented primarily as a reminder that the distinctions therapists draw concerning the way they conceptualize their particular profession should not automatically be attributed to the clients. Clients may very well have their own reasons for referral that have little bearing on our imagined reasons for their showing up at our offices.

Domain: The Setting

The third domain to emerge is related to the setting in which the therapy took place including the room, camera, mirror, and team. The presence of the mirror and team can mean many things. The team has been described as a panel of expert consultants, a jury diagnosing the case, a group of students learning from the counselor, and a group of teachers grading the counselor.

FATHER: The jury.

MOTHER: I think we felt the same, it is the type of thing you hear at the hospital, that many people are diagnosing your case.

FATHER: You always had the feeling you were being watched. Sometimes you have the feeling and you pass it off as paranoia. You knew you were being watched by strange men behind the mirrored glass and they were going to make recommendations on what you were going to do with your family. Sometimes they would knock on the door or window. You get the feeling of 'oh no,' especially if you're talking. It is like being called into the principal's office.

MOTHER: They [the people behind the glass] have drawn this big conclusion obviously. Something triggered them to say 'come here and let's talk' [to the therapist], but they never said to us, 'listen you just said blah, blah.' They knew the answer, they picked up on something, and yet they wouldn't tell us in a manner that we could get results.

The opinions of the team held varying weight with the families. Some people saw the team as being less fallible than the therapist. While these clients might not believe what the therapist said, when the team said it, they were more likely to believe it since it is more difficult to argue with five people. Still other clients reported that although they took comfort in the team's agreeing with the therapist, they were less concerned with the opinion of the team when it differed from the opinion of the therapist. These informants reported taking this stance because the team did not have a personal, in-the-room relationship with them like the therapist, and this relationship was necessary for real understanding to occur.

However, there were times when the difference of opinion between the family and the team worked to the family's advantage and to the therapist's feigned chagrin.

ADOLESCENT: Some of the group's [team's] instructions were a waste. We wouldn't do it. Once they told us to go home and have a fight. That was stupid. We went home and sat down and looked at each other and said 'this is stupid, I don't want to have a fight,' so we didn't. Another time they told me to go home and piss my parents off on purpose. That was stupid, I wasn't going to do that."

The combination of camera, mirror, and team are clear indications that the problems of a family are going to be made public. For some families these signs of technology are comforting and indicative of a modern treatment facility. For other families the use of these tools was demeaning and overly intrusive. This seemed to be more strongly expressed among adolescents.

ADOLESCENT: There is a stigma that there is someone always eavesdropping, if the camera is there, which it always was, and the people behind there, which they always were, that you are being spied on.

Domain: Individual Versus Family Therapy

The fourth domain to emerge related to distinctions the informants drew concerning individual versus family (what they tended to term *group)* therapy. For the most part, the distinctions the informants drew were quite different from those the therapists were drawing. Individual therapy was viewed by many informants as the optimal solution to drug abuse. Characteristics of individual therapy, as viewed by a number of informants, is that "it is deeper," "one can say what one thinks," "it is easier to confess secrets," and "problems do not get back to the group." Furthermore, many parents stated that they believe in a "generation gap," and that few adolescents feel free to talk with their parents present. Individual therapy was described by some informants as more potent because it is intensive and focused on one individual rather than taking a wide view like the "group counseling." These parents saw individual therapy as focusing on the locus of the drug abuse and the adolescent. As a result, the informant's understanding of the nature of the problem sometimes clashed with the therapist's understanding. Yet, these differences were seldom dealt with in the therapy meetings.

FATHER: Maybe if they had some individual counseling they would have said what they thought. Everybody's got secrets or have done things or been involved in things they do not want other people to know about. I don't care if I was confessing to a priest. There were a lot of things that came out [in the family meetings] that were good and we now understand about each other that we didn't know before, but at the same time I feel like there are a lot of things deep inside each individual that did not come out because they did not want anybody else to know about it.

MOTHER: We did not deal with the drug problem. Maybe you have to get to the underlying causes of the interaction in a family that makes one turn to drugs, but the anger . . . the kid cannot sniff gas that many times without causing brain damage. That is where the anger came in. We did not get to that. There were no individual sessions. We did not deal with that issue, and that is frustrating.

Other clients stated that they favored family therapy over individual therapy.

FATHER: I think the pressure from us and the open feelings that came out in the family, how it made us feel, how it was affecting mother, made our son realize that he had a responsibility not just to himself, but also to this family. I honestly and truly, from what I've seen with other people, feel that's the only way you're going to resolve the problem. The whole family has to work with it.

Domain: Characteristics of the Counselor

The counselor's behaviors were described by clients in this study as being quite numerous and diverse, ranging from being impartial, congenial, and sympathetic to being provoking and hurtful. Counselor characteristics that informants mentioned most frequently were: asking lots of questions but giving no answers, making clients figure things out for themselves, helping clients come up with alternative approaches by drawing off their experience, giving suggestions, consulting with the people behind the mirror, becoming a friend, and getting something in his head and not wanting to change it.

MOTHER: Always a pleasure when [the counselor] would stand up and shake hands with you when you had done something good.
FATHER: He would praise you when you needed to be praised and chew you out when you needed it.
MOTHER: When he noticed something he would point it out. He made us aware.
FATHER: He would let you look at your own self, make you aware. [It was] always done in a kind and loving way, even when he shut you down—'You'll get your turn, be quiet.'

Not all clients thought the counselor was sensitive, some even felt they were picked on.

ADOLESCENT: He would just ask questions like he really didn't care . . . just ask you questions and make it hurt.
MOTHER: I remember that statement I made, 'Hope springs eternal.' It was crammed back down my throat! . . .
ETHNOGRAPHER: Are there other words to describe 'getting picked on?'
ADOLESCENT: Tiresome. You know, when you hear someone say bla, bla, bla and give you the same lecture 20 times a day. It gets boring.

Adolescents seemed to prefer working with a counselor who had "been there" just like them. The way a counselor conveys this image is by looking *streetwise* rather than wearing a dress shirt and slacks, and being able to speak the language of drugs as learned first hand rather than from books. Furthermore, a number of adolescents preferred a counselor of the same gender and closer to their age.

ADOLESCENT: Hell, he just reads books. He wasn't experienced [with drugs] . . . It's the looks. Just saying, 'What's up, man' doesn't cut it, but it helps. You need to be able to trust him, and that's how you get trust, if you know this guy's been through the same shit . . . [If] you start talking about it and he doesn't know what the hell you're saying, you're not going to trust the guy. I wouldn't.

While the counselor might at first have been viewed as another authority in the lives of the family members due to the fact that they went to the counselor for help, as the counseling process proceeded the relationship between family members and the counselor often came closer together, perhaps ending in a friendship of sorts. This was especially true when counseling was felt to be successful. Clients reported that perceiving the counselor cared about them as people rather than viewing them as a paycheck was a characteristic of a counselor with whom they could work well.

MOTHER: [The counselor's] being receptive and showing me he cared made me want to talk to him, it made me want to talk about my problems with him because I knew he wasn't just doing the job. With [a bad counselor] I wouldn't want to talk to him. This guy might be able to find the answers to my problems, but he doesn't care or empathize with me. That's important. I would refuse to talk to somebody like that.

Clients preferred a counselor whom they perceived as working with them and as giving suggestions and alternatives rather than giving unilateral directives. They were more likely to cooperate with the counselor when they perceived he understood their concerns and was willing to lead them in a caring manner. Clients were less likely to cooperate when they thought the counselor did not understand them or when they perceived that he was telling them what to do in an authoritative fashion.

MOTHER: If the counselor acts interested and like he really wants to help you. . . .

ADOLESCENT: Like [our counselor].

MOTHER: . . . and makes you feel comfortable, that's good for you. But if you're dreading it and you don't like the person, you eventually quit before it does any good. . . . If they start telling me what I'm going to have to do, force me to make changes, that would turn me off real fast. . . . [Our counselor] would make suggestions. If you wanted to follow them it was really left open to you.

ETHNOGRAPHER: It seems people are saying that without caring, the rest of the counseling skills will not do [the counselor] any good. You will not 'wholeheartedly follow the suggestions' of someone you don't feel comfortable with.

STEPMOTHER: Yes, definitely.

Domain: Adolescent Bullshitting

Adolescents unanimously reported being against the idea of coming to counseling. Some adolescents reported thinking they were stupid for having been caught using drugs. Other adolescents thought counseling was an extreme and unnecessary action taken by their parents. Some adolescents did not want to begin counseling, but upon reflection agreed it was necessary. Adolescents had many ways in which they did not cooperate while in counseling. They often used the cover term *bullshitting* to describe their behavior.

ADOLESCENT: It's easy as hell to bullshit someone who doesn't know . . . say, if your parents find you with something . . . you say 'if that was mine do you think I would be stupid enough to leave it where you would find it?' They think, 'I guess he's right, it's not his.' . . . that's the best one there is.

ADOLESCENT: Make them think they're smarter than you that they found it, and at the same time [think] 'My son's not that stupid,' even though you are.

Bullshitting most often began at home or in the automobile on the way to counseling in the form of withdrawal and a refusal to discuss the matter with their parents or counselor. The best strategy was to keep quiet and listen to what the parents and counselor were saying in order to find out what they knew about the adolescent's drug use specifically, and other drug use in general. Listening closely to what one's parents and counselor had to say was a way of information gathering to have some idea how to respond to later questions or accusations. If asked a question, the adolescent would say as little as possible and say only what he or she thought his or her parents, counselor, and the group would want to hear.

Two of the adolescents interviewed reported that later in the counseling process, when they were not as uncertain about what was going to happen at the meetings, they let their guard down and came to a meeting under the influence of drugs (amphetamines, marijuana, or both). When asked by the ethnographer how this was possible, the adolescents replied that they were good at getting high because they had been doing it for so long. To pass the urine screen, adolescents reported bringing urine from someone who was not using drugs. Another ploy was to take large doses of vitamins and drink large quantities of liquids high in acidity (such as a combination of vinegar and water) a couple of days before a meeting.

While telling the counselor and parents only what they wanted to hear, going to counseling high, and beating the *whiz quiz* were things adolescents termed bullshitting, the list of other methods of bullshitting is long. Some common methods involved: telling parents who have found drug paraphernalia in the adolescent's possession that the adolescent is not stupid enough to get caught with the drugs if the drugs actually belong to him or her; the adolescent's making his or her parents feel guilty; telling parents they were young once, too, and that as an adolescent he or she is just trying to learn things on his or her own; telling parents the counselor does not know what he is talking about or the program is no good; or, if the parents threaten some course of action the adolescent does not think they will take, the adolescent will do something wrong in order to challenge the parents to follow through on the threat. Adolescents reported that bullshitting was used quite often, but that it was particularly important between meetings when parents were trying to put suggestions into practice. Adolescents would bullshit in order to keep the parents and counselor off track and keep counseling from working.

ADOLESCENT: They wanted my parents to write down a set of rules and consequences . . . we came home and they wrote it all down, and me and my little brother talked them out of it.

ETHNOGRAPHER: How did you talk them out of it?

ADOLESCENT: Basically by saying, 'that program's not any good out there.' Sort of forcing that in their head. And, you know, 'this isn't going to help.' Then one of them might agree, 'Yeah, I don't know about this.'

ETHNOGRAPHER: You'd go back to Tech and say you tried it [the counselor's suggestion]?

ADOLESCENT: Yeah. But it really wasn't a lie in my parent's eyes. In my eyes I could see exactly, they were bullshitting, like saying 'Yeah, we did it.' But we didn't live by it like we were supposed to.

Domain: How Counseling Progresses

In general, the process is described as *starting broad* in phase one and *focusing down* as the process nears completion. The following phases and included information were generated and labeled by the informants themselves.

Phase One: The Introductory Meeting

Family members stated that counseling began with an introductory meeting. The primary task was to learn what counseling was going to consist of. Overall, family members did not know what to expect. As a result, this phase was often described as a disjointed experience. Most informants expected actual therapy to take place. Some expected the therapist to meet with the adolescent alone, and some expected the adolescent to be questioned or drilled as to his or her drug use. Some family members expected the adolescent to be put in a group with other adolescents, or to be verbally assaulted by a hardened drug addict. Some stated these expectations were shaped by what they had seen on television.

Instead, when the family members arrived at the clinic for the first time, they were surprised to find themselves filling out forms (measures of individual, marital, and family functioning). Informants often described these forms as contradictory and irrelevant. Some informants reported interpreting items on the forms as implying proper personal and familial behavior. As a result, they began counseling feeling more guilty or defensive because their behavior did not match that implied by the items (for example, "Our family does things together"). Another unexpected activity clients experienced was opening up about their problem with someone they later found was not their counselor (the clients interviewed never used the term therapist), a separate person conducted the intake meeting.

Phase Two: Assessment

Informants stated the primary task during this second phase of therapy involved "getting to know you and draw you out." Assessment took the form of the therapist and family meeting one-on-one and getting acquainted with one another. During this phase, the therapist mostly listened and asked questions designed to convey to the family that he (all therapists were male) was interested in their well-being. The therapist also shared some of himself in order to convey to the family he was normal like them. There was some discussion of the problem and why the family was in therapy, but in general the conversation tended to stay general and focused on the family members as individuals with broad interests.

Parents reported doing most of the talking during this phase of therapy. They shared personal information about themselves such as their hobbies and interests. This served to help the parents become comfortable. Parents also reported that when they shared information about family problems and why they were at therapy it served to relieve some of the burden they had been carrying since now they were receiving professional help.

Adolescents reported feeling scared during this early phase of therapy. Upon entering the therapy room, adolescents reported trying to avoid being seen by the camera or the people behind the mirror, and would say as little as possible to anyone. For many adolescents, the early phases of therapy involved sitting quietly and listening to the parents and therapist to see how much they knew about the adolescent's actual behavior, and saying only what the therapist and parents want to hear.

Adolescents reported that this information gathering would be useful later in therapy when they would devise methods by which to mislead or bullshit the therapist and parents. Adolescents continued to be annoyed by the surveillance equipment (video camera and one-way mirror) throughout the entire therapy process.

Phase Three: Getting Down to Basics and Generating Suggestions

The primary task during phase three was that the problem was defined or uncovered and possible courses of action were generated. This phase was described as the most emotionally intense and time-consuming phase of the therapeutic process. During this phase the therapist would ask questions which were more focused on the problem. The therapist would not answer questions, although he would sometimes bring in and expand upon different ideas and draw off of his experience in order to zero in on the problem. Rather than answer questions, the therapist would draw answers out of the family members.

Informants reported that this cycle of questioning and answering went around many times as the therapist and family members tried to get down to the cause of the problem, sometimes going through layers and layers of other problems. Family members reported that during this phase the therapist would dig down and probe all of the family members for weak spots and problem areas that needed addressing so that the problem could be rectified. The reason for this repeated questioning and digging was so that the therapist could get to the bottom of things and find the cause of the problem in order to generate suggestions and alternatives for the family to try in attempting to resolve the problem. Most informants preferred a therapist who they perceived was offering suggestions and alternatives rather than "trying to tell us what to do."

The parents often found this phase stressful. It was during this phase that the family became aware of or realized other problems. While some parents thought that this interaction was necessary in that it allowed problems that were already present to surface (such as marital issues), other parents reported therapy created problems in the family that were not relevant or not present before therapy began (such as marital issues). Some family members felt they were being picked on, torn down, or not understood by the therapist, the group behind the mirror, or other family members as the problem was discussed and suggestions were offered. Family members reported it was difficult to watch the same thing happen to other members of their family. As such, family members reported they would become impatient if progress toward resolving the problem was not being made quickly enough.

Some families reported being stuck in this phase for a considerable amount of time and thought about discontinuing therapy.

For the adolescent, phase three continued much as did phase two. Many adolescents were still trying to avoid being seen or heard and were simply waiting quietly, listening, and gathering information in order to find out what was going to become of the therapy and plan ways to sabotage future interventions. Also, by this time the adolescent's sibling(s) had usually concluded that therapy was boring and they should not have to go, especially since they were not the one(s) in trouble. Many family members expressed surprise and often disappointment that there were no individual meetings with the adolescent during this phase. Most families stated they would have preferred a mix of meetings, with the therapist sometimes meeting individually with the adolescent and sometimes with the entire family.

With regard to the group behind the mirror, clients often conceptualized it as a necessary evil. The group was described as offering some good suggestions and keeping the therapy on track, but was also described as insensitive and intruding, especially by adolescents. Overall, most family members treated the group's opinions as secondary to the therapist's opinion because the therapist was the one who had a personal relationship with the family.

Phase Four: Putting Suggestions into Practice

While the task in phase three was described as identifying the problem(s) and generating suggestions regarding possible ways to resolve them, the task during phase four was described as putting the suggestions into practice. The parents would take a suggestion home and implement it and then report what happened to the therapist at the next meeting. Parents reported that their understanding of what happened at home was often undecided and they turned to the therapist to help gauge whether they should continue what they were doing, modify what they were doing, or go back to phase three and attempt to generate a different suggestion altogether. When the family perceived the therapist was just doing a job and did not really care about them as a family, or when the therapist's questions and suggestions indicated to the family that he did not really understand what family members were thinking or feeling, the family was less likely to whole-heartedly put a suggestion into practice and try living by it.

In general, adolescents stated they continued to stay quiet and listened to what others were saying in order to gather information *during sessions* in this phase. However, adolescents reported they became more active *between sessions* during this phase. Activity the adolescents often referred to as bullshitting became pronounced as the adolescent tried to persuade his or her parents not to follow through on a suggestion. Adolescents tried to instill doubt in their parents about the correctness of a decision they were trying to make or capitalizing on any second thoughts the parents might be having about how to proceed.

Phase Five: Sharing Successes with the Counselor

Informants reported that when phase four was perceived to be successful, the interaction became one of moving to phase five where the task involved the clients sharing successful experiences with the therapist. The therapist at this point was described by some informants as becoming less of an authority figure and more of a confidant and friend. The therapist served as a sounding board rather than someone who needed to ask questions. Parents reported they felt stronger and more confident during this phase when there were successes to report, and used their time in the meetings to tell the therapist about their successes. The adolescents of these families reported feeling less inimical toward the therapist and often thought therapy was for a good cause. These adolescents reported they either greatly reduced their drug use or discontinued drug use altogether.

However, not all families experienced this sharing of successful experiences. The parents of one family said that reaching phase five "was something we would have liked to do, we just never got there." When there were no successes to report, or when the parents felt stuck (as discussed in phase three), the parents reported feeling frustrated, sick, and helpless. The adolescents of families that did not participate in this phase of therapy reported they continued to bullshit the therapist, the group, and their parents. Some of these adolescents reported their drug use was increasing as therapy progressed. Some adolescents stated they thought they would have been more honest and willing to make therapy work if there were some individual meetings for the adolescent along with the family meetings, and if the therapist would have impressed them as having had some personal drug experience and not been so easy to bullshit.

Phase Six: Troubleshooting and Following-up

This is the last phase of the therapy process that informants described. Again, not all informants experienced this phase. The task consisted of parents asking the therapist for suggestions about what to do if various situations arose in the future. The therapist's role at this point was simply to help the family generate suggestions as to possible courses of action. The length of time needed to generate the suggestion was short because the therapist and family members knew each other. As a result, there was not the need for the many cycles of questioning and digging that were necessary in phase three.

DISCUSSION

In a dissertation on physician-patient interaction Skinner (Leiter, 1980) tape-recorded examinations and then interviewed patients and physicians separately about what each had understood the other to mean. Accounts of the conversations did not agree, but at the same time both physicians and patients unanimously reported that they were understood. Apparently there was the illusion of social coherence and common understanding in the conversation despite the substantive meanings of the other being misunderstood. What Skinner's study did not do was follow physicians and patients over a series of interviews to examine how meaning is maintained or becomes ambiguous over time.

The word ambiguous comes from the Latin word *ambigere* which means to wander and can be broken down further into two root words *ambi* meaning about and around and *agere* which translates as to go. That which is ambiguous in meaning wanders between meanings while the individual searches to understand (Webster's New World Dictionary, 1966). Successful family therapy requires at least a minimal amount of sustained social coherence and shared substantive meaning over many contacts. While individuals can maintain a sense of shared meaning where it does not exist, as for example during one examination in a physicians office, the challenge of maintaining this shared meaning even over a limited number of sessions in brief therapy may lead to a sense of ambiguity on the part of clients and therapists.

The results of this study suggest that family therapy might be thought of as an ambiguous experience, at least in the domains specified. It seems possible that much therapy is conducted under the assumption of subjective agreement between participants while at the same time there is little consistency regarding the ways clients and family therapists conceptualize expectations of counseling, the disciplines that perform such services, the setting or environment in which these services are performed, the value placed on family therapy versus individual counseling as a means of treatment, or characteristics of the counselor.

For example, conceptualizing problems within a contextual framework is the hallmark of all systemic approaches to therapy, and many informants agreed with this approach. Yet, there were also many informants in this study who defined the problems of the drug-involved adolescent as being individual problems. When a family member's approach did not mesh with the therapist's (as for example when the therapist did not work with the adolescent alone), the client seldom brought this to the attention of the therapist. Furthermore, if there were differences of opinion within the same family about how to approach the problem, some family members concluded therapy was creating more problems than it was solving. These differences in opinion may be characteristics that distinguish successful from unsuccessful therapy for families and influence whether families complete treatment.

Many therapists also believe matter-of-factly that people seldom take advice and as a result emphasize more of a Socratic dialogue (Maranhao, 1986), asking questions the answers to which lead the client to an answer previously concluded by the therapist. Yet, at least with adolescent drug abuse as a presenting problem, the therapist's questioning of the adolescent and advice giving is frequently expected by the client(s). This focusing on questions without providing answers as an aversive part of therapy may also be one of the characteristics that distinguish unsuccessful from successful therapy, and influence whether families complete treatment. On the other hand, the client's acceptance of the therapist's questions may be due to a process of acculturation with families who have members with previous counseling experience, or whose members are not operating under the assumption of a medical model. One mother stated, "If medicine to treat disease and physical illness is not an exact science, certainly psychology and counseling for emotional problems cannot be an exact science."

All referrals to counseling are ultimately self-referrals. This means that each client and/or family must decide when and to whom referral is appropriate. They distinguish among pastors, counselors, psychologists, social workers, psychiatrists, and other categories of treatment providers. Each of these different disciplines defines itself as having distinct areas of knowledge and expertise. Yet, this study suggests that the definitions held by clients can be at considerable variance with those held by the different disciplines, and these differences may not become issues until the therapy experience has already begun. These differences in understanding may also influence the client's continuation in and successful use of the therapy experience. Clearly for adolescents appearing to be a streetwise, counselors reduced to bullshitting may have retained some adolescents in therapy.

It is interesting to note, that the informants in this study made no reference to the field of counselor education as a service they might use.

Family therapy also seemed to be an invisible profession to these clients despite the fact that the clinic was conspicuously labeled *The Family Therapy Clinic.*

Most family therapists believe that clients are nervous about the camera, but quickly forget that it is there. For the most part this opinion was borne out. Adolescents reported being particularly sensitive to the presence of the camera. While most adults reported forgetting about the camera, at least some adolescents continued to remain sensitive to its presence. Some of the adolescent girls in this study reported they often dressed up for the camera. Many adolescents stated that they would situate themselves in the room so their back was to the camera, or in a corner where it was more difficult to see them on the camera.

While there were vaying opinions concerning the mirror and team, people reported being more reactive to these than to the camera. One adolescent recalled being scared the first time the team called the therapist out of the room by knocking on the glass. She thought someone was trying to break into the room. The results of this study suggest that, at least for some people, too many intrusions by the team behind the mirror can lead to an unfavorable opinion of the therapy experience.

Adolescents were generally opposed to counseling—viewing it as unnecessary, an invasion of their privacy, and embarrassing. Just the ordeal of coming to therapy persuaded one adolescent to quit taking drugs. Adolescents had many ways to not cooperate while maintaining a protective posture about their drug use and gathering information. When possible, adolescents used the ambiguity of counseling to raise questions in their parents' minds concerning the advisability of continuing counseling.

Given the structural-strategic orientation of the therapists in this study, it is not surprising that this client-based description closely parallels the therapeutic processes described by Minuchin (1974) and Haley (1976). For example, Minuchin's joining and Haley's social stage components are analogous to what informants labeled *assessment.* Minuchin's assessment of dysfunctional family structure and Haley's problem definition components are analogous to what informants labeled *getting down to basics.* Minuchin and Haley's giving directives and tasks are analogous to what family members described as *putting suggestions into practice.* And Haley's disengaging from family members component is analogous to what family members described as *sharing successes with the counselor,* and *troubleshooting and follow-up.* Yet, while many informants experienced all of the phases of the therapy process and were satisfied, other informants described how their family was not able to experience all of the phases and were dissatisfied. In this study, informants described two primary reasons for these differences in experience. Both centered on the therapist.

The Counselor as Caring and Able. Two of the therapist characteristics informants discussed most often included perceiving the therapist as (a) caring and understanding, and (b) able to generate relevant suggestions. Good counselors were described as warm, caring, and genuinely interested in the clients as people. Only if the clients felt these qualities were present would they respond with openness and trust. Once the caring relationship was established the counselor's suggestions were better accepted. When the counselor did not seem to be interested in them as people or appeared condescending, openness and trust were lost. The suggestions of bad counselors were either ignored or minimized.

For example, family members who completed all phases of the therapy process tended to be more satisfied with the outcome and described their therapist as caring and able to help the family generate suggestions that eventually ameliorated the problem. Family members who did not complete all of the phases of the therapy process, but who still described the experience as somewhat satisfying, also described their therapist as caring. However, these family members described their therapist as unsuccessful in generating suggestions that would ameliorate the problem. Finally, there were families whose members did not complete all phases of the therapy process and who did not have a satisfying experience. These family members doubted the therapist's understanding of them and their problem, and questioned his ability to generate suggestions that seemed likely to ameliorate the problem.

These clients' descriptions of family therapy suggest that successes in later phases of therapy often depend upon the successes of earlier phases. For example, if in phase two the family members did not perceive that the therapist was caring and that he was genuinely interested in them as unique people, and that he was easy to bullshit, the family members would be less likely to share relevant information or say what was on their minds in phase three. If the therapist had not gained the confidence and cooperation of the family members, and as a result had not been given all of the relevant information, the suggestions the therapist helped generate or the assignments he suggested would not be accepted by the family members as totally relevant and would only be partially put into practice in phase four (if they were put into practice at all).

The third phase was described as one of the most critical phases of the therapeutic process—getting down to basics and generating suggestions. It is now that the family is being questioned by the therapist in order to become aware of the primary problem and generate suggestions about what to do about it. It is during this stage that the therapist's and family members' understanding of the issues contributing to the presenting problem is brought into the open. While these understandings were often compatible, there were also occasions where differences in understanding became obstacles to the therapeutic process.

Clients sometimes thought the counselor was on too strict a program, that is to say, sometimes the therapist's family therapy model was too rigidly applied. For example, Minuchin and Fishman (1981) state,

> Family members have a discriminating sense of hearing, with areas of selective deafness that are regulated by their common history. . . . As a result, the therapist's message may never register, or it may be blunted. The therapist must *make* the family "hear," and this requires that his message go above the family threshold of deafness (pp. 116–117; emphasis added).

Likewise, Madanes (1981) states, "The therapist should repeat his requests time and time again until he succeeds. A great many of the therapist's tactics within this approach involves repetitiousness and tenacity" (p. 143).

The results of this study suggest that an approach that addresses marital issues and parental power and unity at the same time it addresses adolescent misbehavior is often successful from the clients' perspectives. However, interviews with these family members suggest many parents already believed their own problems were contributing to the adolescent's problem, and this made it easier for the therapist to discuss these issues with the parents. For example, one mother stated, "My husband and I knew our problems were upsetting the boys." The therapist's need for repetition and tenacity was low in these situations.

However, the parents of other families conceptualized their problems as being separate and unrelated to the adolescent's problem. Another mother stated, "I knew my husband and I had problems, but that is not why we were at counseling." It was at this point the therapy process often stalled. For these parents, the therapist's emphasis on parental and marital issues seemed either unconnected or secondary to the child's problem, and the therapist's repeated attempts to go beyond the family's hypothesized threshold of deafness in order to make the family hear did nothing more than lead family members to believe the therapist did not understand their situation. From the dissatisfied client's perspective, it would seem that therapists also have areas of selective deafness that are regulated by their common history, and failures in therapy are not due to resistant clients—but are due to *resistant therapists.*

CONCLUSION

Postmodern ethnographers have moved beyond thinking that people can grasp the world view of any other in accurate and finished form (Clifford & Marcus, 1986; Marcus & Fischer, 1986). The inexorable interaction of the ideas of one's self with the ideas of an other means that whatever one writes (constructs) about people is as much a product of self-interests and self-punctuation as it is an objective representation (Marcus & Fischer, 1986). As such, postmodernists hold that people select what is significant to them from the stream of behavior others produce because it piques their interest, addresses their theories, or appears publishable.

Such an orientation is consistent with a radical constructivist understanding that such constructions at best allow one to adapt his or her thinking in such a way that he or she can interact with an other in as humane, nonintrusive, and as effective a manner as possible (von Glasersfeld, 1986). Emphasizing that a therapist's meaning system is inexorably entwined in the meaning system he or she is attempting to understand leads to the conclusion that a client's meaning system is also entwined in such a system. The same process applies with regard to the construction and understanding of an ethnography. What therapists and researchers are left with is constructing ways of thinking which may fit, but do not match another person's way of conceptualizing his or her experiential world. It is within this constructivist and postmodern orientation that this study and its results can be conceptualized.

Therapists, despite their best attempts at joining (Minuchin & Fishman, 1981) or their clever use of the representational systems of their clients (Grinder & Bandler, 1976), will forever live in a twilight of partial truths. Real understanding of families is but an illusion or delusion that we carry as part of our work. As evidence, if you laughed or were amused while reading this chapter we would like to suggest that this is because you added your voice as counterpoint to what the clients were saying about therapy and for an instant your illusion of social coherence was torn away. The voice of the other, the clients in this study, were not as you expected them to be. As a discipline, we understand very little about the people we work with.

We often over utilize the notion of objectivity and its associated beliefs of explanation, prediction, and control that are the hallmarks of a logical-positivist approach to science. In so doing, we overlook the complementary ideas of lack of prediction, explanation, and control. Yet, if we acknowledge that social coherence is often an illusion, and that we cannot stand outside of the family systems with which we work, then a sole reliance upon ideas such as objectivity and control can be problematic. Moving beyond a sole reliance on objectivity, we must, then, include notions of noncontrol with those of control as they relate to family therapy. Like the drinker who is powerless to control alcohol, the therapist is unable to control the family. The therapist must also admit noncontrol (look to the higher power) of the system of which he or she is a part. When noncontrol is accepted, what remains is personal responsibility for one's own actions that do not cause change, but simply create a context that allows change.

The professional models and theories of families and family therapy that we hold are often reified, that is, treated as concrete objects rather than abstract ideas. Seldom do family therapists question in a self-reflexive manner, their own basic premises or acknowledge their conceptualizations of family functioning as being only one among many, including those of the family members (Schwartzman, 1983). Like ethnographers, therapists should constantly be asking themselves "what is this client trying to say to me," "what are his or her beliefs about what is occurring," and "how does this speak to the pattern that connects?" The therapist should be careful as to how the assumed gaps in this discourse with the client are filled in.

Ideally, we would have liked to have included the voices of the therapists who worked with the families and juxtapose their comments with what the families had to say. Instead we must rely on your voices as family therapists and book readers to fill in the voice of the therapist. We would have also liked to give this material back in recursive fashion to informants to allow them to respond to our attempted representation of their experience of family therapy.

REFERENCES

Agar, M. H. (1980). *The professional stranger: An informal introduction to ethnography.* New York: Academic Press.

Agar, M. H. (1986). *Speaking of ethnography.* Beverly Hills, CA: SAGE.

Caudill, W. (1958). *The psychiatric hospital as a small society.* Cambridge, MA: Harvard University Press.

Clifford, J. (1986). Introduction: Partial truths. In J. Clifford and G. E. Marcus (eds.), *Writing culture: The poetics and politics of ethnography.* Berkeley, CA: University of California Press.

Clifford J., & Marcus, G. E. (eds.) (1986). *Writing culture: The poetics and politics of ethnography.* Berkeley, CA: University of California Press.

De Beauvoir, S. (1952). *The second sex.* New York: Alfred A. Knopf.

Estroff, S. E. (1981). *Making it crazy.* Berkeley, CA: University of California Press.

Fabian, J. (1983). *Time and the other: How anthropology makes its object.* New York: Columbia University Press.

Fessler, R. (1983). Phenomenology and 'the talking cure.' In A. Giorgi, A. Barton, and C. Maes (eds.), *Research of psychotherapy, Vol. IV.* Pittsburgh, PA: Duquesne University Press.

Frake, C. (1962). Cultural ecology and ethnography. *American Anthropologist, 64,* 53–59.

Glaser, B. G. & Strauss, A. L. (1967). *The discovery of grounded theory.* Bawthorne, NY: Aldine Publishing Company.

Glasersfeld, E., von. (1984). An introduction to radical constructivism. In B. Watzlawick (ed.), *The invented reality: How do we know what we believe we know? Contributions to constructivism.* New York: W. W. Norton & Company.

Glasersfled, E. von. (1986). Steps in the construction of "Others" and "Reality": A study of self-regulation. In R. Trappl (ed.), *Power, autonomy, utopia: New approaches toward complex systems.* New York: Plenum Press.

Goffman, E. (1961). *Asylums: Essays on the social situation of mental patients and other inmates.* Garden City, NY: Anchor Books.

Grindler, J. & Bandler, R. (1976). *The structure of magic II.* Palo Alto, CA: Science and Behavior Books.

Haley, J. (1976). *Problem solving therapy: New strategies of effective family therapy.* New York: Harper & Row.

Henry, J. (1971). *Pathways to madness.* New York: Random House.

Honigman, J. J. (1970). Sampling in ethnographic field work. In R. Naroll & R. Cohen (eds.), *A handbook of method in cultural anthropology.* Garden City, NY: Natural History Press.

Joanning, H., Quinn, W. H., Fischer, J., & Arrendondo, R. (1984). Family therapy versus traditional therapy for drug abusers. (DHHS Grant No. 1 R01 DA 03733-01). Rockville, MD: National Institute on Drug Abuse.

Keeney, B. P. (1983). *Aesthetics of change.* New York: Guilford Press.

Keeney, B. P. & Ross, J. M. (1985). *Mind in therapy: Constructing systemic family therapies.* New York: Basic Books.

Kruger, D. (1986). On the way to an existential-phenomenological psychotherapy. In D. Kruger (ed.), *The changing reality of modern man.* Pittsburgh, PA: Duquesne University Press.

Kuehl, B. P. (1986). The family therapy of adolescent drug abuse, family members describe their experience. Unpublished doctoral dissertation. Texas Tech University, Lubbock, TX.

Kuehl, B. P., Newfield, N. A., & Joanning, H. (in press). Toward a client-based description of family therapy. *Journal of Family Psychology.*

Leininger, M. M. (ed.) (1985). *Qualitative research methods in nursing.* New York: Grune & Stratton, Inc.

Leiter, K. (1980). *A primer on ethnomethodology.* New York: Oxford University Press.

Lynch-Sauer, J. (1985). Using a phenomenological research method to study nursing phenomena. In M. Leininger (ed.), *Qualitative research methods in nursing.* New York: Grune & Stratton, Inc.

Madanes, C. (1981). *Strategic family therapy.* San Francisco, CA: Jossey-Bass.

Malinowski, B. (1961/1922). *Argonauts of the western pacific.* New York: E. P. Dutton & Co., Inc.

Maranhao, T. (1986). *Therapeutic discourse and Socratic dialogue.* Madison, WI: University of Wisconsin Press.

Marcus, G. E., & Fischer, M. M. J. (1986). *Anthropology as cultural critique: An experimental moment in the human sciences.* Chicago, IL: University of Chicago Press.

Mead, M. (1953). National character. In A. Kroeber (ed.), *Anthropology today.* Chicago, IL: Chicago University Press.

Minuchin, S. (1974). *Families and family therapy.* Cambridge, MA: Harvard University Press.

Minuchin, S. & Fishman, H. C. (1981). *Family therapy techniques.* Cambridge, MA: Harvard University Press.

Napier, A. Y. & Whitaker, C. A. (1978). *The family crucible.* New York: Bantam.

Newfield, N. A., Kuehl, B. P., Joanning, H., & Quinn, W. H. (in press). A mini ethnography of the family therapy of adolescent drug abuse: The ambiguous experience. *Alcoholism Treatment Quarterly.*

Quinn, W. H., Kuehl, B. P., Thomas, F. N., & Joanning, H. (1988). Families of adolescent drug abusers: Systemic interventions to attain drug-free behavior. *American Journal of Drug & Alcohol Abuse. 14,* 65–87.

Quinn, W. H., Kuehl, B. P., Thomas, F. N., Joanning, H., & Newfield, N. A. (in press). Family therapy of adolescent drug abuse: Promoting transition and stabilization of drug-free behavior. *American Journal of Family Therapy.*

Sass, L. A. (1986). Anthropology's native problem: Revisionism in the field. *Harper's Magazine,* May, 49–57.

Schwartzman, J. (1983). Family ethnography: A tool for clinicians. In C. Salicov (ed.), *Cultural perspectives in family therapy.* Rockville, MD: Aspen Systems Press.

Simon, R. (1985). Structure is destiny: An interview with Humberto Maturana. *The Family Therapy Networker, 9,* 32–43.

Spradely, J. (1979). *The ethnographic interview.* New York: Holt, Rinehart, and Winston.

Steier, F. (1985). Toward a cybernetic methodology of family therapy research. In L. Andreozzi (ed.), *Integrating research and clinical practice.* Rockville, MD: Aspen Systems.

Sturtevant, W. C. (1972). Studies in ethnoscience. In J. P. Spradely (ed.), *Culture and cognition: Rules, maps, and plans.* San Francisco, CA: Chandler Publishing Co.

Tyler, S. A. (1986). Post-modern ethnography: From document of the occult to occult document. In J. Clifford and G. E. Marcus (eds.), *Writing culture: The poetics and politics of ethnography.* Berkeley, CA: University of California Press.

Tyler, M. G. & Tyler, S. A. (1985). The sorcerer's apprentice: The discourse of training in family therapy. Unpublished manuscript. Rice University, Houston, TX.

Varela, F. J. (1984). The creative circle: Sketches on the natural history of circularity. In P. Watzlawick (ed.), *The invented reality: How do we know what we believe we know? Contributions to constructivism.* New York: W. W. Norton & Co.

Varela, F. J. (1986). Steps to a cybernetics of autonomy. In R. Trappl (ed.), *Power, autonomy, utopia: New approaches toward complex systems.* New York: Plenum Press.

Von Foerster, H. (ed.) (1986/1974). *Cybernetics of cybernetics: Or the control and the communication of communications.* (B.C.L. Report No. 73.38) Urbana, IL: University of Illinois, The Biological Computer Laboratory.

Watzlawick, P. (ed) (1984). *The invented reality: how do we know what we believe we know? Contributions to constructivism.* New York: W. W. Norton & Company.

Webster's new world dictionary. (1966). New York: World Publishing.

14

Major Issues from Family Therapy Research and Theory

Implications for the Future

MATTHEW D. SELEKMAN, M.S.W.
Family Therapy Supervisor
Des Plaines Valley Community Center, Summit, IL

THOMAS C. TODD, Ph.D.
Chief Psychologist
Forest Hospital, Des Plaines, IL

At this point, the reader has been exposed to 11 distinctly different approaches to family therapy with adolescent substance abuse. While even more diversity would have been possible, this degree of variety poses quite a challenge for anyone to assimilate. In Chapter 12, we gave our own guidelines for integrating some of the approaches presented in this book and what we consider helpful core assumptions common to the approaches we consider akin to ours. We by no means wish to imply that our guidelines form the only possible basis for combining approaches, or that our set of theoretical assumptions are the only ones that make sense. Instead, we would recommend that the reader attempt to articulate his or her own set of assumptions about effective family therapy and then compare these assumptions for compatibility with those made by the various chapter authors.

Having left the reader with guidance for comparing the previous chapters, we would like to devote the bulk of this chapter to existing research in the area, to see what additional light such research can shed on the many issues in the field. Following that, we will offer suggestions about how clinicians can become more empirical in their own work.

FAMILY THERAPY RESEARCH AND ADOLESCENT SUBSTANCE ABUSE

In reviewing addiction and family therapy literature, we were struck by the paucity of family research studies with adolescent substance abusers, particularly the lack of family treatment outcome studies. The majority of existing research studies have examined various dimensions of family functioning, such as family communications and pathological family structures (Cleveland, 1981; Daroff, Marks, & Friedman, 1986; Friedman, Utada, & Morrisey, 1987; Hendin et al., 1981; Hendin & Pollinger-Haas, 1985; Levine, 1985). Friedman et al. (1987), in using the FACES III and Clinical Rating Scale of the Olson Circumplex Model, found that therapists' perceptions of the levels of family functioning of subject families contradicted the families' own views of their level of functioning. The majority of subject families viewed their family systems as being rigid and disengaged, not being chaotic and enmeshed as reported by the therapists, and as often cited in the clinical literature. Findings like these support the constructivists' warning that the family's *map* differs from that of the therapist, and that neither map is real or better (Efran & Lukens 1988; Efran, Hefner, & Lukens, 1987; Hoffman, 1986; Maturana & Varela, 1988.) O'Hanlon (1988) has discussed the dangers in being a slave to one's theory of family therapy, for example, a structural family therapist may invest a lot of energy in searching for pathological family structures.

One of the most important family treatment outcome studies conducted with adolescent substance abusers to date was the research work at the Spanish Family Guidance Clinic in Miami, Florida (Foote et al., 1985; Szapocznik et al., 1983, 1986). Szapocznik and his colleagues found in their study with Latino male adolescent substance abusers and their families that one-person brief strategic family therapy was as effective in enhancing individual and family functioning as a conjoint strategic family therapy approach after a three-year follow-up. According to Szapoczik and Kurtines (1989), "this research clarifies that what is critical in family work is not who is present in the therapy sessions, but rather how the therapist conceptualizes the problem and the intervention" (p. 163).

Although there are a number of methodological problems with Szapocznik and his colleagues' research, their study has produced some important findings for the family therapy field. Their findings provide general support for the family systems concept of *wholism* (de Shazer, 1985), as an explanation for family systemwide changes with the one-person family therapy families. This finding helps support the MRI and solution-focused theorists' position that it is possible to change an entire family system through one family member. de Shazer (1985) refers to this phenomenon as the *ripple effect*. This finding also challenges the widely held family therapy tenet that the therapist must engage all family members in order to have a successful treatment outcome.

Some of the major limitations of Szapocznik and his colleagues' research study were the small homogenous sample (Latino male adolescent substance abusers) and the lack of a third group of untreated control subjects. Clinically, we wonder whether administering the one-person family therapy approach to the family complainant (the parent or most concerned significant other) rather than the identified client would produce similar or better results. If favorable results were produced from such a modification of the Szapocznik study, this would support the use of the MRI and solution-focused therapy approaches with adolescent substance abusers.

In 1985, the National Institute on Drug Abuse (NIDA), in an effort to fill the research gap of family treatment outcome studies with adolescent substance abusers, awarded large grants to three groups (the University of California, San Francisco, Texas Tech University, and Purdue University) to conduct research in this area. We have both been personally involved in the research and family therapy aspects of the Purdue University study and are also quite familiar with the other two projects. In the next section of this chapter, we will compare and contrast the strengths and limitations of each of these three major family therapy studies as reported by the principal research investigators. Finally, we will discuss the relevance of some of the major findings of these studies for clinical practice.

Purdue Project

The Purdue Brief Therapy Project, D.A.R.E., (NIDA Grant # 1R01 DA-MH 03702-01) has been described by Piercy and Frankel (1989). Their initial model was intended to be an optimum blend of structural, strategic, functional, systemic, and behavioral family therapies. (See Piercy and Frankel, 1989 and Lewis et al., Chapter 8 of this book, for further details.) In preliminary results from their project, 69 percent of those receiving family therapy showed significant improvement on their

Index of Drug Severity, in marked contrast to their Treatment as Usual and Family Education control groups. There were, however, adolescents in all three groups that showed unchanged or even increased levels of use.

Evolution of the Model

As Piercy and Frankel (1989) have described, the Purdue staff found it necessary to modify the model significantly to deal with a subgroup of families that responded poorly to the original model. They found that *no-problem problem* families, typically mandated for treatment by an outside agency, denied the existence of a substance abuse problem. This made the application of a problem-oriented model difficult, if not impossible, to apply. Instead, they found it necessary to adopt a more positively oriented approach, borrowing from de Shazer and others, which joined with the family's view of their strengths and asked them to consider how they could use these strengths in the present and future. (See Eastwood et al., 1987, for further details).

Problems with the Research

One problem with the research noted by Piercy and Frankel (1989) was the handling of the urinalysis results. Initially these results were treated as confidential, but neither parents nor therapists were happy with this. Ultimately, they chose to incorporate these results into treatment and believe that this change probably resulted in greater effectiveness.

Obviously the greater issue, which will be noted with all three NIDA projects, concerns the evaluation of treatment procedures that evolve during the course of treatment They noted the need for a coherent model, to allow any empirical test, but also the need for flexibility to allow refinement.

Texas Tech University

Preliminary results of the Texas Tech project "Adolescent Drug Treatment Program," (NIDA Grant # R01DA03733-01) were summarized by the principal investigator Harvey Joanning (personal communication, August 2, 1988). As with the other two NIDA projects, we will not become involved in discussions of control or comparison treatment, complexities of research design, nor methodology.

Family Therapy Results

According to Joanning, highly disorganized families (marital conflict and weak parental coalition), single-parent families, and well-organized families fared well in therapy using their basic structural-strategic model. Roughly 60 percent of the family therapy subjects showed positive results with this model.

Other families did not respond so well, including families with parental or multiple chemical abusers, chronic adolescent substance abuse problems, or presenting with idiosyncratic problems (financial problems, unresolved losses, community problems, etc., drug use in picture, but not primary problem). The 40 percent of the sample with these characteristics fared better with systemic approaches a la Milan Associates (Boscolo et at., 1987), the Ackerman (Papp, 1983), or Galveston Family Institute (Anderson & Goolishian, 1988). Joanning and his colleagues also found the use of metaphor and rituals to be useful with these types of families. In both groups, family therapy subjects greatly decreased or abandoned marijuana use at follow-up.

Evolution of the Model

As mentioned, Joanning and his colleagues found it necessary to become more integrative with the basic structural-strategic model, or to abandon this model altogether in order to best meet the needs of a subgroup of their subject families. As they describe it, in some cases the family therapists moved from a functionalist to a constructivist method of working with their families.

Strengths of the Research

According to Joanning, one of the major aspects of his project that increased referrals and further enhanced successful treatment outcome was communitywide networking with politicians, police departments, probation departments, community leaders, clergy, and school systems. Joanning's family therapists engaged in a considerable amount of work with larger systems with their cases. According to Joanning, "the whole city was involved" with the project.

Another important dimension of Joannings' research was the use of ethnographic interviews at follow-up with a small subgroup of subject families (Newfield, Kuehl, Joanning, & Quinn, this volume). Anthropologists and professionals trained in anthropological interviewing methods, who had not been involved in the project, went to the subjects' homes and interviewed them concerning their experience in the project. The ethnographic investigations produced rich data about how families perceived the therapist, the therapeutic experience, and their involvement in a research project. An important finding was the importance of fit between the family and the therapy approach. Apparently, when there was a good match between therapist variables/therapy approach and family worldview/family characteristics, families were most likely to have a successful treatment outcome (Newfield et al., this volume).

Limitations of the Project

Joanning believes that some families were done a tremendous disservice by random assignment to treatment conditions. Some families in crisis, or desperately in need of family therapy, received a presumably less potent alternative modality. In future research endeavors with adolescent substance abusers, Joanning plans to abandon the traditional random sampling procedure and conduct a careful assessment at pretest to determine which treatment modality would best fit a particular family. Ethnographic interviews at pre-test and throughout the process of therapy will also be utilized to assist therapists in determining the best fit between family and therapy approach.

Extraneous Variables and the Hazards of Research

Joanning and his colleagues encountered considerable criticism and opposition from the AA and disease-oriented addiction community, which is quite powerful in Joanning's catchment area. According to Joanning, these individuals could not accept a systemic way of thinking about adolescent substance abuse problems. Joanning and his colleagues employed a more diplomatic approach in their interactions with these traditionalists and felt that this helped to reduce some of the tension.

Adolescents and Families Project/University of California Project

Howard Liddle, principal investigator of the Adolescents and Families Project of the University of California, San Francisco (NIDA Grant # R01 DA03714–04) described preliminary results based on 34 out of a projected total of 40 family therapy cases (Liddle, personal communication, October 6, 1988). The family therapy model of the project is known as Multidimensional Family Therapy (MDFT) since it assesses and intervenes into multiple spheres of human functioning, including the affective, cognitive, and behavioral domains of each individual in the family as well as its component subsystems (sibling, parental, and often marital).

Evolution of the MDFT Model

On an affective level, Liddle's team found that many of the project families were caught in a cycle of hopelessness and despair. On a cognitive level, family members (particularly the parents) attribute causation of the substance abuse and other problems to extrafamilial factors over which they have little influence, such as the influence of the peer group or lax enforcement by school officials. Adolescents' attributions include such things as the impossibility of their parents ever understanding the adolescents' viewpoints and their parents' rigidity about family rules. Naturally, such attributions interact with the affective domain and tend to reinforce the sense of hopelessness. Finally, on a behavioral level, the families exhibit a progressively more narrow range of possible problem-solving actions, typically culminating either in expelling the adolescent or abdicating all parental responsibility to extrafamilial agents of control such as the police, probation officers, and the juvenile justice system.

Therapists in the project found it crucial to conceive of the therapeutic alliance not as a singular entity but rather in, literally, a pluralistic sense. Serious consideration is given throughout the course of the 16-week therapy to the therapeutic *alliances* of therapist-parents and therapist-adolescent. With parents, this included paying close attention to factors such as previously mentioned feelings on the part of parents that they could not be influential in the lives of their teenagers. With the adolescents, they found increased success in engagement and outcome when focus was given to key features of adolescent development (e.g., identity formation, personal goals, and life direction), particularly in individual sessions with the teenagers. The MDFT model endeavors to incorporate the latest findings from adolescent development research into the clinical arena. For example, the findings of studies that support the importance of good family relationships in the continued formation of a positive adolescent identity (Grotevant & Cooper, 1983) are reviewed regularly and used to inform the treatment along developmental lines (Liddle, 1988).

Differential Outcome

Although results are at a preliminary stage at present, Liddle and his colleagues appear to be finding support for their hypothesis that there are some families who cannot be successfully treated without addressing directly the affective themes of parental and adolescent hopelessness and despair. This frequently includes issues of attachment, separation, and severe past trauma in the family such as abuse and neglect. They also find empirical support for the importance of differentiating the therapeutic alliance into two separate, but interconnected parts—the therapist-parents alliance and therapist-adolescent alliance. With parents, this means having the parents accept the idea that they have influence over some areas of the teenagers' lives and that, in an overall sense, changes in their families are possible. This involves a frank discussion and reevaluation of the parenting philosophy and style of each parent. Such discussions often proceed best when they exist within a context, carefully established by the therapist, in which parental love and commitment to adolescents has been rekindled. The therapist works along a parallel track with teenagers, helping them accept the premise that therapy might "have something in it" for them. Often, this contract takes the form of adolescents using therapists as allies or consultants—those persons who can help them negotiate to get more of what they want in the family. To the extent that either parents or adolescents are not successfully engaged in this manner, outcome appears to suffer.

Limitations of the Project

Liddle believes that the comprehensive and multifaceted way in which the project deals with families and assesses the outcome of therapy highlights the limitations and frustrations of working with multiple subsystems in a brief therapy context. After only the four months of treatment allowed by the research, therapists usually felt that there was still much to be done on many different levels.

Strengths of the Research

The multidimensional model is also valuable in distinguishing the potentially complex issues in the assessment of therapeutic outcome. When the outcome of a case is mixed, certain questions are unavoidable: What *is* therapeutic outcome? How can different dimensions be compared? From this perspective, it seems more difficult to continue to use global and simplistic categories such as *failure case* vs. *success case.* Liddle hopes that projects such as his can begin to influence clinicians to think about the outcome of their work, and clinical work in general, in a complex multivariate manner.

RESEARCH AND INTEGRATION: IMPLICATIONS FOR THE FUTURE

In this section of the chapter, we will discuss some important ways that family therapy outcome research can inform our clinical practice with adolescent substance abusers. We will first contrast the three NIDA studies with each other and with an important Italian family treatment outcome study with substance abusers. This will be followed by some of our recommendations for future research endeavors with this treatment population.

Despite the heated debate concerning integration in the family therapy field (Fraser, 1984, 1986; Rohrbaugh, 1984; MacKinnon & Slive, 1984; Roberts, 1984, 1986; Colapinto, 1984; Stanton, 1981; Sluzki, 1983), the majority of family therapy outcome studies reviewed in this chapter all seem to point to the need for model expansion and the importance of shifting from one model to another in order to better meet the needs of different families. (See previous section and also Cancrini et al., 1988). These researchers have demonstrated that it is not only possible to integrate other family therapy approaches with the original Stanton and Todd structural-strategic model (Stanton & Todd, 1982), but they have also begun to identify particular types of clinical situations where a systemic approach a la Milan, de Shazer, Ackerman, or Galveston was clearly the treatment of choice.

Each project made somewhat different choices about how the basic model should be modified. It is tempting to imagine what differences in treatment population, context, treatment staff, and so on might account for these differences, but such speculations are beyond the scope of this chapter. Piercy and his colleagues have found it most advantageous to expand the original Purdue brief family therapy model to include deliberate split team disagreements (Papp, 1980) and some of de Shazer's (1985) major interventions as helpful family relapse prevention strategies. Their *no-problem problem* approach is heavily based on the work of de Shazer (1985) and Milan (Penn, 1985; Tomm, 1984).

Joanning and his associates found that chronic adolescent substance abusers and cases with parental chemical abuse in the picture fared best with the Milan, Ackerman, or Galveston systemic approaches. This was also the case for families who presented for therapy in crisis around an unresolved family loss, or some other idiosyncratic problem. Liddle and his associates found it necessary to include a similar focus on belief systems for chronic cases in their population.

In a recent study with adolescent and young adult heroin addicts, Cancrini and his colleagues have developed a useful typology for matching substance abusers with a particular type of family therapy (Cancrini et al., 1988). These researchers found that disorganized, multi-problem families benefited most from a structural-strategic approach—a finding that seems supported by Joanning's and Liddle's research. Families that were highly rigid, characterized by scapegoating and double-binding communications, fared well with the original Milan approach (Palazzoli et al., 1978). Similar to Joanning's research findings, families that presented in crisis following a traumatic family loss benefited from either an individual therapy approach for the identified client (depending on the age of the individual), or the Milan Associates approach (Boscolo et al., 1987).

A common thread that runs through all four of the previously mentioned family treatment outcome studies is a concerted effort on the researchers' behalf to develop helpful guidelines for maximizing the fit between family characteristics and family therapy approach. Joanning and his colleagues discovered through the use of ethnographic interviews at follow-up that subject families who reported a favorable treatment outcome clearly felt that the therapy approach meshed well with their worldview in a meaningful way. Therapist variables were also reported as important factors that contributed to successful treatment outcome (Newfield et al., this volume).

Throughout this chapter, we have alluded to the inherent dangers and ethical ramifications of research teams religiously adhering to one particular family therapy model in its purest form with every family seeking treatment through the research project. Similarly, in the spirit of maintaining scientific rigor, the random assignment to treatment conditions, used in all three of the National Institute of Drug Abuse studies, in some cases did a significant disservice to families in crisis. Joanning sums up this problem best by saying: "the random assignment procedure proved to be either an over-kill or an underkill" (Joanning, personal communication, August 2, 1988). We are in agreement with Jurich and Russell (1985) that ethically "the therapeutic imperatives outweigh the considerations of optimum research designs" (p. 92).

At this point in our discussion, we would like to propose some future directions for family treatment outcome research with adolescent substance abusers. To begin, we believe strongly in allowing family therapy models to evolve either through model expansion or shifting models when necessary. Of course this requires that modifications of the model and principles of model selection should be rigorously articulated. Secondly, researchers need to develop better assessment criteria and treatment assignment procedures for determining the best therapy fit for families at intake. We would like to see more use of ethnographic interviewing as an essential component of future family treatment outcome studies with adolescent substance abusers. Perhaps ethnographic interviews could be conducted at assessment, throughout the course of therapy, and at follow-up. This anthropological research method can provide researchers with accurate assessments of family belief systems and subjective experiences in therapy. Finally, we are in support of the family therapy field's departing from traditional hypothesis-testing research and adopting a discovery-oriented research technology. Discovery-oriented research can give clinicians a closer look into therapeutic events and the interrelationships among therapeutic conditions, methodology, and consequences (Mahrer, 1988).

IMPLICATIONS FOR CLINICIANS

Generalizations from Research

We recognize that most clinicians will spend virtually their entire professional careers without engaging in research, and indeed it is the brave clinician who has even ventured to read this far in a research-oriented chapter. As a reward for this effort, we offer some broad generalizations that should be helpful for clinicians and suggestions of methods for continued refinement of one's clinical practice.

A broad review of the research we have examined suggests several major conclusions.

1. *No approach or method works for all cases.* While this conclusion might seem obvious, the more clinically oriented chapters often seem to offer disappointingly little discussion of limitations of the particular approaches. It is striking, though, that all three NIDA projects evolved in similar ways—in response to clear evidence that a single approach was ineffective with a significant subgroup of cases.
2. *Some scheme of categorizations of cases is needed as a guide to intervention selection.* If no approach is universally effective, how does a clinician match the therapeutic approach to the case? Theorists do not agree on crucial dimensions, but again the NIDA projects may offer important clues. Chronicity of drug use and other problems seems important, but at least as important is the presence or absence of previously unsuccessful treatment efforts. The degree of voluntariness of the referral also seems critical.
3. *Straightforward requests for change seem less successful with chronic, demoralized cases.* Such families seem to react poorly to zealous optimism and pushy methods. At least initially, it seems important to mirror their skepticism and avoid extreme directiveness. Neutral, systemic methods, split team or reflecting team dialogues, and, at times, even paradoxical methods are more promising than direct efforts to convince families that they have the power to change. The cybernetic-systemic approach of White also seems particularly applicable with such families.
4. *Regardless of the method, attention to the therapeutic alliance seems critical.* In our own work, we have stressed the importance of deliberate joining with the family and paying attention to engaging the adolescent client, concerns which are also echoed by

Liddle in his NIDA project. Most of the chapters in the present volume pay little or no attention to therapist factors, but it is hard to avoid the suspicion that the personal qualities of the therapist have an important impact on the therapeutic alliance.

Toward Empirically-Based Clinical Practice

We hope that the reader will not take these generalizations or the claims of the various chapter authors as definitive. Particularly since many of these claims conflict with each other, how can the practicing clinician reach independent conclusions without engaging in large-scale, complicated outcome research? We offer the following suggestions as our concluding advice.

1. *Attempt to make your own theoretical assumptions explicit.* This is similar to Liddle's (1982) call for an "epistemological declaration." This task seems less formidable when one recognizes that all actions by a clinician are based on assumptions about what will be effective and why. Unfortunately, most clinicians do not take the extra steps of making assumptions explicit, examining the consistency of these assumptions, or comparing the fit of their interventions with their own theoretical premises.
2. *Attempt to categorize your cases.* Organize the early information learned about each case in a systemic fashion. If this prompts you to be more organized in the ways you go about gathering information, that is all the better. There are no definitive guidelines concerning which variables are most important, but a useful list could include demographic information about the family, observations of family interaction patterns, drug history, other characteristics of the identified client, and previous treatment. Noting such variables can help the clinician develop an individual scorecard of differential effectiveness.
3. *Make hypotheses explicit and testable.* All clinicians develop tentative hypotheses about their cases and revise them in response to clinical feedback. What is rare is to make this process explicit so that it can be reviewed systematically. Explicit, recorded hypotheses can form the basis of periodic review to ascertain what avenues seem consistently promising, and which ones often seem to be dead ends.
4. *When a treatment plan is revised, do so systematically.* All too frequently, supervisors hear clinicians complain "I've tried everything." A closer look usually reveals that the therapist has

changed approaches frequently in major ways, with little rhyme or reason, rarely giving any one approach a fair trial. We believe that one major reason why clinical research projects have been effective is that they have applied methods consistently and only changed methods in carefully controlled ways, as was true of all three NIDA projects. Unless a clinician makes changes somewhat deliberately and systematically, it is unlikely that successes or failures will ever be instructive.

5. *Collect outcome data systematically, including follow-up data.* Most clinicians rely upon their own informal impressions of their own effectiveness. Psychotherapy outcome research consistently shows, however, that there are major discrepancies between the clinician's own impressions of effectiveness and those of the clients. Often the family members themselves are much more favorable in their assessment of therapeutic outcome than the therapist's assessment, particularly if the therapist has not taken the trouble to remain in contact with the family at the termination of therapy and for a significant follow-up period. Hopefully if therapists can become more systematic in their assessment of therapeutic effectiveness, we can move the family therapy field out of the realm of extravagant claims and marketing hype.

REFERENCES

Anderson, H., & Goolishian, H. (1988). A view of human systems as linguistic systems: Preliminary and evolving ideas about the implications for clinical theory. *Family Process, 27,* 371–393.

Boscolo, L., Cecchin, G., Hoffman, L., & Penn, P. (1987). *Milan systemic family therapy.* New York: Basic Books.

Cancrini, L., Cingolani, S., Compagnoni, F., Constantini, D., & Mazzoni, S. (1988). Juvenile drug addiction: A typology of heroin addicts and their families. *Family Process, 27,* (3), 261–273.

Cleveland, M. (1981). Families and adolescent drug abuse: Structural analysis of children's roles. *Family Process,* 20, 295–304.

Colapinto, J. (1984). On model integration and model integrity. *Journal of Strategic and Systemic Therapies, 3,* 38–42.

Daroff, L. H., Marks, S. J., & Friedman, A. S. (1986). Adolescent drug abuse: The parents predicament. In G. Beschner & A. S. Friedman (eds.). *Teen drug use.* Lexington, MA: Lexington Books.

de Shazer, S. (1985). *Keys to solution in brief therapy.* New York: W. W. Norton.

Eastwood, M., Sweeney, D., & Piercy, F. (1987). The "No-problem problem": A family therapy approach for certain first-time adolescent substance abusers. *Family Relations, 36,* 125–128.

Efran, J. & Lukens, M. D. (1988). The world according to Humberto Maturana. *Family Therapy Networker,* May-June, 23–28, 72–75.

Efran, J., Heffner, K. & Lukens, R. J. (1987). Alcoholism as an opinion: Structure determinism applied to problem drinking. *Alcoholism Treatment Quarterly.*

Foote, F. H., Szapocznik, J., Kurtines, W. M., Perez-Vidal, & Hervis, O. K. (1985). One-person family therapy: A modality of brief strategic family therapy. In R. S. Ashery (ed.). *Progress in the development of cost-effective treatment for drug abusers.* NIDA Research Monograph 58, Rockville, MD: National Institute of Drug Abuse.

Fraser, J. S. (1984). Process level integration: Corrective vision for a binocular view. *Journal of Strategic and Systemic Therapies, 3,* 43–57.

Fraser, J. S. (1986). Integrating systems-based models: Similarities, differences, and some critical questions. In D. Efron (ed.). *Journeys: Expansion of the strategic-systemic therapies.* New York: Brunner/Mazel.

Friedman, A. S., Utada, A. & Morrissey, M. R. (1987). Families of adolescent drug abusers are "rigid": Are these families either "disengaged" or "enmeshed" or both? *Family Process, 26,* (1), 131–148.

Grotevant, H. & Cooper, C. (1983). *Adolescent Development in the Family.* San Francisco: Jossey-Bass.

Hendin, H., Pollinger, A., Ulman, R., & Carr, A. C. (1981). *Adolescent marijuana abusers and their families,* NIDA Research Monograph, No. 40, Rockville, MD: National Institute on Drug Abuse.

Hendin, H. & Pollinger-Haas, A. (1985). The adaptive significance of chronic marijuana use for adolescents and adults. In J. Brook, D. Lettieri, & D. W. Brook (eds.). *Alcohol and substance abuse in adolescence.* New York: Haworth Press.

Hoffman, L. (1986). Beyond Power and Control: Towards a 'second order' family systems therapy. *Family Systems Medicine, 3,* 381–396.

Jurich, A. P. & Russell, C. S. (1985). The conflict between the ethics of therapy and outcome research in family therapy. In L. L. Andreozzi (ed.). *Integrating research and clinical practice.* Rockville, MD: Aspen Systems.

Levine, B. L. (1985). Adolescent substance abuse: Toward an integration of family systems and individual adaptation theories. *American Journal of Family Therapy, 13*(2), 3–16.

Liddle, H. A. (1982). On the problem of eclecticism: A call for epistemological clarification and human scale theories. *Family Process, 4,* 81–97.

Liddle, H. A. (1988). Developmental thinking and the family life cycle: Implications for training family therapists. In C. J. Falicov (ed.). *Family Transitions.* New York: Guilford Press.

MacKinnon, L. & Slive, A. (1984). If one should not marry a hypothesis, should one marry a model? *Journal of Strategic and Systemic Therapies, 3,* 26–39.

Mahrer, A. R. (1988). Discovery-oriented psychotherapy research: Rationale, aims, and methods. *American Psychologist, 43*(9), 694–702.

Maturana, H., & Varela, F. (1988). *The tree of knowledge: The biological roots to human understanding.* Boston: New Science Library.

O'Hanlon, W. H. (1988, February). *Brief therapy: Creating a context for change.* A workshop presented in Chicago, IL.

Papp, P. (1980). The Greek chorus and other techniques of paradoxical therapy. *Family Process, 19,* 45–57.

Papp, P. (1983). The process of change. New York: Guilford.

Penn, P. (1985). Feed-forward: Future questions, future maps. *Family Process, 24,* 299–310.

Piercy, F. P. & Frankel, B. R. (1989). The evolution of an integrative family therapy for substance abusing adolescents: Toward the mutual enhancement of research and practice. *Journal of Family Psychology, 3*(1), 5–26.

Roberts, J. (1984). Switching models: Family and team choice points and reactions as we moved from the Haley strategic model to the Milan model. *Journal of Strategic and Systemic Therapies, 3,* 40–53.

Roberts, J. (1986). An evolving model: Links between the Milan approach and strategic models of family therapy. In D. Efron (ed.). *Journey: Expansion of the Strategic and Systemic Therapies.* New York: Brunner/Mazel.

Rohrbaugh, M. (1984). The strategic systems therapies: Misgivings about mixing the models. *Journal of Strategic and Systemic Therapies, 3,* 28–32.

Sluzki, C. (1983). Process, structure and worldview: Toward an integrated view of systemic models in family therapy. *Family Process, 22,* 469–476.

Stanton, M. D. (1981). An integrated structural/strategic approach to family therapy. *Journal of Marital and Family Therapy, 7,* 427–439.

Stanton, M. D. & Todd, T. C. (1982). The conceptual model. In M. D. Stanton, T. C. Todd & Associates, *The Family Therapy of Drug Abuse and Drug Addiction.* New York: Guilford.

Szapocznik, J., Kurtines, W. M., Foote, F. H., Perez-Vidal, A., & Hervis, O. (1983). Conjoint versus one-person family therapy: Some evidence for the effectiveness of conducting family therapy through one person with drug-abusing adolescents. *Journal of Consulting and Clinical Psychology, 51*(6), 889–899.

Szapoczik, J., Kurtines, W. M., Foote., F. H., Perez-Vidal, A. & Hervis, O. (1986). Conjoint versus one-person family therapy: Further evidence for the effectiveness of conducting family therapy through one person with drug-abusing adolescents. *Journal of Consulting and Clinical Psychology, 54*(3), 395–397.

Szapoczik, J. & Kurtines, W. M. (1989). Breakthroughs in family therapy with drug-abusing and problem youth. New York: Springer.

Tomm, K. (1984). One perspective on the Milan systemic approach: Part II. Description of session format, interviewing style and intervention. *Journal of Marital and Family Therapy, 10,* 253–271.

Author Index

Subject Index